BATTLE-AXE BLENHEIMS

BATTLE-AXE BLENHEIMS

No 105 SQUADRON RAF AT WAR 1940–1

STUART R. SCOTT

FOREWORD BY

AIR MARSHAL SIR IVOR BROOM
KCB CBE DSO DFC** AFC

ALAN SUTTON PUBLISHING LIMITED

First published in the United Kingdom in 1996 by
Alan Sutton Publishing Limited · Phoenix Mill · Far Thrupp · Stroud · Gloucestershire

British Library Cataloguing in Publication Data

Scott, Stuart R.
Battle-axe Blenheims: No 105 Squadron RAF
at War, 1940–1
I. Title
940.544941

ISBN 0-7509-1126-3

Typeset in 10/12pt Times.
Typesetting and origination by
Alan Sutton Publishing Limited.
Printed in Great Britain by
Butler & Tanner, Frome, Somerset.

To the Four Musketeers
and all others who were sacrificed

To live in the hearts
of those we leave is
not to die –
until we Meet
(Anon)

Contents

Foreword

Air Marshal Sir Ivor Broom
KCB CBE DSO DFC** AFC

Sgt Stuart George Bastin, a wireless operator/air gunner, was killed in a Blenheim aircraft of 105 Squadron in the summer of 1941 when his aircraft hit the mast of a ship which it was attacking in the Mediterranean. He was nineteen years old. He had already led a charmed life, and had participated in the accepted quota of thirty operational flights. He was all set to return to the United Kingdom for non-operational duties when he was called upon to make one more flight against enemy shipping – the flight from which he never returned. When the author of this book was born thirteen years later, he was given the name Stuart in memory of Stuart Bastin, his mother's only brother.

This book was triggered off by the author's urge to know more about his uncle, and about the lives of the similar young men who flew Blenheims in 105 Squadron in 1940/1. Ten years of meticulous research into the period when the Squadron operated Blenheims has created this fascinating and factual story which will touch the hearts of young and old alike. Operational sorties are described in great detail – the tactics, losses, successes and failures. The descriptions by survivors of low-level raids against continental coastal targets and against shipping off the Dutch coast in Part 1, and in the Mediterranean from Malta in Part 2, have been correlated and cross-checked with the 1940/1 post-flight operational records. The losses were horrendous, particularly during the anti-shipping raids in 1941. If six Blenheims were despatched to attack enemy shipping at low level (notionally 50ft) in daylight, it was very rare for all six to return – and yet squadron life was carried on with great spirit, determination and *joie de vivre*. Youth is not easily deterred, particularly when well led – as 105 Squadron certainly was.

It is worth recalling, when reading the graphic descriptions of operations in this book, that all aircrew were volunteers. The majority of aircrew in those early days were sergeants aged between nineteen and twenty-two. I recall the occasion when a new pilot arrived to join our Blenheim squadron. He was twenty-six years old, and seemed so old compared with the rest of us – I was twenty-one – that he was immediately nicknamed 'Uncle'.

It is good that this book records for posterity the contributions and sacrifices made by the young men of 105 Squadron – the squadron with the battle-axe in its crest – to preserve the freedoms which we enjoy today and which were nearly lost fifty years ago. I know of no similar study into the operational role of any other Blenheim bomber squadron, but I can say from personal knowledge that it mirrors the contribution which so many Blenheim squadrons made to the war effort in 1940/1. We all owe a debt of gratitude to Stuart Scott for his detailed research and for recording this part of our heritage.

Acknowledgements

I would particularly like to thank the survivors of 105 and 107 Squadrons and next-of-kin of those who did not survive or have subsequently passed on. My thanks go to Eric Applebee; the late David Bennett; AM Sir Ivor Broom; Jack Buckley; Ron Butcher; Jack Cowley; Mrs Peggy Duncan, widow of the late F/L Alfred Duncan; Anthony Edwards, son of the late Air Cdre Sir Hughie Idwal Edwards; Wally Fennell; Tony Frick; John Green, nephew of the late Sgt George Eric Green; Brian Hanafin; Frank Harbord; the late Les Harrison; Mike Henry; R.E. Lee; Bob Lyndall; Eileen Maddocks, sister of the late Sgt Ronald John Scott; Tony Mee; Hugh Morgan, nephew of the late Sgt Kemys L. Morgan; Joan Phillips, sister of the late Sgt Harold Frederick 'Andy' Hancock, and her husband Eric Phillips; Dickie Rook; the late Samuel North; H.H. 'Tom' Rose; Geoffrey S. Rowland; Ron Scholefield; Eddie Smith; David Brandwood-Spencer, son of the late F/O Frank Bertram 'Bill' Brandwood; James Taylor; the late Alan Tuppen; the late Johnnie Turner and Ron Wood.

Additionally, I would like to thank the following: the Aircrew Association and Bill Ingles; the Blenheim Society including Betty and Hugh George; Theo Boitens; Lesley Chester; Stephen Cuffe; John Doyle of Edinburgh; Len Fearnley; the Gibraltar Archive and T.J. Finlayson; the late R.E. Gillman; Peter H.T. Green; James J. Halley of Air Britain; the Imperial War Museum's Department of Photographs and John Delaney; Jonathan Hammé at Maurice of Glasgow; Chris Harper; Charles P. John; Martin Kuriger; the Public Records Office; Angela McMahon; the Ministry of Defence RAF Personnel Management Centre and Naval Historical Branch; Ministerio De Justica – Registrio Civil Central of Madrid; the National Library of Scotland, Edinburgh; Aad Neeven; the New Zealand Returned Servicemen's Association; the National Library of Malta; the *Malta Times*; the Mitchell Library, Glasgow; Registrio Civil de la Conception of Càdiz; Kenneth Poolman; Jack Rawcliffe; the Royal Air Force Museum; the Royal Air Force, including Gp Capt M.C. Darby, S/L A.R. James, and Sgt S.W. Pope; Rusty Russell; the late Michael Scott; Mrs Vera G. Sherring; Edgar Smith; Maurice Smith; Stephen Snelling; Linda Stewart; Graham Warner; the West of Scotland Press Agency, Glasgow.

My heartfelt thanks go to my 'Honorary Uncle', the late Maurice Chapple or 'Chappie', who contributed much information from his diaries, photographs and memories of the Blenheim era, and who, along with his dear lady wife Kit, made me so welcome to their home on so many occasions.

Essential financial assistance and moral support came from my Mother, who was sister to the late Sgt Stuart George Bastin, and from my late Father – two wonderful people who were a constant source of encouragement to me, for whom my love and appreciation is immeasurable. To Catherine I also extend my love and appreciation for helping me patiently over the final hurdles towards completion and publication.

Should I have inadvertently omitted to mention anybody, I offer my apologies, and trust that the enjoyment and possibly the nostalgia of the text may provide some small measure of conciliation.

Every effort has been made to trace the copyright holder of the sketch of the Bristol Blenheim on page 4.

Glossary of Terms and Abbreviations

A/	Acting (Rank)
AA	Anti-aircraft
AASF	Advanced Air Striking Force
AC	Aircraftsman
ACHGD	Aircraft Hand General Duties
Ack-ack	Anti-aircraft Fire
AC1	Aircraftsman 1st Class
ACM	Air Chief Marshal
ADC	Aide de Camp
AFC	Air Force Cross
Air Cdre	Air Commodore
AM	Air Marshal
AOC	Air Officer Commanding
ARP	Air Raid Precaution
ATC	Air Training Corps
AVM	Air Vice-Marshal
(B)	Bomber
BEF	British Expeditionary Force
CB	Companion of the Order of the Bath
CDR	Commander (Naval)
CFI	Chief Flying Instructor
CFS	Central Flying School
CIU	Central Intelligence Unit
CinC	Commander in Chief
CO	Commanding Officer
D/F	Direction Finding
DFC	Distinguished Flying Cross (Officers only)
DFM	Distinguished Flying Medal (NCOs only)
DSO	Distinguished Service Order (Officers only)
ETA	Estimated Time of Arrival
FAA	Fleet Air Arm
Flak	German anti-aircraft fire
F/O	Flying Officer
F/Sgt	Flight Sergeant
Gen	General Information
GP	General Purpose
H/F	High Frequency
HQ	Headquarters
Kriegie	Prisoner of War

LAC	Leading Aircraftsman
lb(s)	Pound(s) weight
LMF	Lack of Moral Fibre
Luftwaffe	German Air Force
MC	Military Cross
MO	Medical Officer
Mk	Mark
MT	Motor Transport
MTB	Motor Torpedo Boat
NCO	Non-Commissioned Officer
MV	Merchant Vessel
OBE	Order of the British Empire
Ops	Operational sorties
OTU	Operational Training Unit
Panzer	Tank (German)
P/O	Pilot Officer
Pom-pom	Naval rapid-firing multi-barrel anti-aircraft gun
Prang	Crash
PRU	Photo Reconnaissance Unit
Q Code	Form of Morse shorthand – e.g. QDM – Course to Base
RAF	Royal Air Force
RAAF	Royal Australian Air Force
Recce	Reconnaissance
Revs (rpm)	Rotational speed in revolutions/minute
RN	Royal Navy
R/T	Radio Telegraphy
Sortie	Aerial excursion
Strafe	Aerial machine-gun attack
SAO	Senior Air Officer
SAP	Semi-armour Piercing
SASO	Senior Air Staff Officer
Sgt	Sergeant
S/L	Squadron Leader
Sqn	Squadron
SS	Steam Ship
U/s	Unserviceable
VC	Victoria Cross
Vic	V-shaped formation
W/C	Wing Commander
W/T	Wireless Telegraphy
WOp/AG	Wireless Operator/Air Gunner
ZZ	Crude bad weather radio approach/let-down procedure

Preface

The extraordinary sequence of events I encountered while researching and writing this narrative almost led me to believe that I had been destined for such a task. This may sound a little clichéd, and strangely fatalistic, but the more I wrote the more the subject matter gripped my imagination. Simple research into family history had gained so much momentum that on putting pen to paper, the text became much more comprehensive than originally envisaged.

I would like to outline some of the occurrences which contributed in no small measure to my opinion. The first striking example took place when I was about fourteen years of age. I was walking with my mother when we met an elderly widow called Belle, who lived alone in a nearby house. Neither of us knew her very well but during the ensuing conversation she proceeded to ask the most astonishing question: 'Tell me, Mrs Scott, did you have a brother in the RAF?' My mother nodded. 'Well, I don't know if you will mind me saying this,' Belle continued, 'but I can see your brother standing beside you!' Such a comment came as a shock and seemed ridiculous given the circumstances – my mother replied that she had indeed had a brother, but he had been killed in 1941!

The lady then reaffirmed her statement, assuring her that he was indeed standing beside her. By way of proof, she said that he had a scar above his left eye. Her observations were amazingly correct. The scar was only barely noticeable, save in one photograph which Belle had certainly not seen. My mother was truly astounded, because for someone to know about her brother's RAF service was not unlikely, but the scar was a different matter.

It transpired that Belle was a medium of some standing and a few days later my mother went along to her house for a 'sitting'. Full of scepticism, I accompanied her to satisfy my curiosity. We sat down and eventually Belle announced that she had contact with Stuart, my mother's brother. I distinctly remember her saying, 'Your brother's here, he's with us in the room now, and has a lot of RAF friends with him. There is also someone else with them – a girl – do you know anybody Spanish?' My mother replied that we had no Spanish relations nor friends, nor specifically did Stuart. In the 1940s travel was much more restricted than today, and the chances of knowing a Spanish girl in 1941 appeared ridiculous. However, Belle was insistent, describing the girl as very attractive with long dark hair and dancing with hands held high, clicking castanets above her head and had the name Maria. From that day on nothing further was heard about the matter, and I completely forgot about it, as probably did my mother. Belle went down to the south of England to live, and we heard little more of her, apart from Christmas cards.

Years passed, and I started to write this book. With time I gained many more contacts, eventually being fortunate enough to meet Ron Scholefield, a former observer with 105 Squadron during the Blenheim era. During a telephone conversation concerning his operational flying, he suddenly interrupted his train of thought and said, 'Oh, by the way, I've just remembered – do you know about your uncle and the Spanish girl? At Gibraltar, a Blenheim had an accident. It was either landing or taking off when it crashed, skidded, and ended up ploughing into a small wood or copse near the border with Spain, where it hit and killed a Spanish girl.' He considered that the incident could have occurred when they were leaving Gibraltar. There had been little squadron discussion of the matter. However, he did vividly remember my uncle's pilot, Sgt Ron Scott (no relation), relating the incident to him. Could this have been the Spanish girl whom Belle saw that day so long ago – I often wonder!

Several other strange incidents have occurred during the preparation of this book. One of them happened while I was researching in Malta, on 26 August 1985, the anniversary of the deaths of my uncle and his crew. I had been swimming from a small protrusion of rocks which lay across the bay from Kalafrana, the 1940s seaplane base location. It was very hot and I was becoming light-headed due to the heat. So around lunchtime, about one o'clock, I decided to find some form of refreshment. When packing my bag, I was thinking that it was almost the same time of day when my uncle and crew would have died so many years ago when I looked across Kalafrana Bay and noticed a stationary ship with two masts, just the type of ship the Blenheims would have attacked in 1941. Suddenly, there was a roar in the distance and an aircraft appeared flying low over the bay. It then flew above the ship, rising up over the headland before disappearing off into the distance. It was strangely like a tribute – to my mind at least.

Anyway, I packed up my bag and decided to take a walk around Marsaxlokk Bay to see if I could see anything or find anybody of interest to speak to. I came across a small café and thumbed through a rack of postcards hanging on a wall outside. All were very pleasant; all were of Malta and some of the fishing village itself. A family were sitting around in chairs in the open air, reading papers, smoking the odd cigarette and generally taking in the sun and enjoying the day. Soon the lady of the shop approached me and said, with a delightful Maltese accent, 'Excuse me.' I looked round in response and found her staring at me curiously. She said pointedly, 'Why you come to Malta?' I thought this was a very strange question but answered her politely, saying, 'Well, I have come to Malta on holiday.' She persisted, 'No, no, no, I mean WHY you come to Malta?' I could not understand why she was so insistent. So I said, 'I came to Malta to research some family history.' 'What sort of family history?' she persisted. 'I had an uncle who was in the Royal Air Force,' I said. 'Oh!', she said, looking very interested and curious, and then asked me if I had any photographs. As I always carried a pack of photographs with me when going about my researches, I reached into my pocket and handed them to her. She studied them with great interest and then stopped at one particular photograph, pointed deliberately at my uncle, and said 'Is this your uncle?' 'Yes', I replied with surprise, not knowing what to expect next. 'I knew this man!', she said. It was over forty years after the war and I very much felt that she had to be mistaken. So I continued my conversation with her as she studied the remaining photographs. However, my raging thirst meant I was not really taking any great notice of what she was saying.

A couple of minutes later a Maltese man arrived wearing a straw hat, shorts and sandals. He was swarthy, slim, around six feet tall and appeared to be in his fifties. He started to talk to the lady in fluent Maltese, and then suddenly turned around and said to me in perfect English, 'Ah, you have photographs!' and asked if he could see them. I handed the photographs to him and he too began to thumb through them. 'Were these chaps here when Ron Gillman was here?', he queried. The late Ron Gillman DFC was the author of an excellent book entitled *The Shiphunters*, which outlines the experiences of his Blenheim crew when serving with 107 Squadron alongside 105 Squadron during the latter part of their Malta detachment.

I replied that when Ron Gillman had arrived on Malta, my uncle and crew had recently been killed. The stranger looked further through the photographs, and picked out one which had my uncle's crew on it, pointing this time not to my uncle but to the observer, Bren Healy. 'I remember this man!' he said positively. Again, I couldn't believe that after all these years he could possibly remember, but I listened to what he had to say. 'I once helped him home after he had one or two drinks too many,' he said. 'He was a big tall lad and heavy to lift.' 'Where were you at the time?' I enquired. 'I was living in a hotel my parents owned,' he replied. It transpired that he was Edgar Smith, the son of the hotel owners mentioned later, and was known to me from Ron Gillman's book.

As I was so interested in the history of the war years, he invited me along to the hotel, by now a private house in which he had lived since his parents had died. There I was presented with a cold beer and a delicious tomato omelette. During the course of our conversation, Edgar remembered that he had a box of memorabilia somewhere in his attic. He excused himself and went to find it, returning five minutes later with the box in his hands. Having opened it, he started to tell me about a chap called Bert Child, a pilot with 110 Squadron from whom 105 Squadron had taken over duties. Seemingly, Sgt Child had been flying on a mission to Sicily and had not returned. Edgar had been a good friend of his and sorely missed him. He always wondered what had become of his friend when he failed to turn up one day at the hotel, never to be seen or heard from again.

Edgar Smith relaxes in the rear garden of his house, formerly the Honeymoon Hotel, Marsaxlokk Bay, Malta in 1984. The lemon trees provided fruit for the drinks enjoyed by the sergeant aircrew visitors. (S.R. Scott)

It transpired that in his box, Edgar had a photograph of Sgt Child taken in 1940 which he was eager to show me. As was usual in those days, people were more keen and perhaps had more time to write details on the reverse of photographs. With this in mind I instinctively looked at the back of Edgar's photo where, to my amazement, the details were not of Bert Child but were in fact of Walter Brendan Healy, my uncle's observer! It read 'W.B. Healy, 978873, c/o RAF Upwood, Hunts.' The only explanation I can offer for this is that Bren Healy probably knew Bert Child when training together at 17 OTU, Upwood, and perhaps having engaged in conversation with Edgar, decided to give him the photograph of Sgt Child as a memento. It was commonplace in those days to exchange photos with friends, probably as life expectancy was so short. As a parting gesture Bren Healy would have put his name and details of where he had met Sgt Child on the reverse of the photograph. Edgar's comment at the time was rather poignant: 'If it had not been for you coming back to this house, this information would probably have remained in my attic for another forty years!'

Another interesting and highly coincidental event occurred in the course of writing this book. One day I was engaged in conversation with my friend Charles John, discussing my desire to research the 105 Squadron Blenheim era, when he told me that a colleague at his place of work was a member of the RAF Aircrew Association, who might be able to provide information which could help me. A few days went by and the next time we met, Charles presented me with a piece of paper which was supposed to be representative of the type of information available. I began to scan through the document, and had reached about the third page when, to my absolute astonishment there was a request for information about an airman called Sgt Stuart George Bastin, serial number 909151. His mother's name was given as Rose Bastin and what had been our family home address was quoted. The airman was my uncle! To have been presented with such a random sample, only to find exactly what I required was truly astounding.

It transpired that the originator was another researcher writing a book about his cousin who had been killed on a 21 Squadron raid on Rotterdam on 16 July 1941, and in which 105 Squadron had participated. Subsequently, we were able to exchange information and contacts which might otherwise never have been made, many of whom contributed invaluable information for my narrative.

These then are three examples of unusual events which have occurred throughout the early and middle stages of constructing my Blenheim history. With these and many others in mind, I realize that there is more behind this book than merely relating a story.

It is important to point out that throughout the text, the rank of certain individuals may occasionally have been 'Temporary' and therefore the word 'Acting' should correctly prefix it. However, for the sake of clarity I have omitted this prefix and trust that this will not unduly upset the reader. Additionally, detailed accounts of awards and citations have only been given when the action for which they were received was undertaken while they were serving with 105 Squadron, during their Battle or Blenheim eras, and even then only when found to be available by research.

The text has been based largely upon information obtained from the Squadron's Operations Record Book (ORB) and other official records, backed up by details from individuals' log books and personal recollections. On most occasions, where there have been minor conflicts of information, corroboration has been taken as substantiation of the facts, otherwise logical reasoning and informed discussion have been employed but not to the detriment of the general accuracy of the narrative. I hope the reader will gain as much understanding and enjoyment by reading this book as I have gained while writing it – it has been a most interesting, yet humbling experience.

Stuart R. Scott
Waygateshaw
February 1996

Introduction

The Bristol Blenheim has largely been ignored in discussions about the exploits of the Royal Air Force during the Second World War. Most people tend to expound, usually at length, about the virtues and exploits of the Spitfire, Hurricane, Lancaster and Mosquito; there is, happily, at least one preserved example of each of these in flying condition, and they appear regularly in public in flying displays and events. For the younger generations these beautifully preserved aircraft present a fascinating view of the past, the realities of which will never be fully known to them. To the more senior, such sights conjure up memories of a very different kind. Some are sad – the thoughts of family or friends who lost their lives in action – but some perhaps happy, reflecting on times of comradeship on a vast and prolonged scale unsurpassed in recent years.

Sadly, however, the Bristol Blenheim, which was one of the most active of aircraft in the first half of the war, has until recently been almost ignored. This twin-engined medium bomber had a crew of three, comprising a pilot, an observer, whose duties included navigation and high-level bomb aiming, and a wireless operator/air gunner, whose function was to provide protection from a turret mounted in the upper middle section of the fuselage.

The Blenheim was the mainstay of Bomber Command's initial offensives of the conflict, and formed the backbone of the activities of No. 2 Group Bomber Command as it struggled initially to support our ground troops and latterly to deny the enemy vital raw materials and munitions shipped from Axis ports of supply. Not only did the Blenheim give service in Bomber Command, it was also widely used in each and every aircraft-equipped command of the Royal Air Force. Many 'firsts' were attributed to the Blenheim: it was the first aircraft to be fitted with Airborne Interception Radar for night fighting duties; the first aircraft to destroy a submarine; and many others.

There were also many awards for bravery issued to crews operating on Blenheims. The highest, the Victoria Cross, was awarded to three airmen, each flying a different mark of Blenheim (only three marks ever having seen production). S/L Arthur Stewart King Scarf was posthumously awarded a VC on 21 June 1946, for an action on 9 December 1941, when flying Mk I Blenheims with 62 Squadron in Singapore. W/C Hughie Idwal Edwards was awarded his VC on 22 July 1941 for a low-level daylight raid on Bremen on 4 July 1941 when commanding 105 Squadron, based at Swanton Morley in Norfolk, equipped with the Mk IV Blenheim. The third recipient, W/C Hugh Gordon Malcolm, was also posthumously awarded the VC on 27 April 1943 for an operation on 4 December 1942, when he was flying a Mk V Blenheim of 18 Squadron in North Africa.

The Blenheim crews suffered grievous losses throughout the war, but their resolve, their firm belief in the right of their tasks, and their absolute belief in their leadership, remained unswayed. Despite the supreme efforts and sacrifice of their crews, the Blenheim still tends to be remembered only by that select group of individuals, the Blenheim crews who were fortunate enough to have survived the slaughter of the first three years of the war, and often had to operate in roles wholly unsuited to the aircraft in which they flew. The Blenheim was made a 'Jack of all trades', being used as a bomber for high- and low-level operations, for reconnaissance, as a night fighter, and as a day fighter – these were but a few of the roles into which it was thrust. Indeed, unknown to most, the Blenheim even flew sorties as part of the Battle of Britain.

The Spitfire, Hurricane, Lancaster and Mosquito undeniably did sterling work in defence of their country, contributing greatly to the war effort, and thoroughly deserving the reputations they accrued. However, the not-so-publicized Bristol Blenheim and its crews deserve equal praise and status in the annals of history. It is hoped that those who read this book will gain an appreciation of the sustained efforts both on the ground and in the air of a Blenheim Squadron, throughout the dark days of 1940/1.

Part One – EUROPE

CHAPTER 1

The Squadron

The squadron was officially formed from 51 Training Squadron on 23 September 1917, but it was not until 3 October that 105 Squadron came into being at Andover, under the command of Capt. H.G. Bowen. On 25 March 1918 command of this new squadron was assumed by Major D.J. Joy.

The squadron provided doughty service in the First World War, its roles being to attack opposing armies, thereby giving support to our ground troops, and also to help to eliminate the maritime threat from submarines. The squadron was to become all too familiar with these roles when the 'Great War for Civilization' was later repeated in the shape of the Second World War.

On 19 May 1918 the squadron and its RE8 aircraft were detached to Omagh in Ireland. During subsequent operations in 1918, the squadron operated in two flights: 'A' Flight found itself in County Galway while 'B' Flight was posted to County Mayo. In December 1918 105 Squadron re-equipped with two-seat Bristol F.2b biplane fighters. When the war ended and the new year dawned, command passed to Major H.J.F. Hunter, who continued their reconnaissance role until the squadron disbanded on 1 February 1919.

On 12 April 1937 the squadron re-formed at Upper Heyford from 'B' Flight of 18 Squadron, and was equipped with Hawker Audax aircraft passed on from 114 Squadron. This aircraft, which was developed from the Hawker Hart, first flew on 31 December 1931, and first saw service with 4 Squadron in February 1932. The Audax was powered by a 530hp Rolls-Royce Kestrel IB in-line piston engine, producing a maximum speed of 170mph at 2,400ft. It was primarily a two-seat biplane, protected by a forward through-propeller firing .303in machine-gun, mounted in front of the pilot.

Additionally, a rear-firing .303in Lewis gun was mounted in the rear cockpit. The aircraft was used in training for bombing attacks at sea, dropping four 20lb or two 112lb bombs, which were mounted in racks under the wings.

The Audax was complemented by the Hawker Hart, which saw service until August 1937, when it was replaced by the Fairey Battle, a monoplane aircraft powered by a single Rolls-Royce Merlin I in-line piston engine producing 1,030hp. This was capable of delivering almost double the power of its predecessor, and gave a maximum speed of 257mph at 20,000ft. The one major difference between the Audax and the Battle was the crew. The latter carried a crew of three, comprising pilot, observer and wireless operator/air gunner, who was provided once again with the standard Vickers 'K' .303in machine-gun, which was to see service until replaced by the .303in Browning. In addition, the Battle's pilot had a .303in machine-gun in the starboard wing to provide a strafing capability. The bombload was also increased: the Battle was now able to deliver a total load of 1,000lb of explosive, normally comprising four 250lb bombs mounted two under each wing. The service ceiling of the Audax was 21,500ft, but the Battle was improved to provide a ceiling maximum of 25,000ft.

In 1937 Nos 52, 63, 88 and 226 Squadrons had also been equipped with the Battle, 105

Squadron being the second (after 63 Squadron) to do so. By October 1937 the squadron was fully equipped with the new aircraft. Under the command of S/L G.W. Tuttle DFC, the Battle was to appear several times in public at air displays, demonstrating their dive-bombing ability. Even the mighty German Luftwaffe came to Andover to see a display! On 19 October 1937 Feldmarshall von Blomberg and his entourage were actually treated to a viewing of the latest aircraft capabilities, as demonstrated by an amalgamation of 63 and 105 Squadrons, complemented by a display by 35 and 114 Squadrons. By 22 May 1939 command of the squadron had passed to W/C D. McFadyen, and the squadron had bestowed upon it the honour of being named the 'Hereford' Squadron. Many squadrons had been affiliated with cities, primarily as a public relations exercise to increase the public's awareness of the RAF. This awareness was to become very much heightened as the months went on.

CHAPTER 2

The Aircraft

In 1937 the front-line fighters such as Harts and Furys suddenly found themselves outpaced by a new sleek twin-engined aircraft, the Bristol Blenheim. Originally introduced into the RAF in March 1937, the origins of the Blenheim lay with the *Daily Mail* newspaper owner Lord Rothermere, whose dream was to build the fastest commercial aeroplane in the world. He turned to the Bristol Aeroplane Company, whose chief engineering designer Frank Sowter Barnwell OBE AFC BSc produced a preliminary design of a twin-engined aircraft of light alloy monocoque construction, with hydraulic, fully retractable undercarriage, variable pitch propellers, landing flaps and an enclosed cockpit, all of which were new features.

Originally the aircraft was equipped with two 500hp Bristol Aquilla I engines and was designated Type 135, until April 1935 when equipped with 650hp Bristol Mercury VIS engines it was known as the Type 142, and was named the 'Britain First'. It was not long before it was demonstrated to the Air Ministry, Bristol's biggest customer. Subsequently Lord Rothermere donated the 'Britain First' to the RAF. In June 1935 the military version of the prototype, Type 142M, arrived at RAF Martlesham, and was given the serial number K7557.

As the Type 142 was ostensibly a passenger aircraft, several modifications were made to suit the RAF's requirements for the Type 142M medium bomber. Space had to be allowed for an observer for navigation and bomb-aiming duties, and so a glass nose was formed, complete with panels behind which bombsights could be mounted. Additionally, the wing was raised from its low position to the middle of the fuselage to make room for a bomb-bay. A mid-upper gun turret was fitted, with an entry hatch just forward of the turret, and elevators and the tail-plane were raised. Following all these modifications, the Blenheim MkI was born.

In December 1936 the green light was given for production and the new 'wonder bomber' was delivered to various operational units, 114 Squadron being the first recipients. The first batch to be distributed totalled 434 in number. A fighter variant was produced with a four-gun pack mounted on the belly; this was called the MkIVF. This could be used as a night fighter, fitted with a crude version of airborne radar, then referred to as Airborne Interception (AI) sets. The Blenheim was the first night fighter fitted with such a device.

Further operational requirements led to a MkII version, with strengthened undercarriage and a greater loaded weight. A MkIII was also produced in three stages, all of which were aimed at increasing the pilot's vision. Firstly, apart from additional fuel tanks, modifications were made to extend the nose section, thereby giving the observer a greater working area and providing a map-table for navigation. Unfortunately the extended nose resulted in impaired vision for the pilot, particularly on landing. Consequently, the roof of the observer's enclosure was lowered, but with little effect. Neither the MkII nor MkIII versions saw production. It was not until the pilot was given a normal close windscreen and a scalloped nose section, those distinctive features of the Blenheim MkIV, that the visibility problem was solved. The result was the Type 149, or Bristol Blenheim MkIV medium bomber, which was used extensively throughout the early years of conflict.

The first MkIVs were MkI versions with the modifications listed above, but from L9294 onwards the true MkIV version was produced. An unofficial version designated MkIVL was produced as the first version to have outer long-range fuel tanks; however, all MkIV aircraft

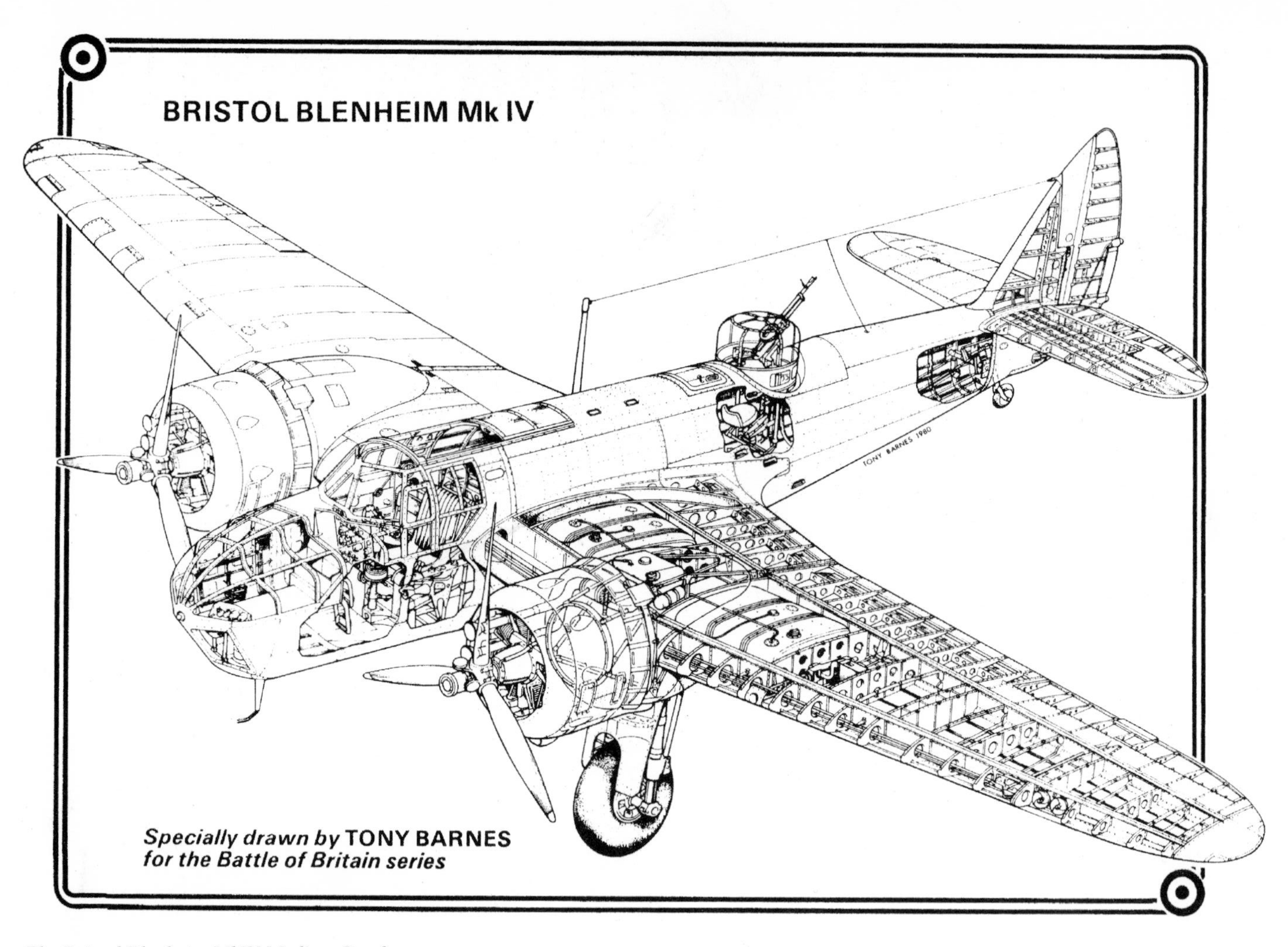

The Bristol Blenheim MkIV Medium Bomber.

were soon similarly equipped. No. 105 Squadron was equipped with the MkIV, although they also possessed a MkI 'hack' aircraft for general duties.

The MkIV had a wing span of 56ft 4in, an overall length of 39ft 9in, and stood at a proud 9ft 10in high with its tail-wheel on the ground. It had two Bristol Mercury XV nine-cylinder, air-cooled, supercharged radial engines, with a rating of 995hp each. Each engine was fitted with a de Havilland-Hamilton two-position, three-bladed metal propeller, hydraulically operated and with a 10ft 6in diameter. The aircraft was capable of a normal cruise speed of 200mph but flat out at sea-level could reach 220mph. Fuel was held in two 140-gallon inner wing tanks, while for longer range sorties, two outer wing tanks each held a further 94 gallons. A fuel jettison pipe was fitted centrally on each wing's under-surface, outboard of the engines, facing to the rear. These pipes permitted fuel to be jettisoned if an emergency landing was required with the aircraft near maximum loading. Should a flight be aborted soon after take-off, fuel could be off-loaded to bring the aircraft back within safe landing weight limits. A further temporary modification could be made by storing extra 100-gallon tanks in the well behind the pilot for very long range trips, such as the trip to Malta described later. This was not, however, a standard modification.

For protection, the Blenheim MkIV had defensive armament consisting of one .303in Browning machine-gun in the port wing. Mounted on a detachable cradle, it was fed from a removable belt-box, which was located behind a detachable panel under the wing. The gun was operated by the aircraft's pneumatic system, as were the brakes. The pilot fired the gun by depressing a button on the yoke with the thumb of his right hand. For safety reasons this button was protected by a brass locking ring, which had to be unlocked before it could be fired. This gun tended to be used on the bomber version for 'hose-piping' rounds over the decks of ships during attacks, to keep the ships' gunners' heads down.

Located to the right of the pilot, the observer had access to a Fraser-Nash FN-54 blister gun, mounted under the nose on the starboard side. This gun could be jettisoned in the event of an emergency, as it was awkwardly mounted around the nose floor escape-hatch. This gun initially comprised a Browning .303in rear-firing machine-gun, operated by the observer by a series of links and linkages. Sighting was by mirrors mounted within the blister. Later versions comprised a two-gun arrangement, enclosed not in a blister but in a fabricated box; this system was designated the Fraser-Nash FN-54A. It tended to be reversed to provide a forward-firing strafing facility for attacking road transports in North Africa. The observer's nose-gun was little used, because once the trigger had been pulled and the initial rounds expended, the nose area filled up with smoke and cordite fumes. This not only made the environment rather unpleasant, but also made accurate aiming impossible. Nevertheless it was available, even though its greatest benefit was probably psychological.

The main protection came in the form of two machine-guns mounted in the mid-upper turret and operated by the wireless operator/air gunner. The turret was initially only equipped with one Vickers gas-operated (VGO) 'K' machine-gun, but subsequent modifications resulted in two .303in Browning machine-guns becoming the norm. The Bristol B.I (and latterly B.X) turret was hydraulically operated by a pump driven by the port engine, which also operated the undercarriage system. Selection of hydraulics to the undercarriage was controlled by the pilot, operating a selector switch. This gave turret control only when in flight. The turret was operated by foot-pedals and twist-grip handles. When the guns were elevated, the gunner's seat would descend to give a better line of sight for aiming. Conversely, when the guns were lowered the seat would rise. The cupola around the guns was designed so that it could be raised and lowered by rotating a handle. This design proved to be rather a problem on occasions, because if the controlling wire snapped, the cupola could drop. Consequently, it was not unknown for an air gunner to end his days with a broken neck.

The turret was rotated hydraulically. A mechanical stop was fitted under the guns, which ran around the raised ring section when it traversed towards the rear of the aircraft. This section formed part of the fuselage and would automatically elevate the guns when they swung towards the tail, thereby preventing the air gunner from scoring an 'own goal' by shooting his tail off. Ammunition was housed in two deep metal boxes on either side of the air gunner's knees, and belts of .303in bullets were fed up to the guns on metal gooseneck-shaped feeders, with spent cartridges being discharged into a container at the rear of the guns. The gun-sight was electrically operated on the later versions. Various modifications were tried, usually at a local or squadron level, to improve the MkIV's defensive capability, including the fitting of rear-firing guns in the engine nacelles. Another popular feature was the fitting of a VGO gun through the nose on a gimble mounting, which was operated by the observer.

Bombs were carried in bomb-bays in the centre plane of the aircraft at its centre of gravity. There were two bomb compartments, each enclosed by spring-mounted doors, which flew open under the weight of the falling bomb and then snapped shut again when the bomb or bombs had passed through. The main bombload comprised four 250lb bombs or two 500lb bombs. Smaller 40lb high explosive or incendiary bombs could be fitted into Universal Carriers, the former fitted two to each bomb compartment. There were other locations where bombs could be carried; outer wing racks were used for practice bombs or flares, and an under-fuselage mounted rack could hold similar types of small munitions. This rack was mounted behind the main bomb-bays. There was a winch mechanism to lift the bomb up into the bomb-bay, often with the steadying influence of the back and shoulders of the nearest armourer, until the bomb could be located on its hook. In general, the most common bombload was four 250lb general purpose or semi-armour piercing types, each fitted with an 11-second delay fuse, particularly for low-level work against ground targets or ships. This delay permitted the aircraft to get far enough away before the explosion, thereby minimizing the risk of being caught in the bomb blast. It was, however, not unknown for the following aircraft to fly through the bomb blast from the preceding aircraft.

The bombs were kept in bomb dumps on the aerodrome and were pulled out to waiting aircraft on bomb trolleys, all clipped together like a small train. The round fins were stored separately and clipped to the bombs before loading. Each bomb's heavy metal casing was filled with a

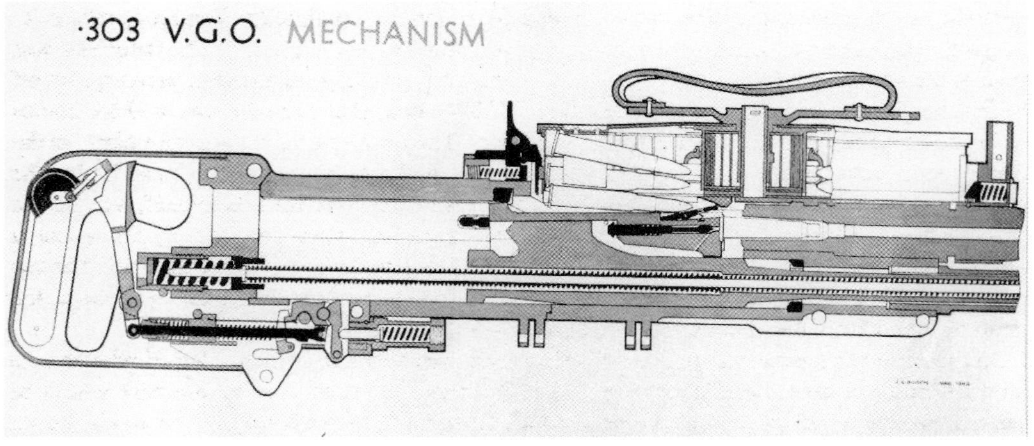

The .303in Vickers Gas Operated (VGO) machine-gun, drawn by 105 Squadron's J.L. Higson in March 1942. This was the WOp/AG's standard defence until it was replaced by the .303in Browning machine-gun. (via Wally Fennell)

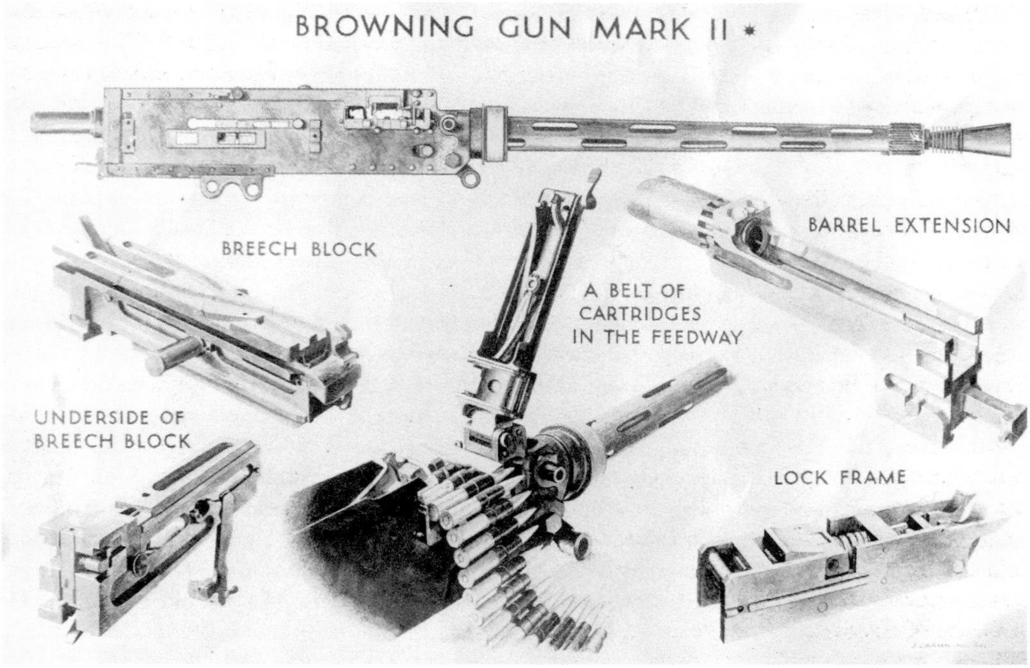

The .303in Browning machine-gun, drawn by 105 Squadron's J.L. Higson in October 1941. This gun replaced the VGO machine-gun and subsequently the WOp/AG's gun turret was equipped with two of these guns. A forward-firing .303in Browning machine-gun was also mounted in the port wing of the Blenheim as a standard item; a later squadron modification resulted in a .303in Browning machine-gun being mounted through the perspex nose panel of some aircraft, for operation by the observer. (via Wally Fennell)

newly introduced explosive called RDX (Research and Development Compound 'X'), now commonly known as Hexogen, which was very new at the time. It was desensitized by mixing it into a melt with TNT. The mixture was quite inert until detonated. Each bomb had a screwed metal plug in the nose and another in the tail and a tube ran the length of the interior from nose to tail plug. This tube was filled with high explosive known as an 'exploder'. The detonator was fixed in the nose or tail. When the bomb hit, the detonator, possibly fulminate of mercury, set off the tetryl exploder which in turn exploded the RDX/TNT mix. If a nose fuse was used the bombs would be dropped from height to explode on impact. The nose fuse had a pressure plate on the front attached to a metal stalk. When the bomb impacted, the stalk was pushed back, hitting the detonator, which exploded the bomb. Between the pressure plate and the bomb itself, was fitted a fork-like device, akin to a large tuning-fork. To prevent the fork from inadvertently falling out, a pin was inserted through it at each end which remained in situ until just before take-off. The top end of the fork was attached to a wire which was in turn attached to the aircraft. As soon as the bomb fell away from the aircraft, the wire pulled the fork out, thus arming the bomb.

On the observer's panel in the nose of the aircraft was a switch, which selected whether the bombs were to be armed or if they were to be jettisoned. In the latter case, the wire would be released from the aircraft along with the fork and bomb. Consequently, there would be no explosion – or so the theory went! It was important prior to bombing to ensure that the selector switch was set to make the bombs 'live'. When tail fuses were used, the nose fuses were not fitted, and nose plugs were screwed in instead. The tail fuse was screwed into the rear of the bomb and comprised a bob weight of brass inside a tube which moved forward on impact, hitting a lightweight spring. The forward-facing stalk on the bob would hit the detonator. A delay was fitted to prevent immediate detonation, each bomb being colour-coded to identify the delay period. Bombs could be dropped singly or in salvos. Selection was made electrically in the cockpit. When dropping salvos, the observer would rotate his 'Mickey Mouse' lever (as it was known), to electrically release the bombs in rotation.

The Blenheim was equipped with two radio sets located behind the gun turret, in what was probably the most difficult position for the wireless operator/air gunner to get at. Initially they were equipped with a T1083/R1082 transmitter/receiver, with its various plug-in coils giving access to different frequencies from 111kHz to 15MHz. It was a most complicated and cumbersome piece of equipment to operate. Later Marconi T1154/R1155 transmitter/receiver sets were installed, which were more efficient and easier to tune, using 'click stop' settings for the transmitter frequencies. These sets were used for Morse code only, and could operate up to a range of about 1,000 miles. Twenty miles out, when returning from operations, the WOp/AG would call up the DF Station and send out the Movement Serial Indicator (MSI). This code of letters/numbers, changed at intervals throughout the day, was a method of identifying friendly aircraft. If he was uncertain of their position, the WOp/AG could request a QDM and then send out a long continuous tone for several seconds; this allowed the ground station to take a direction-finding bearing from the signal so they could advise a magnetic heading for the aircraft to steer.

An Identification Friend or Foe (IFF) set was later fitted to the floor of the aircraft behind the gunner; this was switched off on leaving the coast and was only switched on again when the aircraft was about 20 miles from the coast on its return journey. This system worked in conjunction with the radar stations and friendly aircraft were identified by a different type of 'blip' on the ground radar scope. The Blenheim was also equipped with a small TR9 radio set operated by the pilot. This provided an internal intercom system, and also permitted R/T or voice communications between aircraft and ground. It was operated by a lever to the left of the pilot, which could be pushed forwards, backwards, or returned to a central position. Its range was about 5 miles. If the pilot wanted to talk to the ground control station on the aerodrome, he would choose one of the five channels available, one of which would be home base. Pushing the handle forward gave 'transmit' mode, while pulling it back gave 'receive' mode, hence the origin of the commonly used expression 'over', because when changing to receive mode from transmit mode, the pilot would pull the handle 'over'. When not in use the handle was left in the central 'off' position. The local set had a dedicated frequency called the 'darky frequency' which was used only in the UK, mostly for aircraft lost at night 'in the dark'. The nearest aerodrome would reply and give roughly the location of the aircraft.

The principal manufacturer of the Blenheim I was the Bristol Aeroplane Company, although a handful were manufactured under licence in Yugoslavia for use by their air force. Finland also had a licence to produce airframes and engines at the State Aircraft Factory (Valtion Lentokenetehdas), a total of fifty-five being built to Finnish specifications. These aircraft were equipped with larger bomb-bays to house the larger bombs they used, and some were even fitted with skis for use in snow-covered fields. Nose cones were also fitted to the propellers on some Finnish versions. There were another two manufacturers of the Blenheim I in England: A.V. Roe and Company Ltd manufactured a total of 250 machines, and Rootes Securities Ltd of Speke manufactured a further 318 aircraft. The Blenheim MkIV was mostly manufactured by Rootes Securities Ltd, and also by AVRO at Chadderton. The latter produced 755 aircraft, while Rootes produced some 2,230 aircraft, 84 of which were MkI conversions, with Bristol manufacturing only 300.

This then was the Bristol Blenheim medium bomber operated by 105 Squadron.

CHAPTER 3

The War in Europe and Scandinavia

At 04.45 hours on Friday 1 September 1939, an event took place which was to cost the lives of millions of people the world over. Germany's leader, their Führer Adolf Hitler, ordered the commencement of the invasion of Poland. His two Army Groups, 'North' and 'South' under Field Marshals von Bock and von Runstedt respectively, began a ruthless campaign which lasted only eighteen days before Poland collapsed. The campaign was greatly aided by a Russian invasion from the east. Germany's seemingly inexorable drive across Europe had begun.

Since his declaration of 'Führer' in 1934, Hitler had seen the Rhineland reoccupied in 1936 and subsequently came to the aid of the Nationalists in Spain, where he provided General Franco with men and military hardware. Where else could he find a proving ground for his new found military might, established despite the Treaty of Versailles? Luftwaffe bombers savagely destroyed Spanish towns and villages and their fighters were equally well employed. Although there were several verbal debates regarding their conduct, no direct force was offered to the Germans by anyone other than the defenders. Even when Hitler and his Nazis took over Austria and subjugated Czechoslovakia in 1938, there was no action from Britain.

On 24 September 1938 Prime Minister Neville Chamberlain emerged from his aeroplane at Heston, proclaiming 'peace in our time', and waving his famous piece of paper signed by the Führer, which claimed that German desires were satisfied by the Czechoslovakian settlement and that the foundations for a lasting peace had been laid. Despite this, the French and British had not rested on their laurels, taking the Führer's assurances with no more than a pinch of salt. Mr Chamberlain admitted: 'after Munich our defence programme was actually accelerated and expanded so as to remedy certain weaknesses which had become apparent during the crises.' However much we attempted to boost our forces, with schemes such as the RAF expansion programme, the day had come when action was required to stop the German dictator from overtaking Europe. Consequently, on 3 September 1939 at 11.15 hours, a radio broadcast was made from 10 Downing Street by the Prime Minister in which he stated: 'This morning the British Ambassador in Berlin handed the German government a final note, stating that unless we heard from them by eleven o'clock that they were prepared at once to withdraw their troops from Poland, a state of war would exist between us. I have to tell you that no such undertaking has been received, and consequently this country is at war with Germany.'

Chamberlain further conceded: 'His action shows convincingly that there is no chance of expecting this man will ever give up his practice of using force to gain his will. He can only be stopped by force. We and France are today, in fulfilment of our obligations, going to the aid of Poland, who is so bravely resisting this wicked and unprovoked attack on her people.'

He concluded: 'Now may God bless you all. May he defend the right. It is the evil things that we shall be fighting against – brute force, bad faith, injustice, oppression and persecution – and against them I am certain that the right will prevail.'

Following the birth of the Royal Air Force's Bomber Command, No. 2 (Bomber) Group was formed on 20 March 1936, with its headquarters at Abingdon. Initially equipped with Hawker Hinds and Fairey Gordons, there was a slow transformation as squadrons were absorbed on to

2 Group strength, while others were impressed into other Groups. On 26 January 1937 headquarters moved to RAF Andover. Fairey Battles joined the scene at 63 Squadron. Subsequently, many other Group squadrons began to exchange their Hinds, re-arming with these aircraft. The Blenheim too began to emerge strongly within 2 Group. The first of the Group's deliveries were to 114 Squadron based at RAF Wyton, followed by 90, 139, 110, 18, 62, 82, 57, 104, 108, 101, 34, 21 and 107 Squadrons. The low-flying capability of the aircraft was recognized even at this stage as being its 'stock-in-trade'.

With the events that were taking place in Europe, the outbreak of war was an inevitable conclusion. Nevertheless it still came as a shock when inevitability became reality. But 2 Group was ready and immediately sprang into action – only one minute after war had been declared, blue puffs of smoke thrust from the exhaust stubs of Blenheim N6215, as 139 Squadron's F/O Andrew McPherson prepared for take-off at Wyton along with his crew, Cdr Thompson RN and Corporal V. Arrowsmith. Despite severe icing at high altitude, they returned with an abundance of photographs, including several capital ships of the German Fleet in the Schillig Roads. The first sortie of the war had been successfully completed, but because of the icing up of the radio, plans for any subsequent attacks could only be made having first studied the photographs.

The next day the AOC Bomber Command instructed fifteen crews from 107, 110 and 139 Squadrons to attack the German Fleet anchored off Wilhelmshaven. Destroyers in the Jade River were to be alternative but secondary targets. Despite the atrocious weather, with low cloud and rain, five Blenheims from each squadron duly took off. The aircraft of 139 Squadron failed to find any targets because of the weather conditions, but 107 and 110 Squadrons, led by F/L K.C. Doran of 110 Squadron did find elements of the German Fleet. The *Admiral Scheer* was found by 110 Squadron and they attacked with two bombs which hit the ship and exploded amidships. One Blenheim failed to return. By the time 107 Squadron attacked, the enemy was alerted, and four of their five aircraft failed to return. It was a heavy price to pay – five aircraft lost in achieving only some bomb damage to the *Admiral Scheer*. The cruiser *Emden* was also damaged, sadly as a result of a Blenheim crashing into its bows. So ended 2 Group's first engagement of the war. Such rates of attrition were to become synonymous with the Group as time wore on.

On 2 November 1939, in recognition of their fortitude, both F/L Kenneth C. Doran of 110 Squadron and F/O Andrew McPherson of 139 Squadron were awarded the DFC, the first decorations of the war, which was only a few hours old when their attack was made. The ceremony took place at RAF Wyton and the decorations were personally bestowed by HM King George VI.

Following the signing of a Pact of Non-Aggression in 1932, the Russians made vital territorial demands on her neighbour Finland, which were clearly not acceptable. Consequent upon Finland's refusal to accede to such outrageous requirements, the Russians denounced their Pact of Non-Aggression and on 30 November 1939 launched an attack on Finland. This attack by a country known to be aligned with the Nazis was taken very seriously, particularly with regard to the northern trade routes. It was recognized that on receipt of British aid to the Finns, a foothold might be established in the Baltic within Norway or Sweden. It was also recognized that Germany was obtaining a great deal of iron-ore, a vital ingredient in munitions, from these two countries. These facts had clearly been appreciated by the Germans, who considered it imperative to win a foothold there before their enemy.

Representations were made on several occasions to the Norwegian and Swedish governments to allow military units to cross their countries to reach Finland. Each time, these met with a rebuff and the provision of iron-ore supplies to Germany continued. However, suspicions were aroused in the Fatherland, and it was subsequently decided that Germany must quickly secure her interests in Scandinavia, before the British could secure their own. Britain's only recourse was to mine the waters outside the port of Narvik. On 13 March 1940, at 11.00 hours, there was an armistice in the Russian/Finnish war and a Peace Treaty was drawn up with the Soviets. It was decided, however, that the British would pursue their aims to prevent further Russian incursions in the Scandinavian Peninsula and of course, to control the export of iron-ore. This was recognized by the Germans who responded by launching Operation Weserubung.

On 6 April 1940 the German battle-cruisers *Scharnhorst* and *Gneisenau* were reported at anchor off Wilhelmshaven. That night they sailed, led by the cruiser *Hipper*. Once again, 2 Group sprang into action, and W/C Basil Embry, CO of 107 Squadron, led a dozen Blenheims into the hunt. A total of seventeen ships were found in the convoy. Unfortunately, in the ensuing attack only the *Scharnhorst* had a close call, when a bomb just failed to penetrate it. The curtain of flak produced the same nil result from the second wave of six Blenheims. However, intelligence had been gathered which more accurately defined the force heading north – 2 Group had intercepted the advance forces for the invasion of Norway! By 9 April 1940 Germany had a full grip on Norway. The attention being paid to the two battle-cruisers, coupled with very poor visibility, had masked the activity of the German forces leaving Heligoland Bight to occupy the main ports of Oslo, Arnedal, Kristiansand, Egersund and Bergen.

Having over-run Denmark and now Norway with minimal losses, Hitler had secured the supply routes for his precious iron-ore. It was now down to 2 Group's Blenheims, operating from Lossiemouth in Scotland, to prevent supplies getting to the German garrisons, which in the more remote areas relied on provisions delivered by the Luftwaffe. German-held airfields were therefore targeted. Consequently, operations order no. 10 of 13 April 1940 got into full swing. Airfields, including Stavanger Airfield, and a local seaplane base were attacked. Fighting continued in Norway with the battle for Narvik, which was occupied long enough to destroy the port's facilities prior to withdrawal, so that, in the short term at least, no iron-ore would sail from Narvik to Germany.

The futility of attempting to hold on to Narvik was well recognized, following General Auchinleck's estimates of men and materials necessary, all of which were urgently required to halt the enemy's advances through Europe. But following the destruction of Narvik, iron-ore sailings ceased until January of 1941. The British evacuation of Narvik which began on 3 June 1940, went well, although the Navy ships were engaged on their return journey by *Scharnhorst* and *Gneisenau*. After the valiant attempt to land the ten surviving Hurricanes of 46 Squadron on the deck of HMS *Glorious*, this precious cargo of men and machines were destroyed along with the 22,500-ton ship and its company. On 8 June 1940, west of Narvik, shells from the enemy battle-cruisers rained down on them, leaving only a handful of survivors.

Having secured the supply routes from Scandinavia, Hitler continued his ruthless advances through Europe, with an army of some two million men. They were split into three Army Groups, designated A, B and C. The most northerly, Army Group B, was poised along a line some 200 miles long, along the Dutch and Belgian border. This was to allow a thrust through the Low Countries, while Army Group A was poised to the south of Group B, to skirt around the northern end of the Maginot Line and Dyle line, through Sedan. Lastly, Army Group C were poised along the border to the south of Army Group A, to confront and keep the Maginot Line busy as a diversionary tactic. Army Group B had twenty-nine Wehrmacht divisions including three Panzers, Group A had forty-five motorized infantry divisions including seven Panzers, while Group C had nineteen divisions and no Panzers.

Since the beginning of the war, British plans had intended to send an Expeditionary Force to France in support of the Army. The CinC was to be Viscount Gort VC. The British Expeditionary Force was supported by British Air Forces France under Air Marshal Arthur S.

Barratt, who had two forces subordinate to him. The RAF component under AVM Blount provided five Lysander Squadrons for tactical reconnaissance and photographic work, four Blenheim Squadrons for strategic reconnaissance to the Rhine, and four Hurricane Squadrons as troop supports, as well as to provide protection for the remainder of the RAF component. In tandem with this force, the Advanced Air Striking Force was to provide support in the south under the command of AVM Patrick H.L. Playfair. Playfair had at his disposal ten squadrons of Battle and Blenheim bombers which were to be used in an attempt to attack ground forces, while up to four squadrons of AASF Hurricanes were to protect their bases. Many of these bases were directly in line with the expected thrust of Army Group A. The attacks by the Army units in the north were to be delayed by home-based Blenheims of 2 Group attacking bridges and road junctions where troops would be concentrated. Support by heavy bombers was to be provided from England at night against strategic targets. In particular, Whitleys were to attack rail and road communications routes to the west of the Rhine.

This then was the air support available to the Allied Armies, whose intention was to defend a line along the Belgian borders. It was not considered likely that a German attack on the Maginot Line would be successful and the idea of an advance through the Ardennes was thought equally unlikely. In the event of hostilities, Allied Armies were to advance to a line some 200 miles long running from Holland, south through Belgium and into France. Specifically, the Dyle Line ran from Moerdijk in the north, just inside Holland, to Sedan, further south in France. The defensive line ran from north to south. The French Seventh Army in the north, were to cover an area around Antwerp and the mouth of the River Schelde. South of this, the Belgians were to retreat and fight a rear-guard action, holding the area from Antwerp to Louvain on the south-west of and including the Albert Canal. The BEF was to control the area south of this around Wavre and north-east to Louvain. Further south again, the French First Army was to cover the Wavre to Namur line, while the French Ninth Army covered the Meuse from Mézières to Namur.

Meanwhile, the French Second Army was positioned to attend to any unlikely excursions through the Ardennes to the south, and the Third Army was ably poised to counter any threat from Army Group C should the unthinkable happen and the Maginot Line be breached.

As for the AASF units, they were scattered at airfields in an area south of the Ardennes around the Rivers Oise, Aisne, and Marne. The Battles of 105 Squadron were based at Villeneuve, within approximately 20 miles of 139 Squadron at Plivot and 114 Squadron at Conde, all close to the River Marne.

On 10 May 1940 Hitler's 'Blitzkrieg' commenced and the enemy began a massive penetration into Holland, backed by a large airborne assault. While fighters were already in combat, successfully protecting the BEF from advances towards their lines, the Battles were about to be unleashed on the advancing German troop concentrations through Luxembourg. As Battles and indeed Blenheims were most vulnerable to attack from below, low-level operations were most necessary. As a result, they received a murderous hail of small-arms fire from the columns of troops they attacked. Thirteen Battles out of the thirty-two despatched fell victim to this in the first day of the offensive. One of these aircraft belonged to 105 Squadron (P2200). Clearly, medium bombers were going to suffer grievously.

By the next day it was apparent that the Germans were intending to advance through the Ardennes and through Holland at Maastricht. As a result of a German airborne assault, the bridges over the Albert Canal were captured intact and the German Army, having crossed the Canal safely, now constituted a serious threat to the Belgian rear-guard action. It was therefore decided that 2 Group would reconnoitre the Maastricht area. Twelve crews of 21 Squadron took off in the mid-afternoon to attack the main bridge at Maastricht. Once more, murderous ground fire was met. Out of twelve Blenheims despatched, only one was not damaged and two were shot down. The remainder had taken a severe mauling. To the south, of the eight Battles sent to attack columns of troops near the Luxembourg border, only one returned.

The next day, the 12th, the assault on advancing troops at Maastricht continued, this time by Blenheims of 139 Squadron of the AASF. Nine crews went out and seven succumbed to the usual hail of ground fire – AASF Blenheims were clearly being slaughtered. In view of the seriousness of the situation, a formation of twelve volunteer Battle crews set out to try to stem the advance. This resulted in the loss of five of their aircraft, and the subsequent award of two posthumous Victoria Crosses. As the Battles had been attacking the bridges over the Albert Canal, 2 Group were also busy attacking the Maastricht bridges again. The first attempt was made by 107 Squadron, who were hacked to pieces by a murderous hail of flak and scythed into by fighters. Next into the fray were XV Squadron, who lost eighteen men, and had only two aircraft serviceable on their return. Half of the squadron had been obliterated in a single operation. Then 110 Squadron from Wattisham took their turn and lost two aircraft to fighters. Of their eleven Blenheims, eight were flak damaged. That same evening, 82 Squadron went out on a similar mission, to attack the road along the Albert Canal. This time at least, all returned. Regrettably, in future operations they were not nearly so fortunate.

The next day the medium bombers rested, and news came through that Lt General Ewald von Kleist had commenced an assault on Sedan. Three Panzer Divisions struck to the west of Sedan from a vantage point overlooking the French, supported by a devastating Stuka dive-bomber attack, which lasted all afternoon. The French also took a pounding from the German 88s. Well into the afternoon, the German assault on the river began. Panzer infantry support troops used rubber dinghies and inflatable rafts to paddle across the river, amid ferocious shell-fire. Eventually the French defences crumbled. By that evening, German soldiers were building pontoon bridges across the river and the thrust from the Ardennes started in earnest.

Daily, as the thrust continued, the RAF were called on in an attempt to stem the inexorable onslaught of the German war machine, and grievously they suffered in consequence. On the 14th for example, an all-out attempt was made to attack the Sedan bridgehead, as the AASF attacked columns of troops and bridges. All in all that day, forty medium bombers out of seventy-one were destroyed within a matter of hours. Approximately half of 105 Squadron's Battles succumbed to the gunfire. The worst casualty rate was suffered by 218 Squadron, who lost ten out of eleven aircraft despatched. Subsequently, 2 Group provided support from England and took a similar mauling. Aircraft of 21, 107 and 110 Squadrons set out with fighter escort – of their twenty-eight aircraft, five were lost to enemy fire, two force-landed and at least five were severely damaged. At the end of the day the French troops fighting in the Gembloux gap had to retreat. However, the air assault was causing fatigue within the German ranks and this, coupled with the 2nd Army's attack that day at Sedan, appeared to have held the German advance. This achievement was to be very short-lived.

The next day, 15 May 1940, orders were issued by Air Marshal Barratt that Battles were not to be used on daylight operations unless it was a necessity. This news came as a welcome respite, although 2 Group remained active. Among other raids, 40 Squadron attacked exit points from Sedan. Two Blenheims were lost, one being the CO's machine. And so the carnage continued, as the AASF bases began their retreat to grass landing-strips in South Champagne and at Troyes. The German advance was now turning into a rout, as their army broke through around Gembloux and Louvain – the BEF were suffering badly.

In an effort to stem the enemy advance, 82 Squadron were sent out on 17 May to the Gembloux gap, where they were quickly massacred. Their target was a crossroads at Gembloux. First they met accurate ack-ack at 7,500ft, and when that died down, fifteen Bf 109s pounced on them, delivering very ordered and precise attacks. One at a time these unescorted Blenheims fell prey to the marauding fighters – only one returned. It was in a very battered condition, a complete write-off. The squadron had been decimated. Had it not been for the strength and determination of their CO, the Earl of Bandon, it would surely have ceased to exist. However, despite attempts by Group to disband the squadron, only three days later it had re-formed and was ready to fight again by 20 May.

In view of operational losses, it was decided that 2 Group aircraft should be reserved for night attacks. However, this was subsequently abandoned in favour of the resumption of daylight attacks with fighter escort from 11 Group. The nearer to England the battle raged, the more feasible it was to provide fighter escort for the Blenheim squadrons.

On 23 May 1940 the German armour had advanced to the Channel coast and the BEF had lost their seaports at Calais, Boulogne and Abbeville. It was apparent that only one route home was possible and ironically it was Hitler himself who kept the way open – during a visit to von Rundstedt's HQ at Charleville, he ordered that General Heinz Guderain should not pass beyond a line from Lens to Béthune, St Omer and Gravelines. Otherwise the German Army could have reached Dunkirk within 24 hours. In an attempt to defend the retreating Army, 107 and 110 Squadrons attacked armoured motor vehicles on 26 May. Eleven of the 107 Squadron aircraft were hit.

The RAF flew continuous protective sorties, generally away from the eyes of the troops, many of whom were heard during and after the evacuation to question 'Where was the bloody RAF?'. Perhaps the foregoing will help to answer that particular question!

CHAPTER 4

A New Era Begins

As a component of the Advanced Air Striking Force, 105 Squadron had suffered grievously. They had put up a stern fight in their Fairey Battles, against overwhelming odds. However, having lost both flight commanders in one raid, the survivors of the depleted squadron were given orders to evacuate and make their way back home to England. After a long, tiring and confusing journey, individuals started to trickle back home to their new base at Honnington.

So now, with such sad losses sustained by the squadron, their battles for France were over, and their battles with Blenheims were about to begin! Re-equipment with Blenheim MkIV aircraft began within a week or so of the arrival back at Honnington of those men evacuated from France. As nobody in the squadron had experience of flying the twin-engined bomber, a party of ten pilots proceeded to Bicester under the command of the CO, W/C John G. Hawtrey. They set off on 27 June 1940 to 13 OTU, leaving F/O R.D.E. Pitcairn in temporary command at Honnington.

RAF Honington, c. 1941. The 'hedge' markings are made from waste oil to disguise the aerodrome when viewed from above. 105 Squadron was based here June/July 1940. (via Peter H.T. Green)

Despite the absence of the pilots, the Delivery Units were active. On 28 June the first Blenheim, L9339, arrived and was picketed down at its dispersal point to await the return of its new masters. Three other aircraft, L8778, L9209 and T1826, made up the complement of four, and on the 6 July 1940 the newly converted squadron members returned.

A familiarization period was about to begin, but not before 2 Group had ordered further changes. The new squadron home was to be Watton in Norfolk, and the move was only four days away, on 10 July. Most of the squadron moved off by train to their new base. The four new Blenheims were flown across to Watton, accompanied by a Wellington IC, courtesy of 9 Squadron also based at Honnington. The Wellington went along as an armed guard for items such as parachutes and maps which 105 Squadron had had to borrow from 9 Squadron, such was the lack of equipment at that time. Shortages were to continue for a while and were not solely related to equipment. By the time a further sixteen Blenheims had arrived at their new station, only three air gunners were available for the full complement of twenty aircraft, all of which were proudly dispersed around the aerodrome. W/C Hawtrey protested very strongly to 2 Group Headquarters about the lack of men, but it was not until 22 July that six more air gunners were posted from 13 OTU. On 27 July a further twelve arrived from 103 and 112 Squadrons, and more were now arriving back from France. Now the squadron was up to strength.

The conversion was now virtually complete and there followed a period of intense training, working up to full squadron readiness by the end of July. All parties were to be given practice and their skills tested. The show began on 17 July, when, having at last received all the necessary parachutes, flying training began in earnest.

On 22 July a familiar sight was seen, as Battle aircraft were again in the sky, this time as

An impressive line of 82 Squadron Blenheims at RAF Watton, home of 105 Squadron from July to October 1940. 82 Squadron shared the base with 105 Squadron from August 1939 to October 1940. (via Peter H.T. Green)

target-towing aircraft, pulling drogues over the Wash. This gave the Blenheim air gunners the chance to try out their new power-operated mid-upper turrets and guns. Wainfleet Sands was the venue on 26 July, when each Blenheim practised low-level attacks, dropping 11½lb practice bombs on the bombing range. Low-level work was to be the stock-in-trade of 105 Squadron for a long time to come!

Night flying was also attempted. On two separate occasions 'A' Flight, now operating from the satellite airfield at Bodney, had to cancel their night-flying exercises because of the mist. But success was achieved by two aircraft of 'B' Flight on the evening of the 25th. Two more aircraft from 'A' Flight tried yet again on the 31st, but were once more frustrated in their attempt. This time they received an Air Raid Warning Red at 04.00 hours, but despite a lit flare-path which would have been only too visible to any attacking aircraft, the threat came to nothing.

So the first month of settling in was over and the learning period with their new Blenheims was almost at a close. A total of 323 flying hours had been clocked up, with 8½ hours of night flying. Every aspect of operational work had been practised, and it was now time to test the equipment with its full war load before operations could begin in earnest.

On 4 August 1940 W/C Hawtrey took off at 15.50 hours, accompanied by F/L Mertens and F/Sgt Richardson. The three Blenheims were fully bombed up and armed ready for battle. They practised formation flying at high altitude and it was found that above 19,500ft formation work was most uncomfortable; a lesson usefully learned in advance. Two days later, the squadron's newly found skills were demonstrated. In conjunction with Northern Command, air affiliation exercises were carried out. These comprised attacks on mechanized moving forces along the Corbridge–Risdale road in Northumberland. Finally, on 7 August 1940, the honeymoon was over and the squadron was put to operational readiness.

A 105 Squadron Blenheim on the ground at Watton in 1940. A crew member relaxes on the port wing. Note the pitot head covers flapping in the wind. (RAF Museum: P018943)

The squadron's first operational flights were attempted by W/C Hawtrey, Sgt Costello-Bowen and F/O Carter on 8 August 1940. It was all too obvious that without fighter escort and with no cloud cover during daylight hours the Blenheim crews were in a very precarious position indeed, and it was therefore no surprise when all three flights were abandoned. Another attempt was made on the 9th, but lack of cloud cover again resulted in abandonment of the task.

The first result came on 10 August, when P/O Murray and his crew, Sgt Chadwick (Observer) and Sgt Cameron (WOp/AG), opened the innings at 11.25 hours with an attack on the enemy-occupied aerodrome at Schiphol in Holland. Flying at 1,000ft, two 250lb bombs were dropped on their first run, followed by twelve 40lb bombs on the second run. The second run was in itself an act of bravery, since the enemy were well aware of the attack by then. Anti-aircraft guns opened up on the Blenheim and accurate fire punched holes in the tail unit and fin, severely damaging the aircraft. The crew were unhurt, but Blenheim L9339, the first machine to enter service, had suffered such damage on its first operational flight that it was rendered unserviceable for some time.

The same day, Sgt Costello-Bowen and crew attacked the aerodrome at Flushing, while S/L Key made an abortive attack on the aerodrome at Knokke – his attack terminated at the Belgian coast because of the lack of cloud cover. The remainder of August was taken up with attacks on several enemy aerodromes in France and Holland; many of these attacks also had to be abandoned because of the lack of cloud cover.

However, alternative targets would occasionally present themselves en route. One example of this arose on 27 August when Alkmaar aerodrome was the target for P/O Prosser and crew of 'B' Flight. Lack of cloud cover prevented an attack on the primary target, but a large concentration of shipping was found in the Zuider Zee at location 53° 02'N, 5° 13'E. A 5,000-ton merchant ship was sitting with its hatches off, presenting a perfect target and inviting the attention of one of the 250lb bombs. Equally tempting were the barges which were subsequently bombed from 1,000ft, and five camouflaged lorries which were also machine-gunned as they moved along the road west from the ship. A total of two 250lb and twelve 40lb bombs were dropped.

Two days later, two convoys were found as alternative targets. The first was discovered once again by P/O Prosser in T1887:S, at a location off Den Helder where no less than eleven ships presented themselves as targets, instead of the aerodrome at Rotenburg. Although sticks of bombs were released across the merchant vessels, results were generally not observed, although the crew did get a view of three ocean-going ships in the outer dock basin and cargo ships and cruisers in the inner basin. No doubt the bombs had done some damage, but the operation had been a greater success from a reconnaissance viewpoint!

F/O Pitcairn in T1886 was due to attack a munitions factory at Weitzendorf, 7 miles south-east of Soltau, when en route he too found a convoy at position 35° 50'N, 07° 20'E. He attacked a merchant ship with one 250lb bomb, missing it by about 30 yards. A further fourteen trawlers were also available for punishment, 5 miles north of the Frisian Islands; this time the remaining 250lb and twelve 40lb bombs were dropped, leaving a trawler slewing around billowing black smoke skywards.

Near the end of August, W/C Hawtrey departed from the squadron to take up a new appointment as Inspector to the Royal Iraqi Air Force, having spent six months moulding the squadron into its present form. A replacement CO was soon appointed in the shape of W/C Cyril Kenneth Joseph Coggle, who assumed command on 27 August.

By the end of August 1940, ninety-two hours of operational flying had been expended without loss, which was largely due to the abandonment of thirty-two sorties out of forty-six attempted, largely due to lack of cloud cover in the good summer weather. Although the good

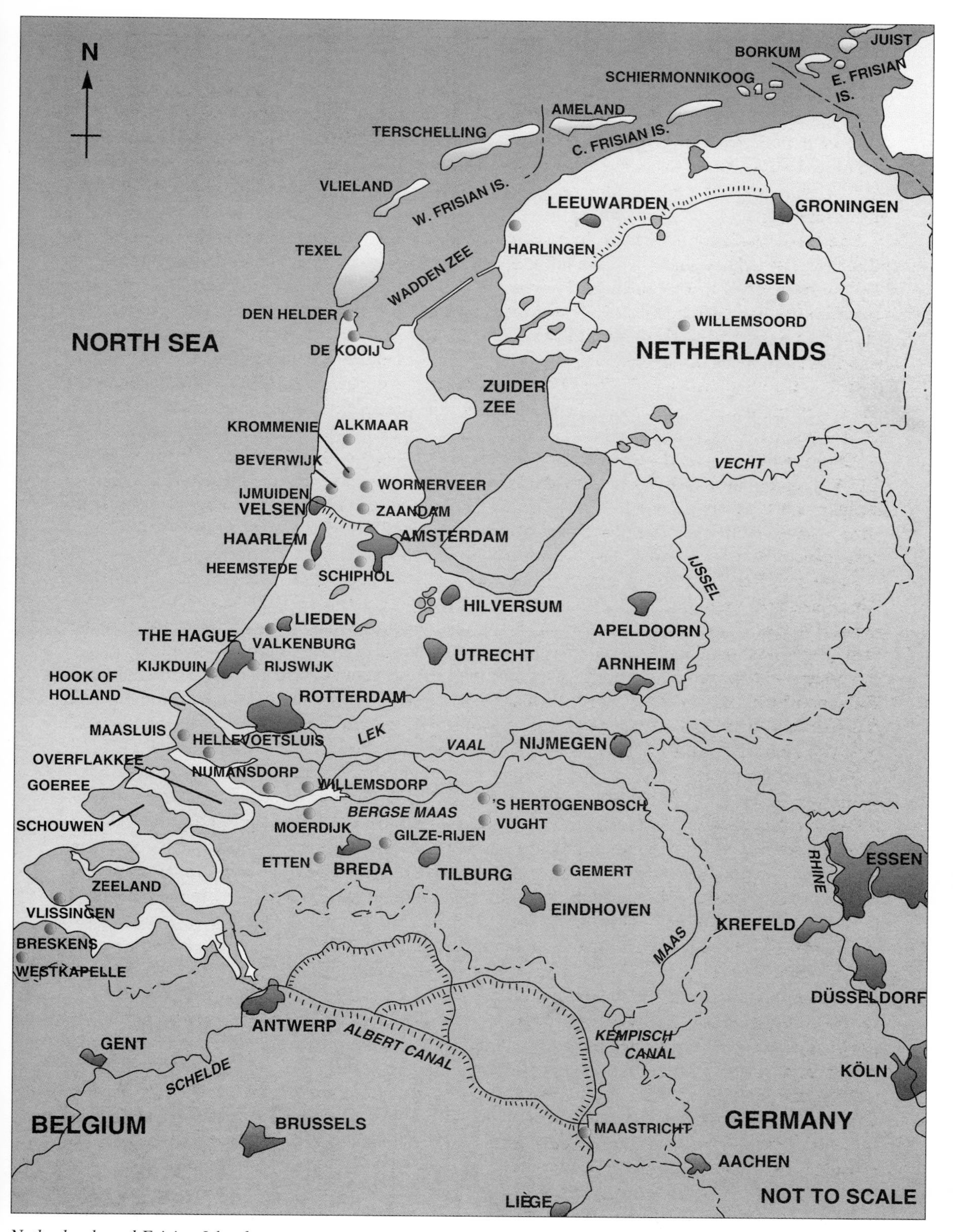

Netherlands and Frisian Islands.

weather continued into September, with the consequent abandoning of sorties, losses began to increase. The first targets of the month were to be industrial in nature.

On 1 September P/O Prosser was once more in the air heading for the Dortmund–Ems Canal, accompanied by Sgt Wilson and crew at 14,000ft. Oil refineries at Hamburg and aircraft parks at Paderborn and Diepholz were also targets for this day but in the event all aircraft abandoned the task owing to insufficient cloud cover.

However, it was not to be plain sailing for one aircraft; P/O Prosser, flying T1877, was over the Zuider Zee when he decided to abort his attack, and in order not to waste bombs, he began looking around for a target to attack. Suddenly a heavy barrage of anti-aircraft fire opened up. One shell burst on the nose of his aircraft, blowing out the perspex where his Observer Sgt Duncan was sitting; Duncan consequently received a severe shoulder wound. The pilot held on at the controls and put down at Mousehole aerodrome from where Sgt Duncan was taken to a civilian hospital for treatment. Sadly though, despite Prosser's efforts, the squadron suffered its first operational loss, when shortly afterwards Sgt Duncan died of his wounds. He was buried on the afternoon of 6 September 1940 at Linthorpe in Middlesbrough. The funeral was private, but was attended by P/O Prosser, Sgt Partridge and Sgt Gresty in the capacity of squadron representatives.

As was typical of operational life, many promotions and postings to and fro occurred. F/O J.N.G. Carter was promoted to Acting Flight Lieutenant. He and his Observer Sgt Woodhouse had been with the squadron for over three years and now they and their WOp/AG, Sgt Williams, were to move to 114 Squadron. Sgt Williams had joined the squadron in France, and according to the squadron's Operations Record Book, had 'achieved a certain notoriety when, some considerable time after he had returned from a raid in a badly battered aircraft, he eventually confessed that several shrapnel splinters had penetrated the seat of his trousers and were embedded in the fleshy portion of his lower abdomen'.

On the 7th, the squadron hosted the first visit to the Blenheim Station by Group Captain Hugh Pughe Lloyd MC DFC, at that time Senior Air Staff Officer of 2 Group. (Group Captain Lloyd was to be long associated with 105's Blenheims, as will be seen later when the squadron was detached en masse for operations from Malta. Then, as an Air Vice-Marshal, he was the Air Officer Commanding RAF Mediterranean.) The afternoon was given over to a discussion with the CO and his two flight commanders about operational training. At 16.00 hours a Bomber Command signal was received – an Invasion Alert was on, and given that the first heavy bombing attack on London was reported, full attention was paid to the signal. A previous invasion alert, which in the event had not amounted to anything, had resulted almost immediately in a change of operational emphasis. The reconnaissance of harbours and inland waterways on French and Dutch coasts was to be given priority, since if an invasion force was indeed mustering, it must be sought out and destroyed.

By dawn on the 8th, all serviceable aircraft were ready and waiting with full war load; all crews were confined to the station and all leave was cancelled. Those fortunate enough to be already on leave had their break cut short and were ordered to return to Watton. No training was allowed and the station waited in a state of readiness. That evening, following a photographic reconnaissance sortie and an attack on Boulogne, crews were permitted to venture out of the station as long as they were no more than 5 miles away after 18.00 hours. A good look at the enemy concentrations was required and consequently the next morning four crews were on their way to view the enemy coastline; once again the weather was very good and, lacking the safety of cloud cover, three of the crews returned to base. However, Sgt Hodson and his crew, Sgt Palmer (Observer) and Sgt Green (WOp/AG) failed to return in T1894 from their first operational flight; they were last seen by F/L Swain 8 miles south of Den Helder in the Dutch coast area being pursued by two single-engined enemy fighters. Without cloud cover it was

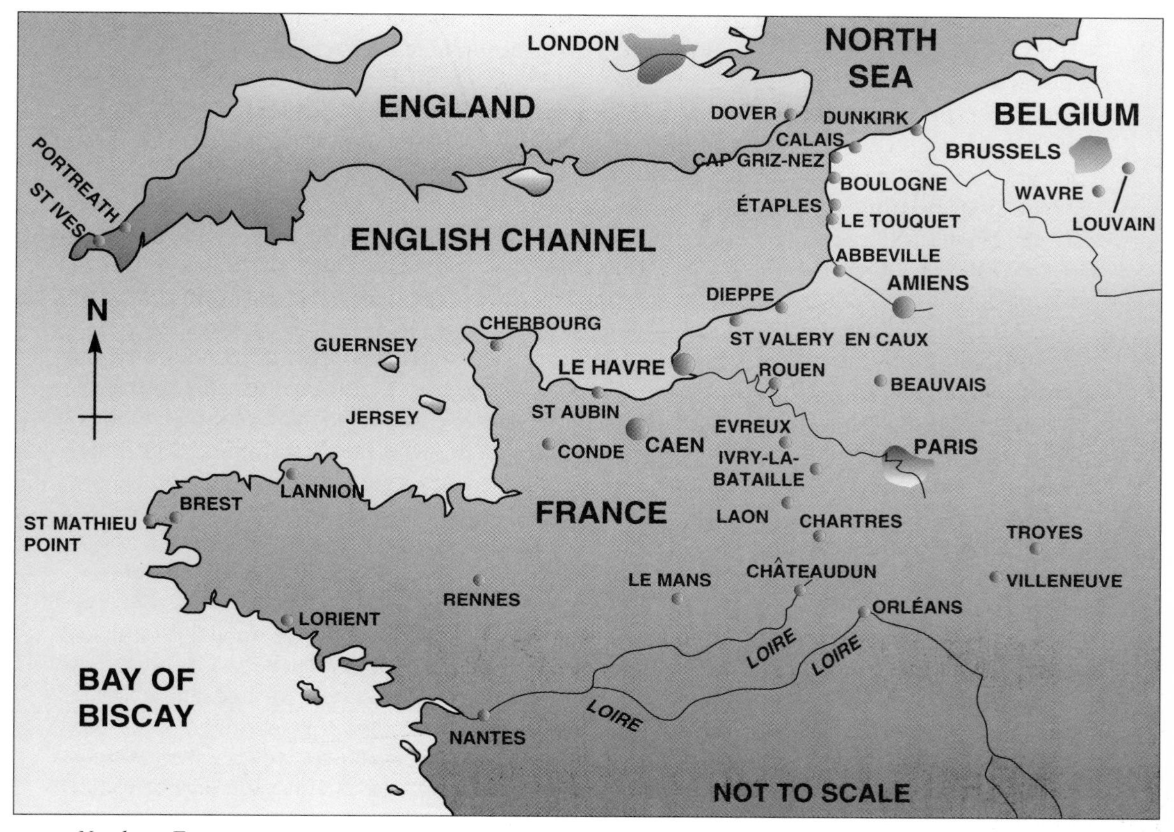

Northern France.

impossible to hide from such attacks and F/L Swain and his crew also had to fend off three similar fighter attacks, assisted by the emergency +9lb of boost on the engines.

The reconnaissance work continued with sorties on the 14th and the 17th, with full squadron effort required on the Dunkirk–Flushing coastline and inland waterways. Of the eight aircraft sent out on the 14th, seven returned owing to lack of cloud cover, and by 11.15 hours only P/O Murray was able to reach a target, leaving the southern part of the aerodrome at Haamstede on the Island of Schouwen en Duiveland in the Netherlands suffering the wrath of his payload, discharged from 3,200ft. On the 17th a further six crews set off. This time only three abandoned the task while the remainder attacked an aerodrome half a mile north-east of The Hague. Two convoys were also attacked, one near Zeebrugge which consisted of five cargo boats, and the other 6 miles north of the Hook of Holland.

Interspersed between reconnaissance sorties were further attacks on the enemy at Cap Gris-Nez, where the gun emplacements had a visit from two crews on the evening of the 14th, complemented on the 15th when three crews led by S/L Key launched an equally successful attack, dropping a total of eleven 250lb Semi-Armour Piercing bombs on the gun emplacements.

Three days later, on the 18th, there was yet another operational loss when five aircraft were despatched to attack the barge concentrations in the harbour at Ostend. The attack formation, led by W/C Coggle, left in the early evening. Despite considerable ground-fire, the attack was pressed home successfully. Some crews fared better than others – Sgt Costello-Bowen reported that his aircraft had been flung on to its back when caught in his own bomb blast at a height of 1,500ft! Miraculously the Blenheim righted itself and the crew arrived back at base at 21.40 hours, very shocked but safe.

Sadly, Sgt Bowles, an original member of the squadron and his crew Sgt Radford (Observer), and Sgt Lackenby (WOp/AG) were killed during the operation. Sgt Radford had recently been accepted for pilot training and Sgt Lackenby was new to the squadron.

Operations continued throughout September with more reconnaissance of the coastline between Calais and The Hague, as well as attacks on shipping in the harbour at Calais and Dunkirk. As operations were now largely undertaken in the evening or early morning, results were much more encouraging. However, one daylight reconnaissance sortie was again attempted on the 23rd and predictably the task was abandoned because of the lack of cloud protection.

Finally, on 26 September 1940, it was announced that Watton was to become a Night Operational Station. As the month drew to a close, the Secretary of State for Air, Sir Archibald Sinclair, made an official visit to the station on the 28th. The end of September saw two raids: the harbour at Calais was bombed on the 29th and Boulogne was bombed from 6,000ft in the early hours of the morning on the 30th, both without loss but leaving much devastation behind them. Altogether seven young men, two entire crews, had been lost in September; almost double the August losses. October was to increase this toll still further.

Evidence of the multiple role capability was again displayed by the Blenheim on 1 October, when an exercise was carried out by three aircraft performing reconnaissance and photography roles in close support of the Army, during a practice motor-transport move of some 600 vehicles of the 129th Infantry Brigade from Saffron Waldon to Hawkspur Green. However, on the 2nd it was back to operations again. Three aircraft set off in mid-evening to attack a marshalling yard at Gremberg, 2 miles north of Dendermonde in Belgium. Once more the weather took its toll, this time ice with rain and low cloud forcing the crews back to base, unable to even see their targets. In the midst of similar conditions, two other crews set out to attack the invasion port of Calais where shipping concentrations were to be bombed, but the weather made it impossible to locate the target so a concentration of searchlights were bombed instead. Nevertheless, Blenheim T1896 failed to return and its crew, Sgt Lord (Pilot), Sgt Bundock (Observer) and Sgt Dunbar (WOp/AG), who had been with the squadron since February 1939 and were by now 'old hands', were a sad loss to the unit. They crashed south-west of Calais near Pihen-lès-Guînes.

The month rolled on with attacks on oil storage tanks at Zeebrugge, an oil refinery at Salzbergen, aerodromes at Flushing and Diepholz, shipping off the Dutch coast and in Boulogne harbour, and the invasion ports of Dunkirk and Ostend. All met with a high degree of success, as did another trip to the gun emplacements at Cap Gris-Nez.

The first attack by the squadron on Germany's industrial heartland, the Ruhr, was made on 12 October when S/L Key, followed at approximately 45-minute intervals by F/Sgt Houghton and then F/Sgt Philips, attacked the marshalling yards at Hamm. The rivers were used as navigational aids across the mist-laden ground terrain, and each aircraft dropped its four 250lb loads of high explosive, despite accurate heavy anti-aircraft fire aided by a nest of searchlights. All aircraft returned safely to base.

Fog and mist was also becoming acute at home base, hampering operations for the next week or so and consequently operations gave way to recreational activities and an instructional film, 'Interrogation of Prisoners', was shown instead. The bad weather continued but sorties were flown. One crew had a bit of a 'shaky do' on the 20th when the squadron targets were an enemy-occupied aerodrome at Hingene and the docks at Antwerp. Returning from the latter, F/Sgt Richardson and his crew, Sgt Donlon and Sgt Gifford, narrowly escaped death when their Blenheim, T1936:P, strayed into the balloon barrage at Harwich. The starboard wingtip clipped

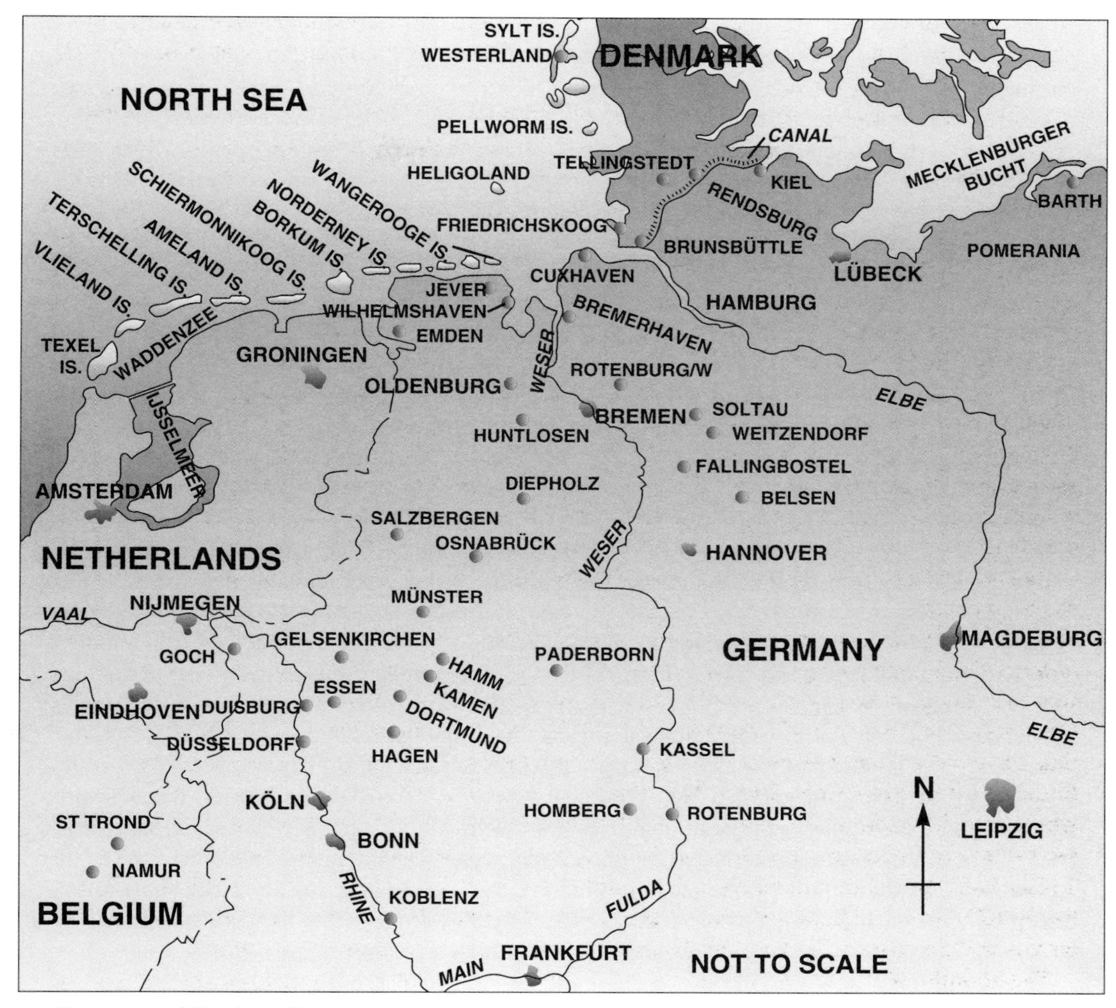

Germany and Northern Coast.

one of the steel balloon cables; another few feet and disaster would have struck. (This did in fact happen to another crew at a later date, and was an ever present hazard, particularly in bad weather.) Only forty minutes after they landed safely back at base at 21.55 hours, the entire Watton station had to be shut down because of the weather!

Five days later, on the 25th, the weather eventually cleared enough to allow resumption of operations. Six aircraft led by S/L Key departed to attack the now familiar gun emplacements at Cap Gris-Nez. Only five of the formation actually reached the target, as P/O Murray and his crew, Sgt Gavin and Sgt Robson experienced engine trouble. The official version reads: 'One aircraft (P/O Murray) experienced engine trouble while flying over the North Sea but located and attacked an enemy-occupied aerodrome at Étaples. After this attack the starboard engine seized up completely, and the airscrew and reduction gear broke away and fell, it is hoped, on some legitimate target in occupied France. P/O Murray succeeded in piloting his aircraft back to England on one engine and made a successful landing on Debden aerodrome.'

The aircraft, T1890, was subsequently repaired and was back in service again by

14 November when P/O Murray successfully attacked Boulogne from 2,000ft. Marshalling yards, shipyards and aerodromes were attacked and Osnabrück, Amsterdam and Schiphol were the targets hit on the 26th. In the evening of the 28th, the squadron suffered the loss of two more crews in two separate attacks.

The first of these comprised an attack by three aircraft flown by F/Sgt Phillips, F/L Swain and P/O Prosser on Ehrang's marshalling yards. The initial target was once again obscured by clouds and they diverted to an alternative target at Koblenz. On the return journey, P/O Prosser and his crew, Sgt Dallas (Observer) and Sgt Hardcastle (WOp/AG), were killed when their Blenheim, T2229, crashed in the vicinity of the Bircham Newton aerodrome beacon. Both pilot and observer were killed instantly and the aircraft burned out. The WOp/AG died of his injuries later in hospital.

The other tragedy occurred when S/L Granum, 'B' Flight Commander, and his crew, P/O Knight (Observer) and Sgt Greenwood (WOp/AG), failed to return in Blenheim T1891. They had been leading a three aircraft operation, targeted at the synthetic oil refinery at Homberg, approximately 19 miles south-south-west of Kassel in Germany. The official record states: 'S/L Grannum was Flight Commander of 'B' Flight and a squadron leader of considerable experience and ability. His loss was a severe blow to the squadron. P/O Prosser had joined the squadron just prior to its evacuation from France. He had shown the greatest keenness and enthusiasm and had carried out twelve operational flights during a period of two months, in which he had exhibited a high degree of dash and initiative. Sgt Greenwood was one of the original wireless operators in the squadron and had done consistently good work during operations in France and subsequently at home when the squadron re-equipped with Blenheims. P/O Knight, Sgt Dallas and Sgt Hardcastle had only recently joined the squadron but had already acquitted themselves nobly.' It was a severe blow with which to end the month.

The squadron was not to continue in the present surroundings, as the bells of change rang out once more. On 30 October the order went out that the squadron was to move from Watton. By 16.00 hours on 1 November 1940, their new home was to be RAF Swanton Morley, a new station situated only a few miles to the north near East Dereham. All the aircraft which were serviceable were flown over to the new station, except those under repair which remained with members of the Maintenance Flight until they were ready for transfer. Swanton Morley was to be the home of 105 Squadron for some months to come and the highest honours were to follow their exploits there.

The new station sported a hanger and annexes which were not quite finished when taken over. Temporary accommodation was made available for both flights in the station headquarters, while parachute and camera sections and the servicing party remained at Watton until their accommodation could be arranged. The accommodation was to be permanent but was built to a different design from the standard 'Expansion Scheme' stations begun in 1934. Groundcrew member Tony Frick commented on the conditions prevailing at the time: '. . . the sad state Swanton Morley was in! No windows, doors, heat, and very little bedding.'

James Taylor, another groundcrew member who had joined the RAF as a 'boy', was promoted to F/Sgt at Kidlington prior to his transfer to 105 Squadron and remembers the new station with affection, despite the initial difficulties: 'Swanton Morley was a good camp with a good Sergeants' mess. Life seemed to consist of trips into Norwich for quantities of beer – if you were hard up, you went into East Dereham. We used to get visits from the ATC from East Dereham – those Air Force Cadets almost used to know more about aircraft recognition than we did!'

The enemy also learned of the new airfield's location and as if attempting to demonstrate the efficiency of their Intelligence, they laid on a welcome of their own. S/L James described it in his book *RAF Swanton Morley – The First Fifty Years*: 'An attack was made at 07.45 hours on 5 November, during which ten bombs fell on the airfield. Luckily, not all of them exploded. However, it was another three months before further attacks took place.'

Teething troubles dogged the squadron for a short while, and they had to rely on Watton HQ for control and Horsham St Faith for D/F facilities. W/C L.B. Duggan took over as Station Commander, having previously been Camp Commandant of the combined 105 and 218 Squadron Camp at Bourgenais, France. At last, on the night of 7/8 November 1940 the first night operations began from Swanton Morley under control of their now completed Operations Room.

The attack was divided between two targets: the submarine base at Lorient for the three crews on their first operational flight, and the Krupps Armament Works at Essen for those with experience. In the event, all aircraft returned to base, although one of the inexperienced crews, Sgt Marshall with Sgt Adams (Observer) and Sgt Gresty (WOp/AG), flying Blenheim T1895, became lost on the outward journey and landed at Boscombe Down. In Blenheim T1866 electrical failure of the release gear meant that Sgt Jenkins only managed to release one bomb, which was seen to explode on the slipway north of Point de Cauden.

Of the experienced crews, S/L Key landed in bad weather conditions, overshot the Glim Lamp flare-path and pranged embarrassingly into the boundary hedge, fortunately without injury. Goose-neck flares were then hastily laid out and lit, enabling the remaining aircraft to land with a greater degree of finesse. Blenheim GB:B was no doubt left to be extracted by the able hands of the groundcrews. Sgt (later W/O) Maurice Chapple, commonly known as 'Chappie', who had joined 105 Squadron in July 1940 on returning from France, remembered the incident:

> One night we were leading an aircraft in, in the flying control van, when the pilot either lost or misunderstood our torch signals. In any event, he chased us clean off the airfield and straight through the boundary hedge! Fortunately, the aircraft stopped on the right side of the hedge.

Maurice Chapple related another amusing incident depicting life at the new station:

> Swanton Morley, like many others, was a grass airfield, and no doubt had been agricultural land. In those days the lanes which had been cut by the new airfield were often blocked by wooden barriers and barbed wire, but these were readily removable probably for airfield exits. Anyway, one morning – an operational morning too – the aircraft were taxiing out. The air gunners were cleaning their guns, which they did by firing a burst into the ground as they taxied out, and I happened to be on the balcony of Flying Control. Suddenly, everybody's head turned and everything stopped, apart from the aircraft engines. There was a trotting horse in the distance. As it drew closer, it was seen to be pulling a trap containing a local farmer and his family, who were evidently not going to take the long way round to Dereham! It was not unlike a Bateman cartoon; officers with purple faces, red Very lights being fired and the horse and trap trotting past Flying Control quite impervious.

Life was not always so humorous at the station however, as Tony Frick remembers:

> I was at Swanton Morley, I think in 1940, when an ACHGD of the MT section fell into a propeller of a Blenheim IV while trying to pull a chock away; with some others, I put him on the Thorneycroft lorry (Dispersal) and the last I saw of him was at the sick bay – his fingers were locked in an iron grip on my overcoat and his back was split open to the spinal column. In late 1945 at Pegu, Burma, on 1348 ASR (Jungle) Flight, we met again – he in an MT on delivery duties. It was quite a surprise, I thought he had passed away from his injuries!

On the 10th another attempt was made to attack the submarine base at Lorient but due to

Blenheim GB:B after S/L Key landed in bad weather conditions at Watton at 02.05 hours on 8 November 1940, overshot the Glim Lamp flare-path and pranged embarrassingly into the boundary hedge. Note the two fire extinguishers sitting ready beside the aircraft. (RAF Museum: P018944)

severe icing and cloud conditions, F/Sgt Phillips was the only pilot of the three despatched who managed to reach the target.

An insight into things to come was provided on the 13th – which nearly proved very unlucky for Sgt Jenkins. He took up a 'Tropicalized' Blenheim, ultimately destined for the Middle East, for a fuel consumption test. He was soon intercepted by three Hurricanes of Fighter Command, who were very suspicious of the Blenheim's behaviour, stooging around without squadron markings on its fuselage. The Blenheim was escorted back to base and was just beginning its approach to land when all hell broke loose as the airfield anti-aircraft battery opened fire. Fortunately, their aim was not all it might have been, and they only managed a single hit on the starboard petrol tank which luckily did not ignite. The aircraft landed safely, and the crew, unharmed but with rather ruffled feathers, survived to tell the tale!

On the 15th, a 2 Group instruction required a maximum effort raid against enemy aerodromes in the area Antwerp–Brussels–Le Culot–St Trond. Enemy aircraft were not to be allowed to leave the ground. In the event, only four aircraft took off because of weather conditions. S/L Key, F/L Swain, Sgt Costello-Bowen and P/O Murray DFC did sterling work bombing aerodromes at Vught, Hingene, Diegem, Evere and Antwerp (Deurne). Searchlight activity encountered at Antwerp was duly machine-gunned, and 40lb bombs dropped on searchlight installations at Breskens. It was later reported that Blenheim T1890, flown by P/O Murray and crewed by Sgt Gavin (Observer) and Sgt Robson (WOp/AG), had been lost during the raid, possibly at Diegem. The crew was laid to rest in the town cemetery. This was only the second operational flight of this aircraft since it had lost its airscrew and reduction gear on 25 October. This was certainly not a contributory factor, as the three aircraft accompanying it reported seeing it being hit by tracer bullets from an aircraft making a very low attack in the vicinity of Diegem, in north-east Brussels. The aircraft was reported to have been engaged by ground defences and was seen to crash in flames. The German High Command later confirmed the names of P/O Murray and his crew, and that they had been killed in action.

The next day, with the previous day's activities still in mind, yet another maximum effort was called for. This time the target was an oil refinery at Hamburg. The target was found by three aircraft, all of which were met by intense flak at 10,000ft but despite this the bombload was delivered. Other crews could not get above the 15,000ft cumulus cloud and bombed the aerodrome on the Dutch island of Schouwen en Duiveland instead. Tragically, another Blenheim, this time T2329, failed to return to base. The crew were Sgt Whitfield (Pilot), Sgt Gilmour (Observer) and Sgt Ashurst (WOp/AG).

Over the next two days various oil refinery targets were attempted with varying degrees of success. Alternative targets were to be attacked when cloud cover was a problem. Sgt Wilson had a narrow escape on the morning of the 22nd, when detailed to attack the Oslebshausen oil refinery at Bremen, a target later to become synonymous with the success, dash and gallantry of 105 Squadron. However, on this occasion lack of cloud cover resulted in an alternative attack on Schiphol aerodrome. This was successfully accomplished, although three Messerschmitt Bf 110 fighters rushed to its defence; due to the skill of the crew and the available cloud cover, disaster was avoided and Blenheim L8788:N survived to fight another day! The raid received recognition from the Air Officer Commanding 2 Group in a congratulatory message which specifically referred to P/O Taylor, who had found and bombed an iron and steel works at Hagen, after spending a very lonely and dangerous hour alone in the target area looking for his objective over the Ruhr!

On 23 November a new crew, P/O George Goode with Sgt Sam Hogan (Observer) and Sgt Geoffrey Rowland (WOp/AG) began operating. The primary squadron targets for the day were an oil refinery at Dortmund and a synthetic oil refinery at Wanne-Eikel, but the new crew had a different target, as Geoffrey Rowland explains:

> The main force went to a normal German target, probably the Ruhr. We, as a new crew, were briefed to go to 'an easy Channel port'. Ostend was expected to take a couple of hours. As we took well over three hours, they were beginning to get a bit worried. In brief, the night was very dark, and Sam had great difficulty in identifying the target in Ostend. In the midst of stooging around at 15,000ft, our intercom faded out! Remembering my training, I then started changing round the wet batteries in the rack, which was quite a job. There were five batteries in the rack, wired up for the transmitter and receiver. This was quite heavy and difficult to access behind the turret. Changing over terminals with freezing hands was not exactly a quick job. (I think at the time we cannot have had a TR9 in the bomb-well as we did later on.) The reason for this failure was because the aircraft, R3838, was probably not allocated to a particular crew, and we had not been allocated to one particular aircraft. Result – nobody's fault! When we had our own machine, I took great pains at all times to know the state of the batteries. Others used to laugh at me for spending so much time on my own aircraft, but it paid off.

The 27th saw two more operations. Sgt Willsher and his crew, on their first operation in Blenheim T1885:F, were to bomb the docks at Boulogne. This they successfully accomplished. The other attack was to be on Cologne and six aircraft bombed the target but one returned with engine trouble prior to reaching its objective. Sgt Costello-Bowen and his crew, Sgt Broom (Observer) and Sgt Cameron (WOp/AG) got caught above ten-tenths cloud. Sgt Cameron tried to summon assistance with his wireless set, but to no avail and their only course of action when the fuel ran short was to bale out. As all three descended by parachute, their aircraft, T1884, crashed at Mottram in Longdale east of Manchester, where it burned out. The crew arrived weary but safe back at base at one o'clock in the morning. Not so fortunate were the crew of Blenheim T1886. P/O Ryan and his crew, Sgt Slade (Observer) and Sgt Meikle (WOp/AG), arrived back very late at 23.25 hours. They were given permission to land but then flew off at low altitude towards the aerodrome beacon at Foxley Wood, where the machine crashed and burst into flames, killing the entire crew. It was the third crew lost this month.

The next day, the target for five aircraft was Düsseldorf. However, Sgt 'Bing' Eagles in T1930:J abandoned the trip when weather became unfavourable and F/O F.A.G. Lascelles (who was reputed to be of the Lascelles family of royal descent) had engine trouble in L9209 and was forced to jettison his bombs. Nevertheless, Sgt Wilson in L8788:N and P/O Shirlaw in T1932:T started fires in the docks area of Düsseldorf. But what of the fifth aircraft? F/L Cyril D. Swain and his crew, P/O E. John Clelland (Observer) and Sgt Maurice J. Cowley (WOp/AG), were flying Blenheim T1893. While they were circling around trying to find the target, what appeared to be an electrical disturbance hit the aircraft, affecting the navigational system. This strange phenomenon is said to have affected a Whitley crew in the same area. After the bombing, over what was supposed to be Düsseldorf, John Clelland set a course of 291° and followed it on his gyro compass. The aircraft proceeded to turn in circles and eventually, over France, it became apparent that the aircraft was not navigable and it was necessary to bale out. In doing so, the crew were temporarily separated. Sgt Cowley had a very smooth trip down on his chute and is adamant that he smoked a cigarette during his descent! Having landed on the one large rock in a well ploughed field, he eventually staggered up and regained his composure, only to be taken 'prisoner' by some French farmers who took him back to a farmhouse and gave him a meal. Sgt Cowley's intention had been to find a church to hide out in, but the offer of a meal seemed to be more acceptable! Suddenly, the door of the farmhouse room burst open and in marched some German soldiers who had obviously been alerted to his presence.

F/L Swain and P/O Clelland were picked up three days later. They all went through various prison camps and Sgt Cowley started his 'kriegie' days on 11 December 1940 in Dulag Luft, west of Frankfurt-am-Main, followed by Stalag Luft 1 at Barth in Pomerania, near the Baltic Sea, then Stalag Luft 3 at Sagan (now Zagań) in Poland, then Stalag Luft 6 at Heydekrug in Poland near the Latvian border, then Stalag Luft 4 at Gross Tychowo again in Poland in Upper Silesia, and lastly Stalag 357 at Fallingbostel in Germany, some 6km from Belsen.

Having been marched between the above camps, Sgt Cowley eventually arrived back at Leighton Buzzard on 11 May 1945, having effected his escape.

F/L Cyril Swain was not so fortunate. Having ended up in Stalag Luft 3, he was involved in what was later to be known as 'The Great Escape', and was last seen alive being taken away in a black car on 31 March 1944. He was thirty-two. It subsequently came to light that he was murdered, along with forty-nine others, in the aftermath of the escape, when all fifty were simultaneously shot in cold blood by the Germans, under Hitler's direct orders. He is buried in Poznań Old Garrison Cemetery in Poland.

A new face had arrived at Swanton Morley on 25 November from 13 0TU at Bicester. Well known to many of the crews as an instructor, S/L Arnold Louis Christian had arrived to become Flight Commander of 'B' Flight, and was ultimately to prove a very popular CO.

On the 28th, Sgt Geoffrey Rowland took part in an air-test to check out the condition of R3682:G. During the thirty-minute flight he found there were again problems with the equipment, and at 11.30 hours he logged the following comment: 'Receiver HT Battery and VR22 valve u/s. Satisfactorily renewed.' The aircraft took off again at 17.15 the same day, this time on operations. The newly arrived S/L Christian and P/O George Goode attacked the docks at Antwerp in P4918:O and R3682:G respectively. Due to the poor quality of the black-out at the target, the town's outline was clearly visible as the two Blenheims dropped their bombs. Searchlights probed the sky for the offending aircraft but were unsuccessful. The raid was effective and the repaired aircraft had performed faultlessly. The two Blenheims touched down back at base after a two hours and forty-five minute sortie.

This brought operations for November to a close after what had been a fairly successful inaugural month at Swanton Morley. However, the number of fatalities was rising continually and the lethal anti-shipping role was yet to come.

December began with a further visit by Group Captain Hugh Pughe Lloyd MC DFC, SASO

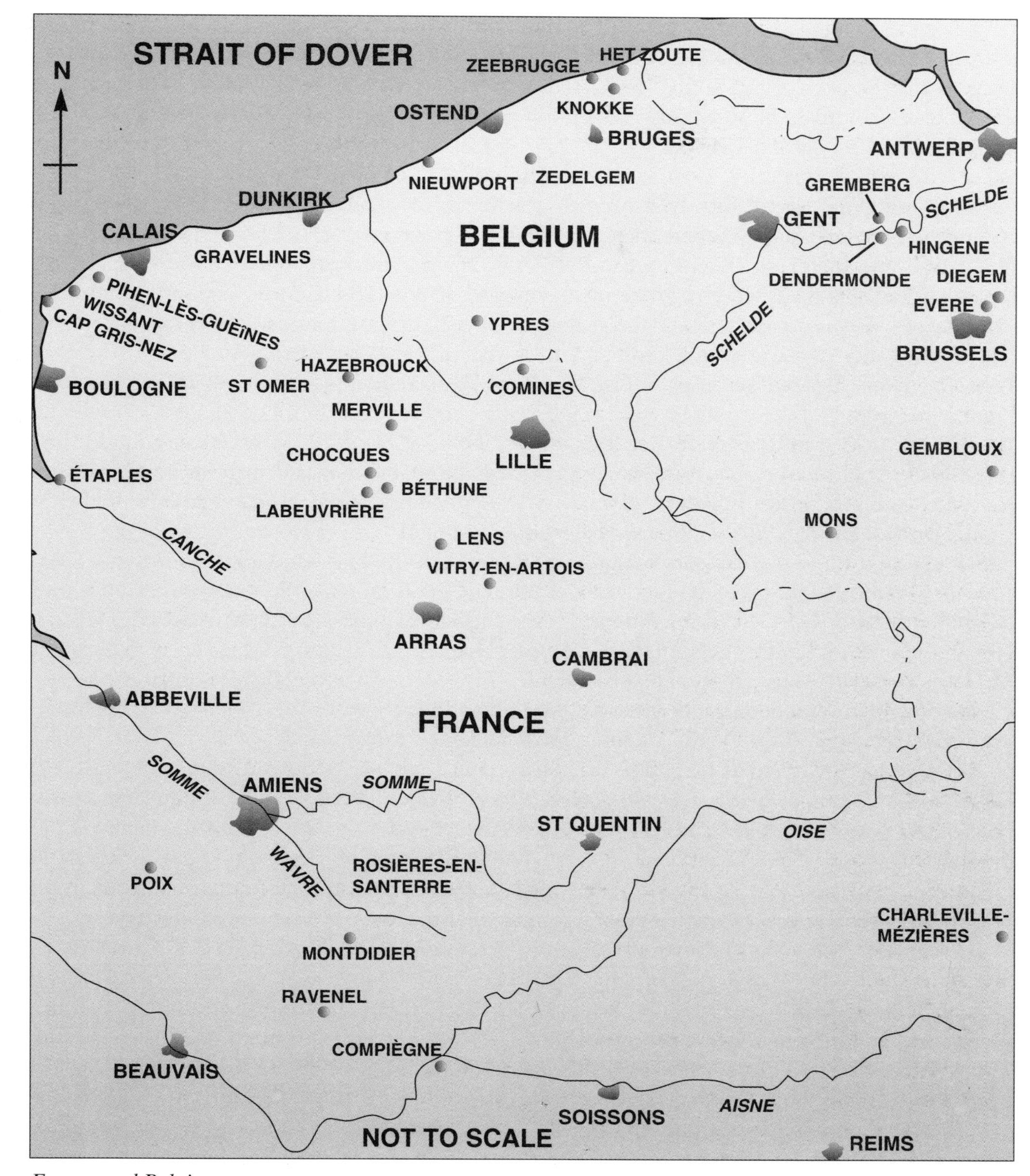

France and Belgium.

2 Group. Concern had been expressed at the length of time many crews had been operating and consequently it was decided that some crews should be allowed to terminate their activities, having spent up to a year on the squadron. They were to be transferred to 13 OTU Bicester, on 'rest'. Some of the squadron's best known personnel departed on the 8th, including F/O Lascelles, F/Sgt Phillips, Sgt Eagles and Sgt Costello-Bowen, all of whom left with their respective crews. Replacements soon arrived, mostly unknowns who were to acquit themselves admirably, particularly later on Malta.

Operations continued amid poor weather conditions, with aerodromes at Lille, Vitry, Cambrai, Amiens, Arras, Merville and Le Touquet bombed on the 6th. Sgt Willsher and his crew, Sgt Higgins (Observer) and Sgt Archer (WOp/AG), took Blenheim R3707:U into a glide attack on Le Touquet aerodrome between 500 and 1,500ft and successfully plastered the landing area with a stick of four 250lb and four 40lb bombs. For good measure, the aircraft parked below were raked with machine-gun fire, as were searchlights encountered on the way home.

The Focke-Wulf aircraft factory at Bremen was the object of attention on the 10th, when it was bombed in freezing conditions and thick cloud. S/L Key's aircraft, R3707:U, was being shadowed by a single-engined enemy aircraft when Sgt Foster opened fire at a range of 150 yards. Amid a shower of red sparks, the fighter broke off the engagement and its demise came in the form of a violent explosion as it ploughed into the ground. All the Blenheims returned safely to base.

The next day, the 11th, three aircraft took off in the early evening to patrol the area Poix–Beauvais–Amiens–Ravenel. Severe weather was encountered so the well known targets of Dunkirk harbour and Cap Gris-Nez gun emplacements were bombed instead. However, Blenheim T1897, captained by F/Sgt Richardson, with Sgt Donlon (Observer) and Sgt Gifford (WOp/AG), failed to return to base, having crashed at Zedelgem near Brugge in Belgium. They were a severe loss to the squadron, as many fine operations had been undertaken by this crew and F/Sgt Richardson was soon to have been commissioned.

For the next eight days events were severely curtailed by fog. One aircraft, flown by P/O Judson, became caught up in the bad weather during a cross-country flight and ended up setting down in a field. A few operations followed, with successful attacks on Gelsenkirchen, Dunkirk, Gremberg and Boulogne. On the latter two trips, contact was at last established with Swanton Morley's own H/F D/F station and subsequently 23 December was officially noted as the first day an operational flight had successfully used the facility.

Whether in an air of celebration or for pure convenience, the remainder of the day was deemed by the RAF to be Christmas Day! The official version from 105 Squadron's Operations Record Book reads: 'The rest of the day was celebrated as Christmas. Despite a slightly unrealistic atmosphere which was inevitable, all ranks managed to acquire at least something approaching the Christmas spirit. Traditional Xmas dinners, with turkey and plum pudding, were served in the Officers', Sergeants' and Airmen's messes and there was an impromptu entertainment in the NAAFI in the evening.' Quite what the impromptu entertainment was remains a mystery!

The next day S/L Arnold Christian was promoted to wing commander and F/L J.S. Dunlevie was promoted to the acting rank of squadron leader as 'B' Flight Commander. W/C Christian took over as squadron commander, when W/C Coggle, having fought off a long-standing illness, was admitted to hospital for observation.

The year drew to a close with attacks on the 29th and 31st on invasion ports and industrial targets in Germany and Holland. On the last operation on the 31st, a factory in Cologne was successfully attacked by Sgt Heape and his crew in T1895:X, followed by an attack on Haamstede aerodrome. Attention was also paid to a flak ship which was machine-gunned for good measure. Sgt Lee and his crew in T1931:K could not attack the Nordstern oil refinery at Gelsenkirchen, again because of the lack of cloud cover, but instead sought out docks at Ijmuiden in Holland as an alternative. P/O Shirlaw in Blenheim T1848:V, tried to reach an oil refinery at Bremen but once again without cloud cover the two crews gave up and began their return trip. Low altitude accurate flak menaced P/O Goode near Amsterdam and his aircraft was damaged; however, both crews returned safely to base.

For the Blenheims of 105 Squadron 1940 had been a year of change and mounting losses – and regrettably, much more of the same was yet to come.

CHAPTER 5

New Year – New Role

The winter of 1940/1 proved to be one of the worst on record at the time. The new year started with snow. Daytime operations were cancelled due to lack of cloud cover, and with deep snow lying on the ground even practice flying proved difficult. Maurice Chapple recalled: 'Night operations continued for some and I have grim memories of seeing aircraft off in blizzard conditions, towing them through deep snow, and sleeping on the site in a tent also surrounded by deep snow!'

However, snow or not, on 3 January, Group Captain Hugh Pughe Lloyd MC DFC visited the station late in the morning, and by 14.30 hours seven crews had been briefed to attack Bremen. The first aircraft took off at 16.45 hours with S/L Dunlevie at the controls. Port engine trouble dogged Sgt Heape and his crew who could not take off in time. The remaining six aircraft reached Bremen, and soon the target was being plastered with ten 250lb bombs and ten containers of incendiaries, all from between 10,000 and 18,000ft. A navigational error resulted in T1814:D missing the target. However, F/O Rotherham made up for things by attacking Huntlosen aerodrome with 250lb bombs and a container of incendiaries. They then proceeded to do the same in the region of Essen railway junction. Doubtless Group were satisfied.

A 105 Squadron airman stands in the remains of the snow at RAF Swanton Morley in the winter of early 1941. Note the guns in place with temporary coverings. (RAF Museum: P018946)

Flying operations then ceased, with the exception of ZZ landing practice for two aircraft at Wyton on the 4th. The ZZ is remembered by Ron Wood as:

> A procedure to enable an aircraft to descend from height through cloud safely, and to continue visually until it reaches the airfield. It was in fact the forerunner of several later procedures: VHF D/F QGH (QGH – descent through cloud); CRDF (cathode ray) QGH; Radar GCA (Ground Controlled Approach); and finally air-interpreted ILS (Instrument Landing System). The ZZ procedure involved the wireless operator transmitting on W/T, with QDMs (courses to steer) being obtained from the ground station, which would enable the pilot to reach home at a safe height above the base. The airfield had a safety lane clear of high ground, which was then used for the aircraft's outbound and inbound legs, and in which the aircraft descended through the cloud until achieving visual contact with the ground and hopefully with the airfield ahead.

Returning to operations, it was not until the 9th that a synthetic oil installation at Gelsenkirchen was attacked. No alternative targets were proposed. S/L Dunlevie took off in Blenheim L9379:Y at 17.15 hours, but only three of the following aircraft were to reach the target, due to low cloud up to 5,000ft. They dropped their load of sixteen 250lb bombs on target, while the other two, P/O Goode in T1848:V and P/O Judson in L8788:N, bombed Düsseldorf and Hamborn (a suburb of Duisburg) respectively.

Some bombing and formation practice followed on the 12th, 15th, and 16th. The remainder of the month was pretty well washed out, with operations having to be cancelled because of the deep snow on the grass runway, and the weather being generally not conducive to flying. In the interim period, lectures were given to the crews. On the 23rd Major Goldsmith delivered a lecture to his assembled audience on the subject of close support for the Army. This was followed the next afternoon by S/L Evans' deliberations on prison camp escape techniques.

The only other operation took place on the 21st, and was attempted by only two crews from an intended force of nine aircraft. The target was Düsseldorf once again. P/O George Goode in R3682:G led Sgts Willsher, Higgins and Archer in R3707:U. The two Blenheims took off at 18.30 hours, and headed towards the target. Low cloud spreading across the Ruhr region prevented P/O Goode from identifying the target area, but it did not prevent him off-loading his two 250lb bombs and a container of incendiaries on an unknown target. Sgt Willsher located and bombed the specified target. Both aircraft returned safely.

February started off on much the same footing as the previous month, with severe winter weather hampering operations. The loss rate was consequently diminished, although this was to be short-lived. Whenever the weather permitted, as on the 4th, full squadron effort was shown. W/C Christian led the squadron against targets in northern France. The docks at Ostend, Dunkirk, and Dieppe were targeted, as were the aerodromes at Évereux, Moiselles and St Omer, all of which were successfully bombed without loss.

Group Captain Lloyd MC DFC, an increasingly frequent visitor, came again on the 8th; his visit was followed by the familiar detail, this time of eight crews, some two hours later. Bad weather delayed take-off until the evening of the 10th, when the eight aircraft left for Hanover and Rotterdam. S/L Dunlevie had engine problems and could not reach Hanover. He chose Ijmuiden's docks as an alternative target, bringing L9379:Y back safely at 01.29 hours. Sgt Jones in T1892:Q and Sgt King in T1826:A, bombed oil tanks in Rotterdam, while the remainder of the force went for Hanover. The only problem encountered was with Sgt Williams' aircraft, T1887:S. Sgt Williams did reach Rotterdam, although a technical failure in the bomb-release gear prevented him from dropping his load on the target.

A synthetic oil plant at Homberg was the target on the 15th, but due to bad weather there

Sgt Willsher (Pilot), P/O Higgins (Observer) and Sgt Archer (WOp/AG) with their Blenheim R3707 GB:U in the snow at Swanton Morley, Norfolk, in the winter of early 1941. Note the mounting on the turret with the guns removed. (RAF Museum: P018947)

Blenheim GB:V, probably V5384, in flight over England in 1941. (RAF Museum: P018942)

were no further operations until the 25th, when several aerodromes in France were attacked. Three days later, on the 28th, Wilhelmshaven received bombloads from five aircraft led by F/L Rotheram, the 'A' Flight Commander. Sgt J.S.H. Heape and his crew, Sgt Jones (Observer) and Sgt Bimson (WOp/AG), failed to return in T1895:X. It was later confirmed that Sgt Heape had survived and was a prisoner of war. Sadly, the other two had not survived. They had been shot down by a night-fighter at Oosterhogeburg, 3 miles east of Groningen in Holland.

March opened with operations being cancelled either because of inclement weather conditions or by orders from 2 Group or Bomber Command Headquarters. Four more aircraft went to Wyton for ZZ landing practice, but it was not until the 10th that any operational work was done against the enemy, when the target was Le Havre. The docks were successfully bombed by S/L Dunlevie, accompanied by F/L Goode, Sgt Willsher and Sgt King. P/O Shirlaw bombed St Aubin aerodrome and Dieppe for good measure in T1932:T. Two others returned to base with engine trouble, Sgt Serjeant arriving back after only twenty minutes in T1848:V, and Sgt Jones putting down safely at Boscombe Down in T1892:Q. The remainder returned to Tangmere, as was pre-arranged because it was felt that the weather at Swanton Morley would not permit a landing back at base. The one hour return trip to Swanton Morley was tackled the next day.

This was followed on the 12th by another night attack. This time the target was Bremen, and eight Blenheims were despatched. First away was Sgt King in Z5903:D, followed at ten minute intervals by the other seven. The last off was F/L George Goode in L8788:N at 21.04 hours. They successfully bombed the target with 14 250lb bombs, and 760 4lb incendiaries. Flak and guiding searchlights were very busy, but all the aircraft survived. The only crew not able to attack was P/O Dore's, who found that the release mechanism would not operate properly on T1931:K, and so he returned with his bombs at 23.48 hours. Following the attacks of the 12th, seven crews set off the next night and repeated the success over Hamburg, despite P/O Dore having had a late take-off, and attacking Bremen again. The last aircraft from the main force arrived back at 05.50 hours, four hours forty minutes from take-off.

The weather struck again, causing operations to be cancelled on the 15th and 16th, when it had been intended to give the inexperienced crew of Sgt Wood, Sgt Turton and Sgt Wilcock a chance. It was normal to allow an inexperienced crew the chance to get adjusted to operations on a relatively 'easy' target, and consequently Rotterdam was chosen for the 17th. However, this was not to be and their trip was cancelled. Despite this, a main force of eight did get sent to Wilhelmshaven, the first up being S/L Dunlevie in P4918:O at 01.54 hours. Intense flak, both light and heavy, was met; nevertheless the target was left well alight. Sgt Williams, having engine trouble in T1892:Q, decided to have a go at Emden, but when his engine started to cut out, discretion was considered the better part of valour and he jettisoned his bombs and headed for home. Arriving back at 07.38 hours, they were at least half an hour later than the others. Due to bad weather, four of the Blenheims landed at Langham, home of 612 (Whitley) Squadron, some 14 miles west of Cromer. Another landed at North Coates, 10 miles south-east of Grimsby, home of 22 (Beaufighter) Squadron. The next day the operation was repeated.

Sgt Wood and his crew got their chance in a separate attack on Ostend, which they successfully bombed in R3682:G, without encountering very much flak, but proving their effectiveness adequately.

Group Captain Hugh Pughe Lloyd MC DFC visited the station again on the 19th and 22nd. On the 21st Lorient, home of the submarines, was to be the target. Six aircraft took off, led by W/C Arnold Christian and his crew who took off in V5828:R at 20.25 hours. The last back after a successful raid was Sgt King and his crew in Z5903:D at 01.25 hours. There was no sign of Q-Queen, Blenheim T1892. P/O Shirlaw and his crew, P/O Dugdale (Observer) and F/O Mair

(WOp/AG), failed to return. In a similar incident to that of 20 October the previous year, when F/Sgt Richardson clipped a balloon cable over Harwich, a balloon cable had been hit at Pilton Hackett, south-west of Birmingham. But this time tragedy had struck: Q-Queen had crashed and the crew were killed.

The next operation, on the 23rd, was to be equally tragic. Five aircraft led by S/L Dunlevie attacked Hanover. One crew, Sgt Wood, Sgt Turton and Sgt Wilcock, were sent in R3682:G to attack Calais. This they did successfully, having encountered no flak at all. Ron Wood remembers the lack of opposition:

> This seemed to surprise the intelligence officer at de-briefing and it was even suggested that perhaps we had not actually got to Calais. I assured them that I had seen the port quite clearly in the moonlight, but it was not until a few days later that I was vindicated – Intelligence had a report that the Germans were training a squadron of night-fighters in the Calais area and their first night flying had been with me!

The crew did have some excitement on their return when their aircraft overshot the goose-neck flare path and at the boundary Sgt Wood had to swing the aircraft round, and the undercarriage collapsed. The crew emerged safe but shaken.

While this was happening, the main force attacked and dropped their full war load on the main target. Sadly, yet another Blenheim, Z5903:D, crewed by Sgt King (Pilot), Sgt Murphy (Observer) and Sgt Gibbs (WOp/AG), failed to return to base. Although Sgt Gibbs rests in Oldenburg at Sage War Cemetery, Sgt King and Sgt Murphy have no known graves.

Following the Hanover raid, the enemy decided to pay Swanton Morley a visit again, the first time since its inaugural Blenheim days, back in November 1940. In a further excerpt from S/L James' book *RAF Swanton Morley – The First Fifty Years* we learn that:

> On 27 February 1941 the airfield was attacked three times during the course of the day. Shortly after 9 o'clock in the morning, a Dornier Do17 flew in from the south-west at 800ft and machine-gunned buildings. Just before lunch, another Do17 arrived from the east and dropped thirteen 50kg and five 250kg bombs, all of which landed within 50 yards of the hangars. Two Bofors and eight other gun posts returned fire; but the excitement wasn't finished. At ten minutes to five, a Junkers Ju88 came in from the north, at a height of only 150ft, and dropped ten 50kg and three 500kg bombs on the south-west side of the airfield. This time two Lewis gun posts returned fire. Fortunately, the aircraft must have been too low for the bombs to fuse properly as none of them exploded. There were no casualties nor damage. The Station Armament Officer, F/L Charlton, was eventually awarded the George Cross for his efforts in dealing with in excess of two hundred bombs, both on the airfield and in the surrounding district.

The last operation of March took place on the 30th, and should have included seven aircraft, but in the event only five took part. One aircraft dropped out because of instrument failure. The other aircraft to abort the operation was crewed by Sgt Ron Wood (Pilot), Sgt Bert Turton (Observer) and Sgt Jimmy Wilcock (WOp/AG). Ron Wood noted:

> The next op planned necessitated the squadron flying down to St Eval in Cornwall. Apparently the *Scharnhorst* and *Gneisenau* had between them sunk twenty-two of our ships on their last foray into the Atlantic and they were now docked in Brest. We were informed that Churchill was loathe to disclose this disastrous loss to the public until he could simultaneously announce that these warships had been destroyed by the RAF. I have never seen so many aircraft assembled on one airfield: Hampdens, Hudsons, Wellingtons and

105 Squadron Blenheim Z5899 GB:J landing at Swanton Morley after a non-operational sortie at low level in February or March, 1941. Note the debris hanging from the pitot tube below the aircraft's nose. Light series bomb racks can be seen under the fuselage just to the right of the port wheel fairing. (The Trustees of the Imperial War Museum, London: CH17171)

> Blenheims all over the place. There were so many that only the squadron commanders attended the briefing, and they then gathered us round to brief us in turn.
>
> Take-off time was when you could see a way out to taxi – it was rather like the car-park at the Open Golf! We had our engines running for over half an hour, waiting to get out, before one coughed and spluttered and cut out. The plugs had oiled up and there was no spare, so we missed the pleasure of that one.

The remaining five Blenheims, led by W/C Christian in P4918:O, departed at 20.18 hours en route to Brest. The armament dropped included, in addition to ten 40lb bombs, ten 500lb SAP bombs. This was the first time such large bombs had been used by the squadron. They appeared to be effective, as bursts were seen in the target area. All aircraft landed at St Eval before returning safely to Swanton Morley. The results were summed up by Ron Wood: 'It was all a bit of a flop, and the ships survived all our efforts.'

During April 1941 a new role and raison d'être began to emerge for the squadron. The feared invasion of Britain had not taken place, although the grinding attacks on Germany's industrial machine were to continue. Shipping in the Atlantic was another worrying factor for Winston Churchill and the War Cabinet. The Merchant Navy was taking a terrible pounding, as German surface ships and U-Boats roamed around our Merchant Fleet, picking off ships almost at will. Churchill ordered Bomber Command to put maximum effort into winning the Battle of the Atlantic, and a blockade of shipping entering and leaving northern Germany was ordered – all ships were to be attacked and sunk. (This was to be echoed some time later, when the squadron was in Malta, and similar instructions were issued regarding the shipping lanes to North Africa.)

The Air Officer Commanding 2 Group, Air Vice-Marshal Donald F. Stevenson DSO OBE MC, who was appointed AOC by Group on 12 February, was given the unenviable task of effectively sealing off the North Sea to enemy shipping, in what was later to be known around the squadron as 'Stevenson's Sea of Carnage!'

But the month got underway with attacks on similar targets to those tackled previously. On the 3rd, Sgt Jackson and Sgt Wood opened the innings with 'freshman' attacks on Ostend and Rotterdam respectively. Port engine trouble on L9244:H forced Sgt Wood to jettison his bombs on searchlights 10 miles north-west of the target, before returning safely back to base. He remembers the sortie as being

> . . . a night trip to Rotterdam where we were attacked by a night fighter. I put in 9lbs boost, and dived to get away. I succeeded in this but unfortunately left the +9lb boost in for rather a long time in my enthusiasm to get away, and once again the Bristol Mercury gave up [a reference to the intended operation of 30 March]. No oiling up of the plugs this time but just engine abuse by the driver, I was told by our flight sergeant on the ground. Anyway, we got back on one engine. The 9lb boost facility was only supposed to be used in an emergency and for very short periods – I was living and learning fast!

Attacks continued, with unsuccessful raids against Cologne and Dunkirk on the 4th. On the 7th Bremerhaven and Emden were the targets, and large fires were started despite heavy flak and probing searchlights. The success of the attack prompted AVM Stevenson to forward his congratulations to the crews. The squadron repeated its performance on the next day, starting fires around Bremerhaven that could be seen from 30 miles away!

On the 10th the squadron was ordered to attack Brest, in order to help Coastal Command. W/C Christian responded and led six aircraft off at 01.25 hours. Four aircraft bombed the target within the time-span requested, dropping their bombs singly to create the maximum nuisance and the longest diversion possible. Of the other two aircraft, S/L Dunlevie had to return with an unserviceable radio, and Sgt Lee armed his bombs later than required and so bombed Lorient instead.

Thus 105 Squadron ended the 2 Group Operations Order No. 11, under which they had operated for the previous nine months, making sporadic attacks on various industrial targets, with specific oil refineries having been allotted to each 2 Group station. The direct order that 'should there be no cloud cover, the operation is to be abandoned', was no longer part of the formula and an order arrived on 9 April stating that the squadron was to go over to daytime operations only.

The new daylight anti-shipping role began on the 13th, when two new words entered the vocabulary of the operational controllers: 'shipping beats'. There were initially six of these 'free bombing lanes', called A, B, C, D, E and F. In order to avoid the enemy radar and achieve surprise it was essential to fly at very low level above the water, with a maximum time limit of only three minutes in the beat area for safety's sake. It was also believed that, should enemy fighters arrive, they would find it much more difficult to attack aircraft 'right down on the deck'; this certainly applied in many cases, although some crews were not so fortunate.

The run to the beat would commence about 30 miles from the enemy coast, with a spread of bombers in line-abreast formation, usually without fighter cover because of the range. From the starting point the aircraft would fly towards the coast until they were about 3 miles away, and then the formation would turn through 90° and fly parallel to the shore for three minutes. Any ship encountered was to be bombed immediately from 50ft or less and the aircraft was then to turn for home. Ron Wood emphasized this point:

> On the daylight low-level shipping strikes one did not hang around after an attack, as it was usually only a slender element of surprise one had, and only a matter of minutes before the fighters appeared. And so it was in, out and away with no time to really see what damage one had done. To resolve this difficulty it was decided to issue Leica cameras to the WOp/AGs before each operation, for them to take pictures, if possible, of the target on leaving. It was optional whether or not they used them and the general feeling was that in most cases using the guns would be of more benefit. It was not long before it was noticed that there were quite a few surreptitiously 'personally owned' Leicas around the 2 Group squadrons. Apparently, the practice had developed that if you drew a Leica for a trip, you left it with a chum who was then a Leica to the good if you didn't come back, the camera of course, in theory at least, being written off with the aircraft.

By the time 105 Squadron had commenced its anti-shipping duties, 2 Group had issued Operations Order No. 27, which extended the beat areas as far as Norway. There were now twenty beats, nearly all of which were to be searched within the next few months. From now on low-level attacks on shipping were to be the main purpose of 105 Squadron and the other Blenheim squadrons of 2 Group. As a result, camouflage changes were introduced: gone were

This 105 Squadron Blenheim GB:X, probably V6374, flying low over the North Sea, is sporting the camouflage of the anti-shipping campaign: dark green and grey upper surfaces and duck-egg blue under surfaces. (Royal Air Force Museum: PC 73/72/24)

the black undersides and green/brown colours on the upper surfaces, the machines being repainted with dark green and grey upper surfaces and a duck-egg blue under-surface.

The first attack took place in the Squadron's new theatre of operations on 13 April 1941, when F/L David Bennett in T1826:A led four other aircraft out from Swanton Morley at 11.50 hours on a daylight operation against any shipping which might be found in Beat 13. P/O Dore abandoned the task when the rear guns on T1931:K jammed, but the remainder had a fairly uneventful trip with no shipping in sight. They all landed back safely at base, the last Blenheim, flown by Sgt Sarjeant and crew, touching down at 15.20 hours. The attack on the 13th on Beat 13 had not been as unlucky as many of the superstitious had imagined! However, these dangerous activities were to take their toll later.

The beginning of the anti-shipping campaign was punctuated on the 15th by an attack at dusk by eight Blenheims on Borkum; they hit a town and barracks on the island. Gun emplacements north of the town were also attacked by P/O Dore. The flak guns replied, hitting R3838:M several times during the engagement. Sgt Sarjeant in L9244:H found the main railway station and dropped two 500lb bombs in from rooftop height. Only one aircraft found a ship – S/L Dunlevie took L9379:Y in to attack a 4000-ton freighter about 1 mile offshore to the south-west of the island. All four 250lb bombs were dropped and eleven seconds later, following a direct hit just aft of the funnel, the centre of the ship blew apart, with debris thrown 200ft into the air. All aircraft returned safely, although several were rather badly shot up. In Michael J.F. Bowyer's *2 Group RAF*, David Bennett recalled his own account of his flight in L8788:N:

> The flak from the E-Boats was intense, and the tracer hose-pipe effect all the more like a Brocks fireworks display in dusk conditions. We all returned safely, although in very poor weather conditions. I had to land at Bassingbourn's satellite, Steeple Morden, and was very nearly shot at by the local AA battery, in spite of firing the correct two star Very of the period. I found out that they had been subjected to an intruder attack the night before by a Junkers 88 and I was lucky since they were trigger-happy.

A further account was written on the day after the raid. In a letter home, Sgt George Eric Green, P/O Rushbrooke's Observer, flying in Blenheim V5384:B reported:

> I was certainly in need of a pick-me-up this morning as last night I had the Honour, mark you, of taking part in one of the cheekiest pieces of work done since this caboodle started. In fact we were told that it was a 'suicide raid', but don't be alarmed, we all made it back! It was my second real 'do', the first was on Palm Sunday, of all days! When you were having your Sunday dinner I was just crossing the French coast (in daylight!) and we had quite a do, but nothing to compare with last night, no sir! Eight planes, twenty-four men, went to Borkum, an island off the German coast where there was a seaplane station, a wireless station and a ship in the harbour. We were told it was a hornets' nest and we took off at half past six in the evening and arrived after flying at only 10ft over the sea in line-abreast formation just as dusk fell. We roared over the island at 280mph, line abreast, and simply dropped four bombs each straight across it. Aerodrome, town, barracks, seaplane station, wireless station and everything including the ship (which the Wing Commander got) went skywards, together with literally thousands of shells and bullets and Lord knows what; talk about a 'Brocks benefit' – it would turn Brocks or Wilders green with envy. We were only flying at 100ft up, we even had to lift a wing to clear a chimney stack and things were beginning to fly around like Billy-ho! In two minutes we were away, before their fighters could get off the ground and we split up and came back singly as night fell all the way across a very empty North Sea. As we neared the east coast we ran thro' clouds and we iced up, blue electrical discharges ran along the wings and

the props looked like Catherine wheels of blue flame. We eventually got out of the cloud as we neared our base and got permission to land. The air-speed indicator and altimeter had gone west and we were very worried as to whether we were going to get down safely after all that we'd been through. As we came down everything seemed to give way and we landed smack on the side of the drome in complete darkness. The whole damn thing seemed to fall apart and as we came to rest we jumped out like scalded cats and waited for it to blow up. Happily it didn't and we salvaged our property and instruments from it and were taken into the HQ for interrogation. I've never been so glad in all my life to sit down and smoke a cigarette and drink a cup of tea as I was then.

Although all aircraft returned safely, the arrival for some of the others was not as elegant as it might have been. Sgt Geoffrey Rowland, WOp/AG in F/L George Goode's Blenheim, remembers that the flare path had been badly laid, with the first flare in the centre of the field. Their Blenheim touched down near the first flare and careered through the boundary barbed wire, leaving T1930:X an apparent write-off. The aircraft was nevertheless repaired, eventually being sent to 13 OTU at Bicester.

The next day, the Air Officer Commanding 2 Group, Air Vice-Marshal D.F. Stevenson DSO OBE MC, visited Swanton Morley to congratulate the crews who had taken part in the raid on Borkum. Sgt Eric Green confirmed this proud occasion in his letter home: 'This morning the AOC, an Air Vice Marshal, came over and congratulated us and shook hands with everyone (including me) and apparently we've made quite a mess of Borkum. You'll probably see something about it in Thursday's papers – I wouldn't be at all surprised.'

George Eric Green, service no. 969371 at No. 1 Initial Training Wing at St John's College, Cambridge, prior to joining 105 Squadron. He was killed in action off Ameland Island on 25 May 1941. (via John Green)

The next operation took place on the 17th. At 06.45 hours participating aircrew were called for their briefing and were addressed by W/C Arnold Christian. At 09.30 hours eight of the squadron's Blenheims were taking off, heading for the Cornish aerodrome at St Eval. They were followed by several more at 10.15 hours. The target was any shipping found in Beats 16 and 17. The first four aircraft away, led by F/L Goode in V5502:U, left St Eval at 13.10 hours, bound for Beat 17 off Lorient on the Brittany coastline. No shipping was found and F/L Goode and Sgt Lister in T1931:K were soon back at base, landing within five minutes of each other, at 18.44 hours and 18.48 hours respectively.

However, the danger of unescorted low-level operations was now to become all too evident, and the other two aircraft were not so fortunate. On the return journey, two Bf 109 yellow-nosed fighters pounced on the Blenheims. Within five minutes Blenheim T2141, crewed by Sgt I.G. Sarjeant (Pilot), Sgt L.L. Evered (Observer) and Sgt K.G. Gresty (WOp/AG), had been shot down in flames. It was the squadron's first loss on anti-shipping duties – the first of many.

The other Blenheim, crewed by Sgt Arty J. Piers, a Canadian pilot, Sgt W. Brendan Healy (Observer) and Sgt Stuart George Bastin (WOp/AG), also came under attack, in an engagement which was to last for twenty minutes. Watching with horror as Sgt Sarjeant's Blenheim fell to the fighters, and with both guns and radio out of action, all the gunner could do was sit and pray. The yellow noses of the Messerschmitts appeared time and time again. Following instructions shouted back from the gunner, the pilot took evasive action, as they slipped and skidded over the sea, churning only feet below them. Eventually, having outwitted the 109s and with considerable damage to their aircraft, they returned to St Eval, where T1885:F crash-landed safely. For the nineteen-year-old air gunner and the rest of his crew, their inaugural operational flight with 105 Squadron had been a memorable one – with a repeat performance yet to come only eight days later on the 25th!

Having taken off some thirty-five minutes later than the first wave on the 17th, S/L Dunlevie led another five Blenheims to Beat 16 off Brest. In the event only one aircraft found a ship, and F/L A.F. Calvert-Booth took V5828:R into the attack. The ship was a merchant vessel of some 5,000 tons, and was located 10 miles south-west of St Mathieu Point. The aircraft ran in at the ship at about 50ft above the wave tops, dropping its bombs into the target in salvos. The flak was intense, but the starboard side of the ship was seen to erupt. A large column of water shot upwards and black smoke billowed out behind it. The ship was claimed as 'possibly sunk'. During the attack P/O Waddington, the Observer in F/L Calvert-Booth's crew, was wounded in the right arm but once R-Robert landed safely back at St Eval, he received medical attention.

The 19th was to see the next operation. Eight aircraft went off to Beat 9 off Texel, this time with the assistance of cloud cover. But despite spending an exceedingly long time (twenty to forty minutes) in the beat area, four aircraft returned without having sighted any quarry. Once more Bf 109s were on the prowl, and a pair of them attacked F/L Calvert-Booth, but the Blenheim crew safely evaded their attackers and arrived back at 15.14 hours. The remainder had successfully found shipping. F/L Goode, Sgt Bruce and Sgt Scott all found targets which they bombed from 500 to 1,500ft. At 52° 45'N, 04° 36' E, a ship of some 4/5,000 tons was attacked with two 500lb bombs, and was left well under and sinking. A convoy was machine-gunned and bombed at 53° 02'N, 04° 38'E, but results were not observed. Two bombs probably hit a 6,000-ton vessel and two overshot when it was attacked in position 52° 45'N, 04° 36'E.

On 21 April 1941 S/L David Bennett issued an order that no aircrew were to leave camp, following which the squadron took part in its first 'Circus Blot' on Le Havre the same day. A 'Circus' was an attempt to draw enemy fighters into combat by flying a formation of high-level Blenheims to a target within range of a strong fighter escort. The 'Blot' operation was a 'fringe' area attack without cloud cover, again escorted by fighters. The 'Circus Blot' was a small, fighter-escorted bomber force, acting close to a main 'Circus' or 'Blot', which served as a diversion to the main episode. The 'Circus Blot' on the 21st was 2 Group's tenth. It was attempted by 105 Squadron accompanied by twelve Blenheims of another squadron based at West Raynham, 14 miles north-east of King's Lynn. They failed to reach Le Havre due to a navigation error by the leading West Raynham aircraft, but undaunted 105 Squadron 'had a go'! Sgt W.H.A. Jackson in L9379:Y, accompanied by Sgt Wood in V6319:F, saw trawlers in position 49° 30'N, 01° 60'E, and let go their seven 250lb, and four 40lb bombs from 3,000ft. It was a spirited attempt, but the bombs fell about 100 or 200 yards ahead of the target. Coincident with the 'Circus Blot' attempt, F/L Goode, accompanied by Sgt Williams and Sgt Scott were in Beat 13, in the region of Dieppe–Cherbourg. The only target they found was a rescue raft at 49°

Sgt Ronald John 'Scottie' Scott (Pilot), service no. 904184 at Swanton Morley. (via Mrs N.A. Scott)

44'N, 01° 36'E. This was bombed by the leader but the attack missed by about 10 yards.

A specific target appeared on the 23rd, when two Blenheims out of a force of five found merchant vessels off Haarlem, 17 miles north of Ijmuiden. The convoy was at a position 52° 43'N, 04° 31'E, and comprised no less than twelve vessels – rich pickings indeed! Unfortunately they could only be attacked by a limited force as S/L Bennett had returned to base with carburettor icing problems, while F/L Calvert-Booth had also returned with an unserviceable air-speed indicator. Sgt Jackson, finding no cloud cover, also returned to base. However, F/L Goode and Sgt Tolman 'had a go' at an 8,000-ton merchant vessel, scoring three direct hits on its No. 1 hatch. Two larger 10,000-ton ships were also singled out and attacked. One was heading north at 52° 30'N, 03° 45'E, and was just missed, two 250lb bombs falling 40 yards to the right of the vessel. The other ship, heading south at 52° 30'N, 03° 46'N, also narrowly escaped a fiery fate, as the bombs landed again 40 yards short.

Meanwhile, in Beat 10 off the Mouth of Schelde, five crews, less their leader S/L Dunlevie, who had returned to base because of insufficient cloud cover in his area, were stooging along like five hounds sniffing out their seaborne quarry. But they did not have to hunt for long, as soon 10,000-ton, 5,000-ton and 2,000-ton vessels were sighted and attacked. The only vessel to be hit was the 2,000-tonner, which suffered one burst against the stern. P/O Needham, Sgt Bruce and Sgt Scott then retired to base, while Sgt Piers was busy dropping four bombs on a coastal boat in the Rotterdam Canal. This boat, a 300/500-tonner, was left to an unobserved fate. One aircraft, having found no ships, did spot an enemy aircraft – a Heinkel III appeared at point-blank range, just in time to receive a stream of one hundred .303in rounds from the Blenheim's turret. The Heinkel disappeared, trailing a long black plume of smoke. Unfortunately, the enemy aircraft was not the only one to suffer, as Blenheim V6318:B was observed by Sgt Bruce, the pilot of R3838:M, to catch fire and crash in the sea off Domberg, Holland, having absorbed fire from minesweeper M1404. The crew, Sgt A.A. Lister (Pilot), Sgt W.T. Heaney (Observer) and Sgt K.W. Porter (WOp/AG), were sadly missed. Sgt Lister rests in Vlissingen in the Netherlands and Sgt Porter in Wendvine Communal Cemetery in Belgium. Sgt Heaney has no known grave.

Anti-shipping operations were beginning to cost dearly in crews, and the next sweep of 25th proved no different. The briefing took place on the 24th at 18.15 hours, and the sweep began in the early hours of the 25th. Six crews took off at 05.05 hours and five ships were found. Near-misses were chalked up against a 1,000-tonner at 52° 25'N, 04° 03'E, which was attacked by two of the Blenheims. Their bombs overshot but both vessels were raked with machine-gun fire. One of these aircraft, V6319:F, belonged to the crew of Sgts Wood, Turton and Wilcock. Ron Wood remembered the attack and the lesson learned: 'On one of my early trips, led by F/L

Goode, I was surprised to see him firing away at some trawlers off the Dutch coast. On our return, I said I had seen a couple of sailors, presumably Dutchmen, on deck waving to us, to which he said that this was a problem but trawlers were known to be positioned there to radio early warning to the enemy.'

At Nieue Waterneg, 1 mile from the Hook of Holland, a 1,600-ton ship received a total of six 250lb bombs, dropped from two aircraft. Only two bombs exploded, but a great column of black smoke and debris was tossed into the air. Sgt Willsher and his crew located twenty huts at a military camp at the Hook, and V6370:T was soon spitting machine-gun rounds at them.

Having attacked a 1,000-ton vessel, P/O R. Needham departed in V6370:T. His Observer on this trip was P/O Thomas Keightley-Smith, who normally flew as part of Sgt Ron Scott's crew, but Sgt Scott had been taken ill with tonsillitis and was not available for duty. Consequently, P/O Keightley-Smith replaced the unavailable Sgt Bruce, P/O Needham's usual Observer. The WOp/AG was P/O Needham's normal operator, Sgt F. Bridgeman. Their aircraft was last seen flying south-east towards some fishing craft, but sadly neither the Blenheim nor its occupants were ever seen again. A few miles west of Westkapelle in the Netherlands they had met fighters and were shot down into the sea. P/O Keightley-Smith rests in Westduin General Cemetery at Den Haag.

The iron and steel works at Velsen, a suburb to the north of Ijmuiden in the Netherlands, was visited later in the day on 25 April. The works produced high grade pig-iron, such as was used for gas engines, cylinder steel, strong low-carbon iron for diesel cylinders, hydraulic presses and pistons.

Four crews left at 09.25 hours. S/L David Bennett in V5502:U led the formation, followed by Sgt Piers in L9244:H, Sgt Bruce in R3838:M, and Sgt Tolman in T1936:P. All except Sgt Piers

The target on 25 April 1941: the Royal Dutch Blast Furnace and Steel Mill at Velsen, Ijmuiden, Holland, with a clear view of the docks. (via Koninklijke Nederlandsche Hoogovens & Staalfabrieken N.V./Aad Neeven)

Squadron Leader David Bennett in Blenheim V5502 GB:U leads the Squadron at low level across a choppy North Sea, bound for the Royal Dutch Blast Furnace and Steel Mill at Velsen, Ijmuiden, Holland on 25 April 1941. (via Mrs N.A. Scott)

attacked the works with full four 250lb bombloads. Gun positions and German soldiers were machine-gunned as the aircraft roared over their target. Sgt Arty Piers and his crew, Sgt Healy and Sgt Bastin, attacked barges and small buildings on the Ijmuiden quay and machine-gunned gun positions. WOp/AG Sgt Stuart Bastin wrote the following account of the raid on his return:

> Lovely clear morning and bright blue sky. Flying a few feet above the sea, we soon saw the Dutch coast about 15 miles away and we were shortly able to pick out our target. Travelling at over 350ft a second, our pilot climbed a little to clear some sandhills. It's a wizard thrill to rush in on the target at this great speed. As we cleared the sandhills the flak started – tracers, and brown and white puffs all over the place – bangs and pops just like a fireworks display. I saw Jerries running all over the place in a terrific panic and one of my pals said afterwards he had seen a fat German doing the ostrich trick behind an exceedingly small bush. Suddenly the kite gave a lurch and several large holes appeared in the wings. I swung the guns over towards the offending gun crew, fired a long burst, and had the satisfaction of seeing the crew fall around their gun – another gun less to deal with. By this time, the plane was wobbling towards the ground with the tall factory chimneys well above us. I yelled to the pilot that there were three big holes in the wings, and he yelled back 'Oh, anyway the starboard engine is stopping.' The observer chimed in with 'we are covered in oil'. I then noticed smoke pouring out of the starboard engine. The pilot managed to get the kite on an even keel again, just in time to miss an overhead pipeline. How the pilot managed to keep her in the air is rather

> beyond me. I heard the observer shout 'Left, left, bombs gone.' The pilot now turned towards the sea and home. I saw the bombs burst across some thickly packed and loaded barges and dockside buildings in the target area. The Jerries were still running all over the place, some towards their guns, mostly towards shelters. One crew never reached their guns. The engine began to pick up again, much to my relief, but there was still smoke and the threat of fire. We got away without further damage. The Germans were putting up a very heavy barrage over the target, fortunately a little too late. Another plane, seeing our predicament, turned and kept guard on us all the way home. I was a bit worried as I could see white trails left behind by fighters, right above us. No machine was more welcome than our guardian. We managed, due to the pilot's skilful handling, to reach our base on ETA.

The 'guardian' aircraft is assumed to have been that of Sgt J.H. Tolman and his crew, Sgt A.W. Hutton and Sgt Fosbrook, who landed before Sgt Piers at 11.27 hours. Sgt Piers in GB:H crash-landed three minutes later at 11.30 hours, skidding to a halt on the grass at Swanton Morley. The *Koninklijke Nederlandsche Hoogovens & Staalfabrieken N.V.* (Royal Dutch Blast-Furnace and Steel-Mill Ltd), Ijmuiden, kindly provided the following damage assessment reports, as written by F.W.E. Spies and here loosely translated into English from the original German. The first report, written at 14.50 hours European Time, reads:

> 'Account of Air Raid on the Ijmuiden Blast-Furnaces.'
>
> This Friday morning at 11.31, four aircraft appeared from a westerly direction very low over the blast-furnaces area. Immediately bombs were dropped. During the entire flight the perimeter defences were firing. Four bombs fell on the east and south embankments of the outer harbours. Three bombs exploded, and a fourth, which lies in the dock, we are not certain about. After that, five bombs fell between the rolling mill and the main works road, and also one bomb south of the steelworks sheds, one by the steelworks return cooling equipment, one in the old iron-manganese sheds, and two on the main works road. Here lies a dud. (Possibly 250lb.) A further stick of four bombs fell to the west of the repair workshop in open land. On the other half of the western perimeter, many incendiaries caused the outbreak of heathland fires. A solitary dud lies near the lamp-gas pumping station.
>
> The material damage was limited to very many panes of glass, a damaged 5,000 cubic meter lamp-gas holder, a damaged ore store and a warehouse, which were completely destroyed. A back-up emission stack for the coke plant was badly damaged. The cleaning cells in the lamp-gas cleaning plant were smashed to pieces. The lamp-gas holder went on fire and was extinguished by the works fire brigade and has been temporarily repaired. A few slightly injured people were treated in the first aid post. In the harbour several ships were slightly damaged.

This shipping, attacked by Sgt Piers and his crew comprised the

> SS *Twiod*, a 203-ton steamship; the RS *Anna*, an 827-ton sailing ship; the RS *Merbaboe*, a 1,740-ton sailing barge; and the RS *Soembing*, a 1,881-ton sailing ship.

The damage caused to the ships as a result of the bombing was fairly minor, with some windows broken and masts damaged. F.W.E. Spies continued:

> Because of the unexploded bomb, the result was that the gas supply to the communities of Ijmuiden, Velsen, Beverwijk, Krommenie, Wormerveer, Zaandam and Haarlem were shut off. The nitrogen plant is partially shut down. The magazine, main repair shop, electrical shop, gas pumping station, lime-saltpetre works were cleared out. The surroundings were closed off with sentry posts.

The threat posed by the unexploded bombs was evident, and at 17.10 hours a further report was produced by F.W.E. Spies, which stated that: 'At 15.45 the two duds were preliminarily disarmed by unscrewing the fuse. (Bomb Disposal Unit, Luftgau Holland, Unteroffizier Kuhrcke.) On Saturday the Bomb Corps will dispose of them by blowing them up. The repairs are in progress and the firm is again running as normal.' The works may well have been 'running as normal', but the cost of repairs, estimated at 25,158.19 Dutch florins (approximately £84,000 at present rates) was still being negotiated, and not all of the damage inflicted had been repaired by the end of April two years later!

As a postscript, this proved to be Sgt Pier's last operation with 105 Squadron. He departed to train on night-fighters, ending up in 264 (Madras Presidency) Squadron, which was based at Colerne, 3 miles north-east of Bath. The squadron flew Mosquito II 'night intruder' missions. On the night of 11/12 March 1943 Night Ranger 14, Mosquito DD 661, crewed by P/O A.W.J. Piers and Navigator/Radio Operator F/Sgt T.B. Hill, departed from Portreath at 21.15 hours. It was shot down over the Rennes area of France and despite intensive searching the next day, neither the aircraft nor its crew were ever seen again. Following his departure, Sgt Piers' Blenheim crew ultimately crewed up with Sgt Ronald John Scott, an experienced pre-war pilot.

A short respite from shipping attacks came on the 27th, when German power stations at Knapsack, Stockum and Quadrath were allocated as targets. In the event, none was attacked due

During the Velsen raid, damage was inflicted when a gun crew in the docks area of the Royal Dutch Blast Furnace and Steel Mill at Velsen opened up on Sgt Piers' Blenheim L9244 GB:H. The WOp/AG, Sgt Bastin, later stated: 'the pilot managed to get the kite on an even keel again, just in time to miss an overhead pipeline'. (The Trustees of the Imperial War Museum, London: C3260)

Having survived the Velsen raid, the battle-damaged Blenheim L9244 GB:H belly-landed on Swanton Morley's convex grass landing area. (via Mrs N.A. Scott)

Front view of crashed Blenheim L9244 GB:H on 25 April 1941. Note the tripod arrangement used to restrain the engine's propeller shaft, and the covers over the twin Browning machine-guns. (via Mrs N.A. Scott)

Flak damage to the port wing root of L9244 GB:H. Note the shrapnel holes in the fuselage close to the turret which must have made Sgt Bastin lift his feet! (via Mrs N.A. Scott)

Close up view of flak damage to the port wing root and flaps of L9244 GB:H. (via Mrs N.A. Scott)

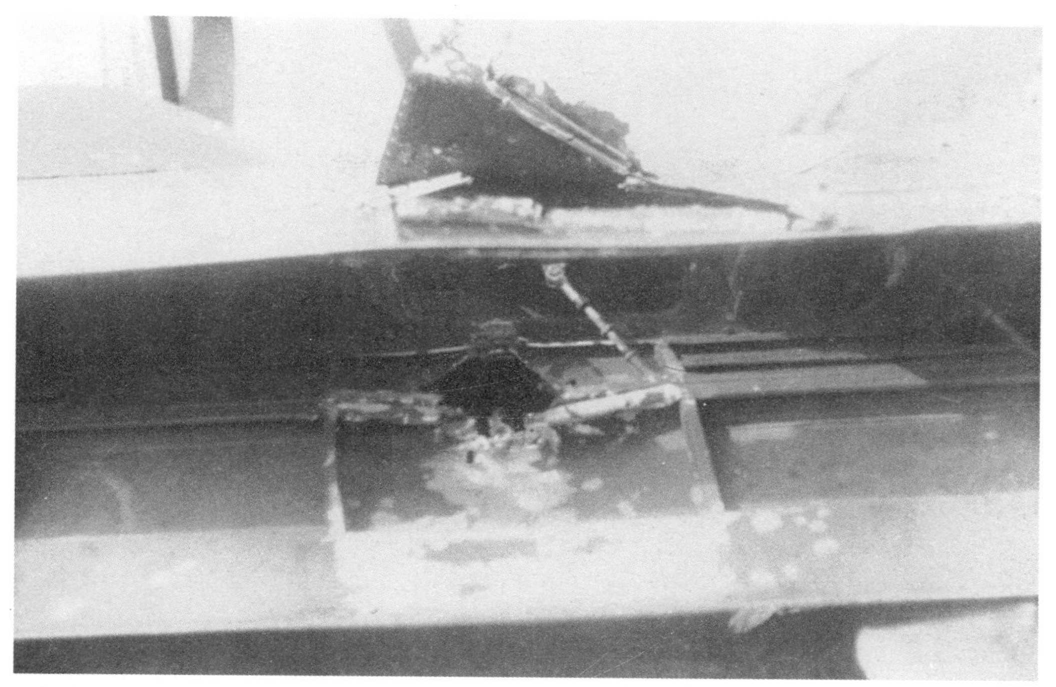

A further view of the port wing root and flaps of Blenheim L9244 GB:H. The entry point of the shell through the flap can be clearly seen, with the exit torn through the wing surface, with consequential damage to the strut. (via Mrs N.A. Scott)

Flak damage to the starboard side of Blenheim L9244 GB:H. Note the close proximity to Sgt Bastin's turret. (via Mrs N.A. Scott)

A closer view of the starboard side flak damage to L9244 GB:H. The splintering in the fuselage can be clearly seen. (via Mrs N.A. Scott)

to lack of cloud cover and two crews attacked only fringe targets, such as the military camp at Gremberg in northern Belgium. Ron Wood recalled the preparations for the Operation:

Standing behind a Blenheim at Swanton Morley are (left) Sgt (WOp/AG) Stuart Bastin and the Canadian Sgt Arthur 'Arty' J. Piers, his first pilot on joining 105 Squadron. (via Mrs N.A. Scott)

This was to be a daylight operation with so-called cloud-cover protection. I remember at the briefing someone voicing most of our feelings in questioning the survivability, even with the promised cloud cover, of nearly 150 miles each way over enemy territory after coasting in. The answer given was that it was not a question of how many got back as long as some got there, and apart from the attack, there was the morale effect of the sounding of the air raid sirens in daylight in Cologne. This despondent infusion from a senior officer (I'm not sure if it wasn't the AOC) who was not going, did not inspire the audience greatly. Fortunately for all of us at that time it was cancelled, although I believe it was done some time later. It all seems hard to believe now, the gladiatorial mood prevailing at that time.

However, it was back to anti-shipping duties again for the last two operations of the month.

A shipping sweep on Beat 14 (Cherbourg) proved fruitless on the 29th, although 2 Group coastal sweep no. 44 in Beat 15 (north-west France) proved more satisfactory. Out of a formation of six, two aircraft found a target. A convoy of two merchant vessels and a tender were found at a position 49° 01'N, 03° 21'E. A 10,000-ton merchant vessel was singled out and attacked by F/L Calvert-Booth in Blenheim V5828:R and P/O Rushbrooke in V6420:K. Eight 250lb general purpose bombs were dropped, each with the usual 11-second delay to allow the aircraft to get well clear of the explosion. For good measure both merchant vessels were machine-gunned prior to departure. The bombed vessel was seen to be damaged and listing to starboard, as the two marauding aircraft sped off back to base, leaving their foe to a watery end. Thus ended the month of April.

May opened with direct orders on the 1st from Group to send three aircraft to sweep between the Hook of Holland and Rotterdam. A further three were to sweep between the English coast and Antwerp. The orders were received at 09.50 hours, and by 12.15 hours two vics of three aircraft, one led by F/L George Goode and the other by F/L Calvert-Booth, were airborne and heading for Rotterdam and Antwerp respectively. F/L Goode, F/O Dore and Sgt Wood were detailed to make use of cloud cover to bomb the docks and any shipping in the waterways. But when they got there the cloud cover was gone, and so F/O Dore in V6028:D turned and headed for home. Sgt Wood, however, took V6319:F into the attack on a 5,000-ton tanker, amid light and heavy flak bursting all around the aircraft. The WOp/AG, Sgt Wilcock, responded with his twin Brownings, and had the satisfaction of seeing the starboard side of the ship erupt in a huge spout of water, just aft of the funnel. At least one of the four bombs dropped had hit its target as the crew sped for home. Ron Wood remembers the operation with some degree of relief:

> Three of us were detailed to attack the docks at Rotterdam. Most unusually, this was planned to be a high-level cloud-cover operation with the aircraft at ten or fifteen minute intervals. F/L Goode was first, which I remember thinking was all right for him, as he would have the benefit of surprise. It didn't turn out that way, however. The cloud cover which we had been assured would extend all the way over the North Sea ran out halfway across. I then decided to continue but at sea-level, and so down we went for low-level protection. We found Rotterdam's waterways and the first ship was good enough for me. I was running in to attack when Bert Turton, my navigator, shouted, 'Pull up, pull up, don't bomb!' This I did and asked what the hell he was playing at, to which he said we hadn't got the 11-second delay bombs (which we always used for low-level attacks) and that we would have gone up with the ship. In fact we found out afterwards that the bombs *were* 11-second delay fused, but for some reason we were not sure at the time, and I suppose it was better to be safe than sorry. I climbed up again, circling, and we started to get some sporadic flak. It seemed quite some time before we found our ship again but eventually we did and had a good run-in to attack, this time it being the navigator's task, with his bombsight in the nose, to drop the bombs. Jimmy Wilcock, our WOp/AG, said he was pretty sure we had hit the ship and Bert Turton said he had seen one bomb hit near the funnel. We didn't stop to look around, we had already been too long over the target area and it was surprising no fighters had appeared. The flak was now more concentrated, which I thought was probably keeping them away and they would be waiting for us on our way back. I dived down to sea-level and we sped back without any trouble. Not so F/L Goode, however; he had been over the target area fifteen minutes or so before us and had attracted five or six 109s on his incursion, and the fighters had very obligingly (for us) followed him away so we missed them completely. F/L Goode had a hairy old time getting back but all credit to him, he made it.

F/L Goode and his crew in V5823:G had gone for the storage tanks. Their attack was right

105 Squadron, Swanton Morley 1941: Sgt Ronald Wood (Pilot), service no. 968970, photographed soon after joining 105 Squadron at Swanton Morley in 1941. (via Ron Wood)

down on the deck, as they released four 250lb SAP bombs. Flak was bursting all around, and it was not possible to positively identify whether the bombs had burst successfully or not. As mentioned above, suddenly no less than five Bf 109 fighters appeared, having spotted the Blenheim on the way home. For twenty minutes the Luftwaffe did their damnedest to destroy their prey, and only by extremely clever flying did F/L Goode eventually escape the streams of gunfire spat at them by the fighters. Sgt Geoffrey Rowland, George Goode's WOp/AG, describes what happened next:

> We were pretty severely peppered and the intercom was failing. Sam Hogan did more than I could to give George evasive instructions, and when the port engine was hit, we had no hydraulics, as it drove the pump. I could only manoeuvre the turret by hand in some small measure, and also fire

Jimmy Wilcock was the WOp/AG in Sgt Ron Wood's crew. (via Ron Wood)

> one Browning by the rear lever, having little chance of aiming it. Goode was injured in one hand, Sam Hogan was injured in one ankle, and I was wounded in my trigger finger. I was able to get a bearing from base, which I passed over the bomb well by hand. I did not even give it a 'priority'.

By now F/L Goode's Blenheim was so badly damaged that one propeller sheared right off, plummeting into the sea, but the wounded pilot and crew flew on. Their traumatic sortie was not yet over, though, as while crossing the English coast, the remaining propeller gave up the fight and also sheared off, leaving the Blenheim gliding, fortunately over England. Geoffrey Rowland continues:

> We crossed the coast somewhere near Southwold, I have always understood, and put the nose down. We pranged in a field near Cookley. It all happened in some sixty seconds, I reckon. The bottom of the aircraft was ripped up, and I had mud up to my knees in the turret. We were very lucky to hit a nice soft field! We clambered out and found a farm house some 150 yards away. The farmer was out, but we went in and I phoned Swanton Morley to report. They got cracking, and after about an hour or more the local ARP from Halesworth came and picked us up in a private car, towing a small ambulance trailer. Hogan was put in the trailer and we were driven to the ARP HQ, which was a pub in Halesworth (or Harleston). From there, after a cup of tea, we were driven to Pulham (the old airship station), which I believe had a small RAF unit, and there transferred to a Swanton Morley RAF ambulance which had come over for us. We were taken to sick quarters at Swanton Morley, and next day to the RAF hospital at Ely, where we were all operated on. After a week or two, we went off for convalescence, they to the Palace Hotel, Torquay, and I to Blackpool.

The incident did not go unnoticed, and two days later, on 3 May 1941, *The Times* newspaper bore the headline 'Home Without Airscrew', while on the same day another newspaper reported 'Plane Had No Props'. Some time later, on 18 July 1941, after their wounds had healed sufficiently, HM The King presented the DFC to F/L Goode and P/O Hogan, while a DFM went to Sgt Rowland. As a postscript to this it is interesting to note that once they had all recovered adequately to return to active duties, there was an unfortunate mix-up. Geoffrey Rowland explains:

> We all wanted to keep together, so after ten days or so I hoped to hear from them that they were going back to Swanton Morley. I never received their letter. The result was that they went back and I knew nothing. At that time their old squadron, No. 90 (which with 35 Squadron had been used to form 17 OTU) was being re-formed. Goode elected to stay on at 105 Squadron with a new crew, and Hogan went to 90 Squadron. This was based at Polebrook, flying the new Fortress Is. He wrote to me complaining that he did not like them, and soon after was lost over the North Sea, on 8 September 1941. Goode went to Malta, and when I reported back to Swanton Morley they had gone and I was sent to another squadron.

Of the other three aircraft in the raid on Rotterdam, F/L Calvert-Booth had bombed four barges with unobserved results but Sgt Jackson abandoned the task due to lack of cloud cover. P/O Alan Judson and his crew, Sgt Richard 'Dickie' Rook (Observer) and Sgt Paddy Murray (WOp/AG), took Blenheim T1887:S into Flushing's harbour area. Dickie Rook takes up the story:

> We were briefed to proceed to the Dutch coast, in the vicinity of The Hague, to fly at minimum height (which meant around 50ft) in loose formation, with the acting 'B' Flight Commander, F/L Calvert-Booth. Upon sighting the enemy coast, we were to separate, and

HOME WITHOUT AIRSCREW

The daylight attacks by the Bomber Command met with strong opposition from the enemy (says the Air Ministry News Service). Everywhere the anti-aircraft fire was intense, and at times our bombers were tackling enemy fighters at odds of three and more to one.

During the attack on oil storage tanks at Vlaardingen, a few miles west of Rotterdam, a pilot had to take violent evasive action to get through the fierce barrage, and even so a shell burst through the nose of the aircraft. The pilot made a good run up and is certain that his bombs damaged the storage tanks. Immediately after he had turned for home five Messerschmitt 109s came up and hotly engaged the single bomber. For 20 minutes the fight went on. Our gunner was wounded, and the mechanism of his gun carriage was put out of action, but he fought on, turning his guns with the hand control. One by one the Messerschmitts broke off the fight, the first four fairly soon, the fifth after returning again and again to the attack.

When the last Messerschmitt gave up the attack oil was pouring from the bomber's port engine In a few moments the engine had stopped, and the airscrew fell off, but the pilot brought his aircraft back over the North Sea. Then, soon after the bomber had crossed the English coast, the second airscrew, which had also been damaged in the encounter, dropped away. The pilot skilfully brought the bomber down, and made a safe landing in a field.

PLANE HAD NO 'PROPS'

FIGHTING off the attacks of five Messerschmitt fighters over Holland, an R.A.F. bomber set course for home with oil pouring from the port engine.

The engine stopped—and the propeller fell off.

Out over the North Sea, on one engine, flew the bomber. The English coast was crossed —and then the second airscrew, also damaged, dropped away.

But the pilot brought his machine down to a safe landing in a field.

He had attacked oil storage tanks near Rotterdam in daylight.

A shell burst through the nose of the aircraft, and then the five Messerschmitt 109s. attacked.

For twenty minutes the fight went on. Our gunner was wounded and the mechanism of his gun carriage put out of action, but he fought on, turning his guns with the hand control.

One by one the Messerschmitts broke off the fight.

Press cuttings reported the story of F/L Goode's extraordinary return flight in V5823:G on 1 May 1941. (via Geoffrey Rowland)

HRH Princess Mary talks to S/L George Goode DFC (right) and P/O Sam Hogan DFC (second from right). Both airmen were convalescing at a hotel in Torquay following their operation to Rotterdam on 1 May 1941. Both airmen were awarded the DFC for their part in this operation, and a DFM went to their WOp/AG Sgt Geoffrey Rowland (not shown). (via Geoffrey Rowland)

our instructions were to follow the coastline in a southerly direction, searching for enemy shipping and if none were located, then to proceed into Flushing Harbour and attack shipping and/or harbour installations.

At 12.15 hours we were airborne in Blenheim T1887, laden with four 250lb SAP bombs fitted with 11-second delay fuses and eight 'flower pot' incendiary bombs on extension carriers beneath the wings. Weather conditions were not good and visibility poor when we eventually came suddenly upon the enemy coastline. As we turned on to our southerly heading, because of the poor visibility it was necessary to fly too close to the coast for comfort. At this stage, our hopes were that we would find some target at sea, sooner rather than later, and avoid the necessity of penetrating the harbour defences at Flushing. However, as ever, easy options seldom present themselves and this was no exception. The further south we went, so the weather conditions deteriorated. Then we turned on to an easterly course into the western Schelde, having failed to locate any shipping en route. We were in low cloud at around 600ft and turning to port, with the intention of descending towards our target on a westerly heading, with a clear run out to sea after the attack. As we slowly descended, all eyes were strained for sight of what lay below and then, at about 400ft, three things happened almost simultaneously, but in exactly which sequence, it is impossible to remember. First we got a fleeting glimpse of the harbour installations, and then through flitting cloud a cargo ship, estimated at around 5/7,000 tons. Secondly, we were hit by anti-aircraft fire with a shell exploding amidships. Thirdly, our bomb priming selection and release took place. The aircraft filled with acrid smoke and wallowed disconcertingly as we headed slowly back into the welcome and all-concealing shroud of thick cloud, no longer the sitting ducks of a few minutes earlier. We felt no further anti-aircraft activity, and once the aircraft became stable, damage was assessed as far as possible. It became clear that all hydraulic controls had been lost, there was no rudder control, and control to the elevators was producing a very sluggish response. Later, it was ascertained that the control cable had, as a result of the explosion and shrapnel, been partially severed. A reasonable degree of stability was possible as we headed for home, taking the shortest possible sea crossing, in case it should become necessary to ditch the aircraft, a thought upon which we didn't dwell.

By now we were climbing gently and contemplating the problems that lay ahead. It was at this point that we realized the intercom to the rear gunner was not working and we had no idea how Paddy had fared in his gun turret. As I made my way to the rear, the centre section was still hazy with smoke, and just forward of the turret, I encountered a hole large enough to fall through in the side and bottom of the fuselage. On reaching the turret, further problems presented themselves. Paddy had been hit in the foot with a small fragment of shrapnel which, while painful, did not appear to be too serious. The greatest problem, however, lay in the fact that the turret was stuck firmly in the raised position, and with the hydraulic power gone, it was impossible to move it in any direction, and he was therefore trapped. Having failed to release him, but having made sure he was in no immediate danger, I reassured him as best I could and then made my way back to the cockpit. We were now presented with a true dilemma, facing three questions:

firstly, had the bombs been released, or had this been prevented through loss of electric power at the time we were hit; secondly, if they had not been released, had they been primed before the loss of electric power; and thirdly, how should we proceed, since because of the turret situation, the option of baling out was no longer available?

All this left us with only one course of action – a crash-landing, trusting that either the bombs had been released or they had not been primed.

We arrived back in the vicinity of base at an altitude of some 3,000ft. It was decided to carry out a simulated approach, to assess the aircraft's behaviour at landing speeds. All went well until the speed was brought down to around 100mph, when the aircraft became difficult to control, and it was obvious that our landing would have to be carried out at a much higher speed than usual. From memory, I believe our final approach speed was over 100mph. The approach was made very low and touch-down effected close to the entrance boundary – all carried out to absolute perfection. Despite this, once contact was made with 'mother earth' we were liberally showered with soil and stones, thrown up through the damaged nose panel. Perhaps the most disconcerting factor in all of this was the front gun mounting, which was threatening to break loose, and be ejected into the cockpit. Fortunately, it remained in place. As we came to a halt, the silence which followed was, in a sense, sweet music, with the only sound being the crackle of hot exhausts. This brief period of peace was shattered abruptly a few seconds later, when a head appeared in the hatch and an agitated voice screamed 'Get out, the bombs are still on board!' Thinking back, one would have expected this to produce a wild scramble to exit, or even perhaps blind panic, but not so. It was as though we had sat down and logically reasoned that if the damned things had not detonated by then, with only

Left to right: Sgt 'Dickie' Rook (Observer); Sgt Paddy Murray (WOp/AG); P/O Alan Judson (Pilot). (via Dickie Rook)

> an 11-second fuse delay, they damned soon would, so why bother to rush around. The feelings of those moments have never left me.
>
> There was no explosion, Paddy was removed from his turret, and after treatment at sick quarters, was soon little the worse for his experience. Such were the times that just two days later, at 18.00 hours, we were off again, this time in Blenheim V6039:Q, and with a reserve WOp/AG, searching for shipping to Den Helder; only 48 hours previously, all this had taken place!

The reserve WOp/AG who took Paddy Murray's place until he was available again on the 7th, was a sergeant, who was affectionately remembered by one who was there as 'Shorty'. The following tale unfolded:

> In the sergeants' mess, there always seemed to be this rather small WOp/AG sergeant, nicknamed 'Shorty'. I thought he must be a real old hand on the squadron. It transpired, however, that he had gone sick soon after arriving and on their first trip with a spare WOp/AG, his crew had failed to return. No one noticed or missed 'Shorty'. 'A' Flight thought he was on 'B' Flight, and 'B' Flight thought he was on 'A' Flight. It didn't bother 'Shorty', and he might have done a full operational tour in the sergeants' mess, if he hadn't blown it by wanting to go on leave, and having to apply to one or other of the flights. Thus his respite came to an end as he was cornered as a spare WOp/AG. One night soon after this, a crew at briefing was short of their WOp/AG, and a message was sent to the sergeants' mess for two spare WOp/AGs to report to briefing. The name of the other one escapes me (it may have been Quinn), but anyway he had been with the squadron in France and had done numerous operations, and sported a DFM. 'Shorty' and the other duly arrived at the briefing, and were asked who was going to go on this operation. I can still remember the laughter

when 'Shorty' piped up with, 'I don't mind standing down if the crew would prefer Sgt Quinn who is a little more experienced than me'.

Some months later, staging through Gibraltar en route to Malta and the Middle East, I recognized the distinctive figure of none other than 'Shorty', looking in a shop window. He said he had been at Gibraltar ten days and was quite enjoying it. I asked him what had caused their delay in getting on to Malta. 'Oh,' he said, 'I had to go sick on arrival and my crew has gone without me and with a spare WOp/AG who was here.' Maybe he saw the war out at Gibraltar!

Meanwhile, on 1 May another sweep was made in Beat 15. No merchant shipping was found, nor was any on the 3rd, when Beats 7 and 9 were patrolled. However, one aircraft on Beat 7 did find a target, as Ron Wood explains:

> We machine-gunned two E-Boats on our way to search for some reported shipping off Terschelling, but as on many of these sweeps, we spent long periods searching without success. These daylight operations were unpredictable. On one of our meetings in Norwich with boys from other squadrons, I remember hearing about one pilot on a squadron who had (so it was said) gone LMF after just three ops, which in itself would seem somewhat unusual, until one heard what those three ops had been like. He had been attacked by fighters on each occasion, with his gunner killed on the last one, and the Blenheim shot up and damaged on both the previous ones. He probably suffered more and saw more action on those three operations than many others did in thirty or more missions at night.

CHAPTER 6

Scottish Venture

At 20.00 hours on 3 May orders were received from Group. The squadron was on the move again, although this time on detachment only. In order to harass shipping entering and leaving the Scandinavian ports, Blenheim squadrons were detached by rota to patrol the seas and fjords of Norway. It was now 105 Squadron's turn to take up its tour of duty.

Lossiemouth in Scotland was to be their new base from where operations would be mounted for the next fortnight or so. An advance party was sent up in three Harrows, closely followed by the main party of essential personnel, including two intelligence officers, F/L Hugh H. 'Tom' Rose and C.R. Tunks. The Operations Officer, F/L Olverson, P/O H.V. Bennett, and the station engineering officer travelled up by road on the 4th prior to the aircrews' departure the next day. The main party was under the command of F/O Francis Edward 'Teddy' Frayn. Having been shot down in France in June 1940 and evacuated with a few of the 51st Highland Division via St Valery en Caux on 13 June, 'Teddy' Frayn had subsequently spent ten months in hospital being 'put together' again! He was also to play a large part in squadron administration during its stay on Malta.

At 14.00 hours on the 5th, seventeen Blenheims departed from Swanton Morley en route to Lossiemouth in three formations, each of five aircraft in a vic, with two more following on behind them. One of the captains, P/O Jack Buckley, flew the three hour trip up to Lossiemouth in V6380:G accompanied by no less than three groundcrew. This was in addition to his own crew of P/O Douglas Ivens, a Scotsman who lived in London, and Sgt Reg Allen his Northampton WOp/AG.

On arrival at RAF Lossiemouth, the weather was cold but pleasant. Nissen-type huts were provided for aircrew and groundcrew accommodation, with a separate hut forming the sergeants' mess. Briefings were held in the 'Intelligence Centre', a hut specially built for the purpose. The location was typical, the walls adorned with photographs, and books of shipping and aircraft all available to be studied. On entry, the crew members would give the customary salute and settle down for briefing. Officers from intelligence, meteorology, radio and navigation disciplines were in attendance. The radio officer doubled as a gunnery officer for the WOp/AGs. The young airmen would sit as crews, and be collectively addressed by the gathered officers before discussing tactics. Then the various disciplines, the pilots, the observers and WOp/AGs would get together to share the necessary 'gen', before jumping aboard the trucks to be dropped off at their respective aircraft. Each would be carrying his navigation bag, codes and so on. The procedure at Lossiemouth was typical of any operational station at the time.

Life at the station was reasonable, with warmth being supplied in each hut by a fire. Aircrew breakfast was served at tables with red chequered tablecloths, but lacking the traditional fried eggs – after all there was a war on! It was possible during spare time to venture into the neighbouring town of Elgin to sample the local hospitality. A few rounds of golf were even put in by the CO, Arnold Christian, on the first evening. For those not so inclined, a brisk walk to the shore was a popular way of passing the time in the evenings. F/Sgt Jim Taylor thought Lossiemouth:

> A nice place – folk were very friendly. There was a pub called the Castle Bar, run by an elderly couple. He was always ridiculing the Germans. Apparently, one night the Germans

came over on an intruder mission and as our boys were landing, they came in and bombed the 'drome. He never forgave the Germans for that!'

Before operations could begin, the 6th was taken up with practice flying, with one hour flights low over the Moray Firth. Bombing-run practices were made against red-sailed fishing boats in the Firth, much to the consternation of the unsuspecting occupants! Once again shipping attacks were divided into beats. Flying in vics as far as the coast, the Blenheims would then split up into pairs and fly parallel to the coast for a three-minute maximum, all in strict radio and Aldis lamp silence lest any prowling fighters be attracted.

The first such operation took place on the 7th. S/L Dunlevie led out a formation of ten aircraft detailed to sweep Beat 1 (West of Denmark) in four sections, but to no avail. The next day, Thursday 8 May, was to be very much more eventful, but in a very unfortunate way. This time six crews were detailed to sweep in pairs on Beat 2 off Stavanger. The Battle Order stated the sweep was to take place at 57° 59'N, 05° 30'E, leaving to the east. The armament was to be four 250lb GP bombs, and briefing was to take place at 03.00 hours. At 05.10 hours, six aircraft, led by W/C A.L. Christian in V5828:R, lifted off into the early morning sea breeze, and set course for the sweep. Four of the aircraft saw no shipping and F/L Calvert-Booth, P/O Broadley, P/O Rushbrooke and Sgt Wood returned to base, the last touching down exactly four hours after take-off at 09.10 hours. Prior to departure, the CO had taken P/O Jack Buckley aside and asked him to keep an eye open to ensure the squadron's formation kept together properly. With this instruction in mind, P/O Buckley tucked his Blenheim T2118:E neatly in at the leader's right side in no. 2 position. He was in this position when a convoy of twenty vessels appeared in the entrance to Hafrsfjord, west of Stavanger. The two captains chose their targets. Two merchant vessels were singled out, one of which Jack Buckley's log details as an 800-ton flak ship. When the first merchant vessel was last seen, it was down by the stern, billowing smoke high into the air. Four 250lb bombs had been dropped, two exploded 10 or 20 yards short but the other two were unobserved. During the attack the ship was raked with machine-gun fire from the front and rear guns.

During his run-in for a beam attack on the flak ship, P/O Buckley was settling his aircraft level, when he realized that W/C Arnold Christian and his crew, F/Sgt Hancock (Observer) and Sgt Wade (WOp/AG), had not reappeared on his port side. Their Blenheim was last seen with the port engine on fire, heading for the Norwegian coast some 2 miles distant. They and their Blenheim, V5828:R, were posted missing. There was, however, a witness to their demise. Herr Leidland, a fisherman, saw the aircraft crash into the water, and he later retrieved a flying boot from the sea; it contained a leather tag with F/Sgt Hancock's name on it. They had in fact crashed south of the entrance to Hardangerfjorden, north of Stavanger.

The loss of the CO hit squadron morale very badly, and was well remembered by the then S/L David Bennett who paid the following tribute in *2 Group RAF* by Michael J.F. Bowyer:

> Arnold Christian, an A1 Category CFS [Central Flying School] Instructor, could fly a Blenheim better than most and inspired us all with his skill and leadership. He was a relative of Fletcher Christian, of 'Mutiny on the Bounty' fame, and Captain Bligh's confrontation with Christian is well known. Like his ancestor, our squadron commander was a stubborn, never-say-die character, with inborn leadership of somewhat rebellious nature, traits possessed by so many 2 Group squadron commanders. He had been responsible for our rapid conversion from night bombing to daylight low-level operations in April 1941. Training was intense and I remember carrying out four sorties in a day, dropping 32 practice bombs in the Wash, as Christian encouraged us to fly accurately over the sea at 50ft and lower. 'The lower the better', were his words, and 'effective jinking manoeuvres near the deck can get you out

of trouble in the target area'. He was right. A Blenheim could be thrown around, and his example inspired us all. Arnold's sense of fun and his good, dry humour, added to his superb airmanship, made 105 a good Squadron!

Sgt Harold Frederick 'Andy' Hancock (Observer), service no. 580443, was killed on 8 May 1941 during an attack on shipping in a Norwegian fjord in Blenheim V5828:R. (Joan and Eric Phillips)

Sgt Geoffrey Rowland, George Goode's WOp/AG, commented, 'W/C Arnold Christian (a relative of Fletcher Christian of the 'Mutiny On The Bounty') was one of the finest COs one could wish to serve under.'

On 9 May 1941 S/L Bennett led a formation of seven saddened crews to sweep in three sections along Beat 1 off Bergen. F/O Judson had to return to base when his turret failed to operate properly and his Blenheim V6039:Q landed safely at 14.25 hours, only one hour and twenty five minutes from take-off. Four of the others found nothing and returned, also having completed their sweep. However, at a position 60° 36'N, 04° 40'E, two fishing boats loomed up on S/L Bennett's and P/O Richard's horizon. The first aircraft made two attacks; in the first he dropped only one bomb in a beam attack and saw an explosion short of the boat. His second run was more successful, with at least one bomb bursting under the hull. By this time the engine on the vessel was out of action and the crew could be seen launching themselves over the edge. The attack on the other ship missed, but having machine-gunned both vessels, the two marauding Blenheims made off. Although all their bombs had been expended, the .303in ammunition was not, and so strafing runs were made as a parting gesture. S/L Bennett arrived home last in V5502:U at 17.32 hours. P/O Richards in T1826:A had beaten him home, arriving eighteen minutes earlier at 17.14 hours.

Since the tragic loss of W/C Christian, the squadron had been temporarily commanded by S/L J.S. Dunlevie. However, they had not long to wait before official command was taken up once more. On 11 May, following his convalescence from tonsillitis, during which period his friend and observer P/O T. Keightly-Smith had been killed, Sgt Ronald Scott accompanied a new crew from Swanton Morley to rejoin the Battle Order. A posting on 10 May had sent this 139 Squadron crew to Swanton Morley for their flight north the next day. But when Blenheim R3907 taxied to a halt at Lossiemouth, in addition to Sgt Scott, the new CO W/C Hughie Idwal Edwards also alighted from the aircraft, accompanied by his crew, Sgt Ashplant (Observer) and Sgt Gerry Quinn DFM (WOp/AG). Hughie Edwards was a tough, pugnacious Australian from Fremantle, aged 26. He was destined to follow a very successful and highly decorated career, boosting both squadron morale and prestige. (*See Appendix I.*)

Following the new CO's arrival, a couple of shipping sweeps were undertaken. On 12 May eight aircraft took off to sweep in pairs along Beat 4 off the Skagerrak. The only pilot to find a target was P/O Buckley, accompanied by his crew, P/O Ivens and Sgt Allen, who machine-gunned a Danish fishing vessel before dropping four bombs, all of which overshot. The other six crews, including Sgt Wood, Sgt Turton and Sgt Wilcock in Blenheim V6420:K saw nothing to attack. Ron Wood explains how the operation concluded and how he had a brush with the new CO in consequence:

> From Lossiemouth, a shipping sweep to the Skagerrak and Kattegat meant that you might not see land for over five hours and this was a bit much with a Blenheim's limited aids. In fact I think we once worked it out that if you were two or three degrees in excess on the homeward course you could miss Scotland altogether. We had a case of one pilot who said he had knocked off a few degrees from the course the navigator had given to him, unaware that the navigator had already knocked off a few degrees from the QDM obtained by the wireless operator – I think they finished up coasting in at Newcastle!
>
> There was no love lost between Hughie Edwards and me at that time but looking back, we were all so young and high spirited and living for the day. I think what started us off on the wrong foot was the incident just after we had lost our ever-so-popular CO, W/C Christian over Norway. It was accepted practice that if one was worried about fuel, and there was a chance that you might not make it back with the bombs still on board, it was perfectly in order to jettison the bombs. After seeing nothing for five hours and with the vague estimate of at least thirty minutes to go, I made the decision to jettison the bombs. On arrival back at base, I was informed that the new CO wished to see me immediately after de-briefing. I thought it was rather nice, until after being ushered in to his presence, when I was greeted not with a welcome, but with 'Why did you jettison your bombs?' I explained the fuel situation and was asked how long I thought I had. I can't remember what I said, but he had my tanks dipped and there was, I think he said, thirty gallons. He then asked me how long I thought I could fly on that, and I said I could probably manage about thirty minutes. He then said he didn't think much of our ability as a crew if we couldn't judge that we had sufficient to get back without jettisoning the bombs. I argued that the reason we had thirty minutes' fuel was *because* we had jettisoned the bombs. He said it was not good enough, and we should bring the bombs back in similar circumstances in future. He asked, did I understand him, and I remember quite well saying, 'Yes, you're the new CO I believe!' I got a glare and took my exit.
>
> I was not alone in my opinions, especially as we all remembered Arnold Christian joining in with the boys, playing rugger with the adjutant's hat, etc. Now this was a different animal and things were going to be different. Hughie Edwards was a 'war winner'; he wanted to send six Blenheims in tight box formation down the Ruhr in daylight. His theory was that with controlled fire-power from the gunnery leader, twelve Brownings would be opposing four enemy fighters' guns. (These were the days before the 109Fs had cannon!) But what made him rather unique was that it wouldn't be five sergeant pilots with a flight lieutenant or flying officer leading, no, *he* would be up at the front!

On 13 May six more crews went out on a sweep of Beat 3 off south-west Norway, but fared little better than they had on the 12th. Due to bad weather T1826:A and V6319:F, captained by P/O Richards and Sgt Scott respectively, landed at Dyce before returning to Lossiemouth the next day.

Since the loss of Wing Commander Christian, morale had been low and the subsequent operations had yielded few results. This would present quite a dilemma for any CO but characteristically Edwards firmly grasped the nettle. He gathered the squadron together and told them that he was going out with them and that they were going to 'find a ship and sink it!'

At 14.25 hours Edwards took off in V6028:D, an aircraft in which he was later to venture to great acclaim. He was followed by P/O Broadley, P/O Clayton, and Sgt Searles. Five minutes later S/L David Bennett took off, accompanied by P/O Richards, Sgt Bruce and Sgt Scott. There

Blenheim L9379 GB:Y flying low over the North Sea on 14 May 1941. At this time 105 Squadron was on detachment to RAF Lossiemouth in north-east Scotland. (via Mrs N.A. Scott)

were eight crews in all, following their new leader. True to his word, targets began to appear. The first sighting went to P/O Broadley in V6399:T and Sgt Scott in L9379:Y, who found a 2,500-ton merchant vessel at a position 61° 20'N, 04° 50'E. The first aircraft made a beam attack from 150ft. Two bombs exploded in the forward section of the ship, leaving a large cloud of white steam rising skywards. Then the second aircraft had a go. One bomb fell short and splashed into the sea and another overshot but the other two found their mark forward of the funnel. There was an explosion and a column of yellowish-brown smoke drifted into the air.

Seeing the action, W/C Edwards and P/O Clayton came roaring across from an adjacent beat and pounced on the ship. Edwards' bombs straddled either side of her, but P/O Clayton's made the mark in a beam attack over the funnel. One of his bombs hit the ship's side, while two others fell short. The fourth was a direct hit, however, thick smoke prevented the results from being seen. The attack had resulted in smoke, which concealed flying planks and debris that was thrown high into the air, and which nearly claimed one of the attacking machines. All crews had been given cameras and the results of this attack were photographed. One of the photographs was subsequently issued to the Press for public issue.

Of the other four aircraft, Sgt Searles found a 200-ton barge at position 59° 58'N, 05° 15'E. His first bomb splashed 6 yards short of the ship, but the fall of the other three was unobserved, as a cliff-face suddenly rose up in front of the aircraft. Sgt Searles pulled away violently, and saved the day! A further three fishing vessels were strafed, each estimated at 80 tons displacement. Meanwhile, at position 60° 08'N, 05° 08'E, Sgt Bruce was harassing an 800-ton coaster. Three of his bombs fell into the sea some 15ft from the vessel, but although some wreckage was seen, the ship continued, heading inland on a different course. P/O Broadley saw

Flying low over the target, a 2,500-ton merchant vessel in a Norwegian fjord, a Blenheim of 105 Squadron views the damage caused by a previous bombing run as smoke billows high into the air. (The Trustees of the Imperial War Museum, London: C1940)

no shipping and took his aircraft home. Unfortunately, Blenheim T2118:E failed to return; P/O Richards and his crew, Sgt North (Observer) and Sgt Snutch (WOp/AG), were last seen heading along a fjord at 50ft on a 90° course. Sgt Snutch has no known grave, but P/O Richards and Sgt North were both laid to rest in Bergen Church Cemetery (Mollendal). Overall, it had been a very successful operation with the shipping successes putting the squadron back on a better footing, but nevertheless it was marred by the sad loss of yet another experienced crew.

Three days later it was all over and F/O F.E. 'Teddy' Frayn resumed command of the main party, southward bound for Swanton Morley. Two aircraft had been lost. P/O Buckley had returned on 12 May to spend a day at Wattisham, which left fourteen aircraft; they all arrived safely at Swanton Morley on 21 May. Once again the main flight was accompanied by the two Harrows containing some groundcrew and equipment.

During the course of researching this book, the author talked with Jack Buckley, who commented that his feeling was that during the operations from Lossiemouth, the results were such that it was almost as if the enemy had been 'tipped off', and knew that the Blenheims were coming. This suggestion was independently corroborated by Ron Wood, who also commented on this rather strange state of affairs:

> It was when we were about to be detached to Lossiemouth for operations off Norway. We were briefed that the purpose of the detachment was to get the shipping which was taking iron ore to the enemy down the Norwegian coast from Sweden, and also to look out for the *Bismarck* which had been reported in that area. [It was in fact in Bergen.] The surprise element was stressed as important, and the secrecy of the move impressed upon us. We were confined to camp after briefing, but the following evening, surprisingly, we were allowed out and the squadron bus was laid on to take us into Norwich. Some time during the evening, my chums and I were in 'Whites Bar' and could hardly believe our ears when the barmaid, I think they called her Penny, said 'I hear you're off to bonny Scotland!' We turned and walked out. Afterwards, I realized that I should have officially reported this, especially as Intelligence reported after our return from Lossiemouth that the detachment had not achieved the success hoped for, and one reason given for this was that the deployment of the squadron had been known to the enemy. There was quite a witch-hunt about it!

CHAPTER 7

Home Again

Once back at base there was to be no respite, and the next day six crews were off to the central Frisian Islands to patrol Beat 7 in pairs. Hampered by sea fog, only Sgt Jackson found a suitable target – a 1,000-ton merchant vessel lying off the Island of Borkum, which was attended to in a stern quarter attack. Bill Jackson's air gunner, Sgt Purves, swung round his turret and poured some 200 rounds along the ship's deck. Unfortunately, he was unable to see if the four bombs had burst, as the vessel disappeared in the sea mist. At 15.05 hours that same afternoon, twenty minutes later than the first wave, another six crews took off, led by Hughie Edwards. They were heading for Terschelling and Beat 8. Again fog at sea-level prevented any sightings. Three hours and thirty minutes later all were safely back home.

The fog was not to last long. On 25 May another sweep was ordered, this time in four sections off the island of Ameland. At 14.05 hours S/L Bennett took off in V6453:E to lead out another seven aircraft. This time visibility was better and the first convoy was found. It consisted of 4,000- and 6,000-tonners, just waiting to be attacked. They did not wait long. F/L Calvert-Booth chose a 6,000-tonner and roared over the ship at mast height in a quarter attack from the bow, leaving a large column of smoke pouring skywards. The other two aircraft in this section had similar luck. Sgt Scott took V6039:Q into a beam attack from starboard on a 6,000-tonner, sending wreckage flying high into the air from aft of the funnel. Leaving in a circling turn, the crew could see the columns of brown smoke billowing upwards from the other two ships. One of these was a 4,000-tonner which Sgt Jackson had attended to, and which was abandoned by the marauding crews at a position 53° 30'N, 05° 36'E.

While all this was happening, S/L David Bennett was 'having a go' at a 1,500-ton vessel at a position 53° 35'N, 06° 05'E. Rising up over the stern quarter of the ship, his bombs jerked free but splashed impotently into the sea 100 yards from the vessel. More accurate, however, were the other two Blenheims, by this time engaging two 4,000-tonners in another convoy, this time at 53° 33'N, 05° 55'E. P/O Buckley, who recorded his ship as a 6,000-ton steamer, made a port quarter attack but didn't get a view of any damage. His wingman also 'had a go', in a beam attack on a 4,000-ton merchant vessel. As R3707:B reared up over the ship, all four bombs dropped from the bomb bays and splashed into the sea. Around 16.00 hours, Jack Buckley watched P/O Rushbrooke and his crew, Sgt Eric Green (Observer) and Sgt Parr (WOp/AG), circling the convoy after the attack. Apparently undamaged, they then flew off towards the Island of Ameland. Possibly the victim of fighters, R3707:B was not seen again. Only two aircraft found nothing on their sweep, F/L Dore and P/O Willsher and their crews returning to base unaware of the afternoon's activity.

While at 13 OTU at Bicester, prior to joining 105 Squadron, Sgt Eric Green wrote the following tragically prophetic remarks about his own and his crews' life expectations:

> Parr, the gunner, is a Yorkshireman, aged 24 and is very quiet but thorough and determined. I'm the oldest of the crew [24 years old], the pilot [Rushbrooke] is only 19! He's a pilot officer and very boyish; only twelve months ago he was still at school and incidentally, made a century at Lords for Harrow against Eton. During the days that lie before us there will be so many occasions on which the lives of all three of us will depend upon the action or thought of one of us; you see, it's so necessary to be absolutely 100% for each other. . . One other

thing; in the very near future I'll be doing the most dangerous job in the whole war; I don't want to worry you but, please, if anything does happen to me, don't fret about it, after all, it's only a job of work and someone's got to do it.

At the same time as the Borkum attack, the three crews who had been despatched to bolster the depleted 18 Squadron took off from their base at Oulton, 12 miles north-north-west of Norwich. A fringe attack on the East Frisian island of Norderney had been ordered. Ron Wood, one of the three pilots, takes up the story, describing what he remembers as 'the worst operation I did with 105!'

It was intended to be a low-level surprise attack on this island off the North German coast, with Luftwaffe bases. Some days earlier a complete surprise attack had been made on Borkum nearby, and the only opposition was the fierce startled glares of the German players and spectators of a football match, as the Blenheims roared across at 50ft. Not so at Norderney, however. The route was on a north-easterly heading, to a point about 30 miles north of Norderney, and then a run-in southward, thus avoiding any landfall.

Unfortunately, while still ten to fifteen minutes from our target, we passed two E-Boats, which obviously alerted the shore bases. The coastal guns opened up at us when we were 4 or 5 miles out, and it looked like a solid curtain of flak up to a few thousand feet over the island. Above this, a couple of Messerschmitts were circling as though waiting for us. Our leader, from 18 Squadron, continued heading in towards this welcoming party for quite some time (it seemed like hours, but was probably only a minute or so), and then started to turn away to port. Our 105 Squadron vic was unfortunately on the starboard side of the formation and the late turn away put us into the concentrated flak over the island. Suddenly, our 105 Squadron vic leader [P/O Ben Broadley], slipped away to the left in a steep turn under and behind the leading vic. Within seconds it seemed there were Blenheims dodging in and out of each other within a few feet of the water, and although we had tried to stay with our leader, it was now impossible, and no proper formation existed. I formated on a Blenheim ahead and someone formated on me, and then the fighters came at us.

After the shambles over the fringe of the island, we somehow got into some sort of order, all heading the same way; unfortunately it was the wrong way; we were heading westward, the shortest way for home, which took us along the Frisian Islands where, of course, we picked up more fighters. The formation/stream/shambles leader at this early stage was none other than one of the 105 support group, Sergeant Bruce – an example of 'enterprise' of which we were to hear more later. The 18 Squadron leader eventually got back in front and we had some gunnery control directed at the attacking fighters but without much success, and we were under attack for some considerable time. During the mêlée, I had seen one Blenheim, with smoke coming from one engine, turning away as though he was hoping to make it to the albeit enemy coast, but I never heard any more of this, and at the time we were fully occupied. I saw another Blenheim go down on the other side of the formation, and then a couple of 109s concentrated with quarter attacks on our side. The 18 Squadron aircraft on my starboard side was getting the worst of it, although our gunners were doing their best. At this stage Jimmy Wilcock, who had been shouting out the directions and timing of the fighters coming in, suddenly screamed with some blasphemy that they had got the gunner of the 18 Squadron aircraft but that the fighters had left us; how long for, of course, we did not know. I dropped back and crossed to the outside of the other aircraft, no heroics but I just thought at least we would have a pair of Brownings to protect this side of the formation. It was quite grotesque, seeing the other aircraft's guns pointing vertically at the sky, and having to formate on a crimson splattered turret. It was a long sad haul home.

It did not all go the enemy's way, however, as training and discipline had paid dividends. Having jettisoned their bombs, they held together in as tight a formation as possible to concentrate their fire-power, and one of the Messerschmitts flew off trailing its undercarriage. As usual, though, the Blenheim formation had come off worst during the assault. Ron Wood continued:

> We landed at Horsham St Faith airfield because of its proximity to Norwich and the hospital. The 18 Squadron gunner was, sadly, dead and I don't know what other injuries there were. Apart from some bullet holes in our aircraft, we were OK.

P/O Ben Broadley in V6373:O and Sgt Bruce in R3838:M both returned safely to Horsham St Faith before returning to Swanton Morley. Sgt Wood in V6319:F had a slightly more eventful return to base:

> I was all set to taxi out to get back to Swanton Morley when an officer appeared in front of the aircraft, signalling me to hold my position. He climbed up the wing and I opened the overhead hatch. He had some groundcrew at the side of the aircraft and asked me to lower my flaps. There was some signalling between him and the groundcrew and then he told me to leave the flaps down and shut down the engines. We all got out and he showed me a row of holes where bullets had gone through the fuselage, and through the flap rod. Miraculously, it had held together during landing but I didn't need to be told what would have happened if it had given way with full flap down on the other side. The squadron sent an aircraft over to pick us up and we were honoured with Hughie himself driving!

Hughie Edwards' log shows an entry for the 15-minute hop, and is recorded as having taken with him to Horsham in V6028:D the new commanding officer of RAF Swanton Morley, Group Captain H.F.V. Battle OBE DFC, together with his WOp/AG, Sgt Gerry Quinn. Group Captain Battle remained at Horsham, while the Blenheim returned with the three 'passengers', referred to in the log entry as '3 others'. Whether the appearance of the group captain was coincidence or was related to the episode described below is a matter for conjecture. Ron Wood concludes the story:

> I thought, how nice of Hughie to come himself for me, but any benevolent feeling was shortlived when we got back and the inquisition started on what had happened, and how had a 105 Squadron aircraft got to be in front coming away from Norderney? Apparently, the 18 Squadron CO was not amused, but there was no court-martial. Although completely innocent, I got some funny looks from Hughie and the next week was drogue-towing for ground gunners, before being required to transfer my services to fighting Rommel and his friends in the Middle East.

Two days later, W/C Edwards led seven other crews to sweep an area off Heligoland, again in V6028:D. Some three hours forty minutes later they were all home again, having found nothing. S/L David Bennett and his crew had returned after only half an hour, due to port engine trouble. In order to reduce weight, they jettisoned the bombs and emptied the outer fuel tanks, and brought V6453:E safely back home to touch down on Swanton Morley's grassy aerodrome.

So May had drawn to a close. It had been a very busy month, with the loss of three fine crews, including the CO. Continued shipping attacks under the new CO had lifted morale out of the doldrums, but it was shortly to be boosted even higher. An operation had now been performed in co-operation with another squadron, a situation which was to prove quite common in the months to come.

June opened as actively as May had ended, with a nine Blenheim attack against shipping in the

The East Frisian island of Norderney, where on 25 May 1941 three 105 Squadron Blenheims joined 18 Squadron to attack the town of Norderney. They met heavy flak and were savagely attacked by German Bf 109 fighters. (The Trustees of the Imperial War Museum, London: C1893)

Kiel Canal. An Operations Order had been received and Fringe targets were now to be attacked in Germany, hopefully, as with Circus raids, luring enemy fighters away from other targets to come to the defence of the Blenheims' target areas. The same afternoon, 107 Squadron Blenheims from Great Massingham, 11 miles east of King's Lynn, and 110 Squadron Blenheims on detachment from Manston, 12 miles east-north-east of Canterbury, had also been attacking targets in northern Germany. Their operations were unsuccessful due to lack of cloud cover.

Not so for 105 Squadron, however, who found sufficient cloud cover to attack their targets in Kiel Canal singly. First into the fray was Sgt Ron Scott in L9379:Y, who bombed a village on Pellworm Island at 54° 32'N, 08° 40'E, using SAP bombs and incendiaries from what was the relatively high level of 1,500ft! No results could be seen due to cloud cover. Their aircraft arrived back at 17.50 hours, some forty minutes before the remainder of the force, who forged ahead to the Canal. Why they chose to attack the island of Pellworm is unclear; whether it was simply a side-show amid the confusion of the main raid, or was aimed at some Nazi installation, or just to affect civilian morale, remains a matter of conjecture.

Arriving unmolested over the target area, the remainder of the force split up and went for any target they could find. S/L Calvert-Booth took V6374:X into a beam attack from 1,200ft on a 3,000-ton merchantman, but again cloud prevented sight of the results. P/O Clayton took V6399:T into a beam attack on a 1,000-ton ship on the River Eider to the north. Yet again, bombing from 1,500ft in cloud, it was impossible to see the results. Not so for P/O Willsher, who had greater success. One of his 250lb bombs slammed into the target amidships. Seconds later, the ship veered to port, out of control, and rammed the canal bank. The remaining two bombs were lobbed at a 3,500-tonner but they overshot. The WOp/AG, Sgt Archer, raked both ships with his twin Brownings before they moved on to the village of Tellingstedt. Here four of their 25lb incendiaries left a sheet of flame stretching skywards above the roof of a two-storey red-brick building. Meanwhile, Sgt Searles found a convoy of six merchantmen in the Canal and proceeded to throw all V6380:G had at them. A 5,000-ton vessel had all four 250lb bombs pitched at its bows with unknown results, while the remaining incendiaries ignited a factory building in Friedrichskoog.

The attack had been relatively effective so far, but what of the others? P/O Buckley had just broken cloud near Brunsbüttle in V5502:U when he saw a naval barracks and parade ground below him, with flags fluttering in the wind. This was too good a target to miss – all four bombs were dropped with accompanying incendiaries at low level, and although the results were not witnessed, the crew were sure that much damage would have been caused. Three other machines also were busy finding targets. P/O Ben Broadley in V6373:O was flying around the Bregstedt Canal when he noticed a 1,500-ton collier and so dropped his load on it. Pulling away from the ship, a gun post on the canal bank opened up and diverted Sgt Marsh's attention. He replied immediately from his turret, but the results of the attack were unobserved. Meanwhile, east of Rendsburg a merchant vessel of some 6,000 tons was bombed and strafed by Sgt Bruce and his gunner in V6039:Q. At the same time, to the south of the town, Sgt Tolman took T1936:P into a bow attack on a 2,500-tonner. Unfortunately, the canal bank fared a lot worse than the ship!

P/O Jack Buckley was the last home, at 18.46 hours, after what he noted in his Form 414 as a five-hour fifteen-minute flight. It had been a very long and concerted attack which was a foretaste of things to come. Bomber Command issued their Intelligence Report No. 1617 on 12 June, which stated: 'A report has been received that on June 12 the Canal was still closed to traffic. The informant stated that on June 6 a ship in which he was interested was ordered to proceed via the Skagerrak instead of its usual route through the Canal. It is said that two ships have sunk in the Canal following the daylight attack of June 2.' The attack had been very successful but had failed to draw fighter response – not that the Blenheim crews would have been disappointed at that result!

Two days later, on the 4th, an attempt was made to attack Valkenburg Aerodrome. Unfortunately, landfall was made to the south instead of north of the target, resulting instead in a visit to The Hague before the error was corrected. Not willing to miss 'having a go', Sgt Bruce found a goods train at a railway junction and left it emitting clouds of black smoke, as W/C Edwards led the formation back over the coast and home.

W/C Edwards' Blenheim V6028 GB:D flying over railway lines on the way to bomb Valkenburg aerodrome in the Netherlands on 4 June 1941. (Public Record Office: AIR37/47 Photo No. 7)

On the 7th, Beat 8 was visited in an anti-shipping sweep off the Frisian Island of Ameland and from Borkum Riff to Terschelling Bank. One crew from 107 Squadron, accompanied by five 105 Squadron aircraft, returned without seeing any action. Another two were not so lucky. In V6380:G Sgt Searles found a 3,000-ton salvage ship alongside a wreck off Terschelling. Sgt Searles manoeuvred his aircraft to run in from the east and made a beam attack, leaving only one bomb, which he believed to have struck either the main target or the wreck beyond. P/O Clayton had also been busy, possibly accounting for another ship which was billowing a large column of grey-brown smoke some 300ft into the air. This was noticed before both aircraft closed up together for the return journey home at sea-level. Suddenly two Bf 109s appeared. The Blenheims separated and engaged the enemy independently. The second Bf 109 paid a heavy price – having been unable to engage the Blenheim from below, due to its very low height above the water, the 109 passed overhead, with fatal results. Immediately, Sgt Bellamy opened up with all his twin Brownings could muster. Streams of .303in rounds rose skywards to rip through the enemy aircraft. To the relief of the air gunner and the observer, Sgt Mitchell, the 109 disappeared pouring black smoke. P/O Clayton was less fortunate, as he was last seen turning away to port with the other Bf 109 attacking him from astern. He and his aircraft, V6316:S, with P/O Phillips (Observer) and Sgt Stiddard (WOp/AG), like many before them did not make it back.

It was another four days before any further operations were attempted. On 11 June, at the briefing for the next operation, it transpired that the targets set were all towns and villages in north-west Germany. One who was there remembers that it was stated at the briefing that 'as the ordinary German civilians didn't know the RAF, so they would be introduced to them!' Bombing military targets was one thing, but civilians! This was quite another prospect, irrespective of what had happened as a result of the Luftwaffe's operations. As the seven crews made their way along dispersal and lined up for take-off, a reluctant W/C Edwards led his formation towards the target area. He did not like the idea himself. However, the task was abandoned due to 'lack of cloud cover'! All seven Blenheims eventually returned with full bombloads, the last touching down some four hours and twenty-three minutes after take-off.

RAF Wattisham was the starting point for operations on the 14th. After a twenty-five minute flight from Swanton Morley, P/O Buckley led two other aircraft to touch down ready to join another nine crews from 110 (Hyderabad) Squadron, for yet another Circus (No. 12). The Circus was to be led by 110 Squadron's W/C W. Peter Sutcliffe, with fighter cover from Tangmere. In the event the sortie only lasted two hours, and had to be diverted because of cloud obscuring the target; the Fort Rouge Aerodrome at St Omer was visited instead, from 10,000ft. Apart from some damage to buildings south-west of the target, no further damage was seen and the formation returned home, touching down again at 08.22 hours. Jack Buckley then led his 105 Squadron formation back on the half-hour return leg to Swanton Morley. That afternoon three other crews tried for a 'Hipper'-class cruiser berthed at Brest, but insufficient cloud cover once again made the attack impossible. The next day the same problem dogged 107 Squadron on the same target.

During wartime, mistakes are frequently made amid the daily struggle, often through spur of the moment decisions made under extreme trauma or because of inexperience. It may have been the latter which was to prove tragically fatal for one crew during the squadron's next operation. Beat 10, off the Mouth of Schelde, was patrolled on the 15th. For this operation W/C Edwards ordered a search in two sections. Edwards himself was to lead F/O Lambert and Sgt Jackson in the first section, while S/L David E. Bennett was to lead Sgt Beacham and F/O Watts in the other. Edwards led the formation out in his usual aircraft V6028:D, and the formation split into the two sections. He found a 4,000-tonner which he left issuing a column of black smoke and with a substantial amount of debris flying into the air. Jackson and Lambert also found targets. The latter raced in on a stern attack on a 3,000-tonner but just as he was about to drop his load on the ship – nothing! Incorrect selection of an electrical switch had rendered the bomb-release gear useless, and the chance was missed. In return, as a parting gesture, a shell went clean through the starboard main plane. Sgt Jackson received similar damage to the port side of R3838:M as a result of his starboard beam attack on a 6/8,000-tonner.

As for the other three aircraft, no targets had been seen as the formation turned line astern to port, on the end of the leg of the Beat. Then, suddenly, a target came into view. Up ahead of the Blenheims, off Kijkduin in Holland, lay ten vessels looking like small motorized ships – a very, very deadly target had been found. S/L Bennett began a turn to starboard, knowing from past experience what the formation was facing. The targets ahead were no ordinary motor vessels, nor anything nearly as benign. There was something much more sinister about these vessels, which were ten heavily armed and deadly E-Boats. In commendable but unfortunate exuberance, the other two aircraft ignored the leader, setting off like hounds after their quarry. Sgt Beacham took V6380:G into a quarter attack from the bow of one boat, and much to his credit, retired with a grey column of smoke pouring up from his target. This he was unable to see, due to the murderous hail of flak which poured at his Blenheim, requiring as much evasive action as could be mustered. Less fortunate was F/O Watts in V6319:F. He and his crew, Sgt Milroy (Observer) and Sgt Murray (WOp/AG), attacked the leading E-Boat. Flak poured towards the aircraft as its bombs dropped, all of them falling short. The anti-aircraft fire stabbed into the machine's starboard petrol tank which erupted into flames. F/O Watts wrestled bravely but desperately at the controls. He appeared for a while to have regained control of his aircraft, but alas it was to no avail, as it plunged into the water, rose again, turned right over and dived straight into the sea below. Ironically, it had been the crew's first operational flight with the squadron since their posting from 17 OTU at Upwood on the 9th – less than a week before! The observer and WOp/AG are buried at Hoek van Holland but the pilot has no known grave.

Although costly in men and machines, the anti-shipping attacks were beginning to bite at the enemy. Consequently, apart from direct fighter interception, the enemy began to think of alternative means to counter the raids, even before the aircraft arrived. Normally, unless no other targets were available to the marauding Blenheims, small shipping vessels were ignored, being considered of little significance. These little vessels therefore became the enemy's new intelligence-gathering stations. With prior knowledge of incoming aircraft, flak batteries could be alerted and if available, local Fighter *Geschwader* scrambled. The trawlers were therefore equipped with various long aerials and radio equipment, and nicknamed 'Squealers'.

Consequently, the Blenheims began to attack *all* shipping, large or small. Two beats were chosen, in which all shipping was to be eliminated: 105 Squadron was assigned to Beat B between Beats 7 and 8. This special operation between the East Frisian Islands and the island of Ameland took place on 16 June. Sgt Bruce didn't find any shipping, but all four of the others were more successful. P/O Buckley found a 60-ton fishing vessel, a 'Squealer', at position 54° 37'N, 03° 52'E, and remembers that it was trailing an apparatus like a buoy, with two vertical rods pointing upwards from it. It was floating about 10ft from the vessel. As the attack began, the ship's crew hurriedly pulled the device out of the water, almost as if they had been tipped off. P/O Buckley considered that it may have been a kind of submarine communications device, although the crews were never made party to such information. However, one thing was certain – whatever the device was, it was *not* being used to catch fish!

A close stick of bombs fell towards the ship. One tore through the rigging, removing an aerial, before plummeting into the superstructure. The other bombs missed, except one which did some damage. To be absolutely sure that the vessel was not going to report on any more Allied aircraft, a total of six runs were made, allowing the air gunner to pour 300 rounds into the ship, which then caught fire and slowly began to sink. Between attacks, one of the vessel's crew was seen pumping a handpump with great vigour. At a position 53° 59'N, 03° 44'E, a 50-ton fishing vessel was similarly bombed by S/L Smithers. Although his bombs fell ahead of the target, they were close enough and when they turned to see the damage, the boat had vanished without trace!

S/L Calvert-Booth found his target lying at 54° 04'N, 04° 01'E, and estimated it was a 60-ton fishing vessel; one of his bombs fell short and two others were seen to have overshot their mark, splashing close to the ship's stern. Sgt Scott had equally bad luck with an 80-ton target at 53° 50'N, 04° 31'E. This time the bombs were dropped in pairs in two beam attacks, the first pair overshooting by 30 yards and the second pair by 50 yards. Some damage was inflicted, however, as on their return, all the ammunition was expended from the port wing's front-firing machine-gun. Additionally, Sgt Stuart Bastin raked the ship from bow to stern with 200 rounds from his twin Brownings before leaving. His Blenheim, L9379:Y, was the last home, touching down at 21.21 hours, after three hours fifty minutes.

This was not to be the last 'Squealer' attack for the squadron though and five days later, on the 21st, another attack was ordered, again off the Dutch coast. This time nothing was found by 105 Squadron's crews. However, another squadron did find a 100-ton fishing vessel at 53° 28'N, 04° 12'E, following a rectangular sweep out to sea.

Apart from the operations mentioned above, the trend for the next few operations was for Circus sweeps over France, in daylight as usual. The 19th saw Circus 24, a Blot on Le Havre, as part of Operation 'Derby'. The squadron fielded six aircraft, accompanied by six from each of 18, 107 and 139 Squadrons. All operated out of Swanton Morley for the raid, while another six from each of 21 and 110 Squadrons operated from Watton. The 105 Squadron aircraft were detailed to operate at high level (5,000ft), along with 18, 107 and 139 Squadrons. The low-level force from 21 and 110 Squadrons was to operate at 1,500ft. Take-off from Swanton Morley was at 15.27 hours, and the squadrons flew first to Tangmere to meet their fighter escort. Four squadrons were to meet the high-level squadrons, who orbited Tangmere twice at 12,000ft. Soon, however, as no fighters arrived, 21 and 110 Squadrons, led by W/C P.F. Webster aborted, as did 18 and 139 Squadrons. This left only 105 and 107 Squadrons. The fighters eventually met up and in typical fashion, W/C Hughie Edwards took command of the formation. Protected by fighters, he showed his true form and carried on to the target irrespective of the loss of most of the force.

The fighter escort provided consisted of four squadrons of Spitfire IIAs and IIBs: 145 Squadron had arrived from Merston in Sussex, while the Polish 303 (Warsaw–Kosciusco) Squadron was also in attendance from their Middlesex base at Northolt. The other two fighter squadrons were 610 (County of Chester) Squadron from Gravesend, Kent, and 616 (South Yorkshire) Squadron from Westhamprett, 2 miles north-east of Chichester in Sussex. In total, eighty-four fighters were up to protect the Blenheims, which had been further reduced to eleven after Sgt Bruce returned in V6399:T after a hatch cover had blown off, reducing his speed to well below that of the main formation.

They flew into Le Havre from the west, surprising the defenders as they arrived out of the sun at 12,000ft. Their 250lb and 40lb bombs were dropped on the ship repair yard south of dry dock no. 1. The central mole of Bassin de Marée and oil storage tanks to the north-east of the dry dock were also hit, with red flashes leaving clouds of dust and smoke rising up from the target area after the attack. The Bassin Pétrole, bombed by 107 Squadron, was emitting a large column of white smoke when last seen. Only two Bf 109s put in an appearance, one being damaged in an engagement with a Spitfire. All the Spitfires and Blenheims returned safely to base this time, although not all Circus raids ended so satisfactorily. The last 105 Squadron Blenheim home belonged to P/O Buckley, who touched down on Swanton Morley's grass strip in V6336:H at 19.10 hours, after a four hour ten minute flight, ready for a well deserved rest.

Jack Buckley spent the next day drogue-towing in the same aircraft as used on the previous day. This unenviable task lasted some two hours forty minutes, and as soon as he landed, the aircraft was handed over for another training sortie. Jack Buckley had just departed on leave, when Sgt Beacham took V6336:H up with his crew, Sgt Griffiths (Observer) and Sgt Appleby (WOp/AG). On board were two 'passengers', AC1 McFadzean and LAC Ballard. As the aircraft took off at 14.10 hours, on the north-east side of the aerodrome, the port engine cut. As usual, when a Blenheim engine cut on take-off, the results were tragically fatal. All aboard were killed instantly as the aircraft hit the ground at East End Farm about 3 miles away at Billingford.

Operations continued on the 21st when yet another 'Squealer' was to be searched out and destroyed. Despite five aircraft hunting in separate beats, nothing was found and all returned early in

Commines power station, France, was the target for Circus Operation C21 on 26 June 1941. However, the sortie was abandoned 8 miles north-east of Dunkirk owing to adverse weather conditions. (The Trustees of the Imperial War Museum, London: C1924)

the evening. A day went by, and on 23 June, yet another Circus operation was undertaken. This time the target was to be the 'Kuhlman' chemical works at Chocques, near Béthune in northern France. The complex was a valuable target indeed. Not only was there a chemical works, but in close proximity, a benzol plant, a power station and an associated railway siding.

For the attack W/C Edwards led ten aircraft from his squadron, supported by six more from each of 21 and 110 Squadrons, a total of twenty-two aircraft, flying at 12,000ft in four box formations, each consisting of five or six Blenheims. Two of the force had to abort and returned to base. The fighter escort was picked up as the formation headed towards its target. Eventually the target appeared and eighty-three 250lb bombs and eighty-three 40lb bombs rained down on the enemy installations below. The power station received some of the load, confirmed by flashes observed at the power house. Not all bombs were seen to explode, and some undershot to the west of the chemical plant. Others overshot to the south. A long building at the southern corner close to a railway was hit, and left a red glowing mess. A further three bursts put paid to nearby railway tracks and a railway shed, also to the south of the target. Some chimneys to the west of the target narrowly escaped demolition as bombs burst close by. The nearby village of Labeuvrière also received numerous bomb bursts. As the formation pulled away, one crew noted the area was covered with a cloud of brown smoke. On the way back, the gun crews at St Omer and Le Touquet opened up and six of W/C Edwards' formation received superficial damage. All landed safely back at base, the last 105 Squadron machine landing at 14.43 hours.

The raid had been an operational success and had been completed without loss of life, at least for the Blenheim crews. Jack Buckley, in an interview with the author of this book, recalled that W/C Edwards did not like the idea of Circus raids, as the fighters could suffer terribly. The intention of drawing the enemy fighters into action had indeed worked on this trip, as no less than seven enemy aircraft were claimed destroyed, with three 'probables' and two 'damaged' by our fighter pilots in the process. But Circus duties were not yet over for the squadron, and one more attempt was made three days later, on the 26th, with almost the same aircraft, except for P/O Broadley who changed his machine from V6373:O to V6399:T – a tribute to the groundcrews' repair skills. S/L Calvert-Booth's position was taken by Sgt Farrow in V6420:K. The target was another power station, also in France, this time at Commines. Eleven aircraft from 226 Squadron and one from 107 Squadron were to accompany 105 Squadron this time. As the Blenheims neared the coast at Dunkirk with their close fighter escort, the weather had closed in so badly that W/C Edwards decided to return and headed the formation back amid some inaccurate flak, landing just after noon. Bad weather had marred what should have been a successful operation. The same problem was to be encountered the next week, with some very interesting consequences as the next target aroused considerable public interest, and the raid was to make the name of W/C Edwards synonymous with dash, initiative, extreme bravery and leadership.

CHAPTER 8

Valiant Wings

In June 1941 a very significant event took place which heralded a change in the squadron's targets for July. At around 03.00 hours on 22 June, a massive German offensive began all along the Russian border, from East Prussia to Poland. There had been several warnings about an impending attack by Germany on the Soviet Union, including a personal despatch from Churchill to Stalin. Hitler had turned on his neighbour and their non-aggression pact was now worthless. It was therefore necessary to maintain the pressure on the enemy in order to capitalize on the division of German strength resulting from their entry into another theatre of war; it was also necessary to attempt to draw German forces into combat, thereby tying them down in Europe.

It was with this in mind that Winston Churchill visited Swanton Morley in late June. In the hangar he praised the assembled aircrew from several squadrons for their anti-shipping operations, and then outlined the necessity of penetrating deep into enemy territory in Europe in order to help the Russians. 2 Group was to be at the forefront. Churchill's rhetoric was as stirring as ever, as he likened the anti-shipping operations to the charge of the Light Brigade. Indeed on 30 August, he wrote in his Personal Minute M852/1: 'The charge of the Light Brigade at Balaclava is eclipsed in brightness by these daily deeds of fame.'

Following his speech, Churchill was introduced to several of the aircrew, including one of 105 Squadron's youngest WOp/AGs: it was a particularly proud and memorable moment for Sgt Stuart Bastin, aged 19. For all the crews, from the youngest to the oldest, such tributes and personal introductions provided a tremendous boost to morale, at a time when it was needed most.

However, no sooner had the great man's words been delivered, than the consequences became equally apparent; Operation 'Wreckage' was born. The target was Bremen – in daylight. Churchill's requirements were to be met in full. An offensive was indeed to be launched into Europe, but not this time on France or Belgium, but deep into the Reich itself. It had been done before, but only at night. This attack was to be different – a precision operation was necessary, employing every means of tactical advantage available if anybody was to survive. The aiming point was to be the built-up area between the main railway station and the docks.

The raid on Bremen took three attempts in all. The first took place on 28 June 1941, and involved a combined force of bombers including 105 Squadron, but led by 107 Squadron from West Raynham. The formation was to be at the target by 07.00 hours. W/C Lawrence Petley was to lead 107 Squadron, and W/C Edwards 105 Squadron; the briefing was held at 21.00 hours. The crews did not find out until the briefing what the target was to be, although rumours abounded – and whatever it was, it was going to be big. When they found out, there was almost stunned disbelief. Hughie Edwards advised his crews of the difficulty of the operation and outlined tactical instructions; and added that a lot of luck would be required if the crews were to get back in one piece. The formation was to proceed between Heligoland and the East Frisian Islands, bristling with fighters and anti-aircraft stations with their early warning radar bases. From here they were to swing south for 40 miles before making landfall, and setting the final course for Bremen and its enormous ground defences.

By 05.00 hours on the 28th, all the crews were going through their pre-flight checks as engines coughed and roared into action. The whole station had turned out to see them off, as they taxiied across the grass ready for take-off. Once airborne they met up with the 107

107 Squadron officers at RAF Great Massingham in 1941. Several of these men took part in the combined raid on Bremen on 4 July 1941. Back row, left to right: F/O L. Ewels; F/O Leach; F/O Bryce (Medical Officer); F/O Redfern-Smith; F/O Dudeney; P/O Sammels; P/O Edrich. Front row: F/L Bailey; S/L Clayton; S/L Simmons; W/C Lawrence Petley (Commanding Officer); F/L Murray; F/L Richardson (Adjutant); F/O Wellburn. (via Mrs Vera G. Sherring/Mr Steven Snelling)

107 Squadron crews at Great Massingham in 1941. Their Commanding Officer, W/C Lawrence Petley is in the centre of the back row. The pilots are in the back row, the observers in the middle row and the WOp/AGs in the front row. (via Mrs Vera G. Sherring/Mr Steven Snelling)

Squadron aircraft which turned up a few minutes later. One aircraft, the formation leader's machine, was missing. Engine trouble had dogged W/C Petley, and he had been forced to give command temporarily to F/O Bill Edrich. But as the main formation headed out to sea, Petley's lone Blenheim was racing over the wave-tops at 50ft to catch up. Eventually he overtook the formation and resumed command, with both engines now running satisfactorily. Unfortunately, faults were shortly to force the return of one aircraft from each squadron, leaving only fifteen machines.

By now, the poorer weather had been left behind and a beautiful cloudless June sky had appeared as the formation raced on over the glistening sea at wave-top height. Lack of cloud cover had always been a good enough reason to abandon such an operation, but Petley pushed on until the formation was north of the East Frisian island of Wangerooge, where their luck ran out. A large destroyer convoy spotted the aircraft and opened fire. Group orders had stated that the aircraft were not to deviate from their objective, even if a large convoy were to be sighted. Although they obeyed the order and ignored the convoy, the element of surprise had gone. It was W/C Petley's judgement that under the circumstances, they should abandon the task and return to base. Many of the crews agreed with his decision and the formation returned home. However, the anti-aircraft fire put up by the escorting destroyers was trifling compared with the barrage of abuse which Petley received from the AOC over the telephone. As AVM Stevenson ripped into Petley, anger rose within the young airman until finally he lost his temper, and responded, 'Well sir, if that's what you think, we'll do the whole bloody show again this afternoon!', and slammed down his telephone.

Characteristically, Hughie Edwards, now back at Swanton Morley, had felt all along that the formation should have pressed on regardless, as he thought that the element of surprise would have been lost anyway because of the 20-mile deep defence zone around Bremen. However, he and Petley had been friends for a long time, and he had the greatest respect for Lawrence Petley. The AOC obviously held similar opinions to Edwards', but any sympathy borne of friendship was absent. Edwards was therefore chosen to lead the repeat effort and 107 Squadron was to be replaced by 21 Squadron, led by W/C Tim Partridge, who was also well known to Edwards from his 90 Squadron days at Bicester.

Sunday 29 June was spent planning the second operation to Bremen, with 107 Squadron now relegated to a diversionary raid on the Westerland fighter base on the island of Sylt. Briefing was held at 11.30 hours, at Watton for 21 Squadron, and at Swanton Morley for 105 Squadron.

At 05.00 hours on Monday 30 June, the Bristol Mercury engines were again coughing into life. By 05.13 hours 105 Squadron was airborne and formating over Swanton Morley, waiting for 21 Squadron to appear. Soon Tim Partridge DFC and his crews arrived, and the whole formation set off on a low-level course across the sea to their target. Initially the weather was favourable, but half-way across, they ran into a fog-bank like a blanket obscuring the path in all directions right down to sea-level. Visibility was nil. In Michael Scott's account of the Bremen raid in *Blenheim On The Deck*, he relates Hughie Edwards' account of what happened next:

> As you know, we flew in dense fog for the next 100 miles or so of the journey to the German coast. I could barely see my two wingmen. When we reached the coast, south of Cuxhaven, the land mass was perfectly clear, but to my astonishment I arrived there with only Sgt Scott on my right and Sgt Jackson on my left. We circled around for five minutes, then, because it was intended to be a raid on Bremen of at least full squadron strength, I sadly decided to return to base.

Edwards touched down at 08.40 hours, his wingmen Sgt Jackson at 08.41 hours and Sgt Scott at 08.45 hours. Of the remaining aircraft, three had emerged from the fog and found targets to bomb, having realized that they would not be going to Bremen as part of a main force. S/L Calvert-Booth and F/O Lambert had latched on to each other when they emerged from the fog, and were met with the sight of fifteen merchant ships, escorted by three naval vessels, north-west of Norderney. They decided to 'have a go'. S/L Calvert-Booth attacked a 6,000-tonner at the rear of the convoy, scoring hits between the bridge and the aft section of the ship. F/O Lambert attacked a 3,000-ton vessel, which resulted in black smoke and a red glow appearing from the stern of the ship, which was left sinking at the stern.

The other aircraft to find a target belonged to S/L Scott, who made several admirable attacks, as reported in his brother Michael's *Blenheim On The Deck*:

> Flying along Terschelling at 07.25 hours, he spotted the masts of the W/T station. He raced in at mast height and dropped one of his 250-pounders, but was away again before his air gunner could observe the result. Swinging a little to port, he roared in over the town and harbour of West Terschelling, dropping two more 250-pounders on the jetty. One landed right alongside the jetty, the other undershot, landing in the street adjoining it. His air gunner was able to confirm the bomb bursts, flashes and black smoke. This time his judgement was good and his WOp/AG, Sgt Conlon, was able to report an explosion right up against the ship's side with foam and smoke rising. It was later claimed by Bomber Command as a 'total loss'.

S/L Scott was the last to return at 08.59 hours. Although the main target had not been attacked, the crews had done the best they could. The crews of 21 Squadron had also been busy, attacking railway marshalling yards. Only one aircraft had managed to get to Bremen. P/O Waples had forged ahead alone in driving rain, and found a timber yard with large chimneys near which he dropped his bombs, sending timber flying high into the air along with other debris. However, the price of his success was a fighter attack on his way home. Initially evading two Messerschmitt Bf 110s, he emerged from cloud cover off Terschelling, where he became the centre of attraction for three Me 109s, which attacked him separately for ten minutes. Good shooting by his WOp/AG brought down one of the fighters and damaged the others. The damage to the Blenheim resulted in a belly-landing at RAF Marham on their return.

Back at base, the AOC had to be faced yet again. However, the station commander, Group Captain 'Bertha' Battle, stood up in support of Edwards, who was subsequently given a third opportunity to complete the mission. The third attempt was intended to take place on 2 July, but was twice postponed under Group orders until Friday 4 July. This time, W/C Petley was to get another chance with 107 Squadron, while the diversion was to be by 226 Squadron.

For 105 Squadron, briefing took place at 21.30 hours on 3 July. The next morning, the crews were called at 03.30 hours. Again, as on the two previous occasions, by 05.05 hours the engines were firing into life. This time the show was on and there would be no turning back. Bremen had been attacked the previous night by Wellington bombers to soften up the enemy anti-aircraft defence positions, in the hope that when the Blenheims arrived the gun crews would either be sleeping, or at least very tired and probably inaccurate. At 05.21 hours the control tower signalled a green light and they were off. Nine crews from Swanton Morley waited over Swanton Morley to rendezvous with six aircraft from 107 Squadron, flown by W/C Petley, S/L Murray, F/L Jones, P/O Charney, F/L Wellburn and Sgt Leven. They joined the formation on the port side of the leader. However, some time later, S/L Murray's WOp/AG tested his guns and found that they were unsynchronized, so they returned to base. Illness struck F/L Jones and mechanical troubles dogged P/O Charney, who could not keep station. Both dropped out, leaving only twelve aircraft to do the job. They raced on in four vics of three. Edwards was in front in his leading vic, with Sgt Ron Scott in Z7361:R on his left and Sgt Bill Jackson in Z7484:K on his right, as they settled down for the long journey ahead.

Once again there was no cloud cover, which was considered essential for survival in the face of fighters, but W/C Edwards pressed on regardless. Then the inevitable happened. Flying some 30ft above the wave-tops, 5 miles north of Norderney, several vessels came into view. It was not yet clear to the ships where the Blenheims were heading. However, at 07.35 hours exactly, the formation was on its final track for the coast when their luck ran out. Michael Scott's account states:

> Just 3 miles north of Wangerooge, there to the right of them, steaming north in the brilliant sunshine were three patrol ships, camouflaged in grey dazzle, and an admiralty yacht.

The formation would now certainly be reported. Flying on a straight track, it was not long before they encountered a large convoy, heading for Wilhelmshaven. They would surely have confirmed the Blenheims' direction. The formation made landfall and dropped even lower, almost to ground level, as they raced towards Bremen. Local farmers waved to the aircraft, hardly believing they were enemy aircraft daring to enter the Fatherland in such an arrogant fashion. At an agreed point, near Heerstedt, where a railway line gave a course check as it disappeared south to Bremerhaven, the Blenheims opened out into a line-abreast formation. Having skirted Bremerhaven, the aircraft spread out with a safe 200 yards between them as they approached the smoky target ahead.

Bremen, Germany's second largest port, sprawls along more than 2 miles of the River Weser's banks, penetrating the city to the Europahaven, the Uberseehaven and the

The River Weser was a useful navigational aid for 105 Squadron on their way to Bremen early in the morning of 4 July 1941. (Public Record Office: AIR37/47)

Industriehaven – with a large number of docks. Additionally, there was a plethora of other military and industrial targets available, including two Focke-Wulf fighter factories, U-Boat and minesweeper construction yards, as well as a foundry, oil refinery and textile factories, to list but a few. It was not surprising, therefore, that Bremen was surrounded by a very considerable number of anti-aircraft defences, all of which had to be penetrated. Many guns were sited on surrounding rooftops, as well as in and around the town itself, at any strategic position imaginable. The heavier 105mm guns were located around the perimeter of the city, with no less than twenty batteries, giving a total of 120 barrels pointed skywards. There were also twenty batteries of 88mm guns, subsequently to become the versatile tool of the Afrika Korps later in the war. Just for good measure a further forty 37mm batteries and twenty 20mm batteries complemented the 'heavies', providing 240 and 120 guns respectively.

In Michael Scott's *Blenheim On The Deck*, the fire-power which was to be brought to bear was summed up as follows:

> Taking the section of the city from the main railway station to the Industriehaven, where all the action finally took place, and where, as has been seen, most of the light flak batteries were concentrated, it is reasonable to assume that the eight remaining Blenheims, flying at 50ft along that front of 3 or 4 miles, would have been facing at least twenty batteries of 37mm and ten of 20mm guns, with a combined fire-power of 62,400 rounds per minute – an average of 7,800 rounds per minute against each aircraft. And this does not include machine-gun fire, either from the flak batteries or from troops in the streets or guarding factories or barracks. No wonder then that Hughie Edwards could write of it later, 'The flak was terrible – I saw nothing like it in my wartime operations before or after.'

105 Squadron Blenheims attacked Bremen on 4 July 1941. It had been attacked the previous night by Wellington bombers to soften up the enemy anti-aircraft defence positions, shown here inactive as W/C Edwards' Blenheim GB:D flies overhead. Sgt Stuart Bastin, WOp/AG in GB:R flying on the CO's left, was able to take photographs instead of having to use his guns. (Public Record Office: AIR37/47)

This then is what faced all twelve aircraft as they approached Bremen. On the approach, some 16 miles to the north of Bremen, six heavy gun emplacements were over-flown at 07.58 hours. The Wellingtons' nocturnal activities must have worked. Not only were there no gun crews, who were probably sleeping it off in their nearby huts, but one of the WOp/AGs, Sgt Stuart Bastin, flying on the CO's left, was able to take photographs instead of having to use his guns. However, before active defences could open up on the approaching crews, a passive menace had to be dealt with – balloons. Special box-shaped balloon cable-cutters, operated by a small explosive charge which detonated when they struck a cable, were fitted to the leading edge of the Blenheims' wings for such operations; they were supposed to cut through the steel cables connecting the balloon to the ground but their effectiveness was subject to some debate. As the twelve machines raced ahead past the balloon barrage, many had close encounters

This 107 Squadron Blenheim OM:W (either V6193 or V6020) was shot down on the morning of 4 July 1941, having fallen foul of flak near the Bürger Park while taking part in the daring low-level daylight attack on Bremen under 'Operation Wreckage'. (The Trustees of the Imperial War Museum, London: HU25727)

with hazards such as pylons, buildings, cranes, and ships' masts, all reaching up menacingly ready to knock the intruders out of the sky. As the pylons appeared with their high-voltage cables all the aircraft in the formation rose up and over the top – all that is except W/C Edwards, who ducked down *under* the lethal wires, missing a pylon by inches. Suddenly, flak started to pour up at the marauding Blenheims from all angles. The 105mm and 88mm gun emplacements sounded the first welcoming shots as the aircraft entered the area from the north. Shell bursts were exploding in and around the formation, which by now was down to ten – W/C Lawrence Petley, who had been so keen to repeat the operation, fell foul of the heavier flak from the Bürger Park in Blenheim V6020 and F/L Wellburn was also shot down there in V6193.

As the formation ploughed its way through the lattice of crossfire, Z7426:B was hit in the petrol tank. Sgt MacKillop bravely wrestled with the controls until they dropped his two bombs (which both fell short of the docks), but then the aircraft could fly no longer, plunging into a factory where it blew up. For the crew the end was instantaneous. Similarly, F/O Lambert with his crew, Sgt Copeland (Observer) and Sgt Charles (WOp/AG), were hit by the hail of anti-aircraft fire. Their Blenheim, Z7486:M, caught fire, veered left, then crashed and exploded in a nearby street. The pains of war were over for the crew in an instant. All twelve 105/107 Squadron crew members were subsequently laid to rest in Becklingen War Cemetery at Soltau.

With only eight aircraft left the formation pressed on, their leader determined to get to the target. They flew on into sheets of smaller fire which hit most of the aircraft. Coloured tracer flashed past with puffs of black and white smoke, as shells detonated all around the aircraft. The Blenheims were hit time after time by shrapnel and machine-gun bullets. They were buffeted all

German officers guarding the remains of a 105 Squadron Blenheim, probably Z7486 GB:M flown by F/O Lambert, which was also shot down during the low-level attack on Bremen on 4 July 1941. (The Trustees of the Imperial War Museum, London: HU25729)

over the place by flak blasts, but they kept going, relentlessly seeking their targets. The sole 107 Squadron survivor found a goods yard where he dropped his bombs before turning for home. The leader's vic pressed ahead, aiming for the Hauptbahnhoff (main railway station).

Sgt Scott in Z7361:R dropped his bombs on the Dyckhoff & Widmann Factory area; one hit the factory, the remainder severely damaged the storage depot, an army vehicle depot, and a stretch of railway lines, in addition to three goods warehouses. During the attack, the aircraft suffered damage to its pneumatic systems. A large shell ripped into the fuselage, exploding in the air gunner's well and severely bruising Sgt Bastin's back, as the shrapnel cut through his parachute harness. The main electrical panel was missed by inches. The leader's aircraft, V6028:D, also suffered severely: one cannon shell lodged itself in the radio rack, while splinters from another ripped into the knee of his air gunner, Sgt Gerry Quinn DFM. Undaunted, Edwards kept going and dropped his bombs on the railway lines, putting the line to Oldenburg out of action, and damaged a signal box. His remaining bombs fell on a tramway tunnel, destroying the overhead installations and damaging eight local houses. On circling away, a train of twenty or thirty carriages was duly attacked. The crackle of small-arms fire on the ground was rapidly met by a reply from the Blenheim's port wing machine-gun, scattering the offending opposition, before the aircraft set course for home.

Sgt Jackson in Z7484:K damaged tram lines as well as twenty houses, the windows of which were blown in. The remaining two bombs overshot and damaged more houses, before the crew turned for home with a severely mauled aircraft. A shell had exploded so close that the undercarriage was useless, and both his Observer, Sgt Williams, and his WOp/AG, Sgt Purves, were wounded. S/L Scott and his wingman were also busy. P/O Ben Broadley aimed V6373:O to drop his bombs on a propeller foundry. This caused great damage, not only to the building and surrounding area, but also to a nearby minesweeper. S/L Scott was also suffering severely from the flak. To quote from his brother Michael's account:

> Now it was Scotty's own turn, buffeted by the shells from the heavy guns across the big Waller Cemetery, to the western end of the Europahaven, where he dropped his full load. They were right on target, scoring a direct hit on Warehouse 8 and doing heavy damage to the building. Pulling around like Broadley in a tight turn to starboard over the Weser, he headed for Oldenburg and the way out.

Of the other two survivors, P/O Jack Buckley flying V6453:F dropped his bombs on the Weser-Flug aircraft factory, damaging several new Ju88 aircraft, as well as the hanger itself. Meanwhile Sgt Bruce was attacking a vacuum oil depot in the Industriehaven, where an empty storage tank was hit, as well as several railway lines. All bombs having been dropped, the surviving crews headed for home. It was every man for himself.

Meanwhile, 226 Squadron made a diversionary raid on the seaplane base on Norderney, which was very successful but cost the lives of W/C R.G. Hurst and his crew who led the raid.

It was mid-morning when the surviving battered 105 Squadron Blenheims began to appear over the horizon, before touching down on Swanton Morley's convex grass strip. Sgt Bruce and his crew were first back in V6380:G at 10.31 hours, followed closely at 10.34 hours by Sgt Scott and crew in Z7361:R. The latter had problems stopping, as the pneumatic brakes were

W/C Edwards' aircraft V6028 GB:D, which returned to Swanton Morley with flak damage after 105 Squadron's daring low-level attack on Bremen on 4 July 1941. Note the shell hole in the letter 'D' below Sgt Gerry Quinn's gun turret, the damage to the upper surface of the wing, and the souvenir debris wrapped around the starboard wheel oleo, collected while low flying. (RAF Swanton Morley)

Sgt Ron Scott's Blenheim Z7361 GB:R suffered flak damage while attacking Bremen on 4 July 1941. One shell entered the fuselage and exploded just behind the mid-upper turret entry hatch, cutting the parachute harness and badly bruising Sgt Stuart Bastin's back while he was at his station in the turret manning the guns. (via Mrs N.A. Scott)

unserviceable, but it eventually came to a halt. Scott's wounded WOp/AG, Sgt Bastin, did not report sick: having miraculously suffered only severe bruising to his back, he considered that if he reported wounded to the MO, he would be taken off operations and would then lose his crew, with whom he got on so well. Third to return was S/L Scott in Z7439:H at 10.37 hours, followed by P/O Broadley in V6373:O at 10.41 hours, and P/O Buckley in V6453:E at 10.53 hours. Sgt Jackson arrived at 11.00 hours in Z7484:K, but owing to undercarriage damage, his aircraft had to belly-land, causing much discomfort to his already wounded crew. Last to arrive was W/C Edwards in V6028:D, with his wounded WOp/AG, Sgt Gerry Quinn DFM. His aircraft was a mess. Apart from the cannon shell lodged in the radio rack, the machine was festooned with telegraph wires. Due to the injury to Sgt Quinn DFM, he was unable to extricate himself from his turret, so willing groundcrew jettisoned the cupola, strapped him up, and with the aid of a 'Coles' crane, lifted him out by the armpits, before taking him off to hospital.

The aircraft were then lined up for the groundcrews to repair – a formidable task! Sgt Chapple's diary contained one very interesting entry concerning the condition of the aircraft:

> Sgt Jackson belly-lobbed – machine and crew shot up (Sgt Williams and Purves), hydraulics shot up.
>
> Sgt Scott's machine, 61:R, badly holed in fuselage – brakes u/s.
>
> P/O Broadley's machine, 73, – untouched.

This last statement would seem contradictory, especially considering later reports that all aircraft were damaged. Doubtless this was a generalization, as the great majority of those machines which survived had indeed suffered severe damage. The squadron had returned, bloodied and bruised, but in greater numbers than could possibly have been expected. Naturally there was sadness at the loss of six young airmen from the squadron, and those of 107 Squadron, who were also mourned, 2 Group being a close-knit 'family'. However, there was also relief that after two abortive attempts, the 'big one' was over, a professional job having been completed.

After the operation, tired as they were from the day's events, Hughie Edwards and his flight commander S/L Scott were summoned to 2 Group Headquarters at Huntingdon, where the success of the operation was related and celebrated. Indeed, the news spread fast and furiously. Soon tributes were flooding in from all quarters. Each was recorded for posterity in the squadron's Operation's Record Book. The citations included the following.

The AOC 2 Group, Air Vice-Marshal Donald F. Stevenson DSO OBE MC, wrote:

Two photographs of shrapnel exit points on the fuselage of Z7361 GB:R. (via Mrs N.A. Scott)

YEAR 1941. MONTH	DATE	AIRCRAFT Type	No.	PILOT, OR 1ST PILOT	2ND PILOT, PUPIL OR PASSENGER	DUTY (INCLUDING RESULTS AND REMARKS)
—	—	—	—	—	—	— TOTALS BROUGHT FORWARD
JULY.	1	BLENHEIM	6028	SELF	SGT. KNIGHT " QUINN	Air Test
		"	6380	"	"	to HEMSWELL & return
	4	"	6028	"	P/O. RAMSEY SGT. QUINN.	Operations. Low level attack BREMEN. Formation 12 a/c – leader. Intense barrage.
	6	"	7488	"	SOLO.	to HORSHAM & return
	8	"	6453	"	F/Lt. L-CAMPBELL SGT. JAMES " FISHER	Practice Formation
	9	"	7427	"	P/O. RAMSEY SGT. BRUCE " FLETT	BICESTER & return
	10	"	7439	"	SGT. S. BOTHMAN	BOBBINGTON & return
		"	6453	"	SOLO	Practice bombing
	14	"	7427	"	SOLO.	BODNEY & return
		"	7427	"	A.S.O. PAINE	Local
	16	"	7439	"	F/Lt. SMITHERS " ROSE F/SGT. SHERWOOD	WATTON & return
		"	7427	"	F/Lt. ROSE	HORSHAM & return
					GRAND TOTAL [Cols. (1) to (10)] 773 Hrs. 45 Mins.	TOTALS CARRIED FORWARD

A page from W/C Hughie Edwards DFC's log book. His entry for the raid on Bremen, for which he was subsequently to be awarded the VC, simply reads: 'Operations. Low level attack BREMEN. Formation 12 a/c – leader. Intense Barrage.' (via Anthony Edwards)

'Please convey to the crews of 105, 107 and 226 Squadrons who took part in today's daylight attack on Bremen and Norderney, my deep appreciation of the high courage and determination displayed by them. This low flying raid, so gallantly carried out, deep into Germany without the support of fighters, will always rank high in the history of the Royal Air Force.'

The CinC Bomber Command, Air Marshal Sir Richard E.C. Peirse, wrote:

> Your attack this morning has been a great contribution to the day offensive now being fought. It will remain an outstanding example of dash and initiative. I send you and your captains and crews my warmest congratulations and the admiration of the Command.

The Chief of the Air Staff, Air Chief Marshal Sir Charles Portal, wrote:

> I have just read the first account of the Bremen raid today. Convey to the units concerned my warmest congratulations on a splendid operation. I am sure that all squadrons realize that besides encouraging the Russians, every daylight attack rubs into the Germans, the superiority of our units. You are doing great work.

Media interest in the Bremen operation was also considerable. Sgt Jackson was invited to broadcast his account of the raid over the airwaves in a BBC Home Service broadcast during the six o'clock news on 7 July.

Not only were high tributes paid to the squadrons en masse, but individuals were singled out for praise four days later, when an announcement was made that a DFC was to be awarded to P/O Alister Stewart Ramsay, Edwards' Observer. To his WOp/AG, Sgt Gerry Quinn, a bar was added to the DFM he had already gained with his former squadron. Three other DFMs were issued. These went to the crew of the Blenheim which had flown on Edwards' immediate right, Sgt Jackson, Sgt Williams and Sgt Purves, all of whom sustained injuries. Hughie Edwards had not been personally consulted about the awards, but regarding his own heroism, he was to discover that the greatest honour of all was to be bestowed upon him – the Victoria Cross. The announcement was made on 21 July 1941 and he became the first Australian airman to win this award. He was also the only Blenheim MkIV pilot to receive it. Having received the award, with typical magnanimity Edwards assembled the entire squadron in the station's large hangar, and declared that it was the squadron's VC, and that he was simply the person presented with it. Several wits were heard to enquire when, in consequence, they would be permitted to wear their VC ribbons! But his gesture was nevertheless much appreciated by all in attendance and the squadron simply glowed with pride. It was expressed in a letter from Sgt Bastin to his sister:

> What do you think of our Wing Commander getting the VC for the Bremen effort? We are all hugging ourselves about it, '105' is on top now. We got no medals for it but it feels great to think we were on the same job, we were flying on his left the whole time. The toughest job the RAF have done to date.

Following the news of the award, the CO treated his aircrew and NCO groundcrew to a night out in a Norwich pub, to celebrate the award of the 'squadron's VC'. One of those who attended was F/Sgt Jim Taylor, who made the following observations regarding the quality of their CO and the squadron: 'Edwards was a great lad – no snobbery about him, he was just one of the boys – very severe though, very severe!' In his opinion, 105 was 'The best squadron I was on!'

The adulation, pride and general morale Edwards had installed in the squadron since the tragic loss of Arnold Christian, surely speaks for itself in the above quotations.

CHAPTER 9

Onwards

Euphoria aside, there was work to be done and on 6 July six aircraft were put on operational readiness to act as a strike force at one hour's notice. Edwards had been excluded; with his VC award impending, Group had decided that he should not be subjected unnecessarily to dangers – at least until the award had been received.

On the 7th, operational orders arrived at Swanton Morley – a joint operation was once more on the cards. Both 105 and 139 Squadrons were to field six crews; they were to fly in two waves and proceed independently to specified points, 139 Squadron to a position 3 miles off the Dutch coast at Ijmuiden, and 105 Squadron to a position 3 miles further south off The Hague on the same coast. At these points 105 Squadron would turn to port and beat north, while 139 Squadron turned to starboard and beat south. They would rendezvous at 12.30 hours at a point half-way between The Hague and Ijmuiden, where they would bomb a convoy.

On this fine, clear July morning, briefing had been set for 10.00 hours. S/L Scott was to lead five other aircraft from Swanton Morley. All except Sgt Farrow and his crew had taken part in

Sgt Scott, Sgt Healy and Sgt Bastin pose with their Blenheim L9379 GB:Y at Swanton Morley after their fifteenth operational sortie in June 1941. Note the early example of 'nose art' in the form of a crest depicting a strutting cockerel and entitled 'Cock O' The Walk'. (via Mrs N.A. Scott)

the Bremen raid of the 4th. S/L Scott and Sgt Scott had both taken their crews on all three 'Wreckage' operations to Bremen. By 11.27 hours all those who were able to, had taken off. Sgt Scott had hit difficulties at the very last moment in L9379:Y, and failed to take off. This aircraft had been decorated with a crest showing a cockerel, strutting proudly above the legend 'Cock o' the Walk', emblazoned on the starboard side of the nose section. Nevertheless, on this day the only way they would reach the target was to walk, and the machine remained with the crew back at base. Sgt Bruce was also having problems in Z7445:P. Engine troubles were threatening to prevent take-off, but in fact he only lost four minutes before lifting off at 11.31 hours to meet up and formate with the others, who by this time were circling overhead. Exact timing was essential if the two flights were to meet punctually at the time specified by Group.

The 'Cock O' The Walk' crest. (via Mrs N.A. Scott)

S/L Scott pressed on, realizing that time was of the essence, followed by P/O Buckley, Sgt Farrow, P/O Broadley and now Sgt Bruce. The vic flattened out to line abreast half-way to the target, and they lowered down to sea-level to escape detection. Just as plans seemed to be back on track again, F/O Jack Buckley, flying V6380:G at zero feet, hit the water, bounced off the wave-tops and badly damaged the underside of the aircraft, deforming the undercarriage. However, with skilful handling the pilot managed to keep the machine in the air, and pulling up, he turned for home, jettisoning his bombs into the sea. On returning to Swanton Morley, the now familiar belly-landing was safely executed, one hour forty minutes after take-off.

Anthony Aloysius MacDonald Scott, later to be squadron leader and flight commander of 105 Squadron, photographed in June 1940. He was killed on 7 July 1941 during an attack on shipping off The Hague. (via the late Michael Scott)

Only four were now left of the 105 aircraft. Undaunted, S/L Scott kept going – he was not going to miss the rendezvous come what may! The formation closed up until S/L Scott, Sgt Farrow, P/O Broadley and Sgt Bruce were only 40 yards apart. The pre-arranged point for landfall was eventually spotted and the formation executed their turn. A couple of shore batteries took an interest and lobbed some 75mm shells at the Blenheims, which swerved between flak bursts, undeterred from their objective. The flight pressed on. Suddenly the target came into view as the aircraft lifted to the customary 50ft, ready for the final run-in to attack. The convoy consisted of eight merchant vessels, ranging from 2,000 to 4,000 tons, and escorted by no less than four flak ships and an E-Boat. Flak ships were well known to the squadron, but they had worse memories of E-Boats, following the disastrous attack on 15 June, when F/O Watts and his crew had fallen foul of one during their first operation. The E-Boat was circling the convoy and the flak ships were ahead on either side. Heavy fire was pouring north – 139 Squadron had arrived!

As the 105 Squadron aircraft roared in, charging at the convoy, the ships' gunners swung round to meet the new challenge from the rear. Sgt Farrow raced at the 4,000-ton *Delaware*, at the rear of the second column of ships. As he released his bombs, two 250lb bombs ripped into the ship, the third splashing into the sea. P/O Ben Broadley then took his machine into a quarter attack on another 4,000-ton merchant vessel, which burst into flames and sank. Next into the fray was Sgt Bruce, who mauled a ship of some 2,000 to 3,000 tons. His bombs tore in amidships, leaving clouds of first black, then white smoke billowing upwards.

S/L Scott's aircraft, V5502:U, and his crew Sgt Dewin (Observer) and Sgt Conlon (WOp/AG), were not seen after the run-in to attack. In his account of the raid in *Blenheim On The Deck*, Michael Scott deduces, with the aid of a photograph, the following about his brother's loss:

> Scotty was just starting to skid around to port as he weaved to put the flak gunners off their aim. A closer study of the photograph shows lines of tracers coming almost horizontally at his aircraft from the flak ships over on the right. At some instant in the next few seconds, his Blenheim was hit and set on fire.

On 7 July 1941 105 Squadron attacked at very low level a convoy between The Hague and Ijmuiden on the Dutch coast. The 4,000-ton Delaware *was at the rear of the second column of ships. (The Trustees of the Imperial War Museum, London: C1936)*

The aircraft of 139 Squadron also had a hard time of it. F/L H.C. Hilton and crew were hit by flak and their aircraft burst into flames and blew up when it hit the sea. A great deal of damage was done by 139 Squadron, with a 4,000-tonner and two 2,000-tonners having been crippled. They had arrived first and bore the brunt of the flak as 105 approached, but whether the flak would have lessened if 105 Squadron had arrived fractionally sooner, is purely conjecture. On the way home, four Bf 109s pounced on the five returning aircraft and shot down Sgt J.A. Causon and his crew into the sea before breaking off their attack. The three remaining 105 Squadron aircraft flew home, Sgt Bruce landing in Z7445:P at 13.22 hours, followed by P/O Broadley at 13.25 hours in V6373:O. Sgt Farrow was the last home in V6421:A, and having sustained flak damage during the attack, made a successful belly-landing at 13.30 hours.

The operation had been brilliantly executed, but it had also been very costly. S/L Scott was a very valuable leader and on hearing that he had been lost, 139 Squadron sent out two aircraft to join three of 105 Squadron searching for the crew of U-Uncle. Alas, the sweep was not successful. Sgt Conlon was laid to rest in Westduin General Cemetery, but S/L Scott and Sgt Dewin have no known graves.

The AOC 2 Group, Air Vice-Marshal Donald F. Stevenson DSO OBE MC, felt compelled to write the following tribute on hearing about the operation:

> The Group is filled with admiration by the determined attack carried out today by 105 and 139 Squadrons, as a result of which an enemy convoy was practically annihilated, two ships only escaping from a convoy of eight. In tonnage, this is a loss to the enemy of some 18,000 to 19,000 tons that he can ill afford to spare. Well done. Please convey my personal congratulations to the crews who took part in this magnificent operation.

Three days later, F/L George Goode DFC, now recovered from his last operation on 1 May, was promoted to acting squadron leader, and took charge of the flight once again. He appeared with a new crew, Sgt Frank Harbord (Observer), and P/O Eric Applebee DFM (WOp/AG). They were to be eased back into operations during the next task which lay ahead.

No operations were flown until 16 July, but there was a considerable amount of movement of personnel and practice flying instead. Jack Buckley's log notes that he made a low-level bombing practice flight on the 10th, and a trip to Edinburgh and back with Sgt Scholefield on the 11th. On the 12th P/O Buckley, along with Sgt T. Williams, Sgt W.A. Williams and Sgt L.T. Weston, proceeded on a twenty-minute flight, touching down at nearby Watton's satellite airfield, Bodney. They were being transferred to be attached to 110 Squadron in Malta. A rumour had been circulating that the squadron was going out to the Middle East, but by the beginning of July, this had fizzled out, and with four crews being posted out to Malta, it now appeared even less likely that the squadron would move. The news of the posting on the 13th for Sgt L.A. Tapp and his crew to the Middle East appeared to be all the movement expected in that direction.

P/O Eric William Applebee DFM (WOp/AG), service no. 44982. (via Eric Applebee)

CHAPTER 10

The Big Effort

On 14 July four aircraft were put on stand-by, along with two from 226 Squadron from Wattisham, to form a Strike Force at one hour's notice. Something was in the air again, but surely it couldn't be as big as the previous two operations? However, the next day, the crews found out that it was. Bremen had been a large, difficult operation – but this one was just as big: Rotterdam again, and in daylight, this time in the company of 18, 21, 139 and 226 Squadrons. Fighter cover was to be provided by 19 and 152 Squadrons from Coltishall, but only on the return journey. On the way there it was every man for himself!

Rotterdam had been a top priority target since it fell into enemy hands in May 1940. It was a major port handling vital goods for the Fatherland, in particular, iron ore from neutral Sweden. A report from CIU at Medmenham confirmed that the docks were even fuller than normal. With no Group Operations Order appropriate for this one-off attack, 2 Group decided that they would hold a mass briefing on the day of the raid, both at Watton and Horsham St Faith. It was therefore scheduled for 16 July, and the plan was revealed to the crews.

The intention was to approach the massive docks complex from the south-east, in the hope that the element of surprise would reduce the casualty risk. The other consideration high on the agenda was how best to traverse the docks with thirty-six Blenheims, all flying at low level, without collisions. There was also the possibility of aircraft being blown out of the sky by the preceding aircraft's bombs, which were primed to detonate 11 seconds after impact. It was decided, in the interests of safety, that the formation was to be split into two waves. Each wave was to comprise eighteen aircraft, flying at approximately one minute intervals. Hopefully, if the times were precisely adhered to, the anti-aircraft defences alerted by the first wave would not be fully ready for the second. That was the theory, anyway!

The first wave, consisting of two boxes of six Blenheims from 21 Squadron and one box of six from 226 Squadron, was to depart from Watton. The leader of the first wave, and indeed of the whole formation, was W/C Peter Fitzgerald 'Tom' Webster, CO of 21 Squadron. The second wave was to be led by W/C Thomas Noel 'Tim' Partridge DFC, CO of 18 Squadron, departing from Horsham St Faith. This wave was to comprise eight aircraft from 18 Squadron, four from 139 Squadron, and seven from 105 Squadron, flying in boxes as before. One of the 105 Squadron aircraft was to act as a marker for fighter cover on the way home. Each wave would fly most of the route in boxes of six, in vic formation, three Blenheims to each vic. Just before the final turn on to the north-westerly track, the formation would change into groups of six in echelon port, finally fanning out into loose vics in echelon port/line abreast as the target approached.

The briefings were short and to the point as usual, as the elaborate presentations of the 'Bomber Harris' era were yet to materialize. The crews heard about a balloon barrage and flak from an area classified as 'heavily defended'. The 105 crews certainly knew the precise meaning of such a statement, for the experiences of Bremen were still fresh in their minds.

Around 15.30 hours, W/C Webster assembled the first wave over Watton, and headed for the rendezvous at Wattisham. W/C 'Tim' Partridge DFC followed from Horsham St Faith. The two waves coasted out near Aldeburgh with separation as planned. The sea crossing was flown at the customary 50ft above the wave-tops to avoid detection by enemy radar. F/O J.B. 'Robbie' Robertson unerringly guided his pilot Tom Webster to the coast, at the western tip of Overflakkee Island. So far, so good, as the formation passed friendly Dutch folk, waving at the Blenheims. The route then took them down the Haringvliet to the vicinity of Numansdorp, and then the final turn for the bombing attack began. Here the plan slipped somewhat. Tom Webster turned slightly early and finished on a track close to due north, while Tim Partridge settled for a track well to the east of north.

Things went fairly well for the first wave, who covered an area from the eastern edge of the largest dock, Waalhaven, to the dry dock of Wilton Feijenoord to the west. The enemy had almost been caught unawares. However, one alert crew aboard flak ship *Vp 1107*, on degaussing manoeuvres in Waalhaven, reacted with typical Teutonic efficiency and blasted 21 Squadron's V6240, YH:B out of the sky. Sgt J.E.S. Bevan (Pilot), P/O R.M. Slade (Observer) and Sgt L.R. Mynott (WOp/AG) were the first casualties of the raid. The bodies of the pilot and observer were recovered by the Germans and buried in the cemetery at Crooswijk, but the WOp/AG's body was never found.

The rest of the wave recorded hits on a variety of ships, experiencing only light anti-aircraft fire in return. The largest target, the 17,000-ton MV *Baloeran* had been moved to Wilton Feijenoord from its former dock north of Waalhaven since the last sortie by 1 PRU on 11 July. It is understandable that the 10,500-ton cargo-liner *Oranjefontein*, lying in Waalhaven, was mistaken for her larger cousin and was set upon severely by 21 Squadron. The 226 Squadron box on the far left of the formation was now reduced to five, after one aircraft, Z7271, MQ:K, had had to return to base with a partially retracted undercarriage due to hydraulic failure. Nevertheless, 226 Squadron had the honour of attacking the *Baloeran*, renamed *Strassburg* by the Germans. Jackie Onions straddled her nicely with his stick of four 250lb bombs, before realizing, to his utter dismay, that she had been converted to a hospital ship, a fact confirmed later by a photograph taken by his WOp/AG 'Butch' Morton. At the very last moment Shaw Kennedy saw the red cross and instead bombed a large red tanker to the left of the *Baloeran*.

The plumes of smoke rising from the bomb bursts of the first wave were easily visible to the following wave. W/C Partridge DFC, probably guided by them, aimed his Blenheim V6267, WV:M at the untouched docks to the east, achieving a sensible overlap at the Waalhaven. As he and his crew, F/Sgt John Smith DFM (Observer) and Sgt George Dvorjetz (WOp/AG), attacked a merchant vessel in Katendrechthaven 2 (probably the 6,000-ton *Hermod*, which was also attacked by S/L Smythe), they were hit by flak from a group of flak ships moored just across the river. Somehow he managed to keep control of his blazing Blenheim, until finally it rolled over and plunged into the canal side at Noordsingel. This crew were also recovered and buried by the Germans at Crooswijk Cemetery; the Dutch later erected a monument at the crash spot in commemoration of these valiant airmen and the many others who died in the liberation of the Netherlands. Another 18 Squadron crew was hit at the same time as Tim Partridge. Sgt R. Rost, their Australian pilot staggered on in Blenheim Z7496, WV:W as far as Ypenburg before crash-landing. Regrettably, Sgt Rost, Sgt Hughes and Sgt Winter all died later that day in hospital.

Just to the left of the 18 Squadron box, S/L E. Sydney-Smith led his 139 Squadron hybrid, which included two 18 Squadron crews to make up numbers. A hail of flak greeted this former *Daily Express* reporter, and the moored flak ships claimed their third victim of the second wave. With outstanding airmanship S/L Sydney-Smith, with one engine of Z7362, XD:V on fire, just cleared a high tower before crash-landing in the centre of Rotterdam, in an area cleared by the Germans on 14 May 1940. He and his crew survived to become prisoners of war for the duration.

Following all this, 105 Squadron arrived on the far left of the wave, their target Waalhaven. Again W/C Edwards DFC, who would have been the logical choice to lead the squadron, had been forbidden to fly, and the formation leader was F/L Bryan Smithers in V6453:E. F/L Ben Broadley found an 8,000-tonner on stocks outside Dock 14, in the care of the Rotterdam Dry Dock Company. Clouds of smoke were seen billowing from it, and the ship was claimed destroyed.

Next, Sgt Bruce lobbed a 250-pounder on to the barges at the southern end of Waalhaven, before letting go of the remainder in the direction of a 6,000-tonner to the east of the great dock. Bursts were seen amidships, with clouds of smoke rising. This ship was also claimed destroyed. Sgt Taylor, on his first operational trip, is reported to have found the liner *Baloeran*, and Sgts Farrow and Scott were reported to have attacked a 7,000-ton liner, all with unobserved results. Sgt Bastin, Sgt Scott's WOp/AG, considered that they had actually attacked a 17,000-ton liner. Given that the *Baloeran* was of a similar displacement, it would appear that this had been the target. However, it had been moved, and as stated previously, may have been mistaken for the 10,500-ton *Oranjefontein* lying in Waalhaven. It would then seem likely that all three had attacked this ship.

As mentioned previously, S/L George Goode DFC and his crew in Z7488:F had been eased back into operational duties with a less arduous but nevertheless very important job. They were circling smoke markers out to sea, from where they ably shepherded out a Hurricane escort from Coltishall to cover the withdrawal of the Blenheim formation.

Despite enemy claims from flak ship *Vp 1107* that in addition to shooting down 21 Squadron's Sgt Bevan and his crew, they had also accounted for a 105 Squadron aircraft, the 105 Squadron formation returned intact. By the time the intelligence officers had correlated all the reports of the returning crews, an amazing tally emerged. The press release stated that: 'In all, seventeen ships of an estimated tonnage between 90,000 and 100,000 tons have been put out of action, either permanently or for a long time to come. Five more vessels, totalling between 40,000 and 45,000 tons were severely damaged.'

Sgt Bastin's comment written on the back of this photograph sums up the Blenheims' method of attack, on this sortie on Rotterdam docks on 16 July 1941: 'Do we fly low!'. Blenheim L9379 GB:Y 'Cock O' The Walk' was passing over warehouses and small ships before bombing the liner Oranjefontein *at Waalhaven docks. (via Mrs N.A. Scott)*

A view over the guns from the turret of a Blenheim turning for home over Rotterdam docks on 16 July 1941. Note the bombs exploding over the target area. (The Trustees of the Imperial War Museum, London: C1950)

The propaganda value at this bleak time of the war, with its consequential boost to morale in 2 Group, must have been considerable. It was not until some time later that it was realized that the actual tally fell well short of the claims. However, this was not unusual in wartime.

For leading the raid, Tom Webster was awarded the DSO, while 105's F/L Ben Broadley's contribution to the Rotterdam raid was mentioned in his citation for the DFC, as was that of Sgt Paton of 226 Squadron. Again congratulatory messages were pouring in. The CinC of Bomber Command, Air Marshal Sir Richard Peirse, wrote: 'My warmest congratulations on the magnificent attack carried out by you today. This is another crushing blow which will have a far-reaching effect on the enemy in the Battle of the Atlantic.' The AOC 2 Group, Air Vice-Marshal Donald F. Stevenson DSO OBE MC, contributed the following:

> I am filled with admiration for the leadership, courage and determination displayed in the crushing blow which was inflicted by you on the enemy at Rotterdam today. My heartiest congratulations to Wing Commander Webster, the formation leaders and crews who took part in this magnificent operation.

Even the Dutch noted the occasion, with a front page story in their local newspaper *Luchpost* [Airmail].

Flak ship escorts were becoming an all-too-familiar hazard to 105 Squadron. Having escaped without serious losses at Rotterdam, the 19th was to be the day that their fortunes changed again. This time the squadron was to field five aircraft against shipping off The Hague. At 11.22 hours the flight was airborne and heading out over Cromer, again heading for the coast of Holland. The convoy which was to be 'attended to' consisted of eight merchant vessels, escorted by no less than six of the dreaded flak ships!

The attack was led by F/L Smithers in V6453:E, who found a 6,000-ton vessel in the centre of the convoy. It was seen subsequently to be burning fiercely within an envelope of black smoke. F/L Broadley also tackled a 6,000-tonner with his four 250lb SAP bombs, two of which struck home amidships, leaving the vessel burning and emitting brown and black smoke. A third 6,000-tonner was attacked by Sgt Bill Jackson in Z7445:P. The twin-funnelled ship was attacked with four 250lb bombs, similarly leaving it issuing a high column of brown smoke. The ship was subsequently claimed as a total loss.

Sgt Farrow in Z7439:H successfully dropped his bombs on a 4,000-ton merchant vessel, all four bursting along the stern. The ship exploded, and debris was blown high into the air. Sadly, though, Sgt Farrow and his crew, Sgt Saunders (Observer) and Sgt Robinson (WOp/AG), were unable to claim their victory, as they fell victim to the barrage of flak pouring at them. Sgt Taylor and his crew, Sgt Witherington (Observer) and Sgt Sparks (WOp/AG), in Blenheim V6039:Q, attacked the 6,000-ton vessel previously attacked by F/L Bryan Smithers. Unfortunately, their bombs all undershot, but it was of no concern to the crew, as they too were caught by the flak and were shot down with no survivors. Both crews were subsequently buried in Dutch cemeteries, except Sgt Robinson who has no known grave.

The three machines which did survive returned home. F/L Smithers was first back at 13.08 hours, followed by Sgt Jackson at 13.11 hours, and lastly F/L Broadly in V6373:O at 13.15 hours. It had been a very successful raid but had caused the loss of a further two crews, making five lost aircraft and fifteen young men in the month of July alone.

Two replacement crews were brought in from 88 Squadron. F/O Roe and Sgt Bendall with their crews had been posted from Sydenham to Swanton Morley on 8 July, and were officially posted as 105 Squadron replacements on the 22nd. Despite receiving such replacements, the toll on the crews was worrying. Concern turned into horror for those in the know, as soon the rate of attrition was likely to rise even further. Following the attack on 19 July against shipping off The Hague, activity at Swanton Morley took on a different sense of urgency. It had been rumoured amongst the crews for some time that there was a trip planned for the squadron to warmer climes, and it was generally considered that this would mean the Middle or Far East. This was exemplified in a letter, dated 1 July 1941, sent by Sgt Bastin to his sister:

> I have done four ops since I have been back [from leave]. We did that raid on Bremen the papers spoke about today, although most of the stuff now is daylight sweeps over France with a fighter escort. I think the east racket is off now, they think we are doing well enough in this country.

However, from early July there had been a lot of behind the scenes preparations at the base. On the 12th, for example, as previously mentioned, three crews departed en route for the Middle East for attachment to 110 Squadron, who were serving on Malta. As it turned out, these crews did not actually leave for some time. On the 13th, Sergeant Tapp and his crew were posted out to the Middle East, fuelling rumours about a move even further. Moreover, 88 Squadron were shortly to receive many of 105's Blenheims, as the delivery of new aircraft took place. They were not changing aircraft type, but were taking delivery of modified Blenheims. These aircraft had air intakes above the engine nacelles and Vokes tropical air filters over the carburettor air intakes below the engine nacelles; they were painted mid-stone and dark earth on top, with azure blue under-surfaces. They were 'Tropical' Blenheims. Eventually the news broke that the previous rumours had come to fruition. The squadron was being detached, not just to the Middle East, but to Malta! In a further letter to his sister, Sgt Bastin explained that 'I am going to Malta tomorrow for a few weeks, so I should not write to me again until you hear from me there.'

Intelligence officers looked rather concerned, as few crews returned from that particular island. For many, it would indeed prove to be an arduous one-way trip.

Part Two – THE MEDITERRANEAN

CHAPTER 11

The Mediterranean War

Lying some 60 miles to the south of Sicily, Malta commanded the focal point for the great 1,900-mile sea-lanes between the Suez Canal at the eastern end, leading to the Red Sea, with its access to the eastern oil fields and ultimately the Indian Ocean, and Gibraltar at the western end, the great gateway to the Atlantic Ocean.

Throughout the initial stages of the war, the bulk of the Mediterranean countries adopted a neutral stance, or were sympathetic to the Allies. In the east, the oil supplies from Iraq via French Syria and through British-dominated Palestine were secure, because of their controlling governments. Further south, the Egyptian Treaty of Friendship allowed the British the use of the port of Alexandria, thereby giving the Royal Navy a controlling strongpoint in the area.

At the western end of the Mediterranean, Gibraltar was flanked by French Morocco to the

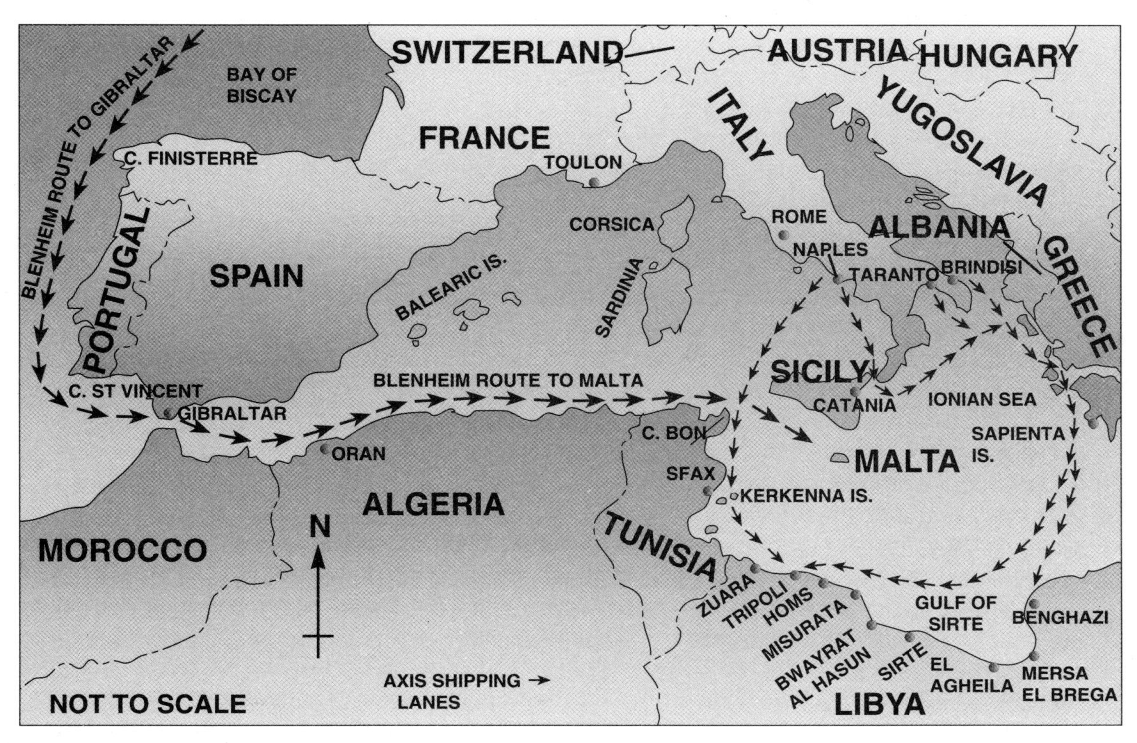

The Mediterranean Sea.

south and Spain to the north, the latter offering a somewhat strained neutrality following the civil war. The French not only had controlling influences in the east, but also boasted large anchorages in Algeria at Oran and Algiers, and in Tunisia at Bizerta, thereby supplementing their own major naval port of Toulon. The remainder of the central Mediterranean remained neutral with Yugoslavia, Greece and Turkey each having Allied leanings, whilst Italy, although still neutral at this stage, had control over Sicily and Libya.

Guarding the Mediterranean was the British Navy commanded by Sir Andrew Browne Cunningham, Chief of the Mediterranean Fleet. His fleet's main base was Alexandria, with a smaller force, Force H, at Gibraltar, and operated not only in the Mediterranean but also in the Atlantic. Hitler's advance into Europe required greater naval activity in the Atlantic, with the result that command of the Mediterranean was divided. Until its capitulation on 22 June 1940 France assumed responsibility for the western side as far as Malta, while to the east of Malta lay Cunningham's domain, although the British also patrolled the whole sea.

Since most of Italy's commodities arrived by sea routes, it was initially thought unlikely that they would take sides against Britain, then in control of these vital sea-lanes. However, with Britain's ambitions in Europe not in Italy's favour, it was just possible that Mussolini might wish to expand the Roman Empire and begin to present a threat. All trade routes through the Mediterranean were therefore brought to a halt until at last Italy declared her intentions were not belligerent. With trade resumed, normality seemed to be restored in the area. The British, however, were determined not to allow the feeding of the Nazi war machine and so adopted a policy of patrolling the Aegean Sea. The other main routes to the Adriatic, and south of the Messina Straits were also policed. Any vessel suspected of carrying supplies to aid the Germans were taken to British inspection ports at Malta, Port Said and Haifa. Preventive measures against supplies passing to the Nazi's proved effective and so orderly had events in the Mediterranean become, that Cunningham settled at Malta with his fleet concentrated in the west, rather than having to protect Mediterranean shipping from Italian aggression which was not forthcoming – or was it?

By early 1940, with thousands of Italian troops massed in Libya, Italy's neutrality began to appear strained. The warning signs were clearly visible to the Allies, and it was obvious that she was intent on entering the war shortly.

Cunningham moved to Alexandria in readiness. The Italian Navy did not own an aircraft carrier, as it was generally considered that Italy herself constituted a land-based carrier – from her central position in the Mediterranean, she could supply any necessary airborne protection. The folly of this supposition was to be learned later.

The 'Duce' now recognized Britain's increasingly weak position in Europe. With this in mind, Mussolini faced the thronging masses in a square in Rome. The people were swept along on a tide of nationalistic fervour, many holding placards calling for the conquest of Suez, Tunisia, Malta and Gibraltar. Their anticipation was rewarded when Mussolini, standing like a peacock on his balcony, declared: 'Fighting men of Italy – to arms! Show the world your will, and your spirit and your valour!'

At last the situation long expected had come to fruition; simultaneously Italy formally declared war on Britain and France and once again trade through the Mediterranean ground to a halt, as shipping took the longer but safer passage around the Cape. Only urgent supplies went through the Mediterranean, proceeding in escorted convoys.

Having declared war, Italy was quick to try to assert her power over Malta. At 06.55 hours on the morning of Tuesday 11 June 1940, the first air raid sirens sounded over the island. Altogether that first day seven raids took place and Malta suffered its first victims of the war: five military personnel, all from the Royal Malta Artillery, and eleven civilians were killed, with another 130 injured. Italy's first air attack marked the beginning of a holocaust that would be stoically endured by the Maltese people.

From the declaration of war and the first air attack on Malta by the bombers of the Regia Aeronautica, Italy had sent wave after wave of aircraft against their new enemy. Flying high-level formations, their dive-bombing expertise proved a severe problem to the Maltese defenders whose anti-aircraft defences consisted of 34 heavy guns and 8 light (40mm) Bofors guns. The air defence force consisted of Gloster Gladiator torpedo-bombers, left behind by HMS *Glorious* when she departed for Norway.

AOC Malta at this time was Air Commodore Forster H.M. Maynard, who lost no time in salvaging six of these machines which had been crated and left in storage at the seaplane base at Kalafrana on the south-east corner of the island. Having obtained Admiral Sir Andrew Cunningham's permission to requisition the Gladiators, Maynard had four of them assembled, only three of which ever flew at any one time. Maynard's assistant flight officer, F/L George Burgess, volunteered his services as a pilot.

Although there were no fighter pilots present, Burgess was soon joined by F/O William J. 'Timber' Woods, P/O Peter B. Alexander, S/L Alan C. Martin, F/L Peter G. Keeble and F/O John L. Waters. All lacked experience, but nevertheless the Hal Far Station Fighter Flight was formed. Training was interrupted when the Maltese authorities ordered that the aircraft were to be returned to their crates; however, this was soon rescinded and the aircraft re-assembled. The pilots of the Hal Far Flight were destined to become heroes in their own right, and three of the aircraft, although not named at the time, later gained fame for their efforts under the names 'Faith', 'Hope' and 'Charity' – an apt set of names which echoed the attributes of the island population at the time. With their faith in God limitless and hope always in their hearts, the people never failed to extend charity to others less fortunate, sharing their food, drink and homes with those who had lost all to the enemy's bombs. Such was the spirit of the people of Malta – but it would be tested to its limits in the months to come.

In view of the intense bombing of Malta, Admiral Cunningham decided to evacuate his warships from Malta to Alexandria. He proposed that two convoys should be assembled to sail from Alexandria to evacuate the women and children from the island. The Maltese people, like the British, were learning to adapt to life in shelters, with black-outs and sandbags.

To protect these convoys the Admiralty planned three naval groups, designated Force A, Force B and Force C. Force A was commanded by Vice-Admiral Tovey in his Leander-class cruiser *Orion*, supported by the cruisers *Gloucester*, *Liverpool*, *Neptune*, *Stuart* and *Sydney*. Force B was led by the Commander-in-Chief Sir Andrew Browne Cunningham in the 30,600-ton battleship *Warspite* with five destroyers at his side. Force C was commanded by Rear Admiral H.D. Pridham-Whipple and comprised two battleships, the larger being the 31,100-ton *Malaya* and the smaller the 29,150-ton *Royal Sovereign*. Force C also had one other crucial ingredient – the 10,850-ton aircraft carrier *Eagle*, together with a screening flotilla.

All of these ships sailed from Alexandria on 7 July 1940, bound for Malta.

However, we should now look back at the events on land and the situation facing the British Army in Egypt.

In June 1940 the Western Desert Force consisted of some 36,000 men from the 7th Armoured and 4th Indian Divisions. The WDF was under the command of General Archibald Percival Wavell, Commander-in-Chief, Middle East. Facing his force were two Italian Armies, comprising some 236,000 men, under Marshal Bolbo. The Italians were pitifully ill-equipped, but on 28 June 1940 Mussolini ordered Marshal Bolbo to invade Egypt. The order never got through, however, as the aircraft in which the Marshal was travelling was shot down by the Italian Army's own anti-aircraft defences. Marshal Bolbo died in the crash. He was soon succeeded by the Army's Chief of Staff, Marshal Rodolfo Graziani, who quickly realized the enormity of his task. He also realized that the coast road to Alexandria was the only communications route and that many supplies and much water would be required. The date for the advance had been delayed to 15 July after Bolbo's death. Marshal Graziani then began to procrastinate, much to the Duce's annoyance – Mussolini was determined that his attack would coincide with Hitler's final blows against Britain.

Graziani had been ordered to advance on Egypt on 29 August; he began to move on 13 September. Within four days of leaving Fort Capuzzo, the Italian Army reached Sidi Barrani, some 60 miles inside Egypt, one-fifth of the way to Cairo. Having gained ground within Egypt, General Graziani decided not to stretch his supply route along the coast road which was vulnerable to naval and air attack, and instead set up seven encampments with fortified perimeters. As time wore on the Italian forces became entrenched in their increasingly comfortable surroundings, allowing considerable relaxation for their troops. This pause also gave the British time to recover from the onslaught and to prepare counter-measures. But with his preparations in full swing, General Richard Nugent O'Connor was to receive a major blow – while the Italians had been preparing to advance into Egypt, their troops in Albania had almost doubled in number to around 125,000 men.

Earlier in the war, Hitler had snubbed Mussolini's ideas of attacking in the Balkans because he was fearful of the Russian reaction to such a move. He further reasoned that since Romanian oil fields supplied much of the German Army's oil, starting a conflict in the Balkans might give the Allies the opportunity to use any territory they might capture as a platform from which to attack the oil fields. Under the circumstances, an attack in Yugoslavia seemed to be out of the question. However, Mussolini was determined not to be excluded from his part in Fascist glory, and decided that Greece could be invaded without unduly upsetting Hitler. On several occasions Greek shipping was attacked by the Italians, both in and out of port. The Greek government played the situation down and turned the other cheek, while at the same time warning the Italians that if attacked, Greece would defend herself. This warning was foolishly taken lightly by the Italians and further appeals were made to Germany to gain Hitler's approval. These were again denied until Britain had been put out of action. Mussolini remained frustrated but obeyed until 20 September, when Hitler struck another blow. In order to protect the Romanian oil fields, Germany invaded Romania, an action provoked by continuing poor relations with Russia. Mussolini was not even informed about the action, and Italian pride was severely hurt in consequence.

Mussolini felt that the only way to repay Hitler's action was to display some face-saving Italian initiative by launching an Italian attack on Greece – without informing the Führer until the deed was done.

Accordingly, on 28 October 1940, the reinforced Italian troops in Albania marched into Greece. The Greek population greeted news of the Italian attack on their soil with derision and, true to their word, they fought back. It was not long before the Italian advance from neighbouring Albania began to meet resistance. Although far outnumbering the Greek defenders in men and munitions, the Italian advance was slowed by deep mud and rivers swollen by torrential rain. They also had to contend with determined Greek resistance, which included sabotage of communications. Eventually the Italians could not push ahead any further and on 4 November 1940, the Greeks counter-attacked and the Italians were pushed back all along the Albanian border. The Greeks, facing an opposing army almost seven times larger than their own, began to drive into Albania. However, by the beginning of

December the Greek Army, which lacked the facilities necessary to afford themselves tank support or anti-tank protection, was waging a mountain-top war. Soon the freezing winter temperatures arrived, as did the snow and ice and consequently the Greek offensive began to crumble. The Italians were reinforced by eight divisions and the Greeks began to withdraw.

While fighting raged in Greece, the RAF were flying reconnaissance flights from Malta. A concentration of Italian naval strength, which included their entire contingent of six battleships, was observed to be moored in the harbour at Toranto. Here was the opportunity for which Cunningham had been waiting, to hit hard at the enemy. The attack was carried out on the night of 11 November 1940 by two waves of the Fleet Air Arm's Swordfish torpedo-bombers flying from the deck of the 23,000-ton aircraft carrier HMS *Illustrious*.

The attack was a daring one, carried out at low level in the moonlight. The first wave of twelve Swordfish from 815 Squadron FAA accounted for two of the battleships, the *Conte Di Cavour* and the *Littorio*.

They lost one aircraft in the process, and the crew were taken prisoners of war. The second wave of nine Swordfish from 819 Squadron FAA also created havoc but lost one aircraft in the process; this time the crew were killed. The entire attack was completed amid very heavy anti-aircraft fire, leaving the harbour apparently full of wreckage and ablaze with black burning oil. The remaining Swordfish arrived back safely on board the *Illustrious*. The result of these nocturnal activities was the destruction of or damage to three battleships (one each of Cavour, Littorio and Duilio classes), two destroyers and two cruisers (one each of Bolzano and Trento classes). The remaining three battleships returned to Naples out of harm's way. Once again the Mediterranean could be described as 'Cunningham's Pond'.

The British Fleet was now at liberty to police the supply routes between Italy and North Africa, thereby allowing troops and munitions to sail in comparative safety to Alexandria, from where General Wavell fortified his army in preparation for a counter-attack. On 6 December 1940 the thrust began. Some 30,000 British soldiers were on the move, covering 75 miles before engaging the enemy. The Italian Army encampments were so far apart that they precluded mutual support. Consequently, General O'Connor attacked the fortifications from the rear, the direction their rations would come from. The encampments fell within hours, thousands of prisoners being taken. Two days later Sidi Barrani fell, and O'Connor was able to use the stockpiled equipment, food, fuel and other materials necessary to sustain an army, to continue his assault further westwards into Libya.

Following a strong supporting bombardment by Air Chief Marshal Sir Arthur M. Longmore's Malta-based Wellington bombers, and by shelling from three battleships and seven destroyers of Cunningham's force, O'Connor pushed onwards. The Italian stronghold of Bardia had succumbed by 7 January 1941, leaving 40,000 prisoners. O'Connor wanted to push ahead to Tripoli but after the fall of Tobruk, and with a total of 200,000 Italian prisoners on his hands, Churchill ordered many of O'Connor's forces to go to the aid of the Greeks, who were by this time suffering badly.

The beginning of 1941 heralded the arrival of the Luftwaffe in the Mediterranean. Their intention was to make up for Axis deficiencies on land and at sea by introducing an aerial presence which could be turned on the Royal Navy with devastating effect. The most revered of the units sent to Sicily was Fliegerkorps X, which had arrived from Norway equipped with the much-feared Junkers 87 'Stuka' dive-bombers and Junkers 88 twin-engined medium bombers.

There were fifty-eight raids during the month of January, most of which were attempts to destroy the *Illustrious*. On the night of 23 July, during a pause in the fighting, she slipped out of dock in a damaged condition. Sufficient repairs having been effected, despite the atrocious conditions, she was able to head under her own steam. Escorted by the fleet, she steamed towards Alexandria, where she could be repaired properly beyond the range of the Luftwaffe. 'Cunningham's Pond' was to be ravaged by the Luftwaffe in the coming months, and once again all convoys required protection as they steamed along the North African coast. The Germans had certainly established a formidable presence in the Mediterranean, but the worst was yet to come.

On 12 February 1941 Lieutnant General Erwin Rommel and his Afrika Korps arrived at Tripoli. Their task was to aid the Italians, with the intention of tying down the British and covering the southern flanks of Europe. The small Afrika Korps was at first enhanced by bluff, as Rommel ordered that dummy tanks were to be assembled in an attempt to make the force look much larger and more formidable than it was, until the remainder of his Panzers could arrive. Hopefully the British would take time to build up forces to repel such a large force; a breathing space Rommel desperately needed. His plan worked, aided by Churchill's order on 4 March that British troops were to be sent to Greece, leaving Wavell's army sadly depleted. The British had by this time advanced as far west as El Agheila, where on 24 March, the German offensive began. Faced with an apparently vastly superior force, backed by a formidable display of 'tanks', the British Army commenced its withdrawal.

Rommel forged on to Mersa el Brega and in just twelve days pushed the British back some 500 miles to Egypt. Thousands of British troops were taken prisoner, including Lt-Gen Philip Neame and Lt-Gen Richard O'Connor. Neame had replaced O'Connor in command of Cyrenaica, while O'Connor had been promoted to command the British troops in Egypt; O'Connor was, however, brought back by Wavell in an attempt to arrest the British withdrawal, which had turned into a rout. The only stronghold not to fall to the Germans was Tobruk, which the British desperately needed for its port facilities. Tobruk provided the only point of replenishment of rations and supplies, which otherwise could only be brought into Tripoli or Benghazi. Try as they might, the Afrika Korps could not take the besieged town, which was initially held by an Australian garrison and later reinforced by Polish, South African, Indian and British troops. Rommel tried time and time again to take Tobruk but failed. He became increasingly enraged and frustrated until on 27 April, having lost a thousand men in his latest attempt to take the town, the German High Command intervened and stopped him. During the ensuing stalemate, there was time to take stock of tactics.

Churchill ordered that a consignment of tanks be delivered directly to Alexandria to aid General Wavell in a new offensive. The shipment arrived on 1 May 1941, although the tanks were poorly made.

Operation 'Brevity' ensued as a precursor to the main offensive, code-named Operation 'Battle-axe'. On 15 June, as the British tanks trundled into Halfaya Pass, they were very effectively ambushed by the thunderous might of concealed German Krupps 88mm anti-aircraft guns, dug into the side of the cliffs with their barrels levelled at the oncoming advance. The tanks didn't stand a chance and were summarily blown to pieces. As a result, Halfaya Pass became known to the British soldiers as 'hellfire pass'. Having taken such a mauling and with much equipment lost due to mechanical breakdown, Operation 'Battle-axe' proved to be a disaster, in which around a thousand men lost their lives. Subsequently Churchill ordered that General Wavell be replaced by General Sir Claude Auchinleck, soon commonly referred to as 'the Auk'.

On 24 April 1941 the first evacuations of Greek and British forces sent to the aid of Greece began. In a Dunkirk-style operation, the Royal Navy rescued nearly fifty thousand men. The evacuation was completed on 1 May. The large British anchorage at Suda Bay, Crete, took in some twenty thousand men between 25 and 28 April; they arrived in a variety of sailing craft, from cruisers and destroyers to caiques.

The German invasion of Crete began on 20 May, with German parachutists dropped from Ju 52 transport aircraft leading the assault on Maleme on the north-east coast, defended by New Zealand infantry. Valiant defence was put up throughout the island, with the Royal Navy doing all it possibly could to give support but suffering grievously at the hands of the Luftwaffe. Eventually, overwhelmed by the German onslaught, evacuation began on the night of 28 May from the village of Sphakia, on the south-east shore of the island. This courageous operation lasted for three nights under the protection of the RAF who flew protective sorties from North Africa. Further garrisons in the north, at Rethymno and Heraklion, also required evacuation. However, the evacuation of Rethymno did not happen at all. The Australian troops there fought to the last. Eventually, overwhelmed by German might, some of the survivors took to the hills while others surrendered. For the present at least, Crete belonged to the Germans.

From Italy's initial declaration of war, Malta had endured an aerial onslaught, heightened when the Germans brought Fliegerkorps X to their new base in Sicily. The 'Battle of Malta' had begun and was destined to continue well into 1942. Malta became the most bombed place on earth. Yet despite the bombings, Malta's aircraft continued to provide photographic reconnaissance of enemy movements in Sicily, Italy, North Africa, Greece and the Greek Islands, providing vital information as the war raged in the Mediterranean.

When Hitler attacked Russia, Fliegerkorps X was required to give aerial support at the Russian front. By the end of May 1941 they had departed, leaving the Italian Regia Aeronautica to wage war against Malta on their own. Thus Malta received some respite from the intense daily bombardment by the Luftwaffe and a period of relative quiet began, allowing vital stores to be brought to the island. In May, July and September 1940 large convoys had arrived, replenishing the island's stocks of fuel, munitions and food. For the moment at least, supplies of everything were plentiful. Thus the opportunity was at last afforded for Malta to go on the offensive.

In May 1941 Air Commodore Sir Hugh Pughe Lloyd MC DFC arrived to take up his position as AOC, with the task of creating an offensive capability to be wielded against all shipping at sea loaded with supplies for Rommel's campaign in North Africa. Shipping in port was also to be attacked. If no targets could be found at sea or in port, secondary land-based targets were to be sought. In addition to the valiant actions of the Malta-based British 10th Flotilla whose U-class submarines were waging a war of their own against the enemy's sea-lanes, the FAA's Swordfish were to strike at night, as were the RAF's Wellington bombers. The RAF's newly arrived Bristol Blenheims were to attack at mast height by day. The opportunity was also taken to build up defences, as in July, when the Malta Night-Fighter Unit was formed, consisting of night-fighting Hawker Hurricanes.

The relative lull in enemy activity was shattered on the night of 25 July, when a daring raid was attempted by the Italians. They endeavoured to breach the defences of the Grand Harbour with a force of midget submarines, supported by a number of E-Boats, in order to attack a newly arrived convoy berthed there. It was a brave attempt, but proved tragically fatal for the Italians. The attack left twenty Italian dead and eighteen prisoners were taken.

This then was the state of play in the Mediterranean theatre of war at the end of July 1941, when Malta was about to play host to the Blenheims of 105 Squadron in the continuation of the war of attrition waged daily against Rommel's supply convoys.

CHAPTER 12

Onwards to Malta

There was feverish activity at RAF Swanton Morley as the new 'Tropicalized' Blenheims were air tested in readiness for the trip to Malta. Following a few days of embarkation leave for several aircrew, all the crews were kitted out with their new tropical kit. This consisted of a tropical hat with an RAF flash on the side, khaki shirts, big, baggy khaki shorts, socks and ordinary shoes; not particularly stylish clothing, but a lot better suited to the climate than the standard issue blue serge worn in the UK! Nevertheless, the new kit was a novelty. Stuart Bastin wrote in his letter of 23 July: 'You should see me in my tropical kit, I look a real "Poonah Man".'

On the 23rd, the squadron assembled for an official farewell photograph, which included not only the aircrew who were going to Malta but also members of the groundcrews. Sgt Chapple wrote in his diary: 'Selection of groundcrew to go to Malta was made by flight sergeants of A and B Flights tossing a coin. My Flight won – or lost.' He then listed the groundcrew personnel: 'Chiefie Sergeant, myself, Cpl Sommerville, Cpl Eldridge, Cpl Woolven, Cpl Chambers, Sgt Marriot, F/Sgt Taylor, Sgt Balfour, and LAC Eeles.' However, these, with the exception of F/Sgt Taylor, were not the groundcrew who appear in the squadron photograph. Those in the photograph were those available at the time.

Sgt Ron Scholefield (Observer) of 105 Squadron modelling the standard tropical kit outside one of the limestone barrack blocks at Marsaxlokk Bay, Malta. (Mike Henry)

By now the Blenheims were ready, with new equipment for the crews on board. This included a new pocket watch for navigational purposes, located in a drawer underneath the navigation table, as well as a new stopwatch, and a navigator's ruler, all of which were eagerly snapped up by the lucky finder. All that was left to do was load up with all the items required for their long trip. Conditions on Malta were known to be somewhat primitive, so every effort was made to take as many necessities of life as possible for the squadron's operational good. Spares of all types were taken, loaded in the bomb well area between the cockpit and the gun turret.

Due to the long distances to be covered, an auxiliary fuel tanking arrangement containing an extra 100 gallons had been fitted within the bomb well, around which all the kit was stowed. The tank had to be pumped manually by

105 Squadron at Swanton Morley on 23 July 1941, prior to their departure for Malta. (via Frank Harbord)

105 Squadron officers, July 1941. Left to right: S/L B.W. Smithers DFC ('A' Flight Commander); W/C Hughie Idwal Edwards VC DFC (Commanding Officer); S/L H.H. 'Tom' Rose (Intelligence Officer); F/O R.E. Lee (Intelligence Officer); F/O F.E. 'Teddy' Frayn (Gunnery Officer); F/L Wyness (Navigation Officer). (via F.E. Frayn)

105 Squadron officers, July 1941. Left to right: F/O F.E. 'Teddy' Frayn (Gunnery Officer); W/C Hughie Idwal Edwards VC DFC (Commanding Officer); F/L Wyness (Navigation Officer). (via F.E. Frayn)

'Zwicky pump' to transfer the fuel into the wing tanks. This was invariably the task of the passenger – the groundcrew member allotted to the aircraft for the flight. It was no mean task, as the pumping could take up to one hour to complete!

Finally, there was a short pre-flight briefing by the CO, Wing Commander Edwards VC DFC, and the men then said their farewells to those left at the station.

Then it was time to go. Sgt Chapple noted in his diary that initially plans did not go as expected: 'Thursday 24 July 1941: All set to go to Malta. Stood by all day till 17.00 hours, when trip was postponed 24 hours.' However, the next day the weather was beautiful, and the squadron departed for their destination in the late afternoon. Swanton Morley was not to be the point of departure, as the trip had had to be planned with the utmost regard to fuel economy. Instead they were leaving from the fighter station at Portreath in Cornwall, where the Blenheims were to assemble for the long journey to the Mediterranean.

The flight to Portreath started mostly in squadron strength, with twelve aircraft and crews departing around 18.00 hours. Hughie Edwards led with F/O Frayn, Sgt Knight and Sgt Quinn as his crew in 'H', taking two hours ten minutes, while others went via Brackley and Bath to Portreath in two hours thirty minutes.

P/O Brian Hanafin and his crew, Sgt Charles Hill (Observer), P/O Cheney (WOp/AG) and groundcrew/passenger F/Sgt Jim Taylor, flew down to Portreath on the 26th. They had left Swanton Morley on the 25th in the late afternoon but diverted to Mount Farm, a satellite airfield for Benson, home of the PRU, perhaps to pick up the squadron's camera equipment. In particular, each WOp/AG was to receive a hand-held Leica camera to take photographs of their attacks, and it was probably these which were being collected by P/O Hanafin in his capacity of photographic officer for the detachment to Malta. Following take-off from Benson, however, all did not go according to plan. En route to Portreath, the aircraft, V7504, developed trouble in one engine and a forced-landing was successfully made at RAF South Cerney, where the Blenheim was left in the able hands of local groundcrew to rectify the problem. Too late to proceed to their destination, the crew and passenger were given a billet for the night in quarters considered appropriate to their respective ranks and status. Jim Taylor remembers:

> When we force-landed at South Cerney, we had to stay for the night. We were given mugs of tea, watched by a big flight sergeant, a Yorkshireman, who kept saying 'Half a mug, half a mug!' Such charity!

P/O Hanafin and crew arrived at Portreath after their overnight stay, ready to join up with the squadron once again.

Left to right, Sgt Scott, Sgt Healy and Sgt Bastin enjoy the sunshine beside their Blenheim GB:R, prior to departure for Gibraltar and Malta. (via Mrs N.A. Scott)

Another example of 'nose art' proudly displayed by Sgt Scott, Sgt Healy and Sgt Bastin on the nose of 'Tropicalized' Blenheim GB:R on 23 July 1941. The crest, entitled 'Cock O' The Air' depicts a flying cockerel holding a bomb ready for release over the target. (via Mrs N.A. Scott)

Sgt Brendan Healy, Sgt Stuart Bastin and Sgt Ron Scott get a measure of their new 'Tropicalized' Blenheim GB:R, on 23 July 1941, ready for their flight to Malta via Gibraltar. (via Mrs N.A. Scott)

On arrival at Portreath on the 25th, the squadron was billeted in bell-tents. Sgt Chapple's diary recalls:

> Friday 25 July 1941: Again standing by. Set off this time at 17.30 hours for Portreath. I flew in 'M' with Sgt Bruce (pilot), Flett and Gibson. An uneventful trip. Weather splendid. I flew 'M' for about an hour. Arrived about 20.30 hours. Covered up kites and sorted out the refuelling party. Also changed a couple of tail wheels. No maintenance party available so had to do 'dailies' on three kites myself. Portreath set amid splendid scenery. Found mess and had a good supper and a drink. Slept in a tent miles from anywhere.

However, F/Sgt Taylor was not so impressed with his new surroundings:

> Portreath was a terrible place, the fighter boys there hated us. Walking about with their top buttons undone, they were living in the glories of the Battle of Britain. We sat in the Mess and they ignored us. We were in tents, with a big marquee for a dining hall, and even W/C Edwards noticed it. He didn't criticize them, but you could see by the way he hung his head what he was thinking. He had done more than any of them of course!

The next day all was set for a 10.30 hours take-off, but due to bad weather further south departure was postponed, and the aircrew were given a bus trip into St Ives instead. It was glorious weather, and a splendid day was had there. Sgt Jackson and a few of the others hired a boat and went out to fish for mackerel. On their return to the harbour, they threw their catch to the local bystanders because they wouldn't have been allowed to cook the fish themselves. Then they decided that it was time to eat, and later sought out the nearest hostelry for several

Crew members gathering 'gen' on 23 July 1941, prior to their departure to Malta. Left to right: Sgt Stuart George Bastin (WOp/AG); Sgt Arthur 'Arty' J. Piers (Pilot); Sgt Ronald John Scott (Pilot); and Sgt Walter Brendan Healy (Observer) beside 'Tropicalized' Blenheim GB:R. Sgt Piers did not go with them, as he had transferred to another squadron; he was killed some time later in a Mosquito over the Rennes area of France. (via Mrs N.A. Scott)

beers. Much later that evening, having drunk their fill, they attempted to gain access to a local dance, but were 'refused permission'. So, a little the worse for wear, the troop of young aviators managed to find their way back to their bus, some having left the contents of several pint pots deposited for posterity at various points around the local area. All arrived back safely at Portreath to sleep off their hours of enjoyment. For many of them this was to be the last time they would ever go out on the town in England, and so we can surely forgive such youthful exuberance!

For the groundcrew, however, there remained work to be done. Sgt Chapple noted:

> Saturday 26 July 1941: Met ex-105 bloke in Spitfire squadron who gave me a hand with the dailies. Working all afternoon on S/L Smither's kite adjusting propeller fine pitch.

It was not all work though, as he continues: 'Went down to the village in the evening. Rather charming and sea beautiful. Had a few jugs then back to tent.' Other groundcrew had a more eventful evening, especially F/Sgt Jim Taylor and fellow Scot Sgt 'Jock' Marriott. Jim Taylor explains:

> Balfour told me he was going to a wedding. He had received notification from a pal who joined up with him at Halton, and was an instrument maker. He got married at Redruth. We went to the wedding there, and it was a real Cornish wedding too, the drink and rough cider were flowing and we sampled the Cornish clotted cream as well. When we came back at

This farewell photograph was taken on 23 July 1941. Sitting on the port wing are, left to right: groundcrew (unknown); Sgt Ronald J. Scott (Pilot); Sgt W. Brendan Healy (Observer); Sgt Stuart G. Bastin (WOp/AG); Sgt Bill Jackson (Pilot); groundcrew (unknown). (via Mrs N.A. Scott)

night in the dark, we couldn't find our way back to the camp. The two of us were walking over rocks, I will never forget it. I can't remember how we eventually got back to the camp as there were rocks everywhere, which seemed to get mixed up with the sheep!

The first leg of the journey was to be flown past the Scilly Isles, across the Bay of Biscay, and on to Cape Finisterre, then for 20 or 30 miles parallel to the Portuguese coast as far as Cape St Vincent, before continuing on to the Straits of Gibraltar and landing at Gibraltar itself. Formal briefing was given by W/C Edwards prior to departure, and then suddenly, on the morning of Sunday 27 July, word went out that a favourable weather report had been received, and departure was imminent. Bags of mail were squeezed into the bomb-bays at the last moment, having been delivered by a small red post office van. The crews got on board their machines, having said their goodbyes rather pointedly, and started up their engines. Pre-flight checks completed, they lumbered their way nervously to the end of the runway. Each aircraft was fully laden with fuel, spares and men, and to make matters worse, the runway terminated at the edge of a sheer cliff face.

Some were in a worse predicament than others regarding weight. P/O Hanafin in V7504, GB-G had to carry F/Sgt Taylor as a passenger, and extra weight in spares and toolboxes, as well as two spare main wheels with tyres, plus a spare undercarriage leg! There was nothing else for it but to rev the engines up to full throttle with the brakes on, and with the Blenheim surging with power, the sudden release of the brakes would surely give the machine enough impetus to get airborne once over the edge of the cliff – such was the theory anyway! In reality, once the machine had broken free, the air speed at the threshold was barely enough to allow flight. As the machine launched over the edge, the pilot had to push the stick forward to initiate a dive to the sea to gain sufficient flying speed to be able to level out and then attempt a climb away.

F/O F.E. Frayn, the gunnery officer from Swanton Morley, flew out to Malta with W/C Edwards in Z7423, GB-H, again accompanied by Sgt Knight and Sgt Quinn, to take up his post of squadron adjutant on Malta. He remembers the squadron's departure from Portreath:

> . . . proceeded to Portreath in Cornwall to await favourable weather conditions for the flight to Gibraltar. A few days later the met forecast was good and twelve aircraft took off, led by Wing Commander H.I. Edwards VC DFC. I flew with Edwards in the leading aircraft, with P/O Ramsay as navigator. The squadron flew in vics of three, separated at take-off by 5 minute intervals. We were to proceed in W/T silence at low level to hit land at Cape Finisterre and thence to follow the coast (but well out to sea), to reach Gibraltar.

Some of the aircraft managed to formate over the Scilly Isles, but they soon ran into fog at sea-level and became separated. Several of the familiar 'Squealer' fishing boats were seen off the French coast, but this time they had to be ignored, for to go after them would not only have made the Blenheims conspicuous but would have wasted very precious fuel, and the crews were all too aware of the limitations they were under in this regard. En route there was the chance that if an aircraft were to run into fuel difficulties, then it was possible to put down in neutral Portugal.

This did in fact happen to one Blenheim, and Sgt W.A. Williams, Sgt Griffin and Sgt Kay were subsequently interned. They later effected their escape and returned to their unit. This particular crew had been posted to Watton on the 12th, with P/O Buckley, Sgt T. Williams and crews, and it may be that they were travelling to Gibraltar with the latter who went out to Gibraltar on the 18th, albeit that P/O Jack Buckley and Sgt T. Williams were at Gibraltar at the same time as the main strength of the squadron. However, the official squadron records have the date of acknowledgement of their forced-landing in Portugal as the 27th! It is unknown whether or not Sgt Williams was carrying a passenger, but P/O Buckley was carrying S/L George Powell-Shedden DFC, a fighter pilot who saw action in the Battle of Britain, and who was now going out to command the Malta Night Fighter Unit.

P/O Hanafin remembers the long trip as follows:

> We flew fairly low most of the first two to three hours because it would have been wasteful of fuel to attempt to gain much height. I think we were at about 1,500–2,000ft until we were abreast of Cape Finisterre on the north-west coast of Spain. We had kept well out to sea until abreast of Portugal to avoid any chance of meeting enemy aircraft. Portugal was listed as a safe landing area if we were in any trouble. Our passenger [F/Sgt Taylor] sat alongside me and the Observer [Sgt Charles Hill] in the navigation position in the nose. I think they swapped position a few times to relieve the boredom. The hand-pump for transferring the fuel from the extra tank, situated in the area between the pilot and the WOp/AG, was operated by the passenger alongside the pilot, and could also be operated by the pilot. I think I did a token few strokes to relieve Taylor and Hill!
>
> I think the first land we saw after leaving the Scilly Isles was the north-west Spanish coast. I am sure we were both low and far away from the French coast when passing Brest. We remained in sight of Portugal, probably 20 to 30 miles to seaward until Cape St Vincent and then flew direct to the Straits of Gibraltar, being very careful to keep outside the limits of Spanish waters. For landing at Gibraltar we had been warned to keep over the runway if over-flying, or having to go round again. The Spanish border, only some 400–500 yards

from, and parallel to, the runway, was guarded by light flak which could be fired vertically from positions on the Spanish border. Aircraft which strayed across the border, usually inadvertently, had been fired on, and I believe some were either damaged or shot down.

By the time the Blenheims had been airborne for a few hours most, if not all, were running on separate tracks, with theoretically enough fuel for half an hour's flying when they arrived after their seven and a half hour flight. The fuel consumed often exceeded expectations, and many of the crews made sure that they did not need to go around again, for fear of running out of fuel within the circuit.

Arrival at Gibraltar could be hazardous in the extreme as W/C V.E. Pepper DFC found out when five of his 139 Squadron detachment arrived at about 20.00 hours on Sunday 11 May 1941. Maria Corrales Moya was a forty-year-old Spanish maid-servant, born in Gaucin, near Ronda, who lived in La Linea and worked for an Indian in Gibraltar. She had left her labourer boyfriend, Jose Portela Amusco, in La Linea to go to work and was standing beside some trees at the North Front main road (west side) with Maria Silva Sierra and two soldiers from the Gibraltar Defence Force. Until the incoming aircraft had all landed they were supervised by the police before being permitted to proceed across the road into Gibraltar. The last aircraft to land was Blenheim T2134, XD:B, flown by Sgt J.N. Dennis, who stated in a subsequent RAF Court of Inquiry on 12 May 1941 that:

> On arrival at Gibraltar I did a circuit of the rock and then made an approach which was too high so I did another circuit of the rock and made a second approach; this approach was very low and I had to open up the engines to clear the edge of the landing ground when I immediately closed the throttles. I floated across about half the areodrome when I decided to take off the flaps and attempt to go round again; this I did but immediately on taking off the flaps I stalled and hit the ground. I then decided that I could not get off again. Having touched down I was about 300 yards from the road which runs across the landing ground; not knowing that the road was there and having the sun in my eyes I imagined this to be the water and decided to swing the aircraft to the right into the wood, which I did. The aircraft ran through some barbed wire on the edge of the landing ground and knocked down three or four small trees; when I swung the aircraft and the sun was no longer in my eyes I saw some people running from in front of the aircraft but by this time it was too late to avoid them. Four people were hit by the aircraft or by the trees when I knocked them down.

Maria Sierra and the soldiers were injured, and Maria Corrales Moya was taken to hospital where she died of a fractured skull. The verdict was 'Death by Misadventure' and the recommendation made by the court was that:

> Pilots of aircraft are shown and made to understand diagrams of the Gibraltar landing strip before leaving England, and that they are told accurately the size, shape and nature of the ground on which they are going to land. That if possible the public are kept further back along the road so that the edge of the landing strip is free from people for at least 100 yards.

Ron Scholefield, Sgt Jackson's Observer for the flight, remembers:

> Our instructions at Gibraltar, when it did appear, were to approach the rock at an angle of 180 degrees, that is from due south, and flash the letter of the day at that time at the rock. So with the Aldis lamp pointing at the point of the rock when we approached it, I flashed the letter of the day, and a light half-way up the rock flashed back the appropriate sign. We made a circuit around the right-hand side of the rock. Now, it was most important that we made the landing 'first time go' because there probably wasn't sufficient fuel to do an overshoot to go

right round the rock and come in to land again. However, Bill Jackson did a marvellous approach, put the wheels down, put a bit of flap down, and came in on a powered approach very low over the sea, and dropped it down right on the beginning of the runway. We made a perfectly good landing and taxied up to the end.

A further account of the arrival at Gibraltar comes from Brian Hanafin:

I think we landed from east to west, and I well remember that the normal airfield circuit consisted of flying down the runway (to have a look at the *very* short strip) then doing a left-hand circuit over Gibraltar harbour and completely round the rock, keeping out to sea all the way. We were warned that over-flying the rock was very dangerous due to downdraughts caused by the wind eddying round and over the rock. Due to the very short runway we approached low and slow over the sea, aiming to touch down as early as possible, and to endeavour *not* to over-run into the sea at the other end of the strip. The start of the runway at the east end was right at the water's edge, but raised about 10ft above sea-level. At least one wrecked aircraft was visible just on the beach, having made too low an approach and hit the lip of the runway.

Edward Smith, P/O Duncan's Observer who flew Z9603, GB:F, to Gibraltar, recalls the first night's accommodation as follows: 'We slept in tents near the aircraft on the landing strip, which had formerly been the old racecourse, and seemed to consist mainly of very fine black ash, and everything was filthy.' Others were luckier and managed to find accommodation in a building near the cliff face for the night. In the evening a group were shown around Gibraltar, including a trip to see the big guns, hidden high in the rock, each of which ran out on rails to be fired. Later the party went into the town and found a restaurant for a meal, following which they ventured further in search of 'refreshments'.

The next day, Monday 28 July, the weather was again favourable, and the squadron made ready for departure, planned for 10.00 hours. The journey was to be direct to Malta in formation. Not all of the crews held formation, however, as the following accounts of the trip will show. Sgt Bill Jackson's Observer, Ron Scholefield recalls:

The following day [29th], we took off from Gibraltar on the very short runway, the engines overheated, spat and missed quite a bit when we got off the ground flying over Gibraltar harbour, in between the ships. We had to weave about in between the ships while the engines cleared as they had become oiled up whilst we were waiting for take-off. We then flew the whole way along the north coast of Africa, not seeing another aircraft at all, until we got just beyond the

En route to Malta, the squadron landed in Gibraltar. Their overnight accommodation consisted of bell-tents in the vicinity of the aerodrome, which itself was a disused horse-racing track. (via Ron Scholefield)

The disused race-course landing ground at Gibraltar, with several Blenheims parked in the distance, and the town of La Linea and the hills of southern Spain beyond. In the centre of the picture is the little wood where Blenheim T2134, XD:B is alleged to have crashed, hitting and killing Maria Corrales Moya. (The Trustees of the Imperial War Museum, London: CM6247)

north coast of Africa when gradually Blenheims started to appear from all directions and we slowly closed up into formation, went down to 20ft, and flew the last 150 miles or so to Malta. What a relief it was to see this little yellow streak on the horizon come into view.

Edward Smith further remembers:

We took off the following morning at 10.30 hours and we nearly didn't make it – some idiot had put most of the mail for Malta in our aircraft, which was already overloaded, as we carried our own spares as well. The only thing that got us off the ground was the fact that we ran off the airstrip, dropped on to the road leading to the frontier, and this bounced us into the air as we proceeded across the harbour, through the ships, flying below deck level! It was some time before we were able to reach about 700ft. We arrived in Malta at 18.00 hours, just after sunset, leading another aircraft who joined us en route. On the final leg, Bob Lyndall got a wireless bearing on Malta which was quite a bit different from my course, and it was getting quite hazy near sunset. Dunc asked me what I thought we should do. I replied, 'Stay on this course', which he seemed relieved to do. Some time later I caught a gleam of light on stone. We were dead on track for the island and a perfect landfall, which was good, because I think we had about 15 minutes of fuel left. Some aircraft I understand cut out on landing and had to be towed to dispersal!

Brian Hanafin in Z7504, GB-G, remembers:

Departure next morning was fairly early again, and I think from east to west. I seem to remember a very lumbering take-off and departure over the harbour, rather close to the ships' masts! I do not think we went to Malta in formation, although I do remember seeing other aircraft. Formation flying, due to having to alter throttle settings continuously, is more expensive in fuel consumption than flying as individual units. Due to the long distance which our overloaded Blenheims were flying, we were using the most economical power settings we could obtain. However, I remember using higher power settings when passing the Italian-occupied islands of Pantellaria and Linosa, just in case they had any airfields which might have had some Italian fighter aircraft. I think we carried a little over 8 hours' fuel at normal cruise speed, and as both the UK to Gibraltar and Gibraltar to Malta legs were over 7 hours each, there was not much to spare, in particular if you had to use maximum power to get away from trouble or to make a big diversion to avoid a convoy. We arrived at Luqa in the late afternoon of 29 July, just as an air raid was finishing or just about to start!

The question over the air raid was settled by 'Teddy' Frayn, who flew in W/C Edward's aircraft for the trip. He recalled:

> Good luck was necessary to reach Malta; an air raid in progress at the time of arrival could have wrecked the whole operation due to running out of fuel and the risk of attack from Italian fighter aircraft. We made it!

Most of the 105 Squadron Blenheims arrived safely in Malta after their flight. Sgt Ron Scott, Sgt Brendan Healy and Sgt Stuart Bastin had set out from Swanton Morley in Blenheim GB:R. Sgt Chapple kept a list in his diary for operational reasons, thus ensuring that aircraft were 'on the line' when needed. His entries cover all the Blenheims of 105 and latterly 107 Squadrons which arrived on Malta. There is, however, no entry for a 105 Squadron R-Robert at any time in July or most of August for that matter. The only 'R' which arrived was a 107 Squadron Blenheim, Z7643 which arrived on 28 August. The 105 aircraft apparently did not arrive at Luqa in Malta! So where did it go?

It is interesting, however, to note Derek Ransom's comment regarding the Gibraltar episode in *Battle Axe*, which states 'One aircraft had hydraulic failure and belly-landed at Gibraltar'. Furthermore, Sgt Chapple recalled that one of the groundcrew stood on a hydraulic pipe when loading an aircraft at Gibraltar! Although the squadron started operations on the 31st, it was not until they had completed three operations under both flight commanders that the very experienced crew of Scott, Healy and Bastin first appeared on the battle order three days later on 3 August!

So the squadron, or most of it, had arrived. Some crews, who had been sent on ahead from Swanton Morley to Watton, arrived on Malta the day before, on the 27th; these included P/O Jack Buckley in V6032, who was delayed in Gibraltar with his crew, P/O Douglas Ivens (Observer) and Sgt Reg Allen (WOp/AG). This particular crew had set out on Tuesday 18 July for Malta, but had had to return to Gibraltar because of engine problems. The CO had still not turned up, having been delayed in Gibraltar with spark plug problems, finally arriving on Malta on the 30th. W/C Edwards was not officially allowed to take an active part in flying operations, as the recent award of his Victoria Cross meant it was considered too great a risk as the authorities had other plans for him, as we shall see.

CHAPTER 13

Life on Malta

When the Blenheims arrived at Malta they touched down on the rough tarmac runway which stretched for 1,200 yards along the aerodrome at Luqa, a village centrally located on high ground south-east of and overlooking the Grand Harbour, with all the hustle and bustle of naval activity. This was the only tarmac strip on the island, although there were two other aerodromes. Luqa was primarily the home of the Blenheims, Marylands and Wellingtons, while the Fleet Air Arm's Swordfish (or 'Stringbags' as they were affectionately known), were based at Hal Far, to the south-east of Luqa. Hal Far overlooked the sea to the south of the island and had been a pre-war station. Between the two aerodromes lay a pair of landing strips called Safi; the intention was eventually to connect Luqa to Hal Far by this means, and providing a dispersal area for the aircraft. Ta'Qali, the third aerodrome, and the main fighter base, was located in the centre of the island, overlooked by the citadel of M'dina, and flanked by the large, imposing military hospital at Imtarfa.

Having arrived, the crews had to be found accommodation. The officers were given billets at Luqa, as were the NCOs for the first night only. Many pints of local lemonade were consumed that night as the crews attended to their initial dehydration. The officers' quarters were remembered by Brian Hanafin:

An aerial view taken from a 107 Squadron Blenheim captained by Sgt Johnnie Turner. (via Johnnie Turner)

> We were billeted at Luqa in stone buildings made from local rock. We were not far from the Officers' Mess which in our case was a large marquee. Our sleeping quarters had no glass windows, only wooden shutters. I cannot remember if this was to prevent any damage due to glass flying around in an air raid or whether the windows were designed not to have glass. The kitchen for our Mess was alongside but underground.

Due to the amount of bombing sustained so far by the island, this standard of accommodation was not surprising. However, as the German Fliegerkorps X had temporarily departed, the intensity of bombing on the island had been greatly reduced, at least for the moment. The worst was yet to come, but it wouldn't come until some time later. A few Italian raids were launched but these consisted mainly of incendiary devices dropped on the limestone rock buildings, which did less damage than high explosive. Jim Taylor recalls the onset of raids on Luqa Aerodrome:

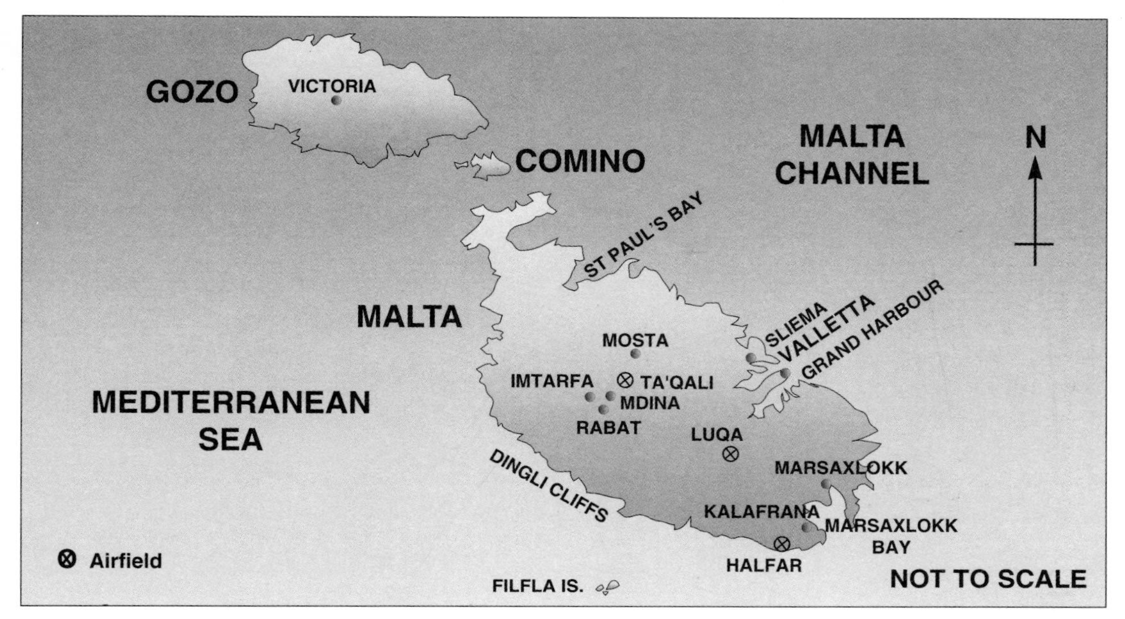

Malta, Comino and Gozo.

> Before the air raids started, the Maltese, who were working at the aerodrome in their hundreds, could be seen racing off across the 'drome with dust flying in their wake. The lads used to say, 'See that, Jock? There's an air raid due in two or three minutes!' And so it was, that the sirens would start two or three minutes later. Whether they had inside information or not I don't know, but they seemed to have a sixth sense and knew everything that was happening.

Other Maltese habits were also noted by Jim Taylor: 'They kept pinching our bikes, which we used to get out to our aircraft at dispersal. The Station CO, Group Captain Cahill didn't prosecute them however!'

Exchanges of fire occurred, notably in the evenings, as Frank Harbord recalls: 'At night the Italian bombers would come over, and as long as they did not come near to overhead, we would go and watch the flak and sometimes an exchange of tracer with the night fighters.'

F/Sgt Taylor also remembers the enemy's nocturnal activities: 'The anti-aircraft gunners were good, and the searchlight crews used to be able to pinpoint the enemy, and get them in a triangle. Our fighter boys would then go in and get them. You could see them coming down on parachutes. It was said that the Maltese used to chase after them and take their heads off with machetes, but I found that hard to believe.'

The lighter side of life was manifest, however; Jim Taylor remembered the mornings following such incidents: 'The first thing you would check when you woke up, was the smoke coming out of the brewery chimney. "Oh, it's all right boys, the brewery's still smoking!" would be the cry.' The chimney's smoke not only indicated the continued flow of local refreshment, but acted as a reliable wind direction indicator for many pilots on their approach to Luqa!

The next day, following their arrival, the NCOs were taken by bus to the picturesque little fishing village of Marsaxlokk on the south-east coast. The route followed some 5 miles of rough, stony, dusty roads, twisting their way down towards the sea. Eventually the bus passed

The 105 Squadron Officers' Mess at RAF Luqa consisted of a tent on the airfield. Seated outside are, left to right: F/O F.E. 'Teddy' Frayn (Adjutant); S/L Bryan Smithers (Pilot/Flight Commander); F/L Alfred 'Dunc' Duncan (Pilot/Flight Commander). (via F.E. Frayn)

the junction that led to the seaplane base at Kalafrana to the right, or to Valletta to the left. The NCOs' destination lay about 1½ miles ahead. However, prior to their arrival a tank obstacle comprising a roundabout composed of large concrete blocks had to be negotiated – it was eagerly and skilfully tackled by their Maltese driver. Further down the road, lay yet another tank trap, in the form of a light wooden bridge over a concrete-lined pit, its presence indicated by a pole erected either side of the bridge supporting a sign reading 'Fasten on to Farsons'. (This was the beer from the local brewery, which the air and groundcrew generally thought tasted rather synthetic. 'Blue Label' was generally considered to be the lesser of the two evils when compared to the 'Red Label', and both were available for about 6d a bottle.) The bus rattled inexorably towards the village past this last obstruction. The final obstacle was a steep hill, at the bottom of which, on the left-hand side, stood a large church overlooking a T-junction, immediately beyond which lay the bay. The church boasted two clocks, one on each spire. Only one of the clocks showed the correct time, allegedly so that if the Devil should be foolish enough to attempt to ascertain the time, he would surely be confused.

Looking ahead, Marsaxlokk Bay stretched around to the left in a sweeping curve as far as the rugged Delimara point. To the right along the sea-front, was a plethora of little fishing boats and barbed wire entanglements to deter any would-be invaders. The route took the bus along the sea-front road, past the local fishermen's houses and the 'Honeymoon Hotel', which was destined to become very popular with the crews. It was a large, two-storey building with a sea-view balcony on the top floor overlooking the bay, and was located on the corner of a street running away from the bay (it is now called Our Saviour Street). The hotel was owned by an Englishman with many years of naval experience, who had married a Maltese woman and settled down to live on Malta. Their son, Edgar Smith, was a tall lad, good at fishing and extremely proud to have been befriended by several of the aircrew, who frequented the hotel for meals and drinks, and with whom he would go fishing between their operations. He was enormously patriotic, and was able to recognize any aircraft which flew by. Indeed, when F/L George Burgess shot down the first enemy aircraft over Malta, Edgar went to the scene to collect a piece of canvas from the downed aircraft, a souvenir which he still has to this day!

The favourite dish at the hotel consisted of a plate of eggs and bacon, cooked in the traditional English way, the eggs coming fresh from the chickens which were resident on the roof. Drinks were always popular in the seething heat of the summer months, the best-liked being a 'Tom Collins' or a 'Lemon-Lemon' drink made from fresh lemons picked from the fruit trees in the hotel's little rear garden, fortified with a dash of red vermouth, and topped up with lemonade. Such refreshments were usually consumed in the little terraced courtyard, again located to the rear of the hotel, where the lady of the house would happily attend to the catering, as the airmen relaxed, reading copies of *The Times of Malta* and chatting amongst themselves.

Further around the bay lay a small slipway, opposite which, on the other side of the little dusty road, was a small hanger. The bus eventually stopped in a cloud of dust a few hundred yards from the hangar. The crews alighted to investigate their new home. For some this was to be home for much longer than the two to three weeks expected; however, for many others it would be much less, as their life-span was to prove tragically short.

Their quarters consisted of four, long, single-storey, flat-roofed, barrack blocks, made of yellow limestone, and situated one behind the other on a terraced hillside. The blocks were overlooked by a Bofors gun emplacement on the top of the hill above. There were twenty bed spaces in each block, with two little rooms at one end of each one. A further block situated at the foot of the terracing, nearer to the road, was used as an ablutions block. Attached to each bed in the barrack blocks was a mosquito net. At night when retiring for the evening, the airmen would carefully tuck in their net on three sides, but one side was always left free, so that if there was an air raid, the occupant could easily roll out and take cover beneath the bed. This probably provided a psychological benefit rather than providing physical protection, although it did protect them against injury from minor projectiles.

On the landward side of the road, with the barrack blocks to the left and behind, stood a yellow sandstone building. Formerly a private house, it had been taken over by the military, and was commonly known to the locals as 'the tea-pot'. This was to be their new mess building for the duration. A notice board was attached to the right of the door, which was used frequently for general information and also for posting battle orders. Inside, the mess villa was quite pleasant, with a room at either side of a central hall, and at either side to the rear. The hall terminated at a little staircase, which led to another four rooms upstairs.

On the ground floor the rooms housed a bar room on the right, a dining room on the left, with one of the rooms at the back containing a piano, which could be played by anybody. Ron Scholefield remembers:

The Honeymoon Hotel, photographed c. *1941. (via Edgar Smith)*

When we, or anybody, got back from

Interior view of the barracks at Marsaxlokk, Malta. Note the mosquito netting. (via Ron Scholefield)

> operations, if anybody was missing, then Tommy Williams, my pilot, would go to the piano, and very solemnly play with one finger the 'Dead March' from Saul. We would all gather round and sing along to it, and then we would have some beer.

However, the room was also used for happier occasions, when a local singer, affectionately known to some of the lads as 'Moaning Minnie', would give many a rendition to those assembled before her.

A beautiful anteroom was to be found upstairs, with French windows and a balcony enclosed by decorative wrought iron railings overlooking the bay. Here many a young airman would stand in contemplation, absorbing the view out over Delimara Point with the blue Mediterranean beyond.

Life at Marsaxlokk was generally fairly comfortable except for the occasional enemy raid, during which the Bofors gun emplacement would open fire, without warning, from its site above the barrack blocks.

Food at this time was served up in the Mess by Maltese waiters, and was generally of reasonable quality, largely made up of salads, corned beef, fruit, melons, and Maltese sweet cakes, which consisted of a flour-based mix with currants throughout. Ron Scholefield remembers that the bread was 'made with 60 per cent potato instead of flour, obviously because of the shortage of flour. Strangely, it was quite palatable, with a faint memory of the old potato-cakes which Grandma used to make. It was rather heavier than ordinary bread, and greyish in colour, but nevertheless was certainly quite edible, and I don't recall any shortage of butter.'

At this time, therefore, food was in reasonable supply, if not generally abundant. On one occasion P/O Applebee DFM, billeted at Luqa, was invited to dinner with some Navy

105 Squadron's Sgt Kindell enjoying the view across Marsaxlokk Bay, Malta, from the sergeants' mess. (via Ron Scholefield)

personnel. It appeared that the Navy brought food in from Alexandria, and so were not too badly off. Indeed when P/O Applebee arrived at the party in a wardroom at Sliema, he was confronted with a table liberally adorned with food. In pride of place was a boar's head, with an orange firmly wedged in its mouth. The relationship with the Royal Navy on the island was generally good, with parties such as the one described above. There were other social gatherings, such as an invitation received by P/O Applebee and his pilot, S/L George Goode DFC, flight commander of 'B' Flight, to attend a party at a large private house, again in Sliema. It was a grandiose, expensive occasion, attended by several naval officers, and after which the two RAF officers returned to Luqa by taxi. This rapport was not unique to the officer classes, and friendships were struck up between many naval ratings and squadron NCOs. This became a particularly strong bond when the submarine *Utmost* rescued three 105 Squadron sergeants from their dinghy, after they had ditched in the sea following a shipping attack on 12 September 1941. The only aggravation occurred when the three airmen returned to Marsaxlokk only to find that their chocolate and cigarette rations had already been shared out in the expectation that they were no longer on this earth! (Their story follows later; see page 175.)

Ron Scholefield remembers some of the other facilities available to the aircrew:

> We used to get a newspaper in the Mess every day and there was also a radio programme which was called 'Redifusion Malta'. The service radio from Malta was exceptionally good and all the wireless operators used to be very highly in praise of it, not only of its service but of the direction finding and of the clarity of its signals. It was explained to us at that time that the reason it was so good was that it was all pre-war equipment and all the equipment used had matched components.

As was inevitable, casualties began to result. The tradition in the RAF was for each man to nominate a friend, who, in the event of his death, would assemble his personal belongings, sharing out those items which would not survive a trip back home, or which may have been in such desperately short supply as to warrant their retention and use by others. This in itself was a demoralizing procedure, but it became even more so when the barrack blocks became so depleted that there were more empty beds than filled ones. In an effort to avoid this situation, and to keep morale up, it was common practice to keep people on the move, relocating the surviving airmen into the next block lower down on the hill, and thereby giving the impression that the occupied barrack blocks were full at all times. It was never possible to forget the casualties, but this way the reminder was not always present. However, the rate of attrition with regard to crews was severe, and no matter what was done to camouflage the fact, it was always sorely felt. Eddie Smith remembers:

> My time on Malta I didn't enjoy at all, in fact I hated the place, and to see day after day the empty chairs in the Mess growing more numerous, and particularly in the latter weeks, was very depressing.

However, on a lighter note, spare time was often spent swimming from the rocks adjacent to the barrack blocks or around the headland in a little bay below the rocky protrusion which overlooked Kalafrana. Swimming in the crystal clear waters was bliss after the blistering heat of Malta's summer sun. Frank Harbord further recalls:

> When we were not required at Luqa, we used to sunbathe on the slipway at Marsaxlokk, although we were always on call. We would swim in the creek where a Sunderland had been shot up and sunk by the Germans. It could be clearly seen through the water. While we were there an attempt was made to move it: hawsers were fixed to it and powerful tractors pulled them, but they only succeeded in pulling bits off. Walruses would alight on the water in the creek, and as they approached, they would extend their wheels and taxi up the slipway to the hangar.

Swimming near Kalafrana. Sgt Bill Jackson (Pilot) is in the centre, with Sgt Williams (Pilot) on the right. (via Ron Scholefield)

The hangar and the slipway were at the centre of some strange occurrences. Inside the hangar was kept a captured German Heinkel float-plane, perhaps an He 115 as it was taller and bigger than a Blenheim, which fitted neatly into the hangar where it sat quietly in its unobtrusive matt-black camouflage paint. Ron Scholefield noticed that:

> Into the bar in the Mess from time to time came two quite mysterious characters. Two men who were older than us presumably; looking back they were in their thirties. Both of them wore the ubiquitous khaki shirt and shorts. One wore an army sergeant's stripes on his arm, but no regimental badges of any kind. The other just wore a khaki shirt and shorts with nothing on them at all. They used to come in and were very friendly but talked rather guardedly about going over to North

Blenheim aircrew relaxing at Marsaxlokk Bay, Malta. (via Mike Henry)

> Africa from time to time, and having a lot of contacts over there. They wouldn't answer any questions about how they got there, or what they did when they were there, except that they had a lot of friends and they went from time to time and brought back information. This went on for quite a long time, and then one evening the German seaplane was wheeled out of the hangar, the first time we had seen it moved. It was taken down to the bottom of the slipway and launched. These two chaps came along and got into it, started up the engines, taxied round and eventually faced towards the exit to the harbour and took off. We watched the take-off and the seaplane disappearing into the distance. When it was almost out of sight, it suddenly turned into a bright flash of light, and presumably exploded. It was very mysterious for we never heard anything more about it, whether it had been shot down, whether it had been sabotaged, or whether there was an accident; the only thing we knew was that we never saw the two men again.

Sandfly fever was a major health menace, as was a complaint similar to dysentery and known locally as 'Malta Dog'. Sandfly fever in particular struck several of the squadron members during this period of service on the island. It was especially dangerous as it could – and certainly did – strike whilst the men were in the air as well as on the ground. Invariably this led to periods of local hospitalization, often within the confines of the large hospital at Imtarfa. The crews did not loathe Sandfly fever as much as might be anticipated, since many thought of it as a way of living for a few more days, escaping the grim reaper. The other unfortunate aspect of such sickness was that men who had fallen ill would be replaced by a stand-in crew member, and should the aircraft not return from an operation, this would result in other crews becoming decimated as well.

The aircrew relaxed by swimming and sunbathing in between operations. One minute they were relaxing, the next they were fighting for their lives. (via Mike Henry)

There were, however, lighter moments in the course of incarceration due to illness, as Brian Hanafin remembers:

> I was put into the Army hospital with severe Sandfly fever. I do not know what causes it but it has similar symptoms to malaria. A few others from 105 Squadron also got Sandfly fever. In the next bed to me in hospital, was a Hurricane pilot who, as he got better, used to go out of the window at night, taking a pillow case with him in order to bring back bottles of beer. As we were on the first floor, some 12ft from the ground, I am not sure how he managed the return journey without the Army nurses catching him! When I came out of hospital, I was sent for five or six days to a convalescent hospital on the shores of St Paul's Bay. We were woken up there one night to help rescue a Swordfish crew who had ditched in the bay about a mile off shore, on a moonlight night. The Swordfish sank, but the crew were saved, and celebrated their rescue with us until breakfast time. By then they were so full of the local beer and wine, that they did not want to go back to the airfield!

Apart from spare time spent in and around Marsaxlokk, occasional trips were made in the yellow and green camouflaged liberty bus to Valletta, which had been severely bombed. The bus would return in the evening from Floriana. Frank Harbord noted that the Maltese were:

> very pro-British at that time, and whenever a building was knocked down by bombs, the locals would crawl out of the rubble and write on any bits of wall still standing, 'bomb Rome' in white paint or something similar. The King awarded the George Cross to the island, and everyone deserved it for the way they stood up, but they never did get the satisfaction of seeing Rome receive the same treatment they had suffered.

Brian Hanafin recalls that the trips into Valletta were, by necessity, tempered by caution:

> Whilst on Malta we were all required *not* to wear our aircrew badges [pilots' wings, or

Marsaxlokk Bay, Malta. Note the twin-spired church and the flying boat in the bay. (via Ron Scholefield)

> navigators' and air gunners' half-wings] in order to lessen the tension which sometimes erupted between the Army and the Air Force. The British Army personnel based in Malta became somewhat resentful of the attention and publicity given to the activities of the Air Force and Navy, and it was felt that we should not emphasize our aircrew status. Also, medal ribbons (such as Hughie Edwards' VC) were not worn. The Army, through no fault of their own, felt frustrated at being unable to take an active part in the war. The only Army units taking an active part in the Battle for Malta were the anti-aircraft gunners, many of whom were members of the Maltese service units.

Nevertheless, visits to the capital were very much enjoyed and provided the opportunity to get haircuts, meals, drinks, souvenirs and to visit clubs and so on. There were also the seedier parts of the town, such as the end of the long Strait Street (or 'The Gut' as it was known), which narrows as it terminates near the harbour and Fort St Elmo. This was a must for sightseers, but for any self-respecting young aircrew lad, was to be viewed whilst avoiding any involvement. The

A Maltese street, c. *1940. The piles of rubble in the right foreground were the result of bomb damage. (via Ron Scholefield)*

youngest squadron member, Sgt Stuart Bastin, had an interesting experience here, as remembered by Eddie Smith:

> Stuart was the baby of the Mess and looked like a schoolboy – I remember not long after we arrived, we all went on the liberty bus to Valletta and of course went down to 'The Gut'. Two 'ladies' at the door of an 'establishment' took a fancy to Stuart and tried to get him inside, but he managed to escape, which was a source of great amusement for days after.

Jim Taylor had similar memories, and those of 'The Gut' were never to be forgotten:

> I went out with the aircrew lads and we went down to 'The Gut'. It was a really tough area. We went into a place for a drink, and had bottles of beer. Half-way through our drinks, whilst we were not in the slightest bit inebriated, this big fat woman came out and started dancing and singing lewd songs. She used 'different' actions; the boys were disgusted, so we all stood up and walked out! I couldn't describe it, it was horrible. I thought I had seen everything before that, but no!

It must be remembered that the groundcrew were also very active on the island, their lifestyle revolving around maintenance of the aircraft to the highest standards possible with the limited facilities available, and repairing damage to the returning aircraft, often badly battered and holed, and sometimes covered in the blood of the poor young unfortunates who had endured hell within. Sgt Chapple summed up the life of the groundcrew:

> Luqa was a permanent station, so the basic camp had permanent buildings with temporary additions. Our billets were bungalows and I shared a small room [known as a 'bunk' in the RAF] with a very nice chap [aircrew] who had been injured in a Wellington prang. He had recovered and was awaiting transport to North Africa. He was very good when I had Sandfly fever, fetching and carrying for me. We had no mosquito nets, as these were in short supply, so operational aircrew had priority. The Mess was a permanent building but had received a direct hit so was only half of its original size, the open end having a tarpaulin draped over it.
>
> We occasionally got out. Some excursions were only as far as the local village, to take in and collect laundry. Occasionally we got into Valletta which meant a very rocky trip in a bus, a walk around the town and a look at the shops; not much in them but we always looked. Then a visit to 'The Gut' for the odd beer and a meal and a look at the harbour.
>
> Evenings were usually spent in the Fleet Club, untouched then, for more beer and another meal. I remember we used to sit on the battlements and watch the air raids. We were not often bothered during the day, but were shot up on the odd occasion by Macchi C.202s.

A typical Maltese street, c. *1941. (via Ron Scholefield)*

Strada Reale, Valletta, Malta. (Grand Studio, via A.G. Mee)

The groundcrews did sterling work in extremely difficult conditions on Malta, earning a great deal of respect from the men who flew the Blenheims they serviced. Here 105 Squadron groundcrew are working on the starboard engine of one of their Blenheims at RAF Luqa, Malta. (via Maurice Chapple)

The groundcrews' daily food at camp during the Malta detachment was described by Maurice Chapple:

> Our meals hardly varied from beans or tinned bacon at breakfast time and tinned stew, the famous Machonochie M and V! On our excursions into Valletta, we were able to get eggs, bacon and chips; I don't think it ever varied.

It was not unknown, however, during air raids, when the local Maltese had temporarily departed from the scene, for large quantities of grapes to be taken into 'permanent custody' from the vineyards adjacent to Luqa Aerodrome. Also adjacent to the aerodrome were rifle ranges, where the groundcrew would expend many rounds of ammunition, much of which had been removed when not required in the aircraft. The daily practice sessions at the rifle range were actively encouraged, as there was always the threat of impending invasion.

Maurice Chapple described the groundcrews' work and the associated technical difficulties encountered on the island:

> On Malta we changed complete engines in the open. Changes were usually due to loss of power caused by the ingestion of dust. The engines were fitted with sand filters, but they were either not efficient enough or became clogged so quickly that we had to remove them. The biggest job on Malta was the removal of crashed aircraft from the take-off strip. The only lifting equipment was a light mobile crane which was no longer mobile (we had to tow it by tractor), and a hand-wound wooden tripod with one of its supports very horribly bowed! We found a very robust two-wheeled truck which at some time had held fitted equipment of

105 Squadron Blenheim V6014 GB:S waiting in the hot Mediterranean sun at dispersal on Luqa aerodrome, Malta. Note the makeshift limestone 'chocks' inserted in front of and behind the wheels – on Malta necessity was the mother of invention as mechanical shortages mounted. (The Trustees of the Imperial War Museum, London CM1357)

some sort. The drill, if the undercarriage was u/s, was to lift one side a little and chock the wing up with a stone – there were plenty of these on Malta as the soil is very shallow and the rest is rock. (Indeed in the days of sailing ships, soil would be freighted in as part cargo and building stone taken away as ballast.) The fields were small and the stone walls terraced, so we had a good supply of dressed stone. We would lift and chock alternately, until the truck could run under the fuselage. Then we would remove the lifting gear and kick the supporting stones away. This was rather hazardous! With luck, the aircraft would fall with a crunch on to the trolley and we would tow it away. Far from standard practice, this! It was very much frowned upon if further damage was caused by crash removal.

Refuelling equipment was steadily improved as the war went on. At the outset, the standard refueller was a 450-gallon trailer, the pump operated by a frequently temperamental Lister engine. This was hand-cranked and as the engine was about shoulder high, required qualities of strength and determination! We had these on Malta. Petrol was also commonly supplied in very light, tinplate cans. I suspect this was in order to save on weight and thereby carry more petrol per lorry. Two 4-gallon cans were packed in a wooden crate with a nailed top. As the nails sometimes punctured the cans, leaks were quite common, and 'full' cans were sometimes empty. Rough handling also caused leaks and the fire hazard must often have been considerable.

Such therefore was life on Malta, to be endured throughout the days of attrition and carnage which endlessly gnawed away at those who daily put their lives on the line in Malta's defence.

Prior to the arrival of 105 Squadron, 110 Squadron had been operating Blenheims on Malta for 2 Group, and had taken a typical mauling throughout the duration of their stay. One of their number left a poignant reminder of this, and what lay in store for the 'new boys'. Frank Harbord remembers: 'They left a notice over the ops room door for our benefit; it read, "Welcome to 105 – and how!". After a week or two on Malta we realized the depth of the feelings that made them put up the notice.'

CHAPTER 14

Maltese Operations Begin

At last, after all the journeying and settling in, the squadron was put on standby from the morning of Thursday 31 July 1941. At 18.40 hours, S/L George Goode DFC, flight commander of 'B' Flight, flying Blenheim Z7503:J, was at the head of a formation of six Blenheims lined up on the Luqa runway. Rumbling their way into the Mediterranean sky, they formed up over the island into two vics of three, before dropping down to sea-level for the long flight to the Italian-held island of Pantellaria. One hour and three minutes later, the remains of a convoy were spotted about 50 miles from Pantellaria, at an angle of 200°, and the flight prepared to draw first blood in the Mediterranean.

The largest of the four merchant vessels in the convoy was approximately 8,000 tons. The Italians were well aware that it was a prize target, for it was protected by a force of six destroyers and a cruiser! Fighters of the Regia Aeronautica were also in attendance to provide aerial support; four were patrolling above and two at sea-level around the convoy. It seemed suicidal for the Blenheims to attack such a formidable target without cloud protection. Moreover, Standing Orders not to attack naval vessels were still in force, and with so many guarding the prey, any attempt to attack the merchant vessels would mean braving the intense barrage already being thrown up by the naval vessels in anticipation of an attack. As the Blenheims closed in for the attack, discretion was considered the better part of valour, and in order to avoid the total annihilation of his force, S/L Goode decided to abort the attack and the Blenheims set course back to Malta. They didn't escape totally without damage, however.

Although the formation had not flown through the hail of naval gunfire, the cruiser's fire had been very accurate: one of the shells fired at the bombers at a range of a mile had exploded loudly between the wing and tail of Sgt Bill Jackson's Blenheim, Z7240:M, much to the discomfort of the air gunner. Hot shrapnel had scythed through his turret, cutting one of the goose-neck ammunition feeds to his machine-guns, as well as cutting the wireless aerial support which was left whiplashing violently along the fuselage in the slipstream.

As the Blenheims turned away from the convoy, a twin-engined Italian bomber in its distinctive brown camouflage was seen lurking in close proximity; on being sighted it soon flew away. The fighters, however, had different ideas: the two that had been buzzing around the convoy at low level decided to pursue the Blenheims, leaving their four comrades in position to protect the ships. The fighters homed in on Sgt Jackson's already damaged Blenheim, opening fire at 300 yards as they closed for the kill; the damaged turret meant that the Blenheim could offer no answering fire. Despite the repeated attacks from above and below, Jackson's skilful but frantic flying, guided verbally by the WOp/AG, prevailed and the fighters gave up their prey and retreated. Sgt Jackson, Sgt Ron Scholefield (Observer) and Sgt Allan Tuppen (WOp/AG), were left shaken but miraculously uninjured. Jettisoning their bombs to increase speed, the formation headed back to Malta, where by 20.50 hours all had landed safety at Luqa, the last twenty minutes having been flown in darkness.

The squadron's first operation in the Mediterranean was over without loss, and the crews had been given their first taste of bright cloudless skies and a new enemy. However, this loss rate could not, and would not last. It was decided that the convoy was not to be permitted to reach its destination and consequently, F/L Wylde and his crew from 69 Squadron took off at 05.30 hours in reconnaissance Maryland AR714, his mission to locate the convoy. By 07.20 hours the intelligence officers at Luqa had received a report stating that the convoy had been spotted steaming at a steady 10 knots towards Tripoli – the hunt was on. This time it was the turn of the young South African S/L Bryan Smithers, flight commander of 'A' Flight, to lead the rest of the squadron on their first crack at the enemy in Mediterranean waters. In Luqa's old subterranean briefing room below the watchtower, six crews were ordered to attack the convoy, still reported to consist of five destroyers escorting four merchant vessels each carrying vital supplies for the enemy's army in North Africa.

At 08.00 hours the six aircraft were airborne and after two hours and forty minutes all of them were safely back on the island, the crews being debriefed. Why had they not attacked the target? Were the risks too great because of destroyer barrage, or had the agile little CR.42 biplane fighters been too overwhelming in numbers? The answer was somewhat less dramatic – nature had taken a hand in the day's events, reducing maximum visibility at sea-level to only four miles. Having failed to find the target in the designated target area 90 miles off Tripoli, the crews had had to turn around and head for home. It was frustrating for the 'Brass' perhaps, but a relief to the crews that they would live to see another day.

Their respite was not to last long, for at 17.40 hours another three aircraft were finishing pre-flight checks before lifting off along the stony, yellow runway on their way to find another target. On the way back from an early morning reconnaissance flight around Sicily and then south to Lampedusa, F/L Tennant's Maryland located shipping in the harbour at Lampedusa.

F/L Ben Broadley led the Blenheims, closely followed by his wingmen P/O Hanafin and Sgt Bendall in a vic of three. The leader's aircraft, Z9605:U, successfully found the target and F/L Broadley prepared his formation for the run-in. A destroyer lying close to the two target vessels presented a formidable hazard. One of the wingmen, Sgt Bendall, stuck close to the leader during the attack, while P/O Hanafin looked for but could not locate another target and so jettisoned his two 500lb bombs in a position south of the harbour.

Meanwhile, the leader and his wingman were in +9 boost, rushing in low at the two ships. Suddenly, a burst of anti-aircraft fire, presumably from the destroyer, smashed its way into F/L Broadley's starboard engine. Undaunted, he pressed home the attack, both aircraft dropping their bombs on their targets; within seconds, a cloud of debris and black smoke poured skywards as the bombs ripped into the ships' hulls, detonating violently. But success had its price – sturdy as the Blenheim IV was, the flak had taken its toll on the leading aircraft; as it flew off it gradually lost height, until it touched the water, reared up and then dived into the sea to the south of the island.

F/L Ben Broadley and Sgt Victor Marsh (WOp/AG) were picked up from their dinghy some time later by an Italian rescue launch, and became prisoners for the duration. Sadly, P/O Alister Stewart Ramsay (Observer), who had been awarded the DFC on 8 July for his actions during the Bremen raid, died of his wounds and became the squadron's first Mediterranean casualty. Some time later F/L Broadley was held in Stalag Luft 3, the infamous prison camp in Germany whose story was told in *The Great Escape* and which led to the subsequent demise of F/L Cyril Swain in March 1944.

The two remaining crews returned to the island where they landed at 19.10 hours for debriefing, during which they related the sad news to the officer in charge. The next day the Maltese newspaper *The Times of Malta* contained a report on the raid, which stated that 'Two merchant vessels of 300 tons each were hit by several bombs, and wreckage could be seen floating high in the air. Bombers also attacked and silenced machine-gun posts.'

On Saturday 2 August the inevitable telephone call came through to the Operations Room, calling the crews to duty. But this time the target was not sea-borne but land-based; they were to attack the barracks at Misurata, housing troops and ammunition vital to Rommel's campaign in

North Africa. The RAF was required to 'neutralize' them before they could reinforce the German Army and advance further, possibly into Egypt itself. Three aircraft were detailed to carry out the task, led by F/L Jack Buckley, also a veteran of the Bremen raid, with F/O Hubert J. Roe and P/O Peter H. Standfast as his wingmen. Soon after 13.00 hours, the three Blenheims soared up into the sky, bumping over the thermals, and as they left the island, dropped down to 50ft.

Landfall was made to the east of the target and the leader's aircraft, Z9603:F, turned to starboard followed by his two wingmen. As usual when attacking a land target in North Africa, after crossing the coast they had chosen to fly along the Benghazi Road which they followed at low level for mile after mile, until the target eventually appeared on the right hand side. A pile of shells sitting in a yard made a tempting target for the leader's bombs. Turning inland the Blenheims began their bomb run. The formation swooped low over a herd of terror-stricken gazelles, stampeding under the aircraft, their hooves stamping up the desert dust; they presented a strange sight to a crew of Englishmen more accustomed to seeing cattle or sheep fleeing across lush, green European fields. (Even the temperament of the local inhabitants was different. On sorties to France or Germany, farmers would stand, hay rakes in hand, watching sullenly as the low-flying formations of Blenheims thundered across their fields. Arabs tending their flocks of startled goats produced an altogether different reaction, glaring skyward in anger, shaking their hands violently in the air as if wishing to reach upwards and pull the intruders out of the sky. Indeed, it was not unknown for nomadic tribesmen to take a pot-shot at the passing crews. The difference between European and Arab farming people was perhaps a matter of scale as much as ethnic temperament – whereas the European would be upset at having his milk cows disturbed, for the Arab, his small herd of goats and perhaps a camel would constitute his only source of food or income and therefore was arguably much more precious a commodity in relative terms.) However, having duly made their presence felt, the three Blenheims sped off northwards back to base, where they all arrived safely at 16.00 hours.

On Sunday 3 August 1941 Intelligence reported another target – ships in the harbour at the Libyan port of Tripoli, a very highly defended target. At the briefing by W/C Edwards VC, DFC, five crews were detailed to take off at dusk, with S/L George Goode DFC leading the attack. A recce photograph was displayed for the apprehensive crews to study. It had been taken that afternoon by F/O Drew and crew of 69 Squadron, in Maryland BS760. During the sortie they had flown to Tripoli where they discovered no less than twenty merchant ships with an escort of eleven destroyers. The Blenheim crews gathered around, each selecting a target according to their position in the formation for the run-in.

Around 19.00 hours five Blenheims were taxiing along the Luqa dispersal area ready for take-off. This time Z7503:J was in the lead, followed by P/O Alfred L. Duncan, Sgt Jimmy G. Bruce, Sgt Ron J. Scott and Sgt Tommy Williams with their respective crews. By 19.07 hours all five were airborne and forming up above Luqa. As the aircraft left the island, they dropped down to sea-level. The air gunners fired their usual test bursts to check the guns, and operated the turrets to ensure the integrity of the hydraulic control. Shortly after take-off hydraulic problems beset one of the Blenheims. Sgt Jimmy Bruce, with his crew Sgt Adam H. Flett (Observer) and Sgt Henry Gibson (WOp/AG), had to break formation and return to base. Meanwhile, the remainder pressed on, droning their way towards the enemy to claim their targets. After an hour or so their target appeared ahead of them. This time, instead of achieving landfall at a remote point and attacking from the landward side, the formation hugged the waves and approached in a determined spearhead at right angles to the harbour. Along the right hand side of the harbour were several anti-aircraft positions, already well alerted to the incoming enemy, who had been spotted coming from the horizon. As they approached the harbour, the pilots pushed their controls into the +9 boost position and the engines surged with power.

Fortunately for the Blenheims, throughout their run-in the anti-aircraft gunners had had their angle of elevation incorrectly set and their streams of flak arced above the low-flying Blenheims and spectacularly obliterated parts of the shore on the opposite side of the harbour. The largest target, a 12,000-ton ship berthed south of the naval basin in the centre of the harbour, was attacked by the leader's aircraft at 20.35 hours. As the side of the ship loomed up in front of him like a wall of steel, S/L Goode jerked the bomb release and delivered his bombs, smack into the side, amidships. Then, as he hauled his machine up and over the ship's hull, his air gunner had the satisfaction of seeing the explosion several seconds later, as the bombs detonated.

One crew's job was complete, but what of the others? Alongside S/L Goode was P/O Duncan, who with his crew Sgt Smith and Sgt Lyndall, attacked (and is believed to have hit) two medium-sized vessels. Sgt Williams and his crew Sgt Shufflebotham and Sgt Green attacked an 8,000-ton ship lying alongside the 'Spanish Mole'; one of their bombs exploded near the funnel, setting it on fire.

The anti-aircraft gunners, although initially inaccurate, quickly adjusted their sights and hit Sgt Williams' aircraft. Sgt Scott meanwhile dropped his bombs on the local Air Headquarters; during the attack his aircraft was also hit by flak several times, causing damage to the flaps and fuselage.

Having delivered their attacks, the crews broke off and climbed, each pilot finding his own way back to Malta. Three hours after setting out, the Blenheims returned home. Three of them landed without incident, but Sgt Tommy Williams' aircraft, Z7408:K, had been badly hit, not only in the well, but also in the hydraulics and flaps. Without hydraulics, a wheels-up landing was inevitable. It was already after 22.00 hours as he approached Luqa and darkness had well and truly settled in. Although the Mediterranean was not pitch black at night, landing at night with a damaged aircraft was hazardous in the extreme. However, Sgt Williams brought his kite in for a very controlled belly-landing, bringing his crew down safely, if rather shaken, as they ground to a halt.

Through a mixture of good luck and skill, 105 Squadron had returned from Tripoli without loss: they are believed to have been the only Blenheim Squadron to have done so.

On 6 August 1941 *The Times of Malta* reported on the raid saying:

> RAF bombers carried out a successful attack on shipping in the harbour of Tripoli on August 3rd. One merchant ship of 800 tons was hit by heavy bombs and the violent explosion which followed threw a great quantity of wreckage into the air. Two direct hits were obtained on military buildings which were also machine-gunned.

At 10.10 hours on Monday 4 August, a recce mission was flown by 69 Squadron's Sgt Matt and crew in Maryland BS423. They had flown first to Tripoli, where a torpedo boat and nine merchant vessels had been spotted steaming towards the town of Misurata, at the entrance to the Gulf of Sirte on the North African coast. Misurata itself was found to be harbouring a merchant vessel. The Maryland returned in mid-afternoon and two Blenheims were soon despatched to deal with the lone ship, taking off at 17.00 hours.

F/O Roe and his wingman P/O Standfast could not find the intended target, but instead came across an 8,00-ton W/T schooner. The crews fused their 250lb bombs in readiness for the attack. The leader raced in at the schooner but his bombs missed their target. P/O Standfast followed him in, and three of his bombs ripped into the ship. The ship was doomed, and was last seen listing heavily to starboard. In a vain attempt to protect the schooner, shore-based anti-aircraft batteries opened up, but to little effect. Soon the two aircraft were droning back to Luqa, where they landed at 20.00 hours. This was the first ship these crews had attacked since joining the squadron and they had the satisfaction of having done a good job, with a ship to their credit already.

Although the hunting had been good on this day, it was not always to be so. The next day's sweep was to the enemy-held island of Pantellaria. F/L Wylde and his crew from 69 Squadron had been up in their Maryland AR714 between 07.00 and 09.10 hours, on a patrol from Pantellaria to Marittimo Island off Sicily, where two merchant vessels had been spotted nearer the mainland, off Marsalla. Consequently, on Tuesday 5 August S/L Bryan Smithers led P/O Jack Buckley, P/O Alfred Duncan, and Sgt Tommy Williams to find and attack the two merchant vessels off Marsala, Sicily. In the event, the only targets they could find were two small fishing boats lying 6 miles to the south of the northern peninsula of Cape Bon in Tunisia. The boats were east of Pantellaria, heading in a north-westerly direction. Shortly after 13.00 hours the formation pounced, but scored no hits and the aircraft turned away.

Fifteen minutes later, however, a suitable target unexpectedly appeared in the form of a convoy containing several medium-sized merchant vessels and two much larger ones. Having already attacked the fishing vessels, the Blenheims no longer had full bombloads, and just to make matters worse, the convoy also had the protection of two Regia Aeronautica Savoia-Marchetti SM.79 Sparviero bombers, or 'Hawks'. These three-engined bombers were each protected by three 12.7mm Breda-SAFAT machine-guns, with a laterally firing 7.7mm machine-gun housed in the centre. In this close support role, they were a fair match for the Blenheims. Faced with such unfavourable odds and having only a minimal chance of success, the crews abandoned the convoy and returned to base, touching down three hours and ten minutes after setting out. They then reported their find to the intelligence officer at Luqa.

The day's excitement was not over, however, as an anti-shipping sweep had been planned in the Gulf of Sirte at dusk. In the late afternoon two crews took off. Sgt Ron Scott was leading, with Sgt Jimmy Bruce from Buckie in north Scotland flying as his wingman. Sgt Bruce's regular observer had gone down with Sandfly fever and was replaced on this mission by Sgt Ron Scholefield. When the two machines arrived in the Gulf of Sirte, no shipping was to be seen. Consequently, in accordance with their Standing Orders, a land target was sought as an alternative – and what better target than the barracks that stood east of Misurata?

This wireless-equipped 800-ton 'squealer' schooner was attacked and sunk on 4 August 1941 near Misurata, Libya. (via Brian Hanafin/Len Fearnley)

The view from the departing Blenheims after the 'squealer' attack on 4 August 1941. (via Brian Hanafin/Len Fearnley)

The Blenheims ran in fast and low, dropping their bombs smack on target. A great billowing cloud of dust and debris was thrown high into the sky, obscuring the WOp/AGs' view of the resulting damage, but confirming that their presence had been well and truly felt. And so with the action over, the two aircraft swung out to sea, setting course back to Luqa. On the way back darkness closed in and twenty minutes after leaving the target area, the machines were droning back to Malta without any visual navigation aids.

The normal procedure under these circumstances was for the aircraft to navigate back to the island, and when they were a few miles out each wireless operator would break the strict radio silence and transmit his aircraft's MSI to the DF Station. Prior to departure, each aircraft was given a separate MSI; for security, these MSIs were changed at approximately four-hour intervals each day. In addition to this, the IFF (Identification Friend or Foe) set was switched on to indicate the return of a friendly aircraft. Another feature available to the aircraft was the QDM. The wireless operator would send out a continuous note on which the receiving station could take a bearing. They would then transmit the aircraft's exact position to the wireless operator. Naturally, this procedure was only employed when the aircraft was near enough to Malta to be down and safe long before an enemy could intercept.

But it did not all go quite according to plan for Sgt Scott and Sgt Bruce, however. When Sgt Bruce's wireless operator, Sgt 'Gibby' Gibson contacted Luqa, he reported that the ground station was transmitting the words 'Hurry, Hurry'. This was most unusual. In response to a question from the pilot he confirmed that they were indeed using plain language. The pilot, although somewhat amused, considered they were going as fast as they could, and carried on regardless. The transmission was soon to be explained, for as Malta came into sight, the sky above it was illuminated with hundreds of long white spikes of light weaving their patterns in the night sky. It dawned on the crews that an air raid was in progress and they were going to fly straight into it! Their identification signals were duly transmitted and the aircraft were delayed

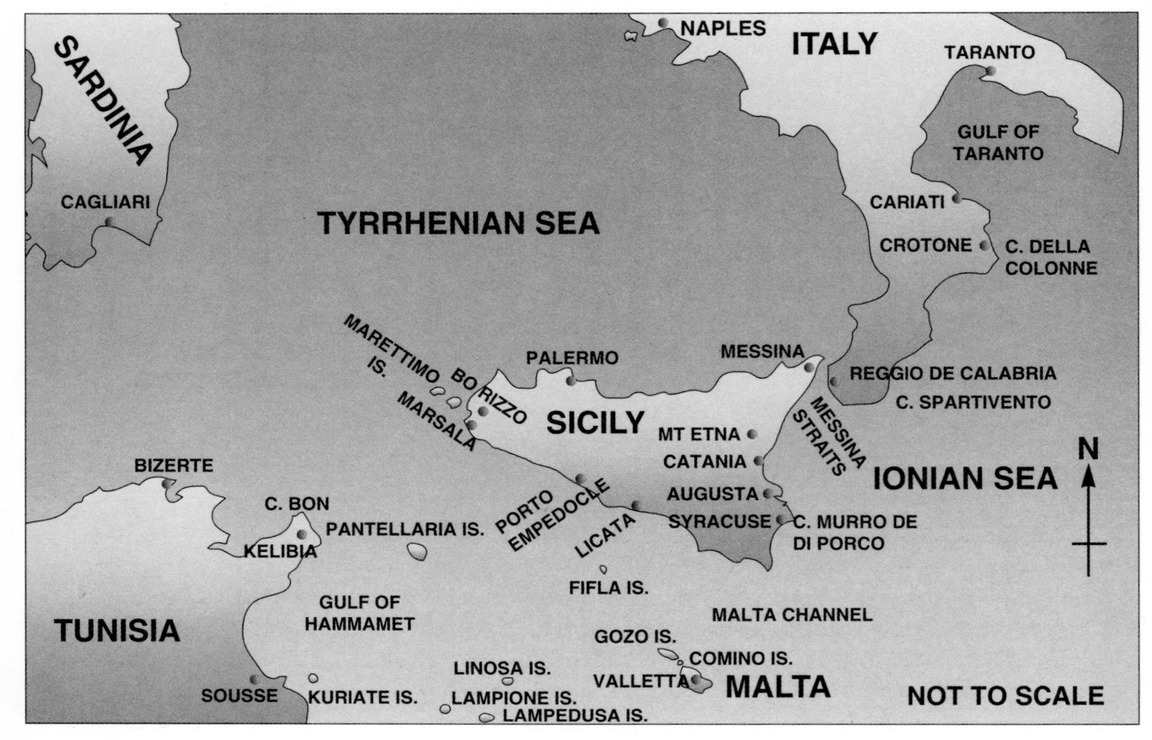

Sicily and Italy.

while a flare path was specially lit for them. Landing some two hours and forty minutes after take-off, they bumped down on to the stony runway, noticing as they slowed down, that the goose-neck flares were being extinguished in the aircrafts' wake with considerable urgency. At the end of the runway the usual little motor truck waited to lead the returning kites to the dispersal point. This too was done much more expeditiously than usual. On jumping down from the wing-root walkway, the crews were met with the rather obvious greeting of 'Hurry up, there's an air raid on!' They then made their way to the underground operations room, below the pile of rubble that served as the control tower, to be debriefed by the waiting intelligence officer.

The air raid had not in fact touched Luqa, although bombs had been dropped on the island. No serious casualties had resulted, but damage had been done to some governmental and civilian properties. The raiders paid a heavy price for their actions, however, as night-fighter Hurricanes based on the island later intercepted them. Three intruders were sent to a watery grave, with one fighter pilot being credited with two of the kills. It was a victorious night for the RAF, and it was also a night for boosting civilian morale, as the downing of the raiders had been witnessed by many of the public, who turned out eagerly to watch in admiration as their protectors engaged in combat far above them.

CHAPTER 15

A Real Stinker

Wednesday 6 August was to see the beginning of a two-day sustained effort to hit hard at the enemy. Tripoli was the destination for six supply vessels, carrying vital supplies for the Afrika Korps. A substantial escort consisting of five destroyers and a torpedo-boat was provided for the merchant ships. Sgt Bibby in his Maryland of 69 Squadron spotted the convoy and its escort south-west of Pantellaria. The convoy was heading south towards Tripoli, passing between the Kerkenna Bank off Tunisia to the west, and the island of Lampedusa to the east. The Blenheims of 105 Squadron were ordered to attack that afternoon.

At 15.00 hours the leader F/O H.J. Roe took off with P/O J. Buckley, P/O A.L. Duncan and P/O B.D. Hanafin and their crews. Having located the convoy, they found that in addition to the reported escort force, there were also three Italian Fiat CR.42 'Falco' (or 'Falcon') fighters. These small, highly agile fighter-biplanes were armed with one 12.7mm and one 7.7mm gun (later types had two 12.7mm guns), and had a maximum speed of 267mph at 17,485ft. With a range of 481 miles the Falcos posed a considerable threat to the under-armed Blenheim. It would have been suicidal for the four aircraft to launch an attack on such a heavily defended convoy in broad daylight. The fighter protection only strengthened the argument. The attack was therefore aborted and the formation returned to base to report.

It was subsequently decided that the convoy should be attacked under cover of darkness. Fairey Swordfish of 830 Squadron of the FAA, operating from Hal Far, were detailed for the task. They took off in two waves, the first wave commencing at 18.45 hours and the second wave ten minutes later. Each aircraft carried a torpedo with a duplex pistol. The attackers were met by a heavy barrage, which lit up the night sky like a fireworks display against a backdrop of target flares. However, the Swordfish carried out their attack with determination, leaving one 8,000-ton merchant vessel sinking by the stern, with another belching flames and also going down.

Although 105 Squadron's Blenheims had not attacked on the 6th, they were off again on the 7th in search of the same convoy. This time the original four were reinforced by another four machines, making a total of eight, and the attack was to take place at dusk, improving their chances of success still further. At 04.45 hours the two waves of four aircraft lifted off from Luqa into the darkness.

The first wave was led by the flight commander, S/L George Goode DFC. He and his three followers, F/O Roe, Sgt Jackson DFM and Sgt Williams, set off and returned without finding the convoy but the other group was more successful. They found the target about 60 miles south of Pantellaria. Each aircraft was carrying two 500lb bombs for maximum effect. For the pilots who found the ships, the attack was to be, in the words of the leader's WOp/AG, P/O Eric Applebee DFM, 'a real stinker'.

First to sight the target was P/O Standfast, who went for an 8,000-ton merchant vessel, while P/O Hanafin attacked another and claimed a 'probable'. Next, P/O Buckley in Z9604:D broke formation and chose a target. Hearing anti-aircraft fire cracking around his aircraft, he had to take sudden violent evasive action as streams of glowing tracer laced their way towards him, interspersed by exploding shells. It was one of the most hairy sorties he and his crew had been on. Meanwhile P/O 'Dunc' Duncan was caught by the anti-aircraft fire. The tail, wing and fuselage of his aircraft were peppered and the tail wheel was severely damaged. Duncan's observer, Edward Smith, recalled:

> . . . Lost the other aircraft in the darkness – came daylight, alone and just about to turn for home when convoy sighted. Dunc asked me what I thought we should do and in my ignorance said 'have a go'. I think this was the worst operation I have ever been on! The convoy escorted by four or five destroyers was of two fairly large cargo vessels and on the run-in we were repeatedly hit by pom-pom fire from the destroyers (we had to pass between two) and unable to make height, I dropped my bombs alongside a ship and we turned on the run-out getting hit repeatedly, but everything kept going. We were just relaxing, thinking we were out of range when a shell hit the tail wheel, removing about half the rudder, damaging the tailplane and making quite a mess. We also lost the trimming control so poor Dunc had the weight of the aircraft on the stick – it was quite heavy, I know, because I held it for a while. We landed with a heck of a screech with no tail wheel and taxied into dispersal. The aircraft was a mess, the wings gashed like it had been done with a tin opener in about seven or eight places from leading edge almost to the ailerons – main spars burst, holes everywhere, but all three crew untouched. The aircraft was propped up on barrels and people on the squadron went out to look at it.

Somehow, all the aircraft had found their way back to base. After two hours and forty minutes of sheer hell, miraculously all landed safely.

The attack of the 7th was over, but the next day was to give no respite. Late in the morning, a lone Hurricane purred its way into the bright blue sky. F/O Adrian Warburton of 69 Squadron was off on one of his lone sorties again. For an hour and a half he stooged around the eastern Sicilian ports of Catania, Augusta and Syracuse. In addition to several bombers and seaplanes, he sighted a concentration of shipping in Catania harbour. When Warburton returned at 11.30 hours, this information was reported and the Blenheims were brought to readiness. That evening, at 19.20 hours, as a green flare flickered its way into the Maltese sky, the Blenheims once again began their take-off rolls down the Luqa runway. On climb-out, they circled and formed up into two neat vics of three, before dropping down over the coast on a northerly heading towards Sicily.

After about half an hour, Sgt Jackson DFM and his crew, Sgt Scholefield and Sgt Kindell, had to return to base with engine trouble, their entire flight lasting only fifty minutes. The remaining Blenheims wave-hopped their way to the target with S/L Goode leading. Eventually, they reached the south-east tip of Sicily and steered a north-westerly course towards Catania, one of the island's main ports. As they entered the inlet, the leader looked with dismay at a formation of enemy aircraft building up at some distance in front of him. Remarking to his crew that he didn't like the look of things, they nevertheless continued for a few minutes until full realization dawned – the enemy aircraft formation consisted of no less than thirty Fiat Falcos! Faced with such formidable opposition, the entire flight would have faced certain death if the attack had gone ahead. Consequently, George Goode swung his aircraft back on a course for home, followed closely by P/O Roe, P/O Duncan and lastly P/O Buckley in Blenheim Z7420:M.

However, P/O Standfast, with his crew P/O Sorenson (Observer) and Sgt Hoare (WOp/AG), was determined to hit the target come what may. Whether they had not seen the leader swing away on a course for home, or whether they thought the formation was splitting for the attack is unclear. Radio silence was mandatory. Whatever their motivation, they reached the harbour and sighted a 2,000-ton merchant vessel tied to the quayside; in they went, releasing their bombs at the target. Ironically, despite their brave efforts, each bomb splashed impotently into the rippling waters beside the ship and failed to do any damage at all. It was a disappointing result from a determined effort. By amazing good fortune, the fighter force did not intercept the lone aircraft. Perhaps the lone Blenheim went undetected, or the enemy were reluctant to break such a large formation for such a small fish; we may never know. However, the marauding crew returned safely, as did the remainder of the flight, all touching down around 21.50 hours for yet another night landing at Luqa.

On the 9th, S/L Smithers was off again in vic formation with Sgt Scott and Sgt Jackson DFM as his wingmen, followed closely by P/O Standfast, P/O Duncan and Sgt Bruce in another vic of three. As they bumped upwards into the Maltese thermals, their intention was to attack a couple of merchant vessels, reported to be steaming along under cover of the North African coast between Bwayrat Al Hasun in the Gulf of Sirte and Misurata, possibly heading for Tripoli or Benghazi. Both ports were in enemy hands since the British forces had retreated back to Egypt in mid-April 1941. The flight proceeded as usual at wave-top height in the blinding sun and heat until they reached the coast just east of Tripoli, where they turned to follow the coast towards Misurata. The search for shipping proved fruitless and so secondary land targets were chosen. The road from Tripoli to Benghazi was the only main road linking the two ports, and because of the nature of the surrounding terrain, this lone highway provided a vital communications link, along which troops, ammunition, food, petrol and general supplies were moved. This provided easy pickings for the RAF, and 'picked' they certainly were!

P/O Standfast and his group decided to have their customary swipe at the Misurata barracks. Their bombs ploughed relentlessly into the barrack buildings, which certainly would seem to have been full of troops, judging by the convoy of about fifteen lorries parked near the roadway, presenting yet another tempting target. They were soon left in varying degrees of dilapidation, some overturned and others a twisted fiery mass. As the bombs were exploding, round after round of .303in bullets were tearing into the vehicles to secure the kill.

So what of the other three aircraft? On a previous sortie in the area, a dump of packing cases had been noticed on the south side of the road. The contents were unknown but it seemed a worthwhile target nevertheless. Sgt Jackson, with his crew, Sgt Scholefield and Sgt Kindell, attacked the dump. Three bombs were seen to explode, sending the debris of the cases and their fragmented contents cascading high into the air. The leader's other wingman, Sgt Scott, found another large dump. This one was protected by an anti-aircraft site, which suggested a degree of importance; Sgt Scott decided to find out why! Their aircraft was thrown into +9 boost and surging with power it was launched at the target. The Blenheim lurched upwards, as the bomb doors jerked open under the weight of the falling bombs. Seconds later, in a blinding flash, the packing cases erupted violently, sending smoke and dust high into the African sky. This had been no small success. Considering the violence of the explosion, the target had almost certainly been an ammunition store and these vital supplies had been completely destroyed. On the way over the target, the aircraft passed the ack-ack site. Sgt Bastin opened up with his twin Brownings, raking the position for good measure. Near the store, several petrol tankers received similar machine-gun treatment.

As for the leader, he had found three auto-trailer petrol tankers but his bombs had missed and the tankers escaped destruction. Not so for the occupants of a saloon car which was, unusually, painted in blue and presented an obvious target for the passing air gunner who strafed it and left it in flames.

After the attack, the course was set for home and Sgt Jackson DFM got to Bwayrat Al Hasun before turning out to sea, harbouring thoughts of safety and eventual sleep following what had been a very satisfactory operation, denying the enemy a variety of supplies left burning on the dusty roadway, and which was to set the trend for similar future attacks.

This petrol tanker was attacked by Blenheims as it drove along the coastal road between Tripoli and Benghazi in Libya. A departing Blenheim is visible in the top left corner of the photograph. (The Trustees of the Imperial War Museum, London: CM1501)

The next day, Sunday 10 August was to be anything but a lazy Sunday. After a recce flight by F/O Williams in his Maryland BS760, news came in of a new target. An unescorted merchant vessel was reported to be at a position 70 miles south-west of Lampedusa, heading north, and its elimination was left to S/L Goode DFC who was detailed to lead F/O Roe, P/O Buckley and a new crew who had been sent as replacements from 88 Squadron, Sgt 'Bill' Brandwood, Sgt Jock Miller and Sgt Tony Mee who were destined to make quite a name for themselves.

By 17.30 hours the machines were surging their way up the Luqa runway. However, as P/O Buckley had been completing his pre-flight checks, he felt uneasy as the port engine revs seemed abnormal but not sufficiently so to require an aborted take-off, which could be easily misconstrued as his going LMF. Shortly thereafter, they were powering up the runway with the yellow stone buildings of the little town of Luqa blurring in the distance as the machines lifted off, but seconds later, to the horror of the crew, the port engine cut out completely. A Blenheim was never terribly good on one engine and for one to cut on take-off often meant ending in a fireball on the ground amid exploding bombs. With this in mind, Jack Buckley utilized every ounce of his vast experience to keep the aircraft in the air; ensuring that the bomb fusing panel was correctly set to jettison the bombload, he jerked the release and his bombs spilled out and fell into the disused quarry which lay at the south-west end of the runway. As previously mentioned, the quarry was a well used site, with many a crashed aircraft seeing its final resting place there, so much so that it became affectionately known as 'The Graveyard'! Buckley's problems were far from over. On impact, after the expected 11-second delay, the jettisoned bombs exploded. This should not have happened, as the bombs were not fused. There was going to be an awful uproar if, or rather when, the C/O heard about it! Buckley turned the Blenheim into the good engine, which was slower but the only safe way to turn the aircraft under these circumstances, and then completed a half-circuit before landing again. A few minutes later, a camouflaged staff car arrived and out stepped W/C Hughie Edwards VC DFC. Aircraft Z7420:M was down and still in one piece and the crew were safe, but the CO wanted to know exactly what had happened and why the bombs had exploded. After exhaustive questioning, he satisfied himself that there had been an engine fault and that the pilot had acted properly; nobody had been hurt so the matter was laid to rest. It had only been a 35-minute operation for the crew, but it had brought them just as close to 'failing to return' as any enemy action could have.

Meanwhile, in the dusk, the remaining three machines ploughed on relentlessly. Eventually, on the last leg of a search to the north-east of the Kerkenna Islands, lying off the Tunisian coast, the hunters found their quarry – and they could hardly believe what they had discovered. The ship was there all right, exactly where it had been reported. However, it was seen to be flying the French flag! When the ship's crew spotted the Blenheims, they started to run up various message flags. After some consideration, it was decided that the vessel was Vichy French. The feeling was that if it was friendly, it would have indicated its position beforehand. It was therefore decreed that it was an enemy ship trying to confuse matters and the leader went into the attack. Unfortunately, all of the other aircraft had the same idea and pounced simultaneously, with the result that most bombs overshot. However, the leader had been more accurate and one of his bombs hit the stern of the ship, which was left sinking. The formation closed up and headed back to base to find out what had happened to their comrades in 'M' for Mother. The next day, a Maryland flight could only find oil floating on the sea – the ship had been committed to the deep.

When first sighted on 10 August 1941, this ship was seen to be flying the French flag. However, when the crew spotted the Blenheims, they started to run up various message flags. After some consideration the leader decided that the vessel was Vichy French and it was attacked and sunk. (via Brian Hanafin/Len Fearnley)

These were not the only events of the day, however, as at 10.00 hours, F/L Wylde of 69 Squadron had taken off to survey the proceedings in the Sicilian ports of Catania and Syracuse. Near Catania they saw 7 Junkers Ju52s, 16 bombers and around 38 fighter aircraft on the aerodrome. However, more significantly for the Blenheims back at Luqa, six merchantmen and a torpedo-boat were harboured in Catania Bay. As the Maryland flew over, the Observer, Sgt Mutimer, logged all the details and photographs were taken. The photos would finally be produced at a Luqa briefing, allowing the Blenheim pilots to select their targets and decide on the overall direction of attack. All went well, until some distance from home, the Maryland's crew radioed in that the aircraft had suffered an engine failure on the starboard side and was limping back on the port engine alone. The ground personnel waited anxiously as the machine came in on its final approach. Tragically, the Maryland crashed just short of the runway at 11.43 hours, killing Acting F/L Paul Wylde and Sgt Richard Mutimer instantly. Sgt Campbell Clark was taken to hospital where he died the next day. All three airmen's bodies were laid to rest on Malta. Sadly this was not the only incident of its kind and was to be repeated often before the war was over. From an operational point of view, however, all was not over. The Observer's log and the camera were found intact, and the information from these was produced at a briefing late that afternoon and formed the basis for another go at the enemy by 105 Squadron.

S/L Smithers led three aircraft which left at 19.15 hours. After half an hour he was back on the ground again with instrument failure, his air speed indicator having packed up. P/O Duncan took over the lead in Z9604:D and with Sgt Scott and Sgt Bruce in formation they headed for the target. As they closed on the ships, the leader's gunner reported that there were still fighters in the area, and looked with horror as the enemy turned towards their approaching Blenheims. Immediately, P/O Duncan wheeled the formation around and with +9 lbs of boost selected, beat a hasty retreat back to base, landing one hour and twenty minutes from departure, as the last machine touched down at 21.30 hours. Regrettably, the reconnaissance information gained at such a heavy price had not resulted in a successful operation, but for the lightly armed Blenheims to have attacked shipping defended by so many fighters could only have resulted in further tragedy.

CHAPTER 16

Meet the Enemy

Taranto Bay in southern Italy had been the scene of the gallant attack on the Italian Navy by twenty-one 'Stringbags' of 815 and 819 Squadrons of the Fleet Air Arm on the night of 11 November 1940. As outlined in Chapter 11, the result was the loss or damage to three battleships with two destroyers and two cruisers seriously damaged or sunk. In fact, nearly half the Italian Fleet was lost, resulting in withdrawal of their navy to the safer confines of Naples at the order of their Supermarina. South of the Gulf of Taranto, however, lies the town of Crotone, which harboured a small factory producing nitrates for explosives. Intelligence officers had focused their attention on this factory, and subsequently the Blenheims of 105 and other squadrons on Malta were to pay it some close attention.

On 11 August 1941 the chemical factory was to be the subject of an attack by two waves of three aircraft, the first leaving at 16.15 hours and the second 37 minutes later at 17.52 hours. The first wave was led by S/L Bryan Smithers with F/O Hubert Roe and Sgt 'Bill' Brandwood as wingmen. Unfortunately, this formation made their landfall too far to the north. Peasants stood in fields tending their hay with rakes, as the low flying Blenheims flew parallel to each other down a small valley. Some walked along with their rakes over their shoulders, watching, while a large man sitting on a donkey was seen in the lead of this party. As well as local peasants, the military were in evidence. Two soldiers in their green uniforms looked up, but unlike their civilian countrymen, on seeing the three aircraft come thundering in low towards them, they took to their heels and ran, terrified, into a nearby pillbox for shelter!

105 Squadron attacked the railway line leading south from Cariati in the Gulf of Taranto on 11 August 1941. Here Sgt Brandwood's bombs explode in the bay. (via Brian Hanafin/Len Fearnley)

The tremendous spray from bombs bursting in the bay during the Cariati attack on 11 August 1941. (via Brian Hanafin/Len Fearnley)

Not all the bombs fell in the sea: here bombs can be seen exploding on the railway line. (via Brian Hanafin/Len Fearnley)

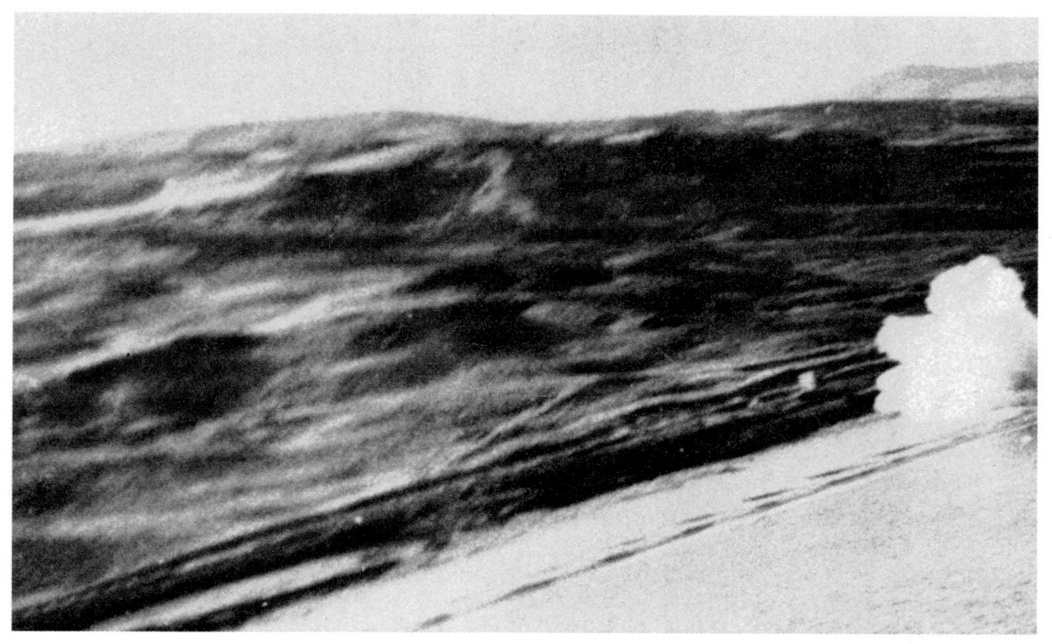

Bombs exploding on the beach near the railway line. (via Brian Hanafin/Len Fearnley)

P/O Eric William Applebee DFM (left), discussing tactics with fellow officers outside Blickling Hall in 1941. (via Eric Applebee)

By 18.10 hours the formation neared the bay. The chemical works was nowhere to be seen, nor was the town of Crotone! They had in fact found the town of Cariati, some miles north of Crotone. A local railway line made a suitable communications target for one of the aircraft, while the others attacked buildings, detailed in the squadron records as barrack blocks. F/O Roe was credited with 'direct hits', while Sgt Brandwood's bombs missed the target, splashing into the bay beyond some fishing boats where they exploded, creating large circular plumes of water but doing little damage. The three aircraft then retreated for home, landing at 20.15 hours.

Navigation by the other three aircraft proved more accurate, but for one crew in particular, the sortie was to prove traumatic. The leader was S/L George Goode DFC, one of the longest-serving flight commanders in the squadron. His Observer, Sgt Nichols, was standing in for Sgt Frank Harbord who had fallen victim to Sandfly fever and was laid up in the military hospital. As usual, the WOp/AG was P/O Eric Applebee DFM, a well-respected member of the squadron.

Apart from having been being personally invited by Hughie Edwards to join the Malta detachment from 18 Squadron, P/O Applebee had gained quite a reputation for developing a technique of shooting down fighters following at sea-level. At just the right range, he would shout to the pilot, who would then throw the engines into +9 boost and haul the aircraft skywards, effectively mimicking a shipping attack. As the machine rotated, forcing its nose upwards, the WOp/AG would get a clear field of fire over the tail. P/O Applebee DFM was reputed to have simultaneously shot down two Bf 109s over the North Sea with this tactic; many another crew would surely have come to grief!

This then was the crew leading P/O Peter Standfast and Sgt Ron Scott. All three machines had lifted off at 17.52 hours, their target appearing ahead of them as the previous three Blenheims were arriving back at base. As usual, the briefing at Luqa had been held in the subterranean limestone room with its hot, stuffy atmosphere. The intelligence officer was asked about the target and the likelihood of it having substantial defences. The confident reply came back, 'Don't worry, old boy, there's not a bloody thing there!' W/C Edwards VC, DFC then brought the briefing to a conclusion and the crews dispersed. The plan had been to arrive in the half-light at dusk, but it was still bright daylight when the crews made their intended landfall, several miles to the north of their target. Racing along at the customary 50ft from the deck, the three aircraft split up and followed each other along the road in a southerly direction to intercept the town of Crotone.

The first into the attack was George Goode, who swooped in low towards his prey. During the run-in, he noticed a staff car heading at speed away from the factory, and immediately signalled his WOp/AG to attack it. This he did with a long burst from the turret's guns. Each aircraft was loaded with two 500lb bombs. As they ran up to the target, S/L Goode operated the bomb release, the aircraft lurching upwards in response. At least one bomb successfully penetrated the building and exploded, but as they prepared to leave the scene, P/O Applebee reported curiously over the intercom, 'I've only seen one bomb go off, George!' It was therefore decided to break off over the harbour and go round again, with the intention of 'shaking' the remaining bomb out over the target, rather than trying to jettison it in the sea on the way home.

Meanwhile, the other two machines were looming up rapidly to the rear. Their attacks unleashed their full bombloads smack into the chemical works, leaving behind a mass of flames and smoke – it certainly wasn't going to be in production again for some considerable time. (It was, however, to become the centre of attention again at a later date.) During these attacks, S/L Goode was making a turn to port to go around again. While crossing the coast, the harbour was seen to be full of little boats, including a number of corvettes. Suddenly, extensive small-arms fire erupted – they had awoken a hornet's nest which was not supposed to exist! As the aircraft banked, the port engine was raked with gunfire and a cloud of what appeared to be black smoke erupted into the slipstream. The gunner quickly reported to the pilot, 'we're on fire!'. 'No, it's not smoke, it's oil,' came the reply. Whatever the nature of the problem, it was causing severe difficulty as they searched for a possible crash-landing site. The aircraft continued its turn and ran over the factory again, but despite the pilot's attempts to shake the bomb off, it appeared to remain attached. By now the limping Blenheim was crossing the harbour once more. Struggling at the controls, desperately trying to gain height, S/L Goode eventually made it over to the other side of the bay. To their left they could see the other two aircraft flying side by side, as they disappeared back to base. Both arrived safely, although Sgt Scott and his crew emerged safely after writing off a probably very flak-damaged V6307:N when coming in to land. The crew were safe but the 'Graveyard' received yet another carcass.

The feeling of isolation was intense back at Crotone, as the pilot and observer strapped themselves in tightly. The gunner, having initially stayed in his turret, moved back into the centre well and lay with his back against the dinghy, in the hope that it would absorb at least some of the impact, as he waited for touchdown.

Eventually, towards the edge of a cliff at Cappo delle Colonna, enough height was gained to reveal a field lying dead ahead. Here at last was the landing site where Z7503:J lurched to a halt. The crew leapt out into the field, and according to instructions, proceeded to destroy their documents. All that was left to be done was to set the machine on fire, thereby preventing it from falling into enemy hands. Hacking a hole into the top of one of the petrol tanks, they struck match after match, but try as they might, almost unbelievably they could not set it alight. They even went to the extent of using Very cartridges and still nothing happened, much to their exasperation. The consensus of opinion was that they would have company at any moment, and their suspicions soon came to fruition when shots suddenly rang out, followed by the swish of bullets above their heads. Hurriedly, the crew threw themselves flat on their faces and on looking up, met the enemy face to face on the ground for the first time. Displayed as if in a pageant, were twenty-seven Italian soldiers, apparently drawn up in ranks. The front row were kneeling, with the back row standing behind them, all pointing their rifles at the three unarmed airmen. As an extra measure of protection, the Italians even had a machine-gun aimed at their captives, with an officer standing to one side, his hand raised to beckon his men to start shooting again should their three captives show any resistance. P/O Applebee stood up with his hands in the air, only to be shot at again. He threw himself to the ground again, surprised but unhurt. Next S/L Goode tried the same thing and received similar treatment. Finally, P/O Applebee stood up for a second time, as the Italian soldiers advanced towards their three captives. When they got closer, the crew were surprised to see that the soldiers actually looked rather frightened, even though they were many in number and armed to the teeth.

Suddenly, amid the confusion a lone shot rang out. An Italian naval officer clambered up from the direction of the coast to join the scene. He was Captain Val Dambrini, who had been in one of the small naval vessels in the harbour, and on hearing the shooting had decided to investigate for himself. Armed with only his service pistol, he took control of the situation and the crew were relieved to be placed in his custody.

Meanwhile, during all this excitement, a small fire had actually started on the aircraft, only to be quickly extinguished by the soldiers. The crew, thinking there was still a bomb on board, wanted to put a safe distance between themselves and the crashed Blenheim. They told their captors of the danger on board, explaining that a violent eruption could be imminent. Nobody seemed to take much notice, even though the officer spoke English. Perhaps they had not been close enough to a bomb to realize what happened when 500lb of RDX/TNT mix exploded! To their relief, a few minutes later the crew were escorted from the scene by Captain Dambrini. At

1	2	3	4	5	6	7	8	9	10	11	12	13	14	15	16	17	18	19	20	21	22	23	24	25

Personalkarte I: Personelle Angaben

Kriegsgefangenen-Stammlager: Stalag Luft 3

Beschriftung der Erkennungsmarke
Stalag Nr. 228325
Lager: IV B

Des Kriegsgefangenen

Name: APPLEBEE
Vorname: Eric William
Geburtstag und -ort: 8.10.19 Liverpool. Engl.
Religion: C.o.E.
Vorname des Vaters: Frederick William
Familienname der Mutter: Wilson

Staatsangehörigkeit: Engl.
Dienstgrad: F/Lt.
Truppenteil: RAF Kom. usw.:
Zivilberuf: Berufs-Gr.:
Matrikel Nr. (Stammrolle des Heimatstaates): 44982
Gefangennahme (Ort und Datum): Italien 11.8.41
Ob gesund, krank, verwundet eingeliefert:

Lichtbild

Nähere Personalbeschreibung

Grösse	Haarfarbe	Besondere Kennzeichen:
1,73	d.braun	

Fingerabdruck des rechten ! Zeigefingers

Name und Anschrift der zu benachrichtigenden Person in der Heimat des Kriegsgefangenen

Feder. Will. Applebee
7. Ridderdale Rd. Liverpool 15. Engl.

Wenden!

Beschriftung der Erkennungsmarke Nr. Lager: Name:

Bemerkungen:

Personalbeschreibung

Figur: schlank
Größe: 1,73 m
Alter: 24 Jahre
Gesicht: oval
Haare: dkl. braun
Bart:
Augen: braun
Nase: etw. Höcker
Gewicht: 65 kg
Schädelform: oval
Gesichtsfarbe: ges. - gebräunt
Gebiß: o. B.
Besondere Merkmale:
Deutsche Sprachkenntnisse:

Der Kgf. wurde am 2.5.44 im Oflag Luft 3
nach Art. 70 Kgf.-Abk. v. 1929 [illegible] vorgestellt.
~~Seine Heimkehrberechtigung wurde [illegible] bejaht.~~
Eingetragen i. d. Befundliste d. Oflag Luft 3, Sagan
Lazarett Ort
vom 4.5.44 unt. lfd. Nr. 1

The identification card of P/O Eric William Applebee DFM, prisoner of war no. 228325 at Stalag Luft 3, Lager IVB. P/O Applebee (WOp/AG) was shot down with his crew while attacking a chemical works at Crotone, Italy, on 11 August 1941. The pilot, S/L George Goode DFC, survived and was taken prisoner with P/O Applebee and their observer, Sgt Nicholls. (via Eric Applebee) gun-point they made their way down to the bay, where the party went aboard his small boat, which was similar to a little corvette. The captain, who also spoke reasonable English, explained that he had an English wife, which made the crew a little less tense for the duration of their brief voyage.

Once at the other side of the bay, they were discharged to a naval station, where they were bundled under guard into a cellar, just below ground level. A small barred window, the top half of which was at street level, allowed fresh air and a degree of sunlight into what was to be their resting place for a week or so. Some of the local women came to take a closer look at the captives and satisfy their curiosity. Their minds alive with hatred over the bombing of their town, they then proceeded to shower the interior of the room and its occupants with spit.

P/O Applebee still had his pocket cigarette case which contained ten 'Craven A' cigarettes, as well as a photograph. On discovery of this precious booty, his captors had confiscated the cigarettes and the photograph, but actually returned the cigarette case, such was the shortage of tobacco at the time. Time passed by slowly and boredom set in. To relieve the tedium, they made up a set of playing cards on some paper, but the Italians, thinking they were formulating some form of secret code, confiscated the lot!

Eventually, the three airmen were removed and taken to Regio de Calabria, from where they were bundled on to a truck, once more under armed guard. After a rough ride, they arrived at an airfield at Centocelle, approximately 5 miles south-east of Rome, where they were again interned in rooms, individually this time. The rooms were very hot and stuffy but at least the occupants were to be well fed. Food was brought to their rooms by an Italian cook, who would arrive every day with his cheerful greeting, 'Whata you wanna eat this day – I got fruits, fishes anda meats!'

It was not all quiet, however, as an interrogator soon arrived from Rome and proceeded to 'interview' the prisoners. After a considerable period of incarceration within their rooms, P/O Applebee demanded to speak to the officer-in-charge. When he eventually met the commandant, he advised him that according to the Geneva Convention they were entitled to at least two hours of exercise each day. Whether this was technically correct or not was irrelevant. That night, each of the airmen was taken up to the roof for exercise, during which time their jailers stood guard on the edges of the rooftop parapet walls; it was not exactly a compound to walk about in, but it provided a welcome if brief respite from their stiflingly hot daytime accommodation.

F/L Alfred 'Dunc' Duncan photographed as a civilian; this picture would have been used on forged documents for him to produce in the event of recapture by the enemy following an escape. (via Mrs Peggy Duncan)

Eventually they were moved on, and after a northerly journey, arrived at Piacenza where they were put into an officers' jail, having left their Observer, Sgt Nicholls, at Centocelle. The jail was an old monastery, of hexagonal shape with a courtyard to the front. They spent some time in the company of captive Greeks, and later they were joined by naval and Army officers. Finally, after making a suitable nuisance of themselves, George Goode and Eric Applebee were decanted to a civilian jail. Situated on top of a mountain overlooking the village of Gavi, approximately 20 miles from Genoa, this was the Colditz of Italy. Conditions were most unpleasant as the building was damp, miserable and inhabited by other 'trouble makers' and scorpions. The commandant was one Guiseppi Moscatelli, who was intensely disliked by all. Here the two 105 crew members remained until Italy capitulated, although the captives were not subsequently released, and after further journeying through Austria and Germany, they ended up in the notorious Stalag Luft 3 – a camp specially erected to contain all their 'rotten eggs in one barrel'. Here they met their old comrade F/L Ben Broadley, who had been the first to be shot down on Maltese operations on 31 July 1941. The prison camp became infamous for its 'Great Escape' and the subsequent disgraceful slaughter of fifty escapees by the Gestapo. Fortunately, unlike many others, these 105 Squadron airmen were not involved. They were, however, involved in the 'Wooden Horse' episode, but that is as they say, another story.

CHAPTER 17

Back to Ships

There was no major operational activity on 12 and 13 August 1941 and the squadron stood down, allowing some time for the pursuit of more leisurely activities. All that is except P/O Hanafin and his crew, whose leisure activity was rudely curtailed late on Tuesday 12 August. On returning from a night out in Valletta, a note signed by the Adjutant, F/O F.E. 'Teddy' Frayn was found pinned to the operations board in the officers' mess tent. It read: 'P/O Buckley (or if not in, P/O Hanafin). To take aircraft F from aerodrome to dispersal at 05.30 hours on Group Captain's orders. Ground crew will stand by at 05.30 hrs.' This was duly complied with and Blenheim Z9603:F was soon dropping bombs on motor transport garages and workshops at Bardia on the Libyan coast some 75 miles east of Tobruk.

However, for the remainder of the squadron only two days' respite were available, and on Thursday 14th, 69 Squadron's F/O Adrian Warburton set off in search of further quarry. While patrolling the coast of Tunisia in the mid-morning sun, he spotted a couple of merchantmen with seaplane escorts off Lampedusa, but it was not until later that he found the day's target: three large schooners and a merchant vessel south-east of the Kerkenna Islands and heading for Tripoli. The Blenheims of 105 Squadron were about to be put to work again. That afternoon, at 15.00 hours, P/O Standfast led Sgt Scott, Sgt Bruce and Sgt Bendall on a square search south of the Kerkenna Islands. However, search as they might, no shipping was found and the tired crews returned three hours later, to touch down once more on Luqa's dusty runway at 18.00 hours, weary after their fruitless search.

Difficult as it may be to believe, returning from a sweep on which the enemy had not been located could be every bit as tiring – if not, strangely, more so – than completing an attack. The pre-sortie nerves, the heat and sweat at take-off took their toll. Would this be the always dreaded time when the engines would fail on take-off? Would the aircraft survive the attack without being jumped by enemy fighters and shot down, or without falling foul of the rain of hot metal pouring skywards to form a deadly cloak around the target? These questions were always in the back of the crews' minds. To prolong the agony of waiting for the moment of commitment when the convoy was sighted and the 'show' was definitely on, was to extend the agony of minds already pregnant with expectations. The result was a total drain of nervous energy, culminating in exhaustion on return.

However drained the returning crews may have felt that day, the next was to prove much more traumatic than fatiguing. Early in the morning of Friday 15 August, the peace was disturbed at 03.00 hours as an air raid alert began. A formation of high-flying fighters appeared over the island, a fairly frequent but irritating occurrence. News came in that a number of merchant vessels were approaching the port of Benghazi, at the eastern corner of the Gulf of Sirte, on the Libyan coast. The vessels were close enough to warrant a fairly early take-off and at 07.00 hours the search began. The sortie was led by F/O H.J. Roe, with his crew F/Sgt J.D. Timms (Observer) and F/Sgt S.R. Samways (WOp/AG), all of whom had joined the squadron on 22 July 1941 from 88 (Hong Kong) Squadron, also based at Swanton Morley. Following closely were the other four aircraft, captained by P/O Standfast, P/O Hanafin, Sgt Bruce and Sgt Bridge.

The sun was rising higher and higher in the sky, as the Blenheim formation headed for the target. The observers checked courses as the air gunners strained their eyes in the glare, looking for fighters. P/O Hanafin's WOp/AG on this trip was Sgt A.G. Mee, who was standing in for his usual gunner, P/O Cheney. As they neared the target area, flying to the starboard of the leader, Sgt Mee noticed a Macchi fighter flying parallel with the coast. It appeared to rise and fall with the shoreline. Immediately the fighter was reported to the skipper, but fortunately it did not intercept. Onwards their machines raced over the waves, flashing in the Mediterranean sun.

Eventually the ships were spotted off the coast at Bwayrat Al Hasun in the Gulf of Sirte. There were two tankers of some 4,000 tons and two three-masted schooners. By this time, as a result of the steady increase in successes against them, merchant vessels were being increasingly protected by on-board guns. While approaching the ships, it was noticed that they had lined up so that they were perpendicular to the distant shoreline, almost as if they knew of their attackers' arrival. Possibly the Macchi had radioed their position earlier. Whatever, the formation flattened out and the pilots chose their targets. F/O H.J. Roe went for one of the tankers, while the other was attacked by P/O P.H. Standfast, with his crew P/O H.G. Sorenson (Observer) and Sgt D.A.D. Hoare (WOp/AG), all of whom had joined 105 Squadron on 11 July from 13 OTU at Bicester. The schooners were targeted by the other three crews.

As the Blenheims raced in towards their prey, anti-aircraft machine-gun fire began. Without tracer, it was not visible to the naked eye, but the tell-tale little spouts of water bursting up from the sea in front of the formation drew the pilots' attention. F/O Roe's aircraft Z7522:E raced in and dropped 500lb of explosive straight into the tanker, which exploded violently. Unfortunately, their aircraft's wingtip smashed into a mast as they roared their way over the ship. Aircraft and crew spun into the sea and were lost. On the left of F/O Roe's attack, P/O Standfast's aircraft, Z9604:D, attacked the second tanker, which was set on fire and left with a pall of black smoke rising skywards. Tragically, the aircraft exploded when it was hit by ship-board gunfire and this crew also failed to return.

Meanwhile, the two schooners were being attacked by the remaining three aircraft. One was left on fire and the other was floating at an unnatural angle in the water by the time the attackers left the scene. Forming up on their return journey to Malta, any elation at the successful attack was eclipsed by sadness at the loss of six very able young men – it had been a successful operation, but as usual an exceedingly costly one.

On Sunday 17 August the crews on the previous day's Battle Order were allowed a day of rest and it fell to Sgt Scott, Sgt Weston and Sgt Bridge to find a convoy to the south of Pantellaria, the small Italian island some 150 miles north-west of Malta, lying between Tunisia and Sicily in the Sicilian Channel. As usual, the convoy had been located by F/O Adrian Warburton in his Maryland, this time BJ427, and consisted of six merchant vessels and six destroyers with fighter escort. As the ships were spotted early in the afternoon, it was possible that the fighter aircraft would have left by the time the Blenheims were ready to take off at 17.15 hours. Although Standing Orders prohibited attacks on naval vessels, six merchantmen made a tempting target.

The three Blenheims lifted off and formed up into a neat vic of three before heading out to sea, leaving the neighbouring islands of Comino and Gozo looking like little yellow stones on the horizon. At precisely 19.03 hours, 108 minutes after departure, Sgt Scott's formation sighted the convoy. Once more it was protected by fighters, which represented a serious threat to the flight long before a run-in could even be attempted. As on previous occasions, the only sensible thing to do was to return to base, which they did, arriving at 20.15 hours. Landing at Luqa often proved hazardous during the day, but in the evenings the light was very bad. The result was that Sgt Weston misjudged his approach and dropped his kite in from about 60ft – it took Sgt Chapple and others of the groundcrew until midnight to get Z7420:M off the runway!

On the 17th, while Sgt Scott and his Blenheims were searching for the convoy, the Fleet Air Arm aircraft were also up in their 'Stringbags', searching for a convoy escorted by five destroyers reported to be 20 miles to the west of Lampedusa. At dusk their attack went in two waves of determined effort. Of the six merchant vessels, ranging between 6,000 and 10,000 tons, one 8,000-tonner was left sinking, another was stopped in the water and a small freighter was ablaze. The anti-aircraft fire had been ferocious and all the 'Stringbags' were damaged. However, it had been a most successful evening for 830 Squadron from Hal Far. After the attack, one of the merchant vessels, the 5,479-ton *Maddelena Odero*, limping along at only 4 knots, was escorted by two of the destroyers towards Lampedusa where it eventually beached. The vessel was spotted in the early hours by S/L Tennant of 69 Squadron, lying disabled outside Lampedusa with a protecting destroyer. There she lay like a beached seal ready for the cull; a task which was shortly to fall to three Blenheim crews.

Among the officers milling around in their marquee-type mess at Luqa, Hughie Edwards was sitting by the telephone when it rang. He answered it immediately, and hearing the report, turned to his fellow officers and calmly announced that a tanker in Lampedusa Harbour had been torpedoed 'last night' and was damaged; a destroyer, three motor torpedo boats and Fiat CR42 Falcos were protecting it. Shortly afterwards P/O Buckley and P/O Duncan were joined by Sgt Shufflebotham, Sgt Allen, Sgt Knight, Sgt Lyndall, Sgt Weston, Sgt Miller and Sgt Mee all of whom had been summoned from Marsaxlokk. The briefing was under way! As the nine airmen listened intently, Hughie Edwards told them how he wanted the attack to proceed. They were to fly in from the north, the east and overland from the west in individual consecutive attacks.

By noon all three aircraft were forming up and heading out south-westwards towards the target. Once over the sea Sgt Weston's WOp/AG, Sgt Mee, fired the customary test burst into the sea. As he did so his guns jammed and their Blenheim was turned around to land back at base after only twenty minutes. Sgt Weston, who just 24 hours previously had crash-landed at night, had been excused today's duty. Meanwhile, P/O Buckley and P/O Duncan roared their way to the target, flying at 50ft above the glinting wavetops. After an hour or so, the two aircraft reached their objective. There she was, and beached indeed – a perfect target! P/O Jack Buckley was first into the attack. As he rushed in very low, the ship's hull eventually rose up in front of the aircraft like a steel wall. He delivered his bombs and hauled his machine up to clear the deck and masts. With the engines coughing because of fuel starvation in the carburettors, the stick was pushed forward to commence the dive down over the other side, ready for the dash for freedom. This was the Blenheim's most vulnerable moment. Just then, one of the MTBs opened up with an Oerlikon-type gun, sending a shell ripping its way into the floor of the cockpit under P/O Buckley's legs. It exploded with a violent crack against the Very pistol, and red hot pieces of shrapnel flew off and embedded themselves in the pilot's leg. The aircraft then fell back down to sea-level ready for the run-out.

P/O Buckley's usual observer, P/O Douglas Ivens, a lad of Scottish descent, was ill in hospital – another victim of the dreaded Sandfly fever – and had been replaced on this trip by the red-haired Sgt Otto Shufflebotham, commonly known as 'Shuff'. As they flew home, Shuff, somehow amused by his pilot's predicament, proceeded to extract the debris from Jack Buckley's leg and then dressed the wound. As if they didn't have enough to contend with, the WOp/AG, Sgt Reg Allen, then shouted that CR.42s were chasing. Four of the fighters had left the area to pursue the Blenheim with its wounded crew member. Two of them took the initiative, attacking from 250 yards range. For twenty minutes, Sgt Allen shouted his instructions across the intercom to his wounded pilot to jink left, jink right, sway back and forth, and other manoeuvres until he saw the fighters break off their engagement. Throughout the attack, matters had been made even worse for the poor WOp/AG as his guns had jammed and he had only been able to point them impotently at his attackers, in the hope of fooling them into evasive action and thereby spoiling their aim. Clutching at straws it may have been – but the crew survived!

During all the excitement, P/O Duncan could see the tanker was well alight. Not being able to attack it further due to the fighters, he went for a two-masted schooner but in all the turmoil missed the target. The two aircraft then began the long trip back to Malta, landing at 14.10 hours. The MO had been alerted and the 'bloodwagon' was standing by to take P/O Buckley to the hospital at Bingi for treatment, followed by a couple of weeks' convalescence. Before he left, however, a welcome tot of brandy was administered to soothe the nerves!

That afternoon, the beached tanker was photographed by a Hurricane of 69 Squadron. F/O Wooton, having completed a reconnaissance sweep of Sicily, dropped in on Lampedusa to see the results of the Blenheim attack. A large pall of thick, black smoke could be seen pouring skywards, drifting in the breeze above the burning ship. In fact, so successful was the attack that the ship burned steadily and was still blazing two days later on the 20th!

In general recognition of the brave efforts of the RAF and FAA on Malta, the following report was detailed for public consumption in *The Times of Malta*'s Saturday 23 August edition. The headline on the first page read: 'Air Secretary Congratulates Airmen'. The article covered a statement made by Sir Archibald Sinclair, Secretary of State for Air, in a telegram to Air Vice-Marshal Hugh Pughe Lloyd MC DFC which read as follows:

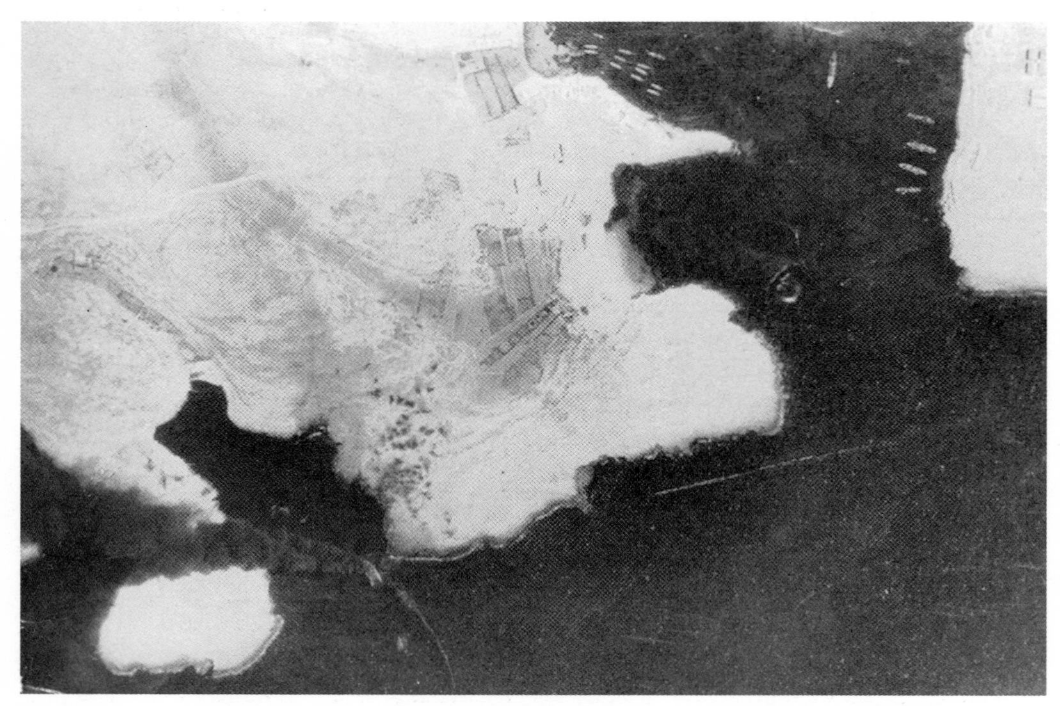

S/L Tennent of 69 Squadron took this photograph from Hurricane V7101 on 19 August 1941. The blazing oil tanker had been attacked on 18 August by 105 Squadron's Blenheims near the entrance of the harbour on the Italian-held island of Lampedusa. A huge plume of black smoke can be seen drifting up from the semi-submerged ship. (via Jack Buckley)

> Heartiest congratulations to you and all ranks of Squadrons operating under your command on the magnificent success of air operations from Malta. The brilliant defence of the Island by 'Hurricanes', the audacious attacks of 'Beaufighters' on enemy air bases, the steady and deadly slogging of the 'Wellingtons' at the enemy ports; the daring and dextrous reconnaissances of the 'Marylands' culminating in the tremendous onslaught of 'Blenheims' and Fleet Air Arm 'Swordfish' on Axis shipping in the Mediterranean are watched with immense admiration by your comrades in the RAF and by your fellow countrymen at home. You are draining the enemy's strength in the Mediterranean. Good luck and good hunting.

Air Vice-Marshal Hugh Pughe Lloyd MC DFC, Air Officer Commanding RAF Mediterranean. (The Trustees of the Imperial War Museum, London: CM2798A)

Such a boost to morale was well received and had been needed. It brought a characteristic response from its recipient, who replied:

> All ranks join me in thanking you for your warm inspiring message of congratulations on our humble efforts. Hunting is certainly good and the hounds are in excellent fettle.

On Friday 22 August 1941 five Blenheims led by S/L Smithers in Z9607:S were busy searching the North African coast between Misurata and Bwayrat Al Hasun in the Gulf of Sirte. The sortie was to last five and a quarter hours in total. After the traditional sweep search had been made to no avail, the 'hounds' headed inland in search of a secondary target. Approaching Bwayrat Al Hasun, the formation came across an army convoy travelling towards the town from the west. As the Blenheims thundered towards the coastal road, the convoy of vehicles came up on their right hand side, and were soon being strafed and bombed. While roaring in low over the road, machine-guns blazing, Sgt Brandwood had a clear view as the rear side door of one of the trucks flew open. An Italian soldier in his green uniform with khaki leggings spilled out and fell across the bonnet. The gunner, Sgt Tony Mee, was engrossed in the scene when suddenly a shell exploded with a large crack directly above his turret. The shock wave blasted him, but fortunately caused no injury. Luck took a hand again some minutes later, as on the way back out to the coast, while following the leader, Sgt Mee's gut feeling was that the aircraft was not far enough out to sea; he told the pilot, Sgt Brandwood, who obligingly moved the Blenheim slightly further out to sea as requested. Seconds after the manoeuvre, the formation flew past a line of coastal guns which opened up fiercely on sight of their enemy, a line of water-spouts indicating the gunfire's contact with the water just short of the aircraft. Had the gunner not reported his anxiety to the pilot, and the pilot not shown respect for his comrade's anxiety, they would have flown directly into the rain of gunfire. For today at least the Grim Reaper had been denied his harvest, and by 13.00 hours all crews were safely back at base.

The next day, Saturday 23 August, S/L Tennent and his crew of 69 Squadron were patrolling the Tunisian coast in their Maryland. At 06.05 hours they spotted a merchant vessel heading south from Pantellaria. Later they found a further two merchant vessels and two schooners also heading on a southerly course, but this time at a position 250° south of Lampedusa. The latter sighting was chosen as the target for the Blenheims, which took off at noon. Another new crew had joined the Battle Order: S/L Barnes and his crew, Sgt Roberts (Observer) and F/Sgt Williamson (WOp/AG) had arrived from 107 Squadron. For their first sortie they joined four other Blenheims, led by S/L Smithers, again in Z7504:G, Sgt Scott, Sgt Jackson DFM and Sgt Brandwood. The two squadron leaders led the formation in a large vic of five, reaching the target around an hour later. The ships were finally sighted at a position 35° 07'N, 12° 28'E, about 30 miles off Lampedusa. S/L Smithers singled out one of the schooners for his attack, after which the ship assumed an ungainly starboard list. Sgt Bill Jackson DFM also had a go at a schooner but his bombs overshot. The only other aircraft to hit the target was Sgt Scott. With his crew, Sgt Healy and Sgt Bastin, he managed a direct hit, following which all aircraft returned safely to Luqa.

The next day, Sunday 24th, at 06.00 hours it was the turn of S/L Barnes to take over as leader. He was followed by P/O Duncan, Sgt Scott and Sgt Bruce. They were to 'fix' a tanker reported to be off Kelibia on the Tunisian coast, some 30 miles south of Cape Bon. The tanker had been sighted by P/O S.W. Gooch and his crew in their Bristol Beaufort I, L9875. (This was one of two Beauforts from 39 Squadron which had been sent to Malta and retained to help in sea sweeps with 69 Squadron.) The tanker was not located by the Blenheims, although two schooners and an escort vessel were. The formation by this time had lost one aircraft: Sgt Bruce had had to turn back when a perspex panel blew out of the cupola, exposing the WOp/AG, Sgt Gibson, to the vicious buffeting of the slipstream.

The remaining three machines went into the attack and S/L Barnes launched himself at one of the schooners which exploded in his wake. The other schooner was attended to by P/O Duncan, who left it listing to starboard. Sgt Scott wielded the remaining aircraft against the merchant vessel, and distinguished himself by completing the hat-trick with a hit on the ship's stern, leaving his gunner, Sgt Bastin, to observe the vessel erupting into fragments in a huge explosion. Being an escort vessel, the large explosion was probably accentuated by the detonation of ammunition. By 12.30 hours the flight was safely back at base once more.

CHAPTER 18

The Irony of War

As crews reached the end of their tours of duty, many having accrued the requisite number of sorties from Malta with some UK operations taken into account, a steady flow of replacements were either being detached for life on Malta or 'hi-jacked' en route and detained on the island to fill the positions of those leaving. By now, one of the longest serving 105 Squadron crews was due for relief. Sgt Ronald John Scott, aged 26, an experienced and highly respected pre-war pilot, was to return to be commissioned. His observer, Sgt Walter Brendan Healy was also to return, along with Sgt Stuart George Bastin, WOp/AG, the youngest squadron member at only 19 years of age. Together they had operated as a very close-knit crew since May 1941. All were now to return 'on rest' to transfer to OTUs and probably split up and go their separate ways. A Sunderland flying boat was to take them on the first leg of their journey home in a few days time.

On 26 August (noted by Sgt Chapple in his diary as the 25th!) a few of the crews were relaxing around the slipway opposite the Marsaxlokk seaplane hangar, as the sun climbed up into the Mediterranean sky. It was to turn into a tragically memorable day.

At the rear of Blenheim L9379 GB:Y are Sgt Walter Brendan Healy (Observer); Ronald John Scott (Pilot); Stuart George Bastin (WOp/AG). (via Mrs N.A. Scott)

While the sergeants were standing around chatting at Marsaxlokk, with the waves lapping their way carelessly up the slipway, the tranquillity of the scene was interrupted by a message from the mess. The day was not to be a quiet one after all; the crews were summoned to Luqa on standby, Sgt Scott's included. He and his crew were reluctant to go on another operation so near to their return and had a strange feeling of foreboding about the trip, which, atypically, they voiced to their comrades. Sgt Bastin had typified the feeling in an uncharacteristic exclamation of 'Oh, God!' when he heard the news. It was commonly considered among RAF aircrews, perhaps with some degree of superstition, that the first and last sorties of a tour of operations were the most likely to end in tragedy. However, off they went, as the bus rolled its way along Marsaxlokk Bay, past the Honeymoon Hotel to the church, where a left turn took them up the hill and around the invasion obstacles as they set course for Luqa.

Arriving at the main gate, the crews spilled from the bus and ambled their way down the dusty track to the Operations Room. Parachute bags belonging to the crews sat in piles on the concrete floor of an adjacent alcove. These did not only belong to the Blenheim crews, but also to those of the Wellingtons and Marylands who shared the aerodrome. Typically, preparation for the day ahead began with the WOp/AGs collecting their grease tins, four by two and pull-throughs to clean their guns. They then would climb aboard the small pick-up truck to be dropped one by one at their respective aircraft, dispersed mostly in the ruins of a nearby bombed village. Once at the aircraft, the WOp/AGs would strip and clean their twin Browning .303in machine-guns with great care – the lives of the entire crew often depended on their doing a good job. The nose and turrets of the aircraft were hooded to prevent the perspex panels from buckling in the hot Maltese sunshine. Although this worked, it also built up the heat inside the fuselage, turning the aircraft into a virtual sauna for the sweating occupant busy with his duties. On this occasion, and unknown to the WOp/AGs, an emergency briefing had taken place back at the Operations Room. The Royal Navy had urgently requested a reconnaissance flight to photograph two enemy transport vessels which had previously been attacked by a submarine. As one of the ships was still afloat, bombs were also to be taken to finish it off.

Two crews only were to go on this 'easy' sortie. F/O Duncan was to have led with his crew, Sgt Smith and Sgt Lyndall, but he was taken ill at the last minute with the dreaded Sandfly fever. Consequently, it fell to Sgt Scott and his crew to take the lead position, with Sgt 'Bill' Brandwood as his wingman. Normally, after sweltering in the turret, the WOp/AGs would have returned to the crew room for a wash and brush-up before briefing, but this day it was very different, for suddenly the pilots and observers were at the aircraft, greeting the gunners with their parachutes and harness, tin hat (or 'battle bowler' as it was affectionately known), along with Syko codes. In addition, Sgt Brandwood's WOp/AG, Sgt Tony Mee, was given a Leica camera to take photographs from his turret, while Sgt Healy, the observer in Sgt Scott's crew, carried an F24 camera to photograph the sinking ship from the Blenheim's nose position.

Shortly before 11.30 hours, Sgt Scott's aircraft was taxiing in the usual cloud of dust around the perimeter to the runway, followed by Sgt Brandwood's machine. Soon the aerodrome was flashing past the two aircraft as they hurtled along the south-east/north-west runway and lifted up into the blue sky. Departing the circuit in a left turn-out, they left on a southerly course. By the time the aircraft reached the coast they had climbed to several hundred feet for IFF recognition and minutes later, as Malta disappeared into its mist cloud, the two crews descended to sea-level for the journey to the target areas, the first of which was in the vicinity of Cape Bon, in north-east Tunisia. For one hour and eleven minutes the two hunters skimmed above the sea towards the target. Suddenly, at 12.41 hours, the first ship was spotted, lying 5 miles east of the Kuriate Islands, off Sousse in Tunisia, and within view of the large white lighthouse at Cape Bon. A report of possible fighter activity created an air of urgency about photographing the first

Two photographs of Blenheim Z7848 GB:T at Luqa aerodrome. The guns and turret were covered to reduce the heat build-up. Note the oil filters below the engines and the extra air intakes at the top of the engine cowl, both features of 'Tropicalized' Blenheims, which were modified for operation in hot, dusty environments. (via Johnnie Turner)

target. Sgt Scott went in for his first run-in to allow his observer to photograph the ship with the F24 camera. Sure enough, as reported, the stricken ship had been severely damaged by the Navy's torpedoes and almost half of the vessel was below the water, with her anchor chain lowered and her bows reaching upward as if to breathe a last breath of air, before its inevitable journey to the depths. Meanwhile, Sgt Brandwood did a slow pass alongside the ship, while Sgt Mee used the hand-held Leica to photograph it from his turret. Having achieved this, 'Bill' Brandwood took his aircraft a few hundred yards to the left and circled patiently, keeping a close lookout for fighters. Much to the curiosity of the circling crew, Sgt Scott did several repeated passes over the ship, presumably to maximize the photographic results – no bombs were needed. Later that same day, the position of the ship was confirmed by S/L Lowry of 69 Squadron. Three men, probably from the stricken ship, sat watching helplessly in a rowing boat, as the two Blenheims disappeared off to the east in search of their second prey.

The next target was not far away, at a point some 35 miles east of the Kerkenna Islands, again off the Tunisian coast. As the machines roared in at sea-level, their first encounter was a dhow, with its crew crowding the deck and peering ahead from every vantage point available to them, their robes fluttering in the strong following breeze. A few points to port and at some distance, the second target was sighted. It was 13.00 hours, with the bright sun high in the sky, as the leader, Sgt Scott, dropped right down on the deck, just skimming the wavetops for a run at the ship. This ship had not suffered the fate of the first and was well afloat with small boats proceeding away from it to the north-west, heading for the coast. One of the dhows was tied up alongside the transport ship as Sgt Scott approached for a quarter attack. The wingman held off

This semi-submerged merchant vessel was damaged by the Royal Navy 5 miles east of Kuriate Island off Tunisia. The photograph was taken on 26 August 1941 by Sgt Tony Mee from the turret of Blenheim Z7357, GB:U. (The Trustees of the Imperial War Museum: C1913)

in a parallel course as this time the run-in was a bombing run, and in this way the aircraft would avoid running into the leader's 11-second delayed bomb bursts. No sign of anti-aircraft fire was evident and no tell-tale blips on the water's surface from small-arms fire could be seen. Closer and closer the Blenheim roared in towards the target. The ship's superstructure grew in relation to the aircraft as it closed in, the masts looming upwards like great endless pillars into the blue sky above. The Blenheim would have been well trimmed out as it pulled up on discharging its bombs into the side quarters of the ship; however, having gained some height, the aircraft mysteriously levelled out and Z7682:N ran headlong into the mast, damaging the superstructure as it exploded, before the remains were hurled into the water beyond.

Three survivors start the long haul back to the Tunisian shores in a rowing boat on 26 August 1941. Their merchant vessel had been attacked by the Royal Navy and then photographed in repeated runs by Sgt Scott's Blenheim Z7682:N. (via Brian Hanafin/Len Fearnley)

For Sgt Scott, Sgt Healy and Sgt Bastin, the pains of war were over in an instant. Two direct hits and two near misses were attributed to the efforts of the tragic crew but it was left to Sgt Brandwood to finish it off with two 250lb bombs, one of which missed while the other tore into the ship which was left sinking slowly on an even keel. A Maryland flight later confirmed the vessel was stationary and down at the stern.

Shocked at the unexpected loss of such a respected crew, on what appeared to be a routine task, Sgt Brandwood set course for their traumatic journey home. The radio on Z7357:U did not receive when Sgt Mee signalled base. On nearing the island, and assuming that his signal had not been received, he repeated it but on a different frequency – again, there was no reply. Shortly afterwards, the south coast of the island appeared. The Blenheim climbed to several hundred feet, and having been recognized as 'friendly' on the IFF, it made a left base arrival on the south-east runway back at Luqa. At 14.20 hours, the lone aircraft taxied sombrely along to its dispersal area, where the crew were met by several of the other crew members who, having arrived on a pick-up truck, were waiting to greet the two crews and probably congratulate Sgt Scott and his crew on completion of their tour, and his impending promotion. The control tower had indeed received Sgt Mee's signals, although his receiver was not working and he was unaware of this fact. Of course, hearing two signals on different frequencies, the Controller

On 26 August 1941 Sgt Ron Scott and crew in Blenheim Z7682:N photographed and attacked this ship, 35 miles east of the Kerkenna Islands, off the Tunisian coast. During the run-in the aircraft mysteriously levelled out and ran headlong into the mast, exploding and falling into the sea beyond. (via Brian Hanafin/Len Fearnley)

Sgt Tony Mee took this photograph from the gun turret of Sgt 'Bill' Brandwood's Blenheim Z7357:U as it circled the stricken ship and the remains of Blenheim Z7682:N. Damage can be seen to the ship's superstructure, while the two plumes of smoke from burning oil or fuel show where the Blenheim's engines were thrown into the sea beyond. (via Brian Hanafin/Len Fearnley)

automatically assumed that two aircraft were returning. It was with a stunned feeling of disbelief that they learned of the day's tragic events. Sgt Scott and crew had been one of the longest surviving crews on the squadron, having seen around four months of action, and they were considered 'old hands'. They were a sad loss to their fellow air and groundcrew, 105 being a close-knit squadron, and their loss was a considerable blow to the whole squadron.

Later the same day, after F/O Williams' Maryland report mentioned earlier, three Blenheims were despatched. The targets this time were three schooners off Lampedusa. The formation was to be led by S/L Bryan Smithers in 'S' for Sugar. The Blenheims searched fruitlessly in the hazy dusk for the schooner, eventually returning to Luqa to land safely two hours fifteen minutes from take-off.

On Wednesday 27 August five crews were led out by both flight commanders. S/L Smithers' formation consisted of S/L Barnes and F/O C. Greenhill, both of 107 Squadron, and Sgt J. Bruce and Sgt L.T. Weston of 105 Squadron. By 07.00 hours the hard-pressed groundcrew had six aircraft ready and just over an hour later, at 08.10 hours, the first of the five to take part was climbing to a holding pattern, circling while the remainder formed up. At last, by 08.25 hours, all were airborne and the formation headed off to the north-east at sea-level to take part in a sweep of the Ionian Sea. The pressure on the Italian convoys off Tunisia was beginning to tell, to such an extent that the Italians started to send more and more cargo to the east, away from the suicidal shipping lanes west of Malta.

This sweep was to be a long, hot, boring journey with no sight of an enemy of any kind, all that is except the formation leader. An hour or so into the flight, S/L Smithers began to feel ill; he was suffering from the stroboscopic reflections of the bright sunshine off the waves. Clearly, he could not continue at less than 50ft to the target – it was enough just to fly the aircraft without having to lead an attack on arrival. His observer, Sgt Frank Harbord, set a course for home as S/L Smithers handed command of the formation over to S/L Barnes to continue the sweep. The aircraft peeled away in a climbing turn from the formation and set off to the west at about 100ft. After half an hour or so flying at this higher altitude, away from the stroboscopic effect of the sunlight, the pilot began to recover. It was never considered quite the done thing to return unless forced to do so under conditions of extreme urgency, and so having suitably recovered, S/L Smithers decided his bombs should be used and not returned for the next sortie; there was a job to be done and he was determined he was going to do it.

105 Squadron's Sgt Ronald John Scott, service no. 904184. He was killed in action flying from Malta on 26 August 1941. (The Trustees of the Imperial War Museum, London: ME723)

The nearest location likely to have a suitable target was the island of Lampedusa. The course was set and they arrived at the island at approximately 10.40 hours. They flew low and fast over the north shore, on a southerly overland course, heading for Lampedusa Harbour where a 5,000-ton merchant vessel and four schooners were found to be waiting for them. Suddenly, intense machine-gun fire erupted. Their arrival had been noticed and the defences alerted. Onward the Blenheim surged until the harbour finally appeared. The 'heavies' then opened up and a barrage of accurate anti-aircraft fire met the crew on their run-in towards the ship, one burst of machine-gun fire scything through the port wing. The pilot dropped the bombs but to no avail, as they landed short on the land. He struggled at the controls until suddenly, only 50 or 100 yards from the harbour, a shell exploded close beneath the aircraft. A piece of red hot shell splinter scythed its way through the thin metal nose of the aircraft and embedded itself in Sgt Frank Harbord's thigh. The aircraft flew on. By the grace of God and good flying skills, the crew survived and set course for Malta.

After three hours thirty minutes of what should have been a long, boring flight, 'S' for Sugar was preparing to touch down once again at Luqa. Frank Harbord remembers the incident:

> We were surprised at the quantity and quality of the ack-ack fire; 20mm cannons and machine-guns. We made off straight back to Luqa. S/L Smithers knew the hydraulics had gone, perhaps because there was no power to the gun turret. We jettisoned the forward escape hatch into the sea just before crossing the coast and landed straight away on the rough earth parallel to and about 50 yards to the side of the runway, routine procedure at the time. The ambulance took me to sick quarters, where I had a bath and the MO prodded about to remove a bit of shrapnel from my thigh. The small wound made a lot of blood. I stayed there a few hours and I presume S/L Smithers and our WOp/AG [Sgt Bob Lyndall] went to report to ops.

Bob Lyndall summarized the raid as follows:

> Lampedusa, where even the lighthouse-keeper was armed with machine-guns! Hits in bomb-bay (bombs gone!) hydraulics u/s, Frankie Harbord wounded, no turret, no undercarriage, controls damaged and locked in +9 lbs boost. Returned over the Mediterranean with the

> bottom hatch open, dinghy at ready and parachutes on. Approached Luqa for belly-landing – too fast and went up again. Debate as to whether one could throttle back in +9 lbs boost without cutting the engines. Decided to risk it – successfully!

As for the remaining crews, their sweep had been fruitless. They returned tired and hungry at 13.35 hours.

While the aircrew returned to the debriefing room, the groundcrew had the job of retrieving the pranged Blenheim. During the afternoon they produced their two trusty tripods and lifted it up. The kite was in a 'rather shop-soiled condition' according to Sgt Chapple. They eventually managed to get the wheels down and the machine was then towed carefully to the 'Graveyard' at the end of the runway. There it stayed until it was claimed by 45 Squadron, who operated from the landing grounds of the Western Desert; Z9607 was eventually struck off charge on 23 November 1941.

At 07.00 hours on Thursday 28 August, the groundcrew were up and preparing the aircraft which were required by 09.00 hours. Seven Blenheims were finally ready for action, sitting warming up in the early morning sun, a strong, hot breeze whipping over their fuselages, cooking the interior and presenting an uncomfortable environment for the occupants. In the event, when the Battle Order was posted, only five were required. Yet another new crew had joined the fight – the pilot F/L Allan Ballands, his observer Sgt Yorke and WOp/AG Sgt C. 'Chuck' Widden, a young Canadian lad, had all joined from 107 Squadron. At 10.45 hours S/L Barnes led the new crew, along with F/O Greenhill, P/O Duncan and Sgt Brandwood in search of two tankers, the larger of which was a captured Dutch vessel. For the new crew their first taste of Mediterranean warfare was to prove fruitless. On take-off, port engine problems beset their Blenheim, and so they peeled off and returned to base – yet another job for the hard-pressed groundcrew to contend with. The remainder of the formation pressed on. At a position approximately 130 miles west of Crete, the tankers were sighted and the 'hounds' raced at their prey. The larger tanker was leading the smaller one, and their port sides presented a considerable target. The attack was delivered in pairs.

The larger ship was claimed by Sgt Brandwood, who, despite the attention of a very accurate machine-gunner on board the ship, managed to drop one or possibly two bombs into the vessel, which was left sinking. The other ship was meanwhile receiving S/L Barnes' attention. One of his bombs fell smack on target. The superstructure forward of the funnel blew off and black and brown smoke belched up into the clear blue sky as thousands of gallons of fuel were destroyed. It was another valuable contribution to the war of attrition against the Axis supplies bound for North Africa. At 16.15 hours Sgt Brandwood, last of the four, was on his final approach at Luqa. As the Blenheim eased down on to the deck, the left wing suddenly lurched precariously downwards. The machine took it upon itself to spin uncontrollably across the runway and met the rough perimeter ground. As the pilot struggled at the controls of the bounding Blenheim, it tore across the hard, dry, Maltese earth, as the crew braced themselves nervously. To their great relief, the Blenheim ground to a halt amid a swirl of dust and stones. Groundcrew awaiting the incoming aircraft made their way over to the stricken machine. On closer inspection they found the root of the problem – machine-gun bullets had ripped their way through the tyre, which had been undetected until their attempt to land. The bullets had then penetrated upwards into the bottom of the engine, through the cowling, and entered the propeller assembly. The IFF wiring had been severed and the tailplane was also hit. Fortunately for the crew they had not been in the way. Having witnessed this unorthodox landing, W/C Edwards VC DFC arrived on the scene in his staff car, as he did on these occasions, to acquaint himself with the circumstances and check on the welfare of his crew.

CHAPTER 19

More Shaky Dos

North of Malta, over the Malta Channel, lies Licata, a small town at the western entrance to the Gulf of Gela, on the southern coast of Sicily. Licata harboured an Axis manufacturing facility engaged in the production of munitions. In addition to the chemical factory, there was a supporting power station. The complete installation was the subject of the briefing on 30 August. By 09.00 hours the groundcrews had nine operational Blenheims awaiting their crews at their dispersal points, and by mid-afternoon six had taken off, led once again by S/L Smithers. The formation included two crews on their first operations from Malta.

On reaching the target area, the formation split into three sections of two aircraft. Four attacked the factory and the remaining two went for the power station. The first to attack was S/L Smithers, accompanied by Sgt Weston and his crew in the second Blenheim. Hits were scored by Sgt Weston, who lobbed two 500lb bombs straight through the large main building's roof. Sgt 'Bill' Brandwood led the second wave, accompanied by one of the 'new' 107 Squadron crews – Sgt Turner, with Sgt Warmington (Observer) and Sgt Robson (WOp/AG).

The second wave went for the same target as the first wave, and Sgt Brandwood's aircraft delivered three 250lb bombs which ripped their way into the north end of the building.

Sgt Johnnie Turner's aircraft followed suit and dropped its load. As usual, the bombs were tail fused for 11 seconds delay, but as Sgt Brandwood's bombs hit the target, something went wrong and as Sgt Turner flew over, the preceding aircraft's bombs detonated directly under his Blenheim. The crew fortunately survived the blast, but the hydraulic system was totally u/s. Additionally, bits of shrapnel and debris perforated the fuselage – yet another example of the sturdy Blenheim absorbing punishment and pressing on. The aircraft limped back after the attack for a crash-landing at Luqa.

In a diary entry, Johnnie Turner described the whole episode as follows:

> Just as I was washing, Robby came to me to say we were wanted in the crew room immediately. We had breakfast first then poodled in to find we were on the Battle Order. Bad

Sgt Johnnie Turner's Blenheim flying low over the Mediterranean Sea. The observer can be clearly seen sitting in position in the nose of the aircraft. (via Johnnie Turner)

show, Joe was on too but not Wally who's been here a day longer than us. Stood by all morning, although at ten o'clock we stooged off to the mess for tea and hot cakes, and spent the rest of the time there. At 12.30 I learned Greenhill and Henry were going off on a recce, as all the Glen Martins [Marylands] are u/s. Good, we don't really get much peace. About 2.30 we were called in for briefing, Joe, four chaps from 105 with whom we operate and us. The target was an easy one, a sulphur works at Licata, Sicily. We took off, stooged over to the coast at low level and then in over the hills. Saw four 'Eytie' bombers way up, they didn't see us. As we approached the factory over a hill, I saw a sentry on the crest and with a burst of the gun, sent him running like hell. Down the hill we went, and over the works. 'R' [Z76443] had dropped a bomb some way in front, and it exploded prematurely in front of us, after about three seconds instead of eleven. Great wads of earth shot up before us from the 500-pounder – we were only about 100ft – and I ducked. My perspex broke, cutting my face slightly, and part of the nose perspex broke and also the blister. A glaring hole appeared in the starboard leading edge. However, the kite flew OK, and we stooged off. About half-way home, the remaining nose perspex blew in with a shower of glass and wind. Reached the island all right, climbed up, tested the hydraulics. Undercart OK but the flaps caused the right wing to drop, so I hastily pulled them up and decided on a no-flap landing.

Meanwhile, as the four aircraft were pasting the chemical factory, the power station was being attended to by the remaining two Blenheims. P/O Duncan with his crew, Sgt Smith (Observer) and Sgt Lyndall (WOp/AG), ran in towards their target. They were accompanied by another crew on their first operation, Sgt Mortimer with Sgt Douglas J. Reid (Observer) and F/O Owen (WOp/AG). A total of six bombs were released and resulted in direct hits, smack on target. P/O Duncan's four 250-pounders exploded, throwing dense black smoke and dust into the air. The destruction was further increased by Sgt Mortimer's two 500-pounders, and a pall of black smoke billowed high above the dust cloud. The operation was looking very successful as the aircraft formed up for their return journey, the damaged Blenheim being nursed along by Sgt Turner. By 16.55 hours all were back safely.

However, due to the blast damage, Sgt Turner had considerable difficulty bringing Blenheim Z7641:C in to land. He further recalled the events:

I made a long, fast approach, gently touched the runway but the right wing began to drop, and I couldn't get it up. Slowly I saw it slide towards the ground. Bounce went the wheel, down again and it collapsed. The wing crumpled, we swung round and the other wheel went and the port wing bent. Clouds of dust enveloped me as I crouched down, my feet on the dash, for this was the first time I'd flown without my Sutton harness buttoned, and without my glasses, both of which I needed. As we came to rest I switched off the magnetos, but the port engine was already burning at the bottom. I shouted a warning. Eddie hopped out, followed by me, but Robby didn't appear. We dashed back, fearing the tanks might go up. Eddie opened the hatch and Robby climbed out, rather shaken and partially collapsed. The jolly old fire wagon came up and put out the little fire. Two hours later, our scratches patched, it was just as if we'd done a day's work in an office.

They had not escaped entirely unscathed, however. Johnnie Turner concluded:

Sunday: Robby and I went to see the MO, but I was glad to find my eye no worse than bruised. Robby was not too good, having hurt his back, and spent the day on his bed. I went to Valletta with Eddie on the 2.30 bus, crossed on the ferry to Sliema and had a glorious swim in the crystal clear water. Returned to Valletta for tea, went to The Carlton and saw 'Man of Conquest', then came home. Weather has been very similar to an August day at home, very windy.

The power station and sulphur works at Licata, on the southern shores of Sicily, were attacked by six Blenheims of 105 Squadron on 30 August 1941. (via Brian Hanafin/Len Fearnley)

Smoke and dust surround the sulphur works at Licata after the attack on 30 August 1941. (via Johnnie Turner)

The pranged aircraft remained in position until the next day. Sgt Chapple spent the entire day lifting it up and removing it from the aerodrome. An old but robust two wheeled trailer was used as the crash-truck. The damaged aircraft was supported on a wall of stone chocks, built up beneath it by the groundcrew. The trailer was placed in position to allow the aircraft to be lowered on to it, when suddenly, 'C' for Charlie slipped. Fortuitously it landed on the trailer, much to the relief of the hard-pressed groundcrew, and surrendered gracefully for its last trip to the 'Graveyard'.

On 2 September, a reconnaissance flight by F/O Adrian Warburton in Hurricane Mk I V7191 proved that both Licata's factory buildings had sustained heavy damage and the operation had indeed been a great success.

While all the day's excitement was centred on Licata, one crew was sent off to fly what turned out to be a most memorable sortie of their own. By this time the hard-pressed 69 Squadron was suffering from a lack of serviceable Maryland aircraft and the Blenheims were called on to take over an increasing number of reconnaissance operations in their support. It was in this role that F/O Greenhill led his crew in the early afternoon, in search of two Italian troopships thought to be en route to Benghazi from the north-west. Unlike the usual low-level bombing operations, the Blenheim was to fly at 10,000ft in its reconnaissance role. At least at this altitude they had a chance to use their parachutes if required, unlike low-level work where the very nature of the task precluded their use. However, the downside of high flying was that in an often cloudless sky, the Blenheim was an easy target to attack from below. Only one (or sometimes two) .303in Brownings could be used as protection. No 'deck' was immediately available to which to dive for cover.

Eventually, after a long flight, the target was located. There were indeed two large liners, uncharacteristically devoid of obvious protection. The only other enemy spotted was a sole CRDA Cant Z.501 Gabbiano, about 5,000ft below the lonely Blenheim. The Gabbiano or 'Seagull' was a single 900hp-engined Italian flying boat, with a stabilizing float braced by struts between the two-stepped hull and the wings. On this occasion the Seagull was being used in a reconnaissance role, but it could also be used as a bomber, with a minimum bombload of 1,404lb. For protection, the five crew had three 7.7mm Breda-SAFAT machine-guns, Italy's answer to the Brownings. The seemingly meek little float plane had quite a sting in its tail. Consequently, it was treated with the wariness it deserved and was left unmolested, apparently in ignorance of the Blenheim's existence.

Having coded the message concerning the liners' whereabouts, the WOp/AG, Sgt Mike Henry, transmitted the co-ordinates back to base, but received no acknowledgement. Unperturbed, the crew set course for home after having circled for a considerable period (which didn't help the observer in setting the course!). The Blenheim dropped down to 1,500ft and droned onwards. Suddenly, to the crew's horror, they recognized in the distance the mountains of Calabria – in southern Italy! The pilot immediately dropped down to treetop height, and they turned southwards, flying parallel to the Sicilian east coast, with Catania and Mount Etna on the horizon. The area was a veritable hornet's nest of fighters but miraculously none was scrambled.

Eventually Malta came into view. The fuel gauges were registering empty as the aircraft crossed the coast at Sliema – the situation was desperate. The crew, by now extremely tense, and having considered all the options open to them, decided to carry on overland. The machine clawed its way above the parched ground, the crew expecting the engines to cut out at any second. Finally Luqa came into view. Up went the observer's red/red Very recognition lights. To their horror came a refusal, as a red light greeted their signal – a Wellington bomber was about to take off. Defiantly, the desperate Blenheim hurtled its way on to the aerodrome, the pilot not even attempting to land on the runway, for all the crew knew that the only consideration was to get down before the engines coughed to a halt; otherwise, it would have been a case of 'so near but yet so far'. As the wheels touched down, the fully bombed-up

A close up view of the damage to the leading edge of the wing of Blenheim Z7641 OM:C. The pipe pointing vertically downwards from the under-surface of the wing was an emergency fuel drain. (via Johnnie Turner)

The damage to the starboard side of 107 Blenheim Z7641:C. The collapsed undercarriage, fractured fuselage near the gun turret, and damage to the leading edge of the wing can be clearly seen. (via Johnnie Turner)

Wellington on dispersal suddenly became an obstruction. The Blenheim swung violently to starboard. On throttling back the port engine, a belch of flame shot out of the exhaust. The pilot hurriedly evacuated the plane, followed by the observer and finally a rather disgruntled WOp/AG. He had climbed up his ladder and got on to the wing, before jumping off – only to be missed by inches by the tail plane which almost decapitated him. The reason? – the aircraft was still on the move and doing about 25mph!

Sgt Chapple recorded in his diary for that day:

After the attack on Licata on 30 August 1941, Sgt Johnnie Turner's 107 Squadron Blenheim Z7641:C arrived back somewhat battered at Luqa, Malta. His Blenheim had been damaged by flying into the premature bomb burst of the leading aircraft flown by Sgt 'Bill' Brandwood. (via Johnnie Turner)

> 'B' landed with one engine on fire. Crew leapt out. Aircraft stopped with one wheel in a hole and began racing around in a circle. An airman ran in and roped the tail, climbed along the fuselage to the cockpit and stopped the engines.

The ginger-haired airman had saved the day in a very brave act. In fact, the engine had only back-fired but to the observing groundcrew and probably the pilot as well, it did seem to be on fire.

Johnnie Turner also remembered the incident and wrote in his diary:

> At 7 o'clock Henry and his kite were missing, but turned up after we had given them up for lost. Thinking they were going to overshoot, Henry and the observer jumped out before it stopped. Greenhill also jumped out and apparently kicked a throttle, as the kite careered round for about five minutes before finally it was recaptured. My God, what a day – two days in fact!

The pilot had rather a lot of explaining to do, especially as the AOC, Air Vice-Marshal Hugh Pughe Lloyd MC DFC had arrived on the scene in his staff car to view the commotion. However, some days later the entire crew were back on the Battle Order once more.

As for the reconnaissance report, it had not been received after all their efforts, and nor had the hurried SOS sent when all seemed lost. The only signal received had been the IFF signal they had sent at about 100ft on the approach. As the aircraft was flying so low it had faded out and the crew had actually been assumed lost. Interestingly, the radio on Z7511:B subsequently caused problems for the next crew to fly it, and it proved to suffer from a fault which only manifested itself in the air.

CHAPTER 20

September Dawns

Monday 1 September was heralded by yet another attack on a land-based industrial target as the squadron embarked on yet another month's stay on the beleaguered island. (Their intended three to four weeks' detachment was extending rapidly.) This time the target was once more the nitrate factory at Crotone, last visited on 11 August. On what was their first trip to Crotone, S/L Barnes and his crew were to lead the formation. A total of seven aircraft arrived at the installation at 13.35 hours. The leader was followed by Sgt Brandwood, P/O Duncan and Sgt Wallace. The flight circled the area once, to ensure they had the correct target, then went in singly to make their attacks. An Italian flying boat was spotted nearby, but was left to its own devices.

The run-in was from the south-east, across the coast at very low level. The first aircraft to find a target was S/L Barnes, who disgorged his bombs on a building to the left of the tanks. A great orange ball of flame erupted into the sky. On his starboard side, Sgt Brandwood, drawing a lot of anti-aircraft fire, turned to starboard, dropping his two 500-pounders smack into buildings close to the tank. The same buildings received four of Sgt Wallace's bombs, which had actually missed their intended target. After the detonation of 2,000lb of high explosive, the building was left in a rather dilapidated condition.

P/O Duncan, having swung north and followed a right turn around the tanks, waited until he met another building to the north of the tanks before dropping his bombs. This larger building was also left in a suitably wrecked condition, as the Blenheim quickly left the scene. Eddie Smith recalled, 'One of our bombs went through the roof and foundered out again, landing in a field next to a house, which was rather bad luck for the house!'

Fortunately, although the ack-ack posts had set their ammunition to the minimum exploding time and were very accurate, the extreme low level of the attack meant that the gunners couldn't get quite low enough to hit the oncoming Blenheims, which were at their most vulnerable when rising up to clear the buildings before dropping down over the railway tracks, carefully avoiding the cabling on the other side.

As well as the main attack, three others were having a go at alternative targets. Sgt Weston left the railway tracks to the south-west in a very buckled state, while the other two crews chose some shipping in the bay. A jetty protruding from the shore harboured a merchant vessel, which was tied up alongside. F/L Ballands and Sgt Mortimer decided to end its association with the factory once and for all. First F/L Ballands and then Sgt Mortimer scored direct hits, leaving the vessel blazing.

After a mere five minutes, the aircraft departed, forming up again beyond the cliffs at Cappo delle Colonna, where they headed out into the Ionian Sea for their return to Malta. All arrived safely back at Luqa. Those who had attacked the alternative targets arrived back at 15.45 hours, and those who went for the buildings some ten minutes later, at 15.55 hours.

Due to its extremely successful results, the main attack of the day attracted considerable publicity. *The Times of Malta* of 3 September, reported on its front page: 'Munitions Factories Successfully Bombed'. In the report, based on a communiqué from Cairo, the paper stated:

> At Crotone, shipping and munitions factories and a railway were bombed. Direct hits on three buildings caused violent explosions with sheets of flame and clouds of blue-black smoke. A merchant ship was hit by three bombs and developed a fire towards the stern. The quays and a seaplane flying in the vicinity were also attacked.

The chemical factory at Crotone, Italy, under attack at low level by Blenheims of 105 Squadron, 1 September 1941. Two aircraft can be seen disappearing into the distance, leaving smoke billowing into the air from their bomb bursts. (The Trustees of the Imperial War Museum, London: ME2260)

The accuracy of that last sentence is a matter of conjecture. About nineteen days after the Maltese announcement, the news broke at home in England, with an article and supporting photograph in the *Daily Telegraph* and *Morning Post* issued on 22 September. Eddie Smith summed up the degree of damage: 'A very successful raid though – the factory was left well alight when we left.' The damage was further substantiated by a report by F/O Wooton of 69 Squadron. On 3 September, while surveying the scene in his Hurricane Mk II Z3053, in addition to spotting several merchantmen in the harbour, he noted that the factory had sustained 'considerable damage'.

Also on 3 September two Blenheims were engaged on a reconnaissance sortie. S/L Smithers was leading, with F/O Wells of 69 Squadron as Observer, accompanied by P/O Duncan with his crew, Sgt Eddie Smith (Observer) and Sgt Bob Lyndall (WOp/AG), in Blenheim Z9608:A. Sgt Smith logged the sortie, a three hours forty minute flight leaving at 11.45 hours, as a 'Patrol looking for convoy south-east Italy – nothing seen'. These trips were 105 Squadron's second association with the reconnaissance role; such sorties were to be repeated thereafter almost on a rota basis.

F/O Wooton's reconnaissance sortie formed the basis for the next 105 Squadron operation. The shipping in Crotone harbour was an important target, having escaped a Fleet Air Arm attack on the night of 2/3 September. The next day, Thursday 4 September, five Blenheims were bombed up ready to follow up the attack on five ships at Crotone. At 14.15 hours F/L Alan Ballands in Z9613:A led Sgt Weston, Sgt Mortimer, Sgt Bruce and Sgt Wallace out to sea. The formation was soon reduced to four when Sgt Bruce began to feel ill and returned in Z9606:V, only one hour into the flight. This was happening more and more as the crews succumbed to Sandfly fever and dysentery, the symptoms of which were most unpleasant and never choosy about when or where they struck.

The remaining Blenheims roared on towards Crotone harbour, known to be something of a hornet's nest and which was well remembered after the reception S/L Goode DFC and his crew had received. Eventually the target came into view and the run-in began. As expected, the flak came in thick and fast. Sgt Weston's aircraft, Z7511:B, lurched as a shell burst into its rudder, tearing away the fabric. The starboard side of his bomb-bay flap was also severely peppered by shrapnel.

Sgt Wallace and his crew, Sgt Parry (Observer) and Sgt Jones (WOp/AG), flew in over the harbour in Z7654:Y, a replacement aircraft for their usual 'O' for Orange which went unserviceable before take-off. As they raced in to the attack the flak caught the machine and blew one wing clean off. The aircraft plunged inverted into the harbour – there were no survivors. They had attempted to attack two ships on the South Mole, but it was unclear whether they had dropped their bombs prior to being hit.

Meanwhile Sgt Mortimer and F/L Ballands attacked a ship at the North Mole, resulting in an explosion at the vessel's stern. The surviving aircraft headed back out to sea and began their return journey, arriving back at Luqa between 18.13 and 18.35 hours. Sgt Mortimer had a problem with Z7403:H, as its radio had packed up, but they managed to get back safely.

Substantiation of the results of the attack on the North Mole was provided in a report from 69 Squadron's F/O Warburton who flew over in a Hurricane five days later, on the 9th. His photographs showed a listing merchant vessel which was put down to the Blenheim attack. Three young lives had been lost to destroy one ship. But that ship carried a considerable cargo, probably of explosives, the use of which would ultimately have resulted in the loss of many more lives of 8th Army soldiers in the North African desert.

The Blenheims were more and more frequently being used to support 69 Squadron's reconnaissance role. On 6 September Sgt Bendall and his crew took off in the early morning to patrol the Ionian Sea.

Two days later, three Blenheims captained by F/L Ballands, Sgt Bendall and Sgt Bridge attempted to find a large merchant vessel, but to no avail. It was not until the next day, Tuesday 9 September, that P/O Gooch in Beaufort I:L9875 located a couple of merchant vessels escorted by a destroyer. They were off Cape Spartivento heading south-east from Messina at 10 knots, probably on course for Benghazi. A Cant Z506 Airone (or 'Heron') seaplane was escorting them but might have gone by the time an attack could be made. Newly promoted F/L Duncan led Sgt Brandwood, Sgt Mortimer and Sgt Weston to find the convoy. Although they failed to find it, a schooner was located off Sicily which was possibly spying, and consequently received similar treatment to the 'Squealers' found in the North Sea – it was sunk immediately. The formation then returned safely to Luqa. Sgt Eddie Smith was convinced that the ship was indeed spying, and noted later in his log:

On 9 September 1941 Blenheims of 105 Squadron attacked and sank this schooner off Cape Passero, Sicily. That it was a radio-equipped 'squealer' was confirmed by its SOS which was intercepted on Malta. (via Brian Hanafin/Len Fearnley)

This ship was attacked and left sinking on an even keel on 11 September 1941, approximately 120 miles west of the Mediterranean island of Crete. (via Brian Hanafin/Len Fearnley)

Search for convoy SE coast Sicily – not found, but saw a schooner off the coast – later confirmed my conviction. This was a Squealer, equipped with radio sending [equipment], sighting information to Italian Fighter Command. Their SOS was intercepted in Malta.

The episode was repeated yet again following a report on Wednesday 10th, by Sgt Harvey in reconnaissance Beaufort I:W6518. A merchant vessel and a destroyer had been sighted on the approach to Cape Spartivento on the south-east coast of the toe of Italy. Once again four Blenheims were despatched at 15.00 hours, led by F/L Alan Ballands. Having penetrated deep into the Messina Straits, all arrived back two hours and fifty minutes later having found absolutely nothing. Frustration reigned until Thursday 11th, when five crews led by S/L Smithers went off on a hunt in the Ionian Sea, determined to find a target. The search commenced in two waves with S/L Smithers, Sgt Bendall and Sgt Weston leaving first at 06.45 hours, and F/L Duncan and Sgt Mortimer fifteen minutes later at 07.00 hours. Plug trouble beset Sgt Mortimer who had to return, landing after only sixty-five minutes. Eventually, the first wave spotted two merchant vessels and an escorting destroyer appeared at a position 35° 33'N, 20° 35'E – about 120 miles west of Crete. Bombs were dropped along the entire length of one merchant vessel by all the aircraft and it was left sinking. The second wave continued the search and was logged by Eddie Smith as a 'solo search for tanker off Sapilange [possibly Sapiéntza] near the Greek coast, actually sunk by other members of the squadron engaged on a similar search'. Five and a half hours after take-off, S/L Smithers in Z7408:K was first to touch down at Luqa, followed by the others. Last back was F/L Duncan in Z9608, who landed at 12.50 hours. At last the squadron had found another target, and bombed it without loss.

The next day found Sgt Bill Jackson DFM taking his turn on the reconnaissance rota, crewed with a 69 Squadron observer. They set course along the Tunisian coast, flying south until they came to the Kerkenna Islands, where a merchant vessel was seen steaming south-eastwards at 10 knots, obviously heading for Tripoli. The crew returned at 10.50 hours to report, and by 15.00 hours two Blenheims were up in search of the lone ship. Sgt Tommy Williams led the sortie in 'S' for Sugar, accompanied by Sgt Bridge. A thorough sweep was made from Tunisia to Lampedusa, but once more no target could be found.

Generally, over the past few days life had been quiet, with no substantial targets to attack. This was, however, the calm before the storm, for the squadron was now to take part in one of the most concerted efforts of combined operations during their stay in Malta – and one of the most costly.

One of two ships sighted on 11 September 1941, approximately 120 miles west of Crete. This ship escaped attack. (via Brian Hanafin/Len Fearnley)

CHAPTER 21

Castaways

On 11 September 1941 a supplies and troopship convoy was spotted by a Fleet Air Arm Swordfish reconnaissance flight. The convoy was on a south-westerly course between the islands of Pantellaria and Lampedusa. There were six merchant vessels, ranging in displacement from the smallest, a 5,000-ton freighter to the biggest, a 12,000-tonner. The Italian Navy were also present in force in their usual role of convoy protection: seven destroyers had been despatched to see the convoy safely to its final destination, the port of Tripoli. In the event, the convoy was to take a dreadful mauling, despite the heavy defences from the destroyers and the greatly increased armaments on board the merchant vessels.

The first to fly into the fray were the trusty 'Stringbags' of 830 Squadron, Fleet Air Arm. At 09.45 hours they spotted the convoy. Its course had been altered, possibly due to a submarine alert, and its new course was taking them further south and parallel to the Tunisian coast. The weather was very hazy as the 'Stringbags' pounced. The first victim was an 8,000-tonner, hit by a torpedo. On hearing the explosion, all hell broke loose, as the full defences on board all the ships opened up. Despite the intense barrage, the 'Stringbags' pressed on valiantly and were well rewarded for their efforts. Their tally was one ship sunk and two badly damaged, both of which had black smoke billowing from the superstructure. One of the two ships was stationary when the 'Stringbags' broke off and returned to base.

Following this attack, Wellingtons of 38 Squadron kept up the pressure. That night, they took off from Luqa, arriving at 03.40 hours to find the convoy 25 miles north-west of Tripoli. It now consisted of five merchantmen escorted by six destroyers in line ahead formation. The Wellingtons went into attack and left two ships blazing. Their attack was aided by the destroyers foolishly pouring out anti-aircraft fire along the water. High-level attacks had not been anticipated due to the previous low-level 'Stringbag' attack. The destroyers then laid a defensive smokescreen, but it was too late, as the damage had been done.

The next day, Friday 12th, Sgt Bridge's Blenheim reconnaissance flight took off from Luqa at 06.30 hours, to survey the situation.

Meanwhile, back on Malta, the Blenheim crews had been called from their quarters. The officers made their way across to their mess tent, as the sergeant aircrew made their usual trip by bus to the aerodrome, from where they ambled down to the sergeants' mess. The air was full of expectation – the word was out that a major 'do' was on. The WOp/AGs carefully cleaned and greased their guns in anticipation of the day's events. By 11.00 hours everyone had been summoned to the ops room, where all was to unfold. It was to be a maximum effort. The station commander, Group Captain C.H. Cahill DFC AFC, was present, as well as the new squadron commander, Wing Commander D.W. Scivier AFC. Based on the reconnaissance report, the targets were detailed as comprising five destroyers escorting seven merchant vessels, accompanied by an escorting fighter. On hearing how heavily the ships were defended, some derisory comments followed. The entire squadron was united in one common opinion – an attack in daylight on such a target was suicidal. The end could not possibly justify the means.

Apart from the ships' fire-power, the fighter would have free range to attack the Blenheims at will, as they concentrated on the ships. This opinion was shared by the wing commander, who agreed with his crews that it would be a waste of effort. The Blenheims probably wouldn't even reach their target before being shot down. A further night strike by 'Wimpies' or 'Stringbags' was thought to be much more appropriate and would surely be much more effective. However, the group captain disagreed, and the op was not cancelled. Finally, the OC, Air Vice-Marshal Hugh Pughe Lloyd MC DFC, was called upon to act as arbitrator – his conclusion was that the 'show' was on!

The apprehensive crews jumped aboard the pick-up and headed out to the dispersal points, to be dropped off one by one at their aircraft. By 12.30 hours S/L Smithers was lifting Z9613:A into the blue Mediterranean sky, to circuit the aerodrome until the last members of the formation joined them fifteen minutes later at 12.45 hours. Shortly afterwards, all eight pilots were lowering their Blenheims to sea-level to start their square search in the target area. Both flight commanders were present: S/L Smithers was accompanied by S/L Charney from 107 Squadron flying Z9603:F. The squadrons proceeded in two elongated vics of four, in an overall echelon starboard formation. On and on they flew, but nothing was seen.

At 14.15 hours, just as they were beginning to think the target would not be found, the convoy was spotted in the mist on the horizon to port and at 90° to the direction of the last leg of their square search. The grey hulls of the enemy ships were just visible above the flat sea, at a new position of 34° 30'N, 12° 10'E, some 40 miles north-north-west of Tripoli. The 105 Flight was on the port side as they wheeled around to face the convoy, followed closely by the 107 Squadron aircraft. The Blenheims were now in line abreast facing the long string of ships. The formation is believed to have been as follows: (left to right) Sgt Brandwood, Sgt Bendall, S/L Smithers, Sgt Weston (105 Squadron) S/L Charney DFC, Sgt Mortimer, F/L Ballands, F/O Greenhill (107 Squadron).

The seven merchant vessels and five destroyers reported at the briefing turned out to be five merchant vessels (one less thanks to the previous night's activities) escorted by seven destroyers. About 5 miles out, the Blenheims were thrown into +9 boost, and the formation spread out, approaching the targets from the south. The vessels were now in line ahead formation. The destroyers were lying in wait on the other side of the ships, expecting an attack from the north, but nevertheless ready for an air attack. Above the convoy the 'Lightning' fighters were buzzing about waiting to pounce.

The approaching Blenheims roared in loudly at 210mph. Firstly, the gunners on board the destroyers opened up with their heavy anti-aircraft guns, the shells plunging into the water in front of the aircraft like bricks thrown into a pond. Their intention, if they failed to hit the aircraft, was at least to send up large enough water spouts to swamp the wave-hopping machines. All aircraft began to side-slip and jink violently to distract the aim of the ships' gunners, as the Blenheims then began to run into the smaller pom-pom fire. The pilots selected their targets as the light-arms fire threw up a lattice of hot steel. Tracer was floating up from all quarters, interspersed with unseen deadly rounds as the sea boiled, throwing up huge spouts of water. The flanking destroyers were despatching their own sheets of glowing tracer, which caught the tail of the port aircraft, creeping up along its fuselage from both sides as it stabbed its way along towards the WOp/AG, Sgt Tony Mee. He sat watching helplessly as the scissor action advanced towards him – and stopped only inches from his turret. S/L Smithers went for the 12,000-tonner with his four 250lb bombs, as did Sgt Weston with his two 500-pounders. All six bombs thudded into the side of the ship. Eleven seconds later, it was left a mass of smoke and flames. To their left Sgt Bendall's aircraft had singled out a 10,000-tonner and rammed two 500-pounders into her, leaving yet another ship burning furiously.

Meanwhile, 200 yards behind and to the starboard of the two ships, S/L Charney DFC and his crew, Sgt Porteous (Observer) and Sgt Harris (WOp/AG), in Z9603:F had been racing through the hail of flak, heading towards another of the merchant vessels, with Sgt Mortimer's machine formating on them. Unfortunately, the destroyers' central gunnery control found S/L Charney's aircraft and locked on to it, shooting them down into the sea. Frank Harbord recalls the incident: 'That day we also lost S/L Charney. I remember a glimpse of his aircraft on fire and cartwheeling into the sea.' Sgt Mortimer's machine, Z7504:G, flying parallel with the squadron leader, also fell foul of the hail of fire. He and his crew, Sgt Douglas Reid (Observer) and F/O Owen (WOp/AG), were also shot down into the sea.

F/L Ballands and F/O Greenhill and their crews did not manage to take a ship. However, F/O Greenhill's WOp/AG, Sgt Henry, added to the damage as best he could, pouring a stream of rounds across the deck of one of the destroyers, with such continuity that his guns seized.

The fighter threat consisted of eight Macchi C.200 Saetta or 'Lightning' fighters. These were single-seater 874hp fighters, each armed with two 12.7mm Breda-SAFAT machine-guns in an upper section above the engine. In the event, only three of them gave chase after the departing Blenheims but they soon returned to the convoy. The whole action was over in just a few terrible moments.

The remaining crews formed up, followed by the odd parting shots from the destroyers. All that is except Sgt 'Bill' Brandwood, who had chosen as his target a large liner sporting four lines of portholes along its side. As the pilot lifted his aircraft high over the stern, the bomb doors sprang open, releasing their load into the troopship. The aircraft dropped again over the other side, and found that one of the destroyers had turned in towards the convoy, thereby blocking the fire of the other ships. Quickly, though, another destroyer turned around and poured a stream of pom-pom fire into the aircraft. Only the Blenheim's armour plating saved the crew. Sgt Brandwood, realizing he was in serious trouble, cleverly feigned his demise by allowing the aircraft to side-slip, then pushed the nose down to make the ships' gunners believe they were going to crash into the sea, in the hope they would ease off – miraculously it worked! The aircraft then pulled up level again and raced off out of range. However, they were certainly not out of danger yet as during the attack the starboard engine had been damaged. Sgt Mee reported over the intercom, in as casual a manner as the situation allowed, that the engine was streaming white smoke and seemed to be on fire. It transpired that the trail of smoke in the slipstream was petrol vapour. In +9 boost the pressure loss on top of the wing had blown the flames out. The engine was quickly switched off, the fuel supply isolated, and the throttle opened to drain off the remaining fuel. Sgt Mee used his Leica camera to photograph the burning ship behind them, as the Blenheim raced ahead on the port engine only, trying to catch up with the others. Eventually they pulled up on S/L Smithers' starboard side. For a minute or so they kept station alongside, but their troubles were far from over. The smell of burning was becoming acute. Sgt Mee reported

Sgt Douglas J. Reid (Observer), service no. 978132, was killed in action on 12 September 1941, on an operation from Malta. (via Jim Taylor)

it to his pilot and as a result, both he and the Scottish observer, Sgt Jock Miller, had to use the fire extinguishers on the bomb well which was well alight. So intense had been the fire that Sgt Miller had felt the heat through the spars before proceeding to tackle the blaze. Once the extinguishers were exhausted, the observer returned to his position in the nose and strapped in. He then began to remove the Very cartridges from their rack, fearing that the heat might set them off. As he did so, the port engine began to surge and power dwindled – like it or not, only 12 miles from the convoy, they were going into the drink!

At 14.25 hours Sgt Frank Harbord, observer in the leader's aircraft, watched as Sgt Brandwood's machine turned away, the fire still raging in the bomb-bay. Apparently out of control it plunged into the sea nose first. In Frank Harbord's words: 'It was while forming up was going on that Sgt Brandwood came up on our right as I remember for a minute or two, when he suddenly turned away from us at right angles and fell into the sea.'

In the centre of the fuselage Sgt Mee was standing on the fuselage skin, just off the wooden walkway, his left arm draped over the 12-volt battery and his back pressed against a spar as the aircraft went in. There was a terrific shock wave. G-force pinned the crew down as the machine thrust its way down below the waves. The impact forced the cupola on the mid-upper turret to break free of its mountings and it bounced about violently as a cascade of dark green water gushed into the fuselage. This was complemented by another jet of water pushing up through the perspex panel below the F24 camera, the framework of which was located on the floor near the escape hatch. The aircraft was filling rapidly, as the forces balanced and the sinking ceased. Briefly the descent stopped as the aircraft started to rise, recoiling to the surface for its last breath of air. As it rose up, the surrounding water turned from dark green to a lighter shade of green before the Blenheim re-emerged temporarily, to surface once more below the clear blue of the Mediterranean sky. As the aircraft had plunged into the water, Sgt Mee had felt an intense pressure and severe pain, due to his spinal vertebrae compacting under the shock. When the turmoil died down, he found himself standing in a couple of feet of water amid the battered structure. Instinctively, he opened the hatch and proceeded in great pain to heave the inflatable dinghy out into the sea.

Meanwhile, as the gunner was getting out, the two in the front were having problems of their own. Sgt Jock Miller had escaped through the collapsed perspex in the nose, and was a few feet away from the aircraft doggy-paddling around to the best of his ability. The pilot, Sgt 'Bill' Brandwood, was bemused to find that the wall of water in which he was engulfed, had pirouetted him through 180 degrees – he was left facing the direction from whence he came, with nothing but the armour plating, which had been behind him, now facing him. Desperately he groped for the release pin on his Sutton harness. Instinctively pushing at his front brought no release, as due to his abnormal position it was now located at his back. Eventually, with his right hand stretched behind his shoulders, he was able to release himself from the straps and quickly clambered up through the 'office' hatch to the surface, and fresh air once again.

By this time Sgt Miller had swum over to the starboard wing. He was holding on tightly as Sgt Mee used his knife to cut the dinghy free. The kit immediately transformed itself from a neat package into a fully equipped dinghy, complete with a knife, two wooden plugs in case of puncture and two paddles. To aid survival, the dinghy was also equipped with three small food packs, each approximately 5in square. A 'pyrotechnic' flare was also included, should the occupants be fortunate enough to be spotted by a friendly party – not that that was to be expected off the coast of Tripoli! First into the dinghy was Sgt Miller. Sgt Mee, by now in severe pain, was being helped by Sgt Brandwood towards the dinghy, which had begun to drift. Sgt Mee was then pulled aboard by his two comrades. By this time their aircraft, Z7367:L, had quietly succumbed to the lure of the depths as she nosed her way gently to her final resting place several hundred fathoms below.

As the three lads settled uncomfortably into their respective sections of the dinghy, there was a heartening reminder that they had not been forgotten. Two of the formation had circled to note the position of the stricken crew; Sgt Brandwood had seen them in the distance and stood up waving his arms aloft. The Blenheims replied as they flew overhead, waggling their wings. S/L Smithers and Sgt Weston then disappeared into the distance and returned to base.

The operation had lasted three and half hours as the last aircraft, S/L Smithers in V6913:A, landed at Luqa.

All the survivors got back safely, if not elegantly. Sgt Bendall, with his wounded observer, Sgt Hindle, and WOp/AG Sgt Brown only just made it. Having been badly shot up over the target area, they landed Z9606:V at 15.15 hours without wheels, skidding along to a halt in a brown cloud of dust and flying stones.

Immediately after their return, P/O Gooch of 69 Squadron was warming up Beaufort I L9875 ready to search the area for the missing crew. At 15.45 hours he and his crew took off. They located the convoy at 33° 56'N, 11° 52'E, heading at 10 knots on a course of 150°. A great deal of wreckage littered the sea, with the forlorn sight of empty life rafts and lifeboats bobbing about on the water amid an oil patch to the north of the convoy. However, in addition, a yellow dinghy was seen, which probably contained the airmen. Meanwhile, the three crew members were busy baling out the water in the bottom of their survival craft. They dried out their clothes and cigarettes as best they could under the circumstances!

On their return, the remaining crews had been debriefed as usual, and the story of the 'L' for Leather's ditching was hurriedly told. Typically, W/C Edwards VC DFC, who was still on Malta, immediately ordered that his crew was not going to spend a minute longer than necessary adrift in the Mediterranean. He went personally to Manoel Island to solicit naval assistance. The next day, Edwards defied the flying ban imposed upon him and soon Blenheim 'T' for Tommy was in the air with Hughie Edwards at the controls, accompanied by F/O Ivens (P/O Buckley's observer), along with his own crew of Sgt Knight and Sgt Quinn DFM and bar. They spent three hours and five minutes searching off Kerkenna and the Tripoli area, but only spotted an Italian Macchi C.200 fighter and a Cant. That afternoon, S/L Smithers in Z7357:U led three Blenheims to a position 35° 15'N, 11° 47'E. However, after having searched in vain for three hours and ten minutes, they were all safely back at base.

They were, of course, wholly unaware of the events which had taken place earlier in the morning. The day previously, as time wore on and nobody had come to their rescue, the three sergeants had settled down for the night at sea. They drifted along beneath the bright stars in the cloudless sky, their brilliance only eclipsed by a large bright moon which illuminated the shoals of silver scaled fish, twisting their way lazily past the dinghy. Despite this apparently tranquil scene, the sea was getting rougher and sea-sickness was beginning to set in.

That night they heard faint rumbles in the distance and saw flashes as 38 Squadron followed up the Blenheim attack. Shipping which had reached the Spanish Quay was getting a pasting. This was followed by an attack by eight Swordfish of 830 Squadron Fleet Air Arm, who had found surviving ships from the convoy 15 miles east of Zuara, heading for Tripoli under the protection of shore batteries. Once again the 'Stringbags' mauled the shipping, leaving a 5,000-tonner ablaze while a large explosion sealed the fate of a 6,000-tonner which was left crippled in the water. The 'Stringbags' returned to Malta, only to be replaced in this relentless onslaught at 03.00 hours by the 'Wimpies' of 38 Squadron, which again attacked the shipping in Tripoli's Spanish Quay. They met a lattice of searchlights, eleven in all, and a thick smokescreen which made visibility difficult, in addition to the light and heavy ack-ack fire. However, by 04.35 hours it was all over, with 27,500lb of bombs having ripped into the target area. As the 'Wimpies' droned their way back home, the dinghy with the three airmen was left bobbing about in solitude.

After some hours of sleep, there came a yellowish light as if dawn was breaking, which proved to be a false dawn. But shortly afterwards, the real dawn broke, with a splendid orange light spilling across the waves rippling from the horizon. As the bright yellow outline of the sun quickly rose into the blue sky, another day began.

That Saturday morning, the crew was not short of company as they drifted along, propelled by a north-westerly wind. Suddenly, as they marvelled at the shoals of blue and red fish which surrounded them, they noticed a much larger and potentially more dangerous visitor. The three airmen watched anxiously as the fin of a large shark circled them. After a while, the fin changed direction and the shark came straight for the dinghy at speed. As it neared, the crew thrashed violently at the surface of the water, shouting loudly in vain hope that the beast would be frightened off, or at least be distracted and miss the dinghy. The shark slipped swiftly past the port side with a defiant sideways flick of its fin, splashing water high into the air as it went – then it disappeared and was gone. Other fish of a less deadly nature also appeared. Shoals of flying fish sported their blue and green bodies in aerial exhibitions before plunging back into the water again and making off into the distance.

At 07.40 hours the crew's excitement grew as a large black object broke the line of the horizon. Slowly but surely it came nearer and nearer. Sgt Brandwood used his steel mirror to flash the sunlight at it and their hopes were confirmed. This was not another strange tropical fish, but a submarine – salvation at last! At 07.45 hours, as the crew paddled towards the object, Sgt Brandwood picked up the 'pyrotechnic' flare. Pulling on its fibre ring, he launched a dozen or so bright stars into the morning sky. They burst a hundred feet in the air, clearly visible to the submarine's crew, now at a position 34° 38'N, 12° 16'E. The submarine drew closer and closer until by 08.00 hours its crew was visible. On the conning tower one of the sailors wore a green shirt. On the hull another was sporting a red one, while others were stripped to the waist. This sight suddenly kindled a dreadful thought: surely the Royal Navy would not allow such attire – they were almost certainly Italians and the crew were going to spend the rest of the war 'in the bag'! The airmen quickly threw wallets and any other belongings over the side, in order that the enemy might acquire as little information as possible when they were captured. However, ten minutes later, as the submarine came alongside, all their fears were allayed. An English voice greeted them loudly from the sub's deck. It was HMS *Utmost*, a U-class vessel, operating from 10th Flotilla based at Manoel Island near Lazzaretto Creek, a tributary of Marsaxmett Harbour which skirts Valletta. The vessel had a complement of thirty-one, which was soon increased to thirty-four. By 08.10 hours the three airmen were on the deck behind the conning tower, having been hauled aboard over the stabilizing fins. Soon they were taken below where each man was handed a traditional tot of naval rum to warm the heart. In the event the only one who drank his tot was Sgt Mee.

Three minutes later, HM Submarine N19 dived once again.

The captain of the vessel was Lt-Cdr R.D. 'Ben' Caley DSO, who had received an official order to look for the airmen following W/C Edwards' appeal for naval assistance. At this point in time, the log entries for HMS *Utmost* read:

06.50. Fixed position by Morning Star.(34° 36'N, 12° 16'E) A/C [Altered Course] 249°.
07.45. Sighted distress firing signal, Bearing 220, 5'.0. In position: 34° 38'N, 12° 16'E. Proceeded as Req. for close.
08.00. Sighted rubber float, 3 occupants. Embarked 3 sergeants RAF.
08.13. Dived, position: 34° 36'N, 12° 15'E. Raised Log [unreliable]. Speed 3 knots. S/W. 058°.

The place of honour was awarded to Sgt Brandwood, who was given the skipper's bunk for the return journey, while Sgt Mee took over the second-in-command's bunk. On the way back the crew were treated for their injuries and then given a guided tour of the submarine. Their hosts proudly showed them all the equipment in the conning tower, as well as the two diesel-electric motor drives, together producing a maximum of 825bhp, which could push the submarine along at a maximum of 9 knots.

Before arriving back at Malta, the submarine had to follow a zig-zag course and navigate its way through the mine-fields that the Italians had laid around the north of the island. The *Utmost*'s log entries further stated:

19.55. Surfaced, position: 34° 55'N, 12° 52'E. Speed 9 knots.
20.00. Fixed position by Evening Star. [34° 55'N, 12° 35'E].
20.10. Commenced zig-zag.
21.00. A/C 060°.

By this time the submarine had travelled a distance of 116.9 miles on the surface, and 35.2 miles submerged. The total time spent submerged was eleven hours and forty-two minutes.

Neither the submariners nor the aircrews could understand how the other could endure the hardships of their respective jobs – there was great admiration on both sides, and in recognition

The crew of Blenheim Z7367 'L' for Leather, left to right: Sgt Tony Mee (WOp/AG); Sgt 'Bill' Brandwood (Pilot) and Sgt Jock Miller (Observer). Having been shot down off Libya while attacking a large troopship liner in a convoy, they were rescued by HM Submarine Utmost *on 13 September 1941. (The Trustees of the Imperial War Museum, London: CM1420)*

HMS Utmost *(N19) moored alongside a supply ship. The dinghy beside the skull and crossbones of the Jolly Roger at the top of the mast was added in commemoration of the rescue of Sgt Brandwood, Sgt Miller and Sgt Mee from the sea off Tripoli on 13 September 1941. (The Trustees of the Imperial War Museum, London: A7726)*

of this, the *Utmost*'s 'Jolly Roger' flag with skull and cross-bones, traditionally flown from the conning tower of submarines when they re-entered harbour, had from that day forth a dinghy emblazoned on it.

At last the three 'Blenheim Boys' stood once again on terra firma! Relief at being home at base again was immense, although their home-coming was slightly marred when they found, much to their disgust, that many of their minor personal belongings had already been shared out among the other crews.

That same day, at 06.30 hours, three Blenheims had made a fruitless search for a tanker in a sortie lasting six hours. They stooged around Cape Matapan in what proved to be a long and boring trip before 'Y' for Yoke, 'H' for Harry and 'B' for Bertie touched down at Luqa once more.

The following few days were allocated as rest days for the 105 Squadron crews, so it fell to the newly arrived 107 Squadron main force to fly all operations until Wednesday 17 September. That morning, at 09.35 hours, F/L Williams of 69 Squadron took off in a Blenheim to patrol the south-east Tunisian coast. At a point 35 miles to the east of Zuara, a town on the coast some 150 miles west of Tripoli, the target was found. Two 800-ton schooners were being towed by a tug towards Tripoli. The aircraft arrived back at base and Blenheims were subsequently despatched. Four aircraft were detailed for the attack. S/L Smithers was to lead the formation, which comprised two waves of two Blenheims. Alongside Smithers would be Sgt Bendall. The other two machines would be those of Sgt Williams and the newly arrived P/O Robinson, who had been on his way to Egypt a few days before. Robinson's crew had fallen foul of the AOC's habit of 'hi-jacking' crews passing through as reinforcements; they soon found themselves on squadron strength on Malta, like it or not!

Early in the afternoon the crews went out to the dispersal area. Just before take-off, a sandstorm blew up in the distance and so the departure was delayed. Sitting around their aircraft, P/O Robinson produced a packet of Players cigarettes and handed them around. To get a real Players cigarette after weeks away from England was hailed as quite a boost to morale. The discussion inevitably turned to combat tactics and eventually, after much discussion concerning the techniques of shipping attacks, P/O Robinson concluded that his technique was not to go around the masts – he was going over the top!

Eventually the sandstorm blew itself out and at 14.30 hours the four Blenheims took off, lowering down over the sea in pairs for their long flight south. Eventually, at a position 35° 15'N, 11° 47'E, the schooners and tugs loomed up in front of the Blenheims. Each aircraft was armed with two 500lb bombs and the fuses were set. As they approached the targets, moderate flak started to rise up from the tugs. In order to discourage shipping attacks from low level, the enemy had increased the height of the masts on some sailing ships by some 30 to 40ft by adding a length of 2 or 3in diameter steel tubing. A wire was then fixed from one mast to another, attached to the tubing, to act as an arrester. Unsuspecting pilots, concentrating on bombing the ship's hull, could not see the wire at a distance and would only find it as they were pulling up – which was too late. Both these schooners were so equipped. P/O Robinson's theory was going to be difficult to achieve, but was to prove tragically irrelevant.

S/L Smithers and Sgt Bendall veered off to attack the farthest away target, while Sgt Williams and P/O Robinson closed formation to attack the other. During the attack S/L Smithers' kite, Z7357:U, was damaged by ack-ack fire. Sgt Bendall and his crew, Sgt Hill and

'Tropicalized' MkIV Blenheim Z7627 arrived on Malta on 10 September 1941 and was available to both 105 and 107 Squadrons as 'N', prior to its transfer to 14 Squadron based at Landing Ground 116 in North Africa, from where it was shot down by 'friendly' fire from a Hawker Hurricane on 30 March 1942. The nose gun mounting has been reversed to permit forward strafing. (The Trustees of the Imperial War Museum, London: ME3802)

Sgt Brown, flying in P4840:Y were killed, possibly as a result of hitting the arrester wires. The other two aircraft were roaring in on their run-in at the other ship when suddenly, only a few hundred yards from the schooner, P/O Robinson's aircraft, Z7755:O, erupted into a fireball, possibly having been hit by anti-aircraft fire. Sgt Williams' machine, only about 20 yards to the right of it, swerved wildly to starboard, as the blazing aircraft dropped on to the deck of the schooner, killing P/O Robinson and his crew, Sgt Brookes and Sgt Burrell instantly.

Sgt Williams took a wide sweep round and, finding the other schooner had not been bombed, attacked it from the other side. As they approached they could see the panic-stricken crew running along the deck and jumping over the rails into the sea to escape the incoming bombs. Both his bombs tore into the side of the ship, which exploded violently eleven seconds later. The two surviving aircraft then left the two crippled ships and formed up for the long flight home.

After three hours and fifteen minutes both crews clambered out of their aircraft to relate the sad tale to the intelligence officer at debriefing. The target had been obliterated, but as usual at a tragically high cost in human life – it had been a bad day for the squadron. The feelings were typified in an excerpt from the diary of 107 Squadron's Sgt Johnnie Turner, who wrote the following about the second operation of the day for his squadron:

> 17 September. Returned from Valletta to learn that we'd lost two of the four kites on the second show. Couldn't find out who they are, or were. Oh God, when will they stop murdering Blenheim crews!
>
> [18th] The two crews we lost were one 105 and P/O Robinson.

CHAPTER 22

New Leader

The next day, Tuesday 18th, the news broke that W/C Edwards VC DFC was to return to the UK en route to a recruiting and publicity tour of America. It was considered that the presence of such a highly decorated officer would considerably help to attract young enthusiastic pilots. Edwards hated the idea greatly and wanted to stay with his crews on Malta. Although he was considered too valuable to actually fly on operations, he had always been very loyal to his crews and wanted to remain with them.

However, the Air Staff won the day, and on Friday 19 September a Sunderland I flying boat, L2160 of 230 Squadron based at Aboukir, was surfing along the bay at Kalafrana, Malta, bound for Gibraltar. W/C Francis was at the controls for the eight and a quarter hour trip and his passengers were W/C Harris, S/L Fletcher, Brigadier Lloyd, two majors, Captain Littlejohn, as well as W/C Edwards and his crew (although which crew is not known). The Sunderland landed at Gibraltar, and took off again on the 22nd and flew back to Mount Batten near Plymouth. From there, after a nine hour and ten minute flight, Edwards continued his journey in a de Havilland DH86 Express light transport plane, flown by F/L Read. He was accompanied by Captain Littlejohn, Brigadier Lloyd and W/C Francis. Eventually, after a further one and three quarter hours, their aircraft touched down at RAF Hendon.

On 17 October Edwards was on his way to the United States, where he started his tour on 26 October as a passenger in a Liberator flown by a Captain Lancaster, bound firstly for Washington in the company of such famous RAF heroes as Bob Stanford Tuck and 'Sailor' Malan. How strange it must have been for them to travel across peaceful skies once more in this brief interlude!

Meanwhile, back on Malta, Edwards had been replaced by the CO of the recently departed 110 Squadron, W/C Donald William Scivier AFC, a pilot of some experience and an instructor known by some of the crews for his work at 13 OTU at Bicester. He took over a nominal force of twenty-six aircraft; few of them, however, were actually serviceable, despite the sterling efforts of the groundcrew. At 08.00 hours on Saturday 20 September the new CO flew his first sortie, a reconnaissance trip, with some of his new crews. His crew was F/Sgt Barnet (Observer) and Sgt Gray DFM (WOp/AG). By 11.30 hours they were back for lunch. The next task Don Scivier undertook was to send three of the squadron on bombing practice. Filfla Island, just off the south-west shores of Malta, was the venue. S/L Bryan Smithers took the lead in Z7357:U, followed by Sgt Tommy Williams in V6014:S and Sgt Ivor Broom in Z7852:C. The log entries of Bryan Smithers' observer, Sgt Frank Harbord, and Sgt Broom's WOp/AG, Sgt Les Harrison, confirm that the bombing lasted for twenty minutes, while Sgt Ron Scholefield, Sgt Tommy Williams' observer, noted that the bombing was executed with 'four 11½lb practice bombs (on wings). Smoke bombs (white).' Sgt Chapple's diary noted that take-off was at 14.00 hours and both 'S' and 'U' were down at 14.55 hours, with 'C' having landed five minutes earlier at 14.50 hours.

Sgt Chapple also made the following diary entry which typified the hardships faced by the groundcrew at the time:

> Saturday 20 September 1941: Bad day. Two kites collided taxiing in from ops. One AG shot his fin and rudder up! By evening only six kites serviceable – and fifteen required for ops!

Woe is us! Practice bombing in afternoon. Working on 'P' putting armour plate in. 105 do not have armour plate!

Sunday 21 September 1941: At work 07.30. Collected tools and rigger and went to fix brakes on 'P'. OK. Went on to view damage on 'C's' elevator. Nothing serious. 'S's' nose damaged in collision with 'U'. Got most of the damaged parts clear by 12.00. In afternoon got spares from crashed 'N'. Knocked off 20.00 hours. Two kites off on ops. S/L Smithers' DFC through. Sgt. Gibson [Sgt Bruce's AG] has DFM. Awards all well deserved.

It is interesting to note that Sgt Gibson was unaware of this award at this time, and was only to find out later as we shall see.

Around this time a large 24,000-ton liner had arrived at Tripoli, carrying troops bound as reinforcements for the Afrika Korps. While it was berthed, 107 Squadron made repeated attacks on the ship causing some damage, and reconnaissance pilots noted oil patches in the harbour. When the liner left Tripoli, it was seen to be towing what looked like a repair vessel, and appeared to constitute part of a returning convoy heading north along the Tunisian coast, no doubt heading for Naples or a similar Italian sanctuary. So it was that on Sunday 21st, the 'two kites' referred to by Sgt Chapple, flew off; one belonged to W/C Scivier AFC, the other to W/C F.A. 'Bunny' Harte of 107 Squadron. They were to attack a large convoy, escorted by six destroyers – it was felt that two aircraft just might do the trick!

They left at 17.40 hours, sighting the convoy nearly two hours later at 19.31 hours. With so many destroyers around it would have been foolish to attempt a daylight attack so the two aircraft stooged around in circles until finally at 19.53 hours, in near darkness, they formed up for the attack and raced towards their target. W/C Harte was first to release his four 250-pounders, which fell directly amidships. He was followed by W/C Scivier AFC who hit the ship towards the stern. It was difficult to observe the results, although steam was seen to rise from the vessel after the attack, during which the destroyers had put up a fierce amount of flak. Nevertheless, by 21.35 hours both aircraft were safely back, although W/C Scivier's Blenheim returned with one engine on fire!

The sortie had been a success, although it was obvious to the intelligence officers that a considerable number of troops would have been disembarked – they had to be stopped before they could further reinforce Rommel's army! The most obvious way to do this was to hit their barracks, two of which were located along the coast to the east of Tripoli at Misurata and Al Khums (Homs). The next day, five Blenheims of 107 Squadron left to fix the Misurata Barracks, which they did quite successfully, causing the requisite degree of havoc.

Simultaneously, a combined force of 105/107 Squadrons was to hit the Barracks at Al Khums; the results of this attack were to be traumatic for the entire squadron and for one surviving 105 Squadron crew in particular. Early in the afternoon of Monday 22 September 1941, three crews from each squadron took off, led by W/C Scivier AFC.

Shortly after take-off, the six aircraft had formed up into two neat vics of three and descended to sea-level to begin their southerly run. As the aircraft flew lower, the formation spread out, as close formation was more tiring for the pilots. The leader's observer, F/Sgt Barnett, was busy working out his course by dead-reckoning and reading out the ETA to the pilot, while the WOp/AG, Sgt Gray DFM, listened to his radio and kept watch for fighters. Meanwhile, the other observers were checking their track and heading with their instruments and magnetic compass, taking 'drifts' and working out their true track to the target as a check against the leader's navigation. The other WOp/AGs were scanning the horizon for enemy fighters. To ensure that the target was correctly identified, landfall was to be some 10 miles to the west of the barracks, leaving Tripoli a good 40 miles further to the west. This landfall

This 114 Squadron crew were en route to the Far East when they were 'hi-jacked' on 18 September 1941 for service on Malta with 105 Squadron and later 107 Squadron. Left to right: Sgt Les Harrison (WOp/AG); Sgt Samuel North (Observer); Sgt Ivor Broom (Pilot). (via Sir Ivor Broom)

ensured that if the dead-reckoning was not as accurate as required, a run along the coast from east to west was sure to locate the target.

Soon the coast of Libya appeared, shimmering on the horizon, and the six hounds closed up ready for the hunt. As they flew in towards the shore they raced over a shallow wadi, its palm trees a bright flash of green against the yellow background.

The formation flew on, and just before reaching the coast road, the leader signalled a shallow turn to port. Tension began to mount – the air gunners were apprehensive about fighter attacks in this area and the pilots and observers were straining for sight of the target. The two formations were now racing along side by side, with Sgt Bill Jackson's vic on the left. On Jackson's right was Sgt Tommy Williams, flying as No. 2, and on his right was Sgt Broom, flying as No. 3. Sgt Broom was to the left of W/C Scivier AFC.

Sgt Harrison, Sgt North and Sgt Broom posing with a 500lb bomb beside their 114 Squadron Blenheim 'V' for Victory. (via Sir Ivor Broom)

The Blenheims were cruising along at about 180mph, when suddenly Sgt Jackson saw the target appear on his left, at an angle of 45°

between the formation and the sea. Immediately he signalled a left turn and began to rise and turn his vic towards the target. His No. 2, Sgt Williams, found it hard to keep station in such a tight turn. (It must be remembered that in order for a vic formation to turn, the outer aircraft had its work cut out to keep station at the best of times, and his air speed had to increase considerably more than the inner aircraft's, in order to be able to see the leader's signals, as the formation rose and turned.) All would have been well if not for the fact that by this time W/C Scivier's vic were overshooting too far to the right. Consequently, he turned his formation tightly to the left in order to get to the target. As he did so, Sgt Broom's aircraft flew *under* Sgt William's machine, which was in turn followed by the wing commander, who was pulling upwards to hold formation, without noticing that Sgt Williams was above him. Sgt Ron Scholefield, the observer in Sgt Williams' machine, looked down through his nose windows and to his horror watched the wing commander's aircraft slide under him from right to left, apparently rising up directly beneath him. With a fearful shout of 'Pull up!' to his pilot, who immediately increased power and pulled the stick back hard, he flung himself backwards away from the nose. Sadly it was too late. A loud bang, clearly audible above the heavy engines' roar, indicated that the two aircraft had collided. The propellers of Sgt Williams' machine scythed into the wing commander's fuselage, cutting Z7423:H clean in two, forward of the gunner's hatch. The machine fell 600ft and crashed to the ground. There was little chance for survivors.

By this time the remainder of the flight were dropping their bombs. Soldiers running for cover into the buildings across the parade ground were being machine-gunned by the marauding Blenheims. Sgt Williams' aircraft was vibrating badly as they lurched towards the Barracks. The observer, Sgt Scholefield decided that if they were to crash, as seemed inevitable, then the enemy was still going to get their bombload (it wasn't wise to crash-land with fused bombs on board, anyway). So he leaned forward and pulled on the 'Mickey Mouse' bomb release and 1,000lb of RDX/TNT explosive fell smack into the Barracks. As they raced over the target, the aircraft was pulled out of +9 boost and returned to cruising speed, but the vibration remained and all seemed hopeless. Suddenly the coast appeared dead ahead, with a long stretch of clear sand skirting it. The observer suggested anxiously to the pilot that they should land there, and 'chance the mine-fields if there are any!' The idea seemed sound under the circumstances, but how much better it would be to get home. Wrestling at the controls, Tommy Williams surveyed the situation. He waggled the wings and seemed to have aileron control; the engine oil and cylinder head temperatures were also checked and all seemed to be in order. Back came the heartening reply 'we're still flying, let's keep going!'.

As they limped out over the vast blue expanse of the Mediterranean, the remaining four aircraft were forming up and heading at speed away from them. In Sgt Ivor Broom's machine the WOp/AG, Sgt Les Harrison, noticed the stricken aircraft dropping further and further behind, and having heard a report that a Fiat CR.42 Falco was in the area, decided that it would be unthinkable to leave one of their members as 'easy meat' for the enemy. (Sgt Broom had flown to Malta with his crew, Sgt Samuel 'Bill' North (Observer) and Sgt Les Harrison (WOp/AG) in Z7618:O on 16 September, having previously served with 114 Squadron at West Raynham. Like many other crews, they were on their way to the Far East, but having arrived at what they believed was a temporary stopover, they found they were to go no further, having been 'hi-jacked' to act as a replacement crew for 105 Squadron's Battle Order.) He reported over the intercom to his skipper, who agreed and peeled away from his leading position in the formation to re-join Sgt Williams on his starboard side. The crew were delighted to see their escort arrive, but were extremely apprehensive at having another aircraft flying so close to them, after their recent experience. To the relief of all concerned, Sgt Broom stayed several wingspans distant. Sgt Samuel 'Bill' North, the observer in Sgt Broom's aircraft, was busy

Blenheim Z9609 GB:T at Luqa showing the damage caused by the mid-air collision with W/C Scivier's Blenheim over Homs on the Libyan coast on 22 September 1941. Note the deformed propeller blades and bomb-bay area; the hole in the starboard wing root and cooling gills; the shattered nose gun blister; the pitot tube bent back at right angles; and the oil pouring down the port wheel fairing. (via Ron Scholefield)

Blenheim Z9609 GB:T at Luqa on 22 September 1941. Despite the possibility of enemy fighter attack, this shattered aircraft was escorted home to Luqa by Sgt Ivor Broom and his crew. (via Ron Scholefield)

working out the course for home. Sgt Scholefield also checked the course as the aircraft commenced their 218-mile journey back to safety. The crippled aircraft had no air speed indication, as the collision had bent the pitot head, which normally hung vertically downwards under the nose, but which now lay horizontally pointing out to the left. The 90° bend had closed the pipe and consequently the air speed indicator could not register. The observer therefore used the Aldis lamp to 'talk' to the other aircraft, and in the process learned that their speed was about 150mph. Onward they shuddered for something just over an hour – it seemed like an eternity. Oil was pouring out of the port engine, which began to play up as they neared base. The edges of the propellors should have looked like shiny disks – such was the collision damage to the blades that they seemed to have a 'fringe' about a foot long. Given its battered condition, it was a miracle that the aircraft was flying at all!

Approaching Malta, it was doubtful if the damaged machine could climb up to height quickly enough near the coast, and so the two aircraft slowly began to gain height earlier than usual and managed to achieve an estimated 1,200ft. Eventually, after what seemed an eternity to the crew, Malta appeared as a shimmering yellow dot on the horizon, and both crews prepared for landing. Turning into the damaged port engine, Sgt Williams began his approach to Luqa. He selected fine pitch, and the resulting vibration was horrendous. However, with dextrous handling both aircraft and crew miraculously landed safely and Sgt Williams taxied to the dispersal point where to his great relief, he switched off the engines, and the propellers clattered to a halt.

The crew were met by the Adjutant, F/O 'Teddy' Frayn, who ran up to the aircraft shouting 'What the hell happened?'. Inspection of the aircraft, Z9606:T, revealed that the underneath of the fuselage was badly damaged and in particular the bomb-bay access flaps were severely misshapen. A large hole could also be seen on the leading edge of the starboard wing where it met the starboard side of the engine cowling. Under the nose, the blister housing the rear-firing .303in Browning machine-gun had been demolished, leaving only a serrated outline of its former presence. With the engines stopped, the propeller blade tips were seen to have been bent in all directions – it was hardly surprising that such severe vibration had been felt. In view of the damage, it was quite amazing that the Blenheim had flown the 218 miles home successfully.

As the severely shocked crew alighted from their battered Blenheim, their horror was compounded on discovering that the aircraft they had collided with belonged to the new CO. They had not noticed that the No. 3 had moved under them first and the crew had consequently assumed it was this aircraft with which they had collided. Nor did they know at the time which crew had acted as their guardian angels on the trip home, but their gratitude was heartfelt. Sgt Ron Scholefield remembers the trip all too clearly: 'Then one [Blenheim] peeled off, returned and rejoined us on the starboard side several wingspans away, thank God. Thirty-eight years later, I learned that this was Ivor Broom. We knew it must have been one of the 'new boys' because no old hand would have turned back because of the possibility of fighters.'

105 Squadron's Sgt Alan Tuppen (WOp/AG) sketched by J.B. Cary at Imtarfa, Malta, on 28 August 1941. (via Ron Scholefield)

The shaken crew members were taken to the MO at Luqa and the brandy bottle was produced; each of the three airmen was given a large 'steadier'. As it transpired, this was the last operation the crew were to fly on together. Although exonerated of any blame, the memory of the episode haunted the individuals ever after. Ron Scholefield summed up their reactions to the horror experienced by his crew on their return: 'I broke down and wept and wept. Tommy, then twenty-two years old, became completely grey, then white-haired a month later. Tuppen never flew again, not to this day.'

CHAPTER 23

The Last Straws

Following the tragic loss of W/C Scivier AFC and his crew, the well respected and admired W/C F.A. 'Bunny' Harte assumed joint command of 105 and 107 Squadrons, until October 1941 when W/C P.H.A. Simmons DFC took command of 105 Squadron.

No further operations took place until Thursday 25 September, when shipping in the Gulf of Sirte was the target. Nothing was found and so the formation of five Blenheims swept inland, east of Sirte. They flashed in low along the coastal road and beat up an enemy motor transport convoy in Tripoli, while the air gunners severely molested the troops on the ground. At a position 31° N, 17° 30'E, their bombs ensured the quick demolition of a building. All aircraft returned around 17.35 hours, six hours from take-off.

Two days later, six crews were detailed to attack the Marsalla aerodrome at Bo Rizzo, Sicily. Hangars and a wireless station were potential targets. Bad weather prevented the primary target being reached, but on the way back, Sgt Weston noticed a granary at Porto Empedocle on the south coast of Sicily and proceeded to bomb and strafe it. The flight then returned to touch down two hours and fifty minutes from departure.

Due to the lack of success at Bo Rizzo, it was decided to return to Porto Empedocle to finish the job. At 15.30 hours Sgt Weston, accompanied by 107 Squadron's Sgt Roath, Sgt Broom, Sgt Kerr, Sgt Hamlyn and Sgt Hopkinson took off again. This time the defences were alert and intense flak floated towards the formation. The plant and its silos were duly bombed, although in the process the port engine of Sgt Hopkinson's machine burst into flames. The aircraft managed to return on one engine. Sgt Roath's Blenheim was hit in the hydraulics, preventing lowering of the landing gear on return. This would probably have given the additional and nerve-racking problem of turret control failure, hence the gunner would be helpless against air attacks all the way home. However, this time Sgt Roath successfully managed to wind the undercarriage down manually, thereby negating the requirement to make a forced-landing. Sgt Ivor Broom's aircraft also suffered badly. On return from the Bo Rizzo raid in Z7852:C, Sgt Broom and crew changed aircraft to Z7644:E. During the attack this aircraft received a direct hit in the instrument panel from an explosive bullet. The panel was destroyed and it was flying skill alone which took the crew home. The others also returned safely to Luqa after a flight which this time lasted one hour and fifty minutes.

For some days, the build-up of Italian naval vessels had been noticeable. Reconnaissance reports had been lengthy, carefully detailing all shipping in and around Sicily. Sgt Chapple noted in his diary on Wednesday 24th, 'Numerous fighter Blenheims and Marylands came in yesterday.' On the 25th he noted: 'Aerodrome lousy with aircraft. Marylands and two squadrons of Beaufighters arrived yesterday and today.' Something was certainly brewing. The aircraft build-up turned out to be cover for a relief convoy which had left Gibraltar bound for Malta. With its imminent arrival, the Beaufighters were to assume a protecting role and ward off any fighters which might attack from the neighbouring enemy territories. Meanwhile, 69 Squadron were keeping up their Maryland reconnaissance sorties. On 28 September W/C Dowland accompanied by his crew, P/O Potter and Sgt Thomas, were up at 06.25 hours in Maryland BS762, on a 'special crossover patrol' to cover the arriving convoy, which was spotted in position 36° 46'N, 13° 40'E, on a course of 130° and travelling at 15 knots. Having

On 27 September 1941 105 Squadron accompanied by 107 Squadron attacked a granary at Porto Empedocle on the south coast of Sicily. This was the last operation 105 Squadron undertook from Malta. (via Brian Hanafin/Len Fearnley)

Bombs exploding during the attack on the granary at Porto Empedocle. (via Brian Hanafin/Len Fearnley)

returned to Malta at 07.40 hours, the crew changed aircraft, and by 08.05 hours they were once again airborne, now in Maryland BS772 for a further 'crossover patrol'.

Operation 'Halberd' was under way. It was the first convoy to attempt to sail for Malta since 'Substance' in July. Nine transports and three empty ships had arrived at Gibraltar on the night of 24/25 September. They assembled in the Straits on the 25th at 09.00 hours, escorted by Force H under Vice-Admiral Sir James Sommerville in the *Nelson*. The supplemented Force H now included the capital ships *Nelson*, *Prince of Wales* and *Rodney*, as well as the aircraft carrier *Ark Royal;* the rest of the force was made up of five cruisers: *Kenya, Edinburgh, Sheffield, Hermione* and *Euryalus,* and eighteen destroyers.

Force H had initially split into two groups which met up again on the 27th. The purpose of this was to give the appearance of a smaller group (Group I) sailing along the North African coast, as Force H normally would, while the other group (Group II), escorting the nine transports headed north-east along the Spanish coast before turning back to the south-east again on approaching the Balearic Islands.

Group I had their share of action en route, attacking a submarine with depth-charges. Group II were spotted by Spanish aircraft. As mentioned previously, the Spanish often involved themselves in informing on British movements; this incident was no different. On the 27th both groups combined. That afternoon, the expected air attack began. Italian BR.20 and SM.79 aircraft, escorted by CR.42s, attacked when the convoy was 90 miles south-west of Cagliari. In all that day thirty aircraft attacked the convoy. Six were shot down by the ships' guns and four more by fighters. Only eighteen fighters got close enough to attack the convoy, but they managed to damage the *Nelson*; the torpedo that exploded against her port bow restricted her speed to a limping 15 knots. Although it was thought that the Italian Navy would engage the force, nothing materialized. At the mouth of the Narrows, the convoy left Force A which drew off to the west to await Rear-Admiral Harold Burrough's return from Malta. Meanwhile, all the cruisers and half the destroyers continued to the fortress island. The only serious casualty from the convoy was the *Imperial Star*. Like the *Nelson*, she too was struck by a torpedo on the port side aft. Her 'cargo' consisted of 300 soldiers bound for Malta, all of whom were safely decanted to the rescue ship *Heythrop*. After a valiant attempt by the *Oribi* to tow the *Imperial Star* to her destination, the task became impossible. She was taking on water too fast and with a flooded engine room, rudder and two screws out of action, the decision was made to scuttle her with depth-charges. In the early hours of the 28th, she met her fiery fate. The depth-charges were assisted by shellfire from *Oribi* to finish her off; another victim of the 'Malta Run'.

On arrival at the Grand Harbour on the morning of the 28th, Rear-Admiral Burrough was met by a tumultuous welcome from almost the entire population of Valletta. They had turned out en masse to welcome in and celebrate the arrival of the first convoy in three months to enter their fortress walls. Amid the brass band accompaniment, the cheers and tears said it all. The convoy was brought into harbour, escorted by the destroyers, led by HMS *Edinburgh* in the early afternoon.

On the 27th, the last operational involvement of 105 Squadron Blenheims was over following the attack on Porto Empedocle. Plucked from the jaws of seemingly certain death, the surviving aircrews were told to get their kit bags packed and be ready for departure. Bob Lyndall remembers this very welcome occasion:

> Our officers were at Luqa, while we were at Marsaxlokk, so the only fraternization was when we were engaged on an operation. Then, at a time when the squadron morale was at rock bottom, we had a surprising request at 7 p.m. – would we invite our officers to our mess at Marsaxlokk? We agreed, and S/L Smithers broke the good news: 'Pack up tonight – you

have to be on board the cruiser *Hermione* in Valletta at 6 a.m; you're going home! So we finished off the Arak and Maltese Blue Label – who cared about sleeping? It was farewell to Malta!

The groundcrews were also to be relieved. Sgt Chapple wrote of the news and arrival of the relief convoy:

It was a wonderful surprise. The night before we left we had been up to our ears in the usual aircraft preparation, only more so, when one of our few remaining officers gave us the news. The weather was brilliant and the arrival of the convoy was an incredible sight – and all in wide-screen technicolour! The sky above Valletta was thick with aircraft, mostly ours; there were a few interlopers being very roughly handled. All Malta turned out to cheer the convoy in. As each ship entered harbour, a naval bugler on the ramparts sounded the General Salute and the bigger ships played themselves in with Marine bands on the quarter deck.

For the first leg of the voyage, the crews were accommodated on board cruisers wherever space was available. Some were assigned to Rear-Admiral Burrough's Fiji-class *Kenya*, others to Vice-Admiral Syfret's Southampton-class *Edinburgh* and the remainder to the Dido-class *Hermione*. During an air raid on the evening of the 28th, under the shadow of darkness and confusion, the ships slipped out of the Grand Harbour. Force X was en route to Gibraltar once again. The track was to take them along the North African coast where, at 10.30 hours the next morning, Force X would join forces once again with Admiral Curteis in the *Prince of Wales*, before continuing to Gibraltar.

The 8,000-ton Fiji-class cruiser HMS Kenya *which took part in Operation Halberd. (The Trustees of the Imperial War Museum, London: A9223)*

Some of the 105 Squadron aircrew travelled from Malta to Gibraltar on the 5,450-ton Dido-class cruiser HMS Hermione, *shown here (centre) with guns pointing skyward. (The Trustees of the Imperial War Museum, London: A5742)*

Such was the plan as the young airmen entered the world of the 'Senior Service'. Once on board, accommodation had to be found. Typically, as on board the *Kenya*, accommodation was allotted wherever possible. Although a hangar was provided for a mess, bunks were provided in a variety of locations, from the torpedo workshop to the Chief Petty Officers' Mess, where bunks were supplemented by blanketed floor space. While on board there was still work to be done. One group of air gunners was allotted the task of manning Lewis guns. These overlooked the four turrets, each of which contained three 6in guns. Observers were also given their Action Stations on a platform high above the bridge, where there were three sets of binoculars mounted on a pillar on each side of the ship. From this vantage point they each searched one-sixth of the horizon, looking to the left and right to find torpedo tracks, mines, periscopes or any other dangers lurking in the waves. Action Stations were manned throughout the entire night of departure and the following day; only when they were approaching Corsica were they allowed to stand down.

The pilots were also given Action Stations duties and although not many tasks available were relevant to their skills, jobs were found in places such as the ship's magazine room. On board the *Edinburgh*, at least one pilot (P/O Hanafin) was given the task of aircraft recognition in conjunction with one of the anti-aircraft guns. Everybody had to play their part. Any time off was spent hanging around the ship's deck or at the canteen where cigarettes and the usual limited selection of sweets and soft drinks could be purchased. A small wooden table in the hangar served as a meeting point for the young aviators.

During the trip there were five submarine attacks, in one of which *Gurkha* was narrowly missed by two torpedoes. Although depth-charged by several of the destroyers, the submarines did claim the *Auda*. The fleet also bombarded the coast of Pantellaria for good measure.

At dusk on the 29th, with *Kenya* leading in her pink Arctic camouflage, the fleet split into two groups. Rear-Admiral Burrough's *Kenya* and Admiral Curteis' *Prince of Wales* surged ahead. Rumour had it that these two had narrowly avoided colliding during the night, but both safely arrived at Gibraltar in the late afternoon. Two ships containing the 105 Squadron personnel, the *Kenya* and *Hermione* reached Gibraltar with the first group on the 30th. The *Edinburgh* was among the second group which arrived safely on 1 October under the command of Vice-Admiral Syfret.

During the period between arrivals shore leave tickets were issued. Leave started about 18.00 hours and was granted only until 23.00 hours. Once ashore, many men snapped up souvenirs such as silk items for mothers and sweethearts back home. Some crews renewed old acquaintances. One instance of this saw a group of four young airmen visiting an Indian storekeeper who was known to one of their company. Although officially closed, he responded

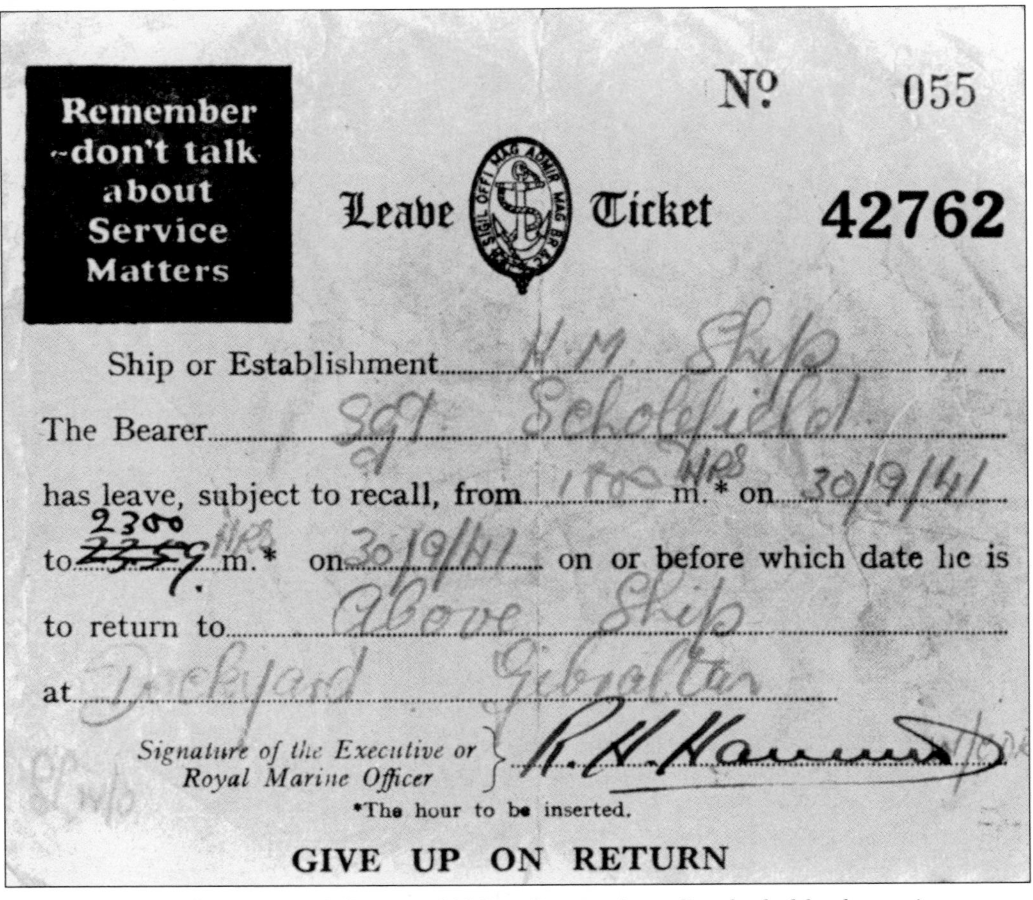
Remember
–don't talk
about
Service
Matters

No. 055

Leave Ticket 42762

Ship or Establishment H.M. Ship

The Bearer Sgt Scholefield

has leave, subject to recall, from 1800 HRS m.* on 30/9/41

to ~~2359~~ 2300 HRS m.* on 30/9/41 on or before which date he is

to return to Above Ship

at Dockyard Gibraltar

Signature of the Executive or Royal Marine Officer } R. H. Ha[illegible]

*The hour to be inserted.

GIVE UP ON RETURN

Leave ticket issued on board HMS Kenya *as 105 Squadron survivors disembarked for the evening at Gibraltar on 30 September 1941. (via Ron Scholefield)* to the knock on the door and rounded off the transactions by providing copious quantities of whisky for his guests.

On return to the ship they all bunked down for the night. The silence was broken by the captain addressing the ship's company over the tannoy, and at 04.45 hours the ship put to sea. One of the RAF crew, Sgt Ron Scholefield, remembers the eventful voyage from Gibraltar as follows:

> The captain explained that we, in company with the *Sheffield*, were to go and look for a submarine supply ship, which had reportedly left Bordeaux one or two days before and was heading into the Atlantic. We had to go and search for it. We travelled with the *Sheffield* for some time, then after a day or so parted company, and each ship went on separate square searches. This went on for two or three days in very, very rough weather. Even some of the seamen were being sick.
>
> The Walrus plane catapulted off several times a day, flying off into the murk, presumably doing a wider search. First of all it would be wheeled out of the hangar, then turned round athwart ships, and fixed on to the steam catapult. Its engine was then started and the crew would climb in, the navigator in the back with his clipboard. They would then open up the throttles wide and the large prop behind the pilot would roar into action. Steam was then released into the catapult, following various shouted orders. The Walrus would then be projected over the side and would sink towards the sea, creeping over the wave-tops, gradually obtaining flying speed before climbing away. After several hours the aircraft would come back again. In order to aid the landing Walrus, the cruiser would swing around

The 9,100-ton Southampton-class cruiser HMS Sheffield *which also took part in Operation Halberd. (The Trustees of the Imperial War Museum, London: A12698)*

in a circle. On the inside of the circle the water was left absolutely smooth. The Walrus then landed on the smooth patch of water, before taxiing up to the side of the ship. The water became rough again by the time the navigator had clambered out of the aircraft with his Mae West around him, and had hooked a winch hook on to an appropriate position above the wings. The whole aircraft would then be winched up level with the deck, before being pulled aboard again.

On a grey September afternoon 'Action Stations' were sounded over the tannoy and we all ran like mad to our stations. Our station was on a high-level platform at the front of the ship. Then the buzz went round that the enemy ship had been found. After a few minutes, in the murky distance, a ship of some 10,000 tons appeared; very much bigger than we had expected. The *Kenya* then increased speed, going faster and faster, until I believe it was doing 33 knots. They told us afterwards that it was travelling faster than it had on its acceptance trials when first built. No notice or warning was given before they opened fire with the forward guns. The gunnery control platform beside us would issue messages to the turrets and then they would order quite quietly 'Fire!'. Immediately the forward guns went off. In quite a short time we were within say half a mile of the ship, and we swung around sideways on. Then they opened up with forward and rear turrets. They then circled, and after several circuits, some 370 rounds of ammunition had been fired at it. We noticed each time we came round that the crew had baled out into the life-boats. We then did another circuit and laid torpedoes. Presumably, having had so much gunnery practice without succeeding very well, only some of the shells hitting, others landing beyond and in front, they decided to fire two torpedoes.

Just about the time they fired the two torpedoes, and in addition to the report of the guns, there was suddenly the most hideous, ear-piercing, shrieking roar; we were all terrified for a few seconds. What had happened was that they had stoked up the boilers so high, the pressure was such that the safety valves blew off, discharging through the steam escape pipe on the funnel about 4 or 5 yards from where we were standing.

We could see the torpedoes go off into the sea and their track as they went towards the ship. Then suddenly, the whole 10,000-ton ship exploded. The whole lot just went up – wham! Comparatively slowly, the red flames and black smoke went up and up into the air. Bits of debris, some very large, flew up into the air before splashing in the sea, some quite near to us. Large plates and huge bits of timber rained down. We then roared away and left them to it. About three quarters of an hour afterwards, when far enough away, we picked up the Walrus which had been flying around.

In the evening, after having been stood down from Action Stations, we were back in the mess having our evening meal when the tannoy erupted. It was the captain, who said, 'You will be pleased to know of the exceptionally good result today when we sunk the submarine supply ship, and I wish to thank all members of the crew for the work they did.' He then said that he wanted to have a word about the crew of the ship which baled out into the life-boats – he said he wished the sea was twice as rough and twice as cold as it was.

The general feeling among 105 Squadron aircrew was that it had been a bloody waste: it had taken 370 rounds and two torpedoes and a ship with about a thousand personnel on board to do what one Blenheim with three crew on board and four 250lb bombs could have done – if they had been able to find it!

It was also noted that the reason the ship did not stop to pick up survivors was due to the threat posed by a submarine lurking in the area. It was considered safer for the ship's company to keep going.

The 9,100-ton Southampton-class cruiser HMS Sheffield *viewed from the decks of the 8,000-ton Fiji-class cruiser HMS* Kenya *bound for Gibraltar and then Scotland, in rough weather. Both ships carried 105 Squadron survivors back from Malta. (via Ron Scholefield)*

Sgt Ron Scholefield and fellow crew member Sgt Alan Tuppen on board HMS Kenya. *(via Ron Scholefield)*

Events on other ships in the convoy were also recorded. Sgt Chapple recalled:

> At Gibraltar, we transferred to another cruiser, I think *Norfolk* and we set sail again. This time we were at sea for nearly three weeks with a convoy which included the Polish liner *Sobieski*. We had various adventures: U-Boat contacts; picking up shipwreck survivors; from Gib we had some escapees and evaders who had managed to get into Spain from the Pyrénées; we passed through the wreckage of a German commerce raider which one of our number, HMS *Kenya* had put down. Only gradually did it dawn on us that we were part of the Atlantic Convoy escort!

Brian Hanafin recalls being on board HMS *Edinburgh*, and has:

> a clear memory of going into the southern part of the North Atlantic, to pick up a convoy of merchant vessels coming from North and South America to the UK. One of the convoy we met was a large Polish passenger ship. We did not lose any ships, although we had a few attacks by U-Boats. The *Edinburgh* did her share of rushing around, dropping depth-charges. All very alarming to us aviators!

A day or so later the convoy came around the north of Ireland, past Rathlin Island and up the River Clyde, past Paddy's Milestone (Ailsa Craig island) as far as Gourock. Before tying up at Gourock, the Royal Marines Band went up on to the fo'c's'le and played music, including the appropriate 'Phantom Brigade'. Once tied up at the quayside, the crews had to get themselves ashore as there was a dock strike on! Nevertheless, they stepped proudly back on to British soil, something many of them had thought they would never do again. As they did so, their thoughts went out to those who never would.

Having at last retrieved their kit from their ship's stores, the airmen changed once again into their 'blues'. It had been a long, cold trip across the Atlantic in their thin tropical kit!

Disembarking in the rain under a dull, grey sky, they headed on to the quayside. Here they had customs to deal with, followed by a trek on to troop trains, which were full to the gunnels.

The 10,000-ton Southampton-class cruiser HMS Edinburgh *was another ship which transported home survivors of the 105 Squadron Malta detachment. (via F.E. Frayn)*

Some went to Glasgow and on to London directly, before completing their journey back to Swanton Morley, while a sizeable contingent travelled on a rather more convoluted journey to the same destination, on a train which left that afternoon and took all night. After journeying via Crewe and Chester, the train finally pulled in at about 03.00 hours at Upton station near West Kirby. Having scrambled on board trucks waiting at the station, they were taken to an airmen's mess where hot meals awaited, consisting of beans on toast and a mug of stewed tea.

The next morning, the sergeants went to their West Kirby mess where they were offered seven days' leave, which was promptly refused by the 105 Squadron crew members. Why, after all they had been through, did they turn down the chance of seven days' leave? – simply because when they got back to Swanton Morley, they knew that they would be entitled to the previously agreed fourteen days' leave! A few hours later, after some telephone discussion, this was verified and the next morning they were permitted to go.

Ron Scholefield remembers an unusual episode which followed:

> That afternoon we went down across the fields into Hoylake, to the Anchor Inn. During briefing at Swanton Morley before leaving, 500 French francs were given to each crew member in a waterproof envelope, in case of ditching near French territory. During the evening at the Anchor Inn, Gerry Quinn DFM and bar, W/C Edward's gunner, had occasion to use the Inn's toilet. Finding there was no toilet paper, he employed his initiative – and costly a visit it proved in terms of foreign currency!

The following morning transport was provided to West Kirby station, where they took the Liverpool train. It was from this train that Sgt Gibson, who had been a waiter on the London–Holyhead train before the war, took some of his sergeant comrades into a canteen located under the platforms at Lime Street station. Here the lady in charge made them bacon sandwiches, a luxury during wartime, before they proceeded to the London Express to go south. On board, Sgt Gibson went along to the dining car and met many old friends. Meanwhile, the remainder of the party had found a copy of *Aeroplane* magazine and were busy checking the decorations section; to everybody's astonishment, there was a DFM for Sgt Gibson. Neither Sgt Gibson nor any of the others knew of this, so when they found him again due congratulations were given. When the restaurant car staff were advised, they invited all the RAF personnel on the train to a free meal at the end of the lunch sittings in honour of the award to Sgt Gibson.

The airmen left the train at Bletchley and got on to another destined for Bedford, and eventually they all ended up at East Dereham. The entire journey had been covered by a travel warrant for fifteen persons from West Kirby to East Dereham. When they got back to Swanton Morley they were made quite a fuss of and then were given the two weeks' leave as agreed.

It would be fitting at this point to quote the words of one of the people responsible for the daily organization of the young airmen, F/O 'Teddy' Frayn, Adjutant on Malta, who also travelled home with the party:

> A bedraggled and low-spirited band of officers and NCOs arrived back at Swanton Morley, to be given leave and then posted to other units. Malta had taken its toll – many friendships had been severed forever and many private tears had been shed. War, however, demanded more from those of us who were fortunate enough to survive and I'm sure we all did so if only to vindicate the loss of our colleagues, whom we should not see again.

None of the aircrew went back on operations at this stage from Swanton Morley. However, after the period of leave, in what must have seemed like a recurring nightmare, one crew learned that there was one final job to be done. Blenheims were required once more, this time to meet up with the aircraft carrier HMS *Ark Royal*. Their point of departure was to be Portreath in

The torpedoing of the 22,000-ton Courageous-class aircraft carrier HMS Ark Royal *by the German submarine U81 on 13 November 1941 put paid to the prospect of a return visit to the Mediterranean for 105 Squadron Blenheim aircrew. (The Trustees of the Imperial War Museum, London: A6332)*

Cornwall, the departure point for the trip to Malta the first time round! On 1 November 1941 F/L Duncan took off in Blenheim R3669 at 15.30 hours, accompanied by his usual crew of Sgt Eddie Smith (Observer) and Sgt Bob Lyndall (WOp/AG). Their destination was Portreath, although due to the inclement weather they actually landed at Perranporth, two hours and twenty minutes after leaving Swanton Morley. The next morning at 09.05 hours they flew the ten minute hop to Portreath. They remained at Portreath for a couple of days, doing a fifteen minute wireless check on the 3rd, and an engine and air-frame test on the 4th which lasted all of ten minutes. The next day, they were at last ready for departure. Bob Lyndall takes up the story:

> On 5 November we took off from Portreath for Gibraltar. Thirty minutes out and we had to return with a duff engine. We heard that we were part of a flight of Blenheims which were to rendezvous with the *Ark Royal* in the Mediterranean, and navigate some Spitfires out east. On 6 November we were sent back to Swanton Morley and who actually went out, I know not. The *Ark Royal* was attacked while returning to Gibraltar on 13 November, presumably after this rendezvous.

The *Ark Royal* had in fact fallen victim to the German 10th Flotilla, and was torpedoed by U-Boat U:81. She sank on 14 November, while still under tow.

Of the remainder of the surviving 105 Squadron Blenheim crews, many went 'on rest' to Bicester as instructors, and some re-trained as navigators or pilots before being posted either back to 105 Squadron, or to other Mosquito Squadrons. One thing was certain – the Blenheim days for 105 Squadron were over. But for those who had survived the slaughter, another four years lay ahead until they could witness what they had all fought for, and so many died to achieve – peace.

APPENDIX I

Air Commodore Sir Hughie Idwal Edwards

VC KCMG CB DSO OBE DFC KStJ (1914–82)

Hughie Idwal Edwards was born on 1 August 1914 at Mosman Park, Perth, Western Australia. His parents, Hugh and Jane Edwards, were both Welsh. His father was an engineer with Perth public works department, having formerly been a blacksmith at the Fremantle gold mine. Hughie was educated at White Gum Valley school and latterly at Fremantle boys' school, before taking up employment as a shipping office clerk in Fremantle.

'Eddie' started his service career in 1934 when he enlisted in a local artillery unit, following which he transferred to the Royal Australian Air Force. By June 1936 Edwards was able to proudly don his wings at Point Cook. He then transferred to the RAF and was commissioned on 21 August 1936.

Hughie Edwards' first posting was as a pilot officer to Abingdon, and then to train with 'B' Flight of 90 (B) Squadron at Bicester, where he flew biplanes such as the single-engined Hawker Hind, as well as the twin-engined Overstrand and Sidestrand. He was appointed Squadron Adjutant on 22 April 1937, and three days later, on the 25th, had his first taste of flying a Bristol Blenheim, under dual instruction with F/L Heffernan in K7048. By the end of the month he had learned about petrol, oil, ignition and hydraulic systems, as well as the correct sequence of cockpit control. At last, on 2 July 1937, P/O Edwards received his 'Certificate of Qualification as First Pilot', confirming completion of his conversion on to the Bristol Blenheim Mk I.

W/C Hughie Idwal Edwards VC DFC, Officer Commanding 105 Squadron RAF, July 1941. (via Jim Taylor)

On 15 November 1937 the squadron was detached to 6 ATC at Wandsford, a posting which lasted until 6 December 1937. It was subsequently detached between 1 and 25 February 1938 to 3 ATC at Sutton Bridge in Lincolnshire, 8 miles west of King's Lynn. On 21 May P/O Edwards was promoted to flying officer, logging his first flight with his new rank on 13 June in Blenheim I, K7126. Accompanied by AC Sherliker they flew as formation leader in No. 1 position.

It was with 'B' Flight of 90 Squadron that Edwards nearly met an untimely end; on 30 August 1938 he was flying a Blenheim I, K7067, on a cross-country flight accompanied by his crew, Sgt Nash (Observer) and AC Theopolis (WOp/AG). Their route was to take them from Bicester to Carlisle and Berwick and back again. Unfortunately the aircraft flew into a snow storm at 7,000ft; the ailerons froze up and control was rendered impossible. He ordered the crew to bale out at 5,000ft, but Edwards characteristically refused to give up. At 700ft the situation had become hopeless and he too decided to escape.

While baling out over Catten near Shap in Northumberland, his parachute snagged on his aerial mast. He plummeted towards the ground with the stricken aircraft. Eventually, he broke free but struck the ground with a great impact. Fortunately a local farmer's wife, Mrs Morris, heard the crash and came running through the snow to help. She raised the alarm, and Edwards was soon rescued by the Redesdale Territorial Army. Edwards spent nine months in hospital as a result of the accident. He had severed a nerve in his right leg which left him with no feeling below the knee. This injury meant that Edwards was declared unfit for flying duties. It was a terrible blow but, typically, he was having none of it. After gnawing away relentlessly at officialdom, he eventually managed to gain a limited flying category. He commenced flying practice again on 13 April 1940, accompanied by F/L Beresford, for a flight to Hornchurch and return to Bicester in Percival Vega Gull P5991.

On 27 April 1940 F/O Edwards was appointed to No. 1 Air Armaments School at Manby, to attend the 29th SAO's course, where he was to fly a variety of aircraft including the Avro 621 Tutor, Fairey Battle, Gloster SS.19 Gauntlet, Handley Page H.P.52 Hampden, Hawker Demon, Hawker Henley, Hawker Hind, Miles M.14 Magister, as well as the Bristol Blenheim MkI. The training covered such subjects as general flying, high- and low-level bombing, air gunnery and turret manipulation, and observing, as well as refresher courses in aerobatics and forced-landings. After forty-three hours and thirty-five minutes of practice flying, he completed his schooling on 23 August 1940, and was posted the next day to 13 OTU at Bicester, once again the proud holder of full flying status, valid both at home and overseas.

Although he still limped and had to support the leg when walking, he was back in the thick of it again. But it hadn't all been plain sailing. On the night of 25 September 1940, Edwards was engaged on a local reconnaissance flying exercise in T1796, accompanied by P/O Osborne and Sgt Raisbeck, when an air raid started which blacked out communications and station identification. Time drew on and eventually Edwards began to think he and his crew would have to bale out, but the attempt was thwarted by a jammed escape hatch. An emergency landing under conditions of total darkness in a field at Litchfield in Whitchurch proved necessary. In the event they landed safely, the only casualties being a damaged tree and a rather bent Blenheim. Miraculously, Edwards suffered only concussion and lived to fight another day.

On 20 February 1941, having completed his re-training, F/O Edwards was posted to Horsham St Faith in Norfolk, where he operated with 139 Squadron before being posted with his crew, Sgt Ashplant and Sgt Quinn DFM, to take up command of 105 Squadron, at that time on detachment from their East Anglian base at Swanton Morley, and temporarily based at RAF Lossiemouth in Scotland.

Later, while operating from Swanton Morley, Edwards was awarded the DFC for an attack on 15 June 1941 against shipping off The Hague. Only days later, he was further awarded the VC for a daring low-level daylight raid on one of the most heavily defended targets in Germany – Bremen.

A subsequent posting took Edwards to Malta with 105 Squadron, where he arrived on 30 July 1941. Forbidden to fly operationally, he nevertheless did fly on occasions, such as during air tests and on local sorties in Blenheims 'A','H','J', and 'K'. One long-range flight lasting three hours and five minutes was undertaken in Blenheim 'T', to search for Sgt Brandwood and crew who were known to be adrift in a dinghy off Tripoli. In addition, a local first solo flight was made on 15 August in Beaufighter 'O', following instruction by S/L Soper. This episode was remembered by Brian Hanafin:

> An officer pilot who was flying out to join his unit in Egypt had his Beaufighter damaged on the ground in an air raid. I think he also had Sandfly fever and a few weeks later, when he and the aircraft were both 'repaired', he got clearance to leave for Egypt. However, Hughie Edwards persuaded the officer to allow him [Edwards] to take the Beaufighter for a short flight. Probably overcome by rank and the VC, the officer gave Edwards some instructions on how to fly the aircraft, but because it was a single-seater aircraft he could not check Hughie out in the air. We all went to the airfield to watch. He took off and flew around for about ten minutes, and then made a not too bad landing. However, as soon as he dropped the tail wheel on the runway, the aircraft started quite a severe ground loop, and he seemed unable to check it. There was a sudden screeching of metal as the undercarriage was ripped off and Hughie was left sitting in a very broken Beaufighter, on its belly, with two bent propellers and engines. Also he was trapped in the cockpit, having not been shown the emergency method of releasing the hood! We eventually released a very apologetic Edwards.

However, it was with a great deal of regret and frustration that Edwards had to relinquish command of his dwindling numbers of 105 Squadron air and groundcrews on 19 September, and proceeded on 17 October 1941 on a recruiting and publicity tour of the USA. At the end of October 1941, Edwards returned to England to take up a new post as CFI at Wellesbourne, Mountford, a few miles east of Stratford-upon-Avon. Here he remained until returning once more to his beloved 105 Squadron to take up command again, this time going back on operations to fly the new unarmed Mosquito MkIV bomber. 105 Squadron was the first unit to be equipped with the type, the first aircraft having been personally delivered by Geoffrey de Havilland Jr, who put on an impressive air manoeuvrability demonstration prior to landing.

Edwards scored many notable successes with the Mosquito, particularly the famous raid on Gestapo Headquarters in Oslo, and a raid on Eindhoven for which he was subsequently awarded the DSO. On 2 February 1943 promotion to Temporary Group Captain saw an end to Edwards' leadership of 105 Squadron. He was given command of RAF Binbrook, a station 10 miles south-west of Grimsby, equipped with Avro Lancasters of 460 Squadron Royal Australian Air Force.

From RAF Binbrook he was posted to Ceylon in December 1944, as Group Captain Bombing Operations RAF HQ, Candy. In January 1945 Edwards became Station Administrative Officer at Headquarters, South East Asia Command. Having graduated from his Bracknell Staff Course in 1949, Edwards was further posted as SASO 21 Group HQ, Flying Training Command, a position he held from 1949 until 1950. Thereafter, he became Officer Commanding RAF Brize Norton's Flying Wing until 1951, following which RAF Wyton and RAF Benson greeted him as their Officer Commanding Flying Wings. Between 1953 and 1956 he was CO of RAF Wattisham in East Anglia, during which period he was given full Group Captain status. Following his Wattisham command he went overseas again, this time to take command of RAF Habbaniya in Iraq, where he remained for two years, until 23 October 1958, when he was further promoted to Acting Air Commodore. On his return to England, he took up the post of Commandant of the Central Flying Establishment at East Anglia's RAF West Raynham.

Full Air Commodore rank was granted on 1 July 1959, and in 1960 he became Aide-de-Camp to Her Majesty, Queen Elizabeth II. Having joined the Imperial Defence College in 1961, Edwards was later made Director of Establishments (RAF) at the Air Ministry between 1962 and 1963. On 30 September 1963 he relinquished his post of ADC to HM The Queen, and retired from service to return to his native Australia. Never one to seek a quiet life, he subsequently became Resident Australian Director of Selection Trust, a major UK mining group, a position he held for ten years between 1964 and 1974.

Thereafter, at the invitation of Labour Premier John Tonkin, he became Governor of Western Australia, following which a knighthood was bestowed upon him. Failing health now began to take its toll and Sir Hughie Edwards was only able to retain the Governor's position for nine months before being forced to retire. Australia's most decorated airman died at his home at Darling Point on Thursday 5 August 1982. He is survived by his son, Anthony, and daughter, Sarah, both to his first wife Cherry (known as Pat) who died in 1966, and by his second wife, Dorothy, whom he married in 1972.

APPENDIX II

Targets

Targets are as listed in the Squadron Operations Record Book and have been corrected where known errors exist. Information is recorded below in the following order: date, location, country, target, result.

Place names in (brackets) represent local supplementary detail.

Place names in [square brackets] represent the commonly used English interpretation.

The following abbreviations have been used :

Abnd	Abandoned	F	France	B	Belgium	J	Jersey
D	Germany	NL	Netherlands	NF	Not Found		

Europe 1940

08.08: Haamstede, NL, Aerodrome, Abnd; Knokke, B, Aerodrome, Abnd; 09.08: Haamstede, NL, Aerodrome, Abnd; Vlissingen [Flushing], NL, Aerodrome, Abnd; Knokke, B, Aerodrome, Abnd; 10.08: Vlissingen [Flushing], NL, Aerodrome, Bombed; Knokke, B, Aerodrome, Abnd; Schiphol, NL, Aerodrome, Bombed; 15.08: Vlissingen [Flushing], NL, Aerodrome, Abnd; Schiphol, NL, Aerodrome, Recalled; 20.08: Brussels, B, Aerodrome, Abnd; Stene [Ostend], B, Aerodrome, Bombed; Schiphol, NL, Aerodrome, Bombed; 22.08: Antwerp, B, Aerodrome, Abnd; Merville, F, Aerodrome, Bombed; Schouwen en Duiveland (Haamstede) , NL, Aerodrome, Abnd; Schiphol, NL, Aerodrome, Abnd; Cap Gris-Nez, F, Gun Emplacements, Abnd; 24.08: De Kooij, NL, Aerodrome, Abnd; Hingene, B, Aerodrome, Bombed; Lannion, F, Aerodrome, Abnd; Schiphol, NL, Aerodrome, Bombed; Schellingwoude [Amsterdam], NL, Seaplane Base, Bombed; 26.08: Paderborn, D, Aerodrome, Abnd; Dortmund–Ems, D, Canal, Abnd; Gelsenkirchen, D, Oil Refineries, Abnd; 27.08: Abbeville, F, Aerodrome, Abnd; Alkmaar, NL, Aerodrome, Abnd; Bauvais, F, Aerodrome, Abnd; Jersey, J, Aerodrome, Abnd; Rennes, F, Aerodrome, Abnd; Schiphol, NL, Aerodrome, Abnd; Zuider Zee, NL, Barges, Bombed; 29.08, Alkmaar, NL, Aerodrome, Bombed; Borkum Island, D, Shipping Convoy, Bombed; Cherbourg, F, Harbour/Seaplane Base, Abnd; Den Helder, NL, Shipping Convoy, Bombed; Gladbeck, D, Target Not Known, Abnd; De Kooij, NL, Aerodrome, Bombed; Diepholz, D, Aerodrome, Abnd; Gemert, NL, Photo Recce, Abnd; Kamen, D, Recce, Abnd; Münster, D, Photo Recce, Photos; Rotenburg, D, Aerodrome, Abnd; Weitzendorf, D, Munitions Factory, Abnd; 30.08: De Kooij, NL, Aerodrome, Abnd; Schiphol, NL, Aerodrome, Abnd; Schellingwoude, NL, Seaplane Base, Abnd.

01.09: Dortmund–Ems, D, Canal, Abnd; Diepholz, D, Aircraft Park, Abnd; Hamburg, D, Oil Refineries, Abnd; Paderborn, D, Aircraft Park, Abnd; 02.09: Cherbourg, F, Oil Storage Tanks, Abnd; Dortmund–Ems, D, Canal, Abnd; Kamen, D, Power Station, Abnd; 06.09: Diepholz, D, Aircraft Park, Abnd; Dortmund–Ems, D, Canal, Abnd; Gladbeck, D, Ammunition Works, Abnd; Kamen, D, Oil Refinery, Abnd; Paderborn, D, Aircraft Park, Abnd; 08.09: Boulogne, F, Harbour, Bombed; NW France, F, Reconnaissance, Recce; 09.09: Location Not Known, Reconnaissance, Abnd; 14.09: Dunkerque/Vlissingen, F/NL, Reconnaissance, Photos; Dunkerque/Vlissingen, F/NL, Reconnaissance, Abnd; Schouwen en Duiveland (Haamstede),

NL, Aerodrome, Bombed; Cap Gris-Nez, F, Gun Emplacements, Bombed; 15.09: Cap Gris-Nez, F, Gun Emplacements, Bombed; 17.09: Location Not Known, Reconnaissance, Abnd; Den Haag [The Hague], NL, Aerodrome, Bombed; Hoek van Holland [Hook of Holland], NL, Shipping Convoy, Bombed; Zeebrugge, B, Shipping Convoy, Bombed; 18.09: Oostende [Ostend], B, Harbour/Barges, Bombed; 20.09: Dunkerque [Dunkirk], F, Harbour, Bombed; 21.09: Dunkerque [Dunkirk], F, Harbour, Bombed; 23.09: Calais–Den Haag [The Hague], F/NL, Coast/Waterways, Abnd; 24.09: Calais, F, Harbour, Bombed; 29.09: Calais, F, Harbour, Bombed; 30.09: Boulogne, F, Harbour, Bombed; Le Touquet, F, Outskirts, Bombed.

02.10: Gremberg, B, Marshalling Yards, Abnd; Calais, F, Harbour, NF, 04.10: Köln [Cologne], D, Marshalling Yards, Abnd; Vlissingen [Flushing], NL, Shipping, Bombed; Vlissingen [Flushing], NL, Aerodrome, Bombed; Hellevoetsluis, NL, Shipping, Bombed; Maasluis [Rotterdam], NL, Barges, Bombed; Zeebrugge, B, Oil Tanks, Bombed; 06.10: Diepholz, D, Aircraft Park, Bombed; Harlingen, NL, Shipping, Bombed; Salzbergen, D, Oil Refinery, Abnd; Willemsoord, NL, Ship, Bombed; 07.10: Oostende [Ostend], B, Shipping/Barges, Bombed; Dunkerque [Dunkirk], F, Docks/Harbour, Bombed; Zeebrugge, B, Target Not Known, Bombed; 12.10: Boulogne, F, Harbour, Bombed; Hamm, D, Marshalling Yards, Bombed; 20.10: Antwerp, B, Docks, Bombed; Hingene, B, Aerodrome, Bombed; 25.10: Amsterdam, NL, Shipyards, Bombed; Cap Gris-Nez, F, Gun Emplacements, Bombed; Étaples, F, Aerodrome, Bombed; Osnabrück, D, Marshalling Yards, Abnd; Schiphol, NL, Aerodrome, Bombed; 28.10: Ehrang, D, Marshalling Yards, Abnd; Vlissingen [Flushing], NL, Aerodrome, Bombed; Goch, D, Flare path, Bombed; Homberg, D, Synthetic Oil Plant, Bombed; Koblenz, D, Marshalling Yards, Bombed; Mannheim, D, Marshalling Yards, Bombed; 31.10: Duisburg–Ruhort, D, Marshalling Yards, Abnd; Etten, NL, Railway Siding, Bombed.

08.11: Lorient, F, Submarine Base, Bombed; Duisburg, D, Docks, Bombed; Essen, D, Krupps Factory [Armaments Works], Bombed; N of Pont de Cauden, F, Slipway, Bombed; 10.11: Boulogne, F, Aerodrome, Bombed; Chateaudun, F, Aerodrome, Bombed; Chartres, F, Aerodrome, Bombed; Étaples, F, Aerodrome, Bombed; Ivry-la-Bataille, F, Aerodrome, Bombed; Knokke, B, Aerodrome, Bombed; Laon, F, Aerodrome, Abnd; Le Touquet, F, Aerodrome, Bombed; Het Zoute, B, Aerodrome, Bombed; Lorient, F, Submarine Base, Bombed; 15.11: Antwerp (Deurne), B, Aerodrome, Bombed; Diegem, B, Aerodrome, Bombed; Evere, B, Aerodrome, Bombed; Breskens, NL, Aerodrome, Bombed; Hingene, B, Aerodrome, Bombed; Vught, NL, Aerodrome, Bombed; 16.11: Schouwen en Duiveland (Haamstede), NL, Aerodrome, Bombed; Hamburg, D, Oil Refinery, Bombed; 22.11: Bremen, D, Oil Refinery (Oslebshausen), Abnd; Köln [Cologne], D, Oil Refinery (Wesserling), Bombed; Hagen, D, Factory, Bombed; Hannover, D, Oil Refinery (Misburg), Bombed; Leeuwarden, NL, Aerodrome, Bombed; Schiphol, NL, Aerodrome, Bombed; Willemsdorp, NL, Docks/ Shipping, Bombed; 23.11: Dortmund, D, Oil Refinery, Bombed; Oostende [Ostend], B, Harbour, Bombed; Schiphol, NL, Aerodrome, Bombed; Texel Island, NL, Aerodrome, Bombed; Wanne-Eickel (Essen), D, Oil Refinery, Bombed;

06.12: Boulogne, F, Docks, Bombed; Köln [Cologne], D, Inland Port, Bombed; Amiens (Glisy), F, Aerodrome, Bombed; Arras (Duisans), F, Aerodrome, Bombed; Arras (Pas-de-Calais), F, Blast Furnaces, Bombed; Cambrai, F, Aerodrome, Bombed; Dunkerque [Dunkirk], F, Docks, Bombed; Gravelines, F, Aerodrome, Bombed; Le Touquet, F, Aerodrome, Bombed; Lille (Ronchin), F, Aerodrome, Bombed; Lille (Vendeville), F, Aerodrome, Bombed; Merville, F, Aerodrome, Bombed; Vitry-en-Artois, F, Aerodrome, Bombed; 10.12: Bremen, D, Focke-Wulf

Factory, Bombed; 11.12: Cap Gris-Nez, F, Gun Emplacements, Bombed; Dunkerque [Dunkirk], F, Harbour, Bombed; 21.12: Dunkerque [Dunkirk], F, Harbour, Bombed; Gelsenkirchen, D, Oil Refinery, Bombed; 23.12: Bonn, D, Marshalling Yards, Bombed, (Leafleted); Boulogne, F, Harbour, Abnd; Gremberg, B, Marshalling Yards, Bombed; 27.12: Boulogne, F, Harbour, Abnd; 28.12: Antwerp, B, Docks, Bombed; Düsseldorf, D, Docks, Bombed; 29.12: Poix–Bauvais–Amiens–Ravenel, F, Area, Patrol; Calais, F, Harbour, Bombed; Dunkirk, F, Harbour, Bombed; Amiens (Glisy), F, Aerodrome, Bombed; Poix, F, Aerodrome, Abnd; Rosières-en-Santerre, F, Aerodrome, Abnd; 31.12: Bremen, D, Oil Refinery, Abnd; Köln [Cologne], D, Oil Refinery, Bombed; Gelsenkirchen, D, Oil Refinery (Nordstern), Abnd; Schouwen en Duiveland, NL, Aerodrome (Haamstede), Bombed; Ijmuiden, NL, Docks, Bombed.

Europe 1941

03.01: Assen, NL, Railway Junction, Bombed; Bremen, D, Not Known, Bombed; Huntlosen, D, Aerodrome, Bombed; 09.01: Düsseldorf, D, Town, Bombed; Gelsenkirchen, D, Synthetic Oil Factory, Bombed; Hamborn, D, Town, Bombed; 22.01: Düsseldorf, D, Town, Bombed;

04.02: Dieppe, F, Town, Bombed; Dunkerque [Dunkirk], F, Town, Bombed; Évreux, F, Aerodrome, Bombed; Moselles region, F, Aerodrome, Bombed; Oostende [Ostend], B, Aerodrome, Bombed; St Omer, F, Aerodrome, Bombed; 10.02: Ijmuiden, NL, Docks, Bombed; Hanover, D, Town, Bombed; Rotterdam, NL, Oil Tanks, Bombed; 15.02: Düsseldorf, D, Town, Bombed; Homberg, D, Synthetic Oil Plant, Bombed; Le Havre, F, Docks, Bombed; 25.02: Beauvais, F, Aerodrome, Bombed; Caen, F, Aerodrome, Bombed; Conches, F, Beacon, Bombed; Dunkerque [Dunkirk], F, Docks, Bombed; Évreux, F, Aerodrome, Bombed; Laon, F, Flare Path, Bombed; Montdidier, F, Target Not Known, Bombed; Poix, F, Target Not Known, NF; 28.02: Borkum Island, D, Target Not Known, Bombed; De Kooij, NL, Aerodrome, Bombed; Emden, D, Target Not Known, Bombed.

10.03: Dieppe, F, Docks, Bombed; Le Havre, F, Docks, Bombed; St Aubin, F, Aerodrome, Bombed; 12.03: Bremen, D, Town, Bombed; 13.03: Bremen, D, Town, Bombed; Hamburg, D, Town, Bombed; 17.03: Wilhelmshaven, D, Town, Bombed; 18.03: Oostende [Ostend], B, Target Not Known, Bombed; Wilhelmshaven, D, Town, Bombed; 21.03: Lorient, F, Various Targets, Bombed; 23.03: Calais, F, Port, Bombed; Hanover, D, Town, Bombed; 30.03: Brest, F, Various Targets, Bombed.

03.04: Oostende [Ostend], B, Town, Bombed; Rotterdam, NL, Docks, Abnd; 04.04: Köln [Cologne], D, Target Not Known, Abnd; Dunkerque [Dunkirk], F, Target Not Known, Abnd; Gilze Reijen, NL, Aerodrome, Bombed; Nieuwpoort, B, Target Not Known, Bombed; Schiphol, NL, Aerodrome, Bombed; 07.04: Bremerhaven, D, Target Not Known, Bombed; Emden, D, Target Not Known, Bombed; 08.04: Bremerhaven, D, Target Not Known, Bombed; Emden, D, Target Not Known, NF; Jever, D, Railway Junction, Bombed; 11.04: Brest, F, Various Targets, Bombed; Lorient, F, Target Not Known, Bombed; 13.04: Beat 13 (Dieppe/Cherbourg), F, Shipping, NF; 15.04: Borkum, D, Town, Bombed; Borkum, D Barracks, Bombed; Borkum, D, Railway Station, Bombed; N of Borkum, D, Gun Emplacements, Bombed; SW of Borkum Island, D, Shipping, Bombed; 17.04: Beat 16 (Brest), F, Shipping, NF; Beat 17 (Lorient), F, Shipping, NF; 19.04: Beat 9 (Texel Island), NL, Shipping, Bombed; 21.04: Beat 13 (Dieppe/Cherbourg), F, Shipping, Bombed; Le Havre, F, Various, Abnd; Off Le Havre, F, Shipping/Trawlers, Bombed; 23.04: Beat 10 (Mouth of Schelde), NL, Shipping, Bombed; Beat

9 (Off Haarlem), NL, Shipping, Bombed; 25.04: Beat 10 (Mouth of Schelde), NL, Shipping, Bombed; Velsen, NL, Steel Works, Bombed; Ijmuiden, NL, Barges, Bombed; 27.04: Gremberg, B, Military Camp, Bombed; 'Knapsack' [Cologne], D, Factory, Bombed; 'Knapsack' [Cologne], D, Power Station, Abnd; Quadrath [Cologne], D, Power Station, Abnd; Stockum [Düsseldorf], D, Power Station, Abnd; 29.04: Beat 14 (Le Havre), F, Shipping, NF; Beat 15 (Cherbourg/Brest), F, Shipping, Bombed.

01.05: Antwerp, B, Docks, Bombed; Beat 15 (Cherbourg/Brest), F, Shipping, NF; Rotterdam, NL, Docks, Bombed; Rotterdam, NL, Shipping in Waterways, Bombed; Vlissingen [Flushing], NL, Harbour, Bombed; 03.05: Beat 7 (Terschelling Island), NL, Shipping, NF; Beat 9 (Den Helder), NL, Shipping, NF; 07.05: Beat 3 (SW Norway), N, Shipping, NF; 08.05: Beat 2 (Stavanger), N, Shipping, Bombed; 09.05: Beat 1 (Bergen), N, Shipping, Bombed; 12.05: Beat 4 (Skaggerak), N, Shipping, Bombed; 13.05: Beat 3 (SW Norway), N, Shipping, NF; 16.05: Beat 1 (Bergen), N, Shipping, Bombed; 22.05: Beat 7 (Central Frisian Islands), NL, Shipping, Bombed; Beat 8 (Ameland/Terschelling Islands), NL, Shipping, NF; 25.05: Beat 8 (Ameland/Texel Islands), NL, Shipping, Bombed; Norderney Island, D, Town, Abnd; 27.05: Area off Heligoland, D, Shipping, NF.

02.06: Bregstedt Canal, D, Shipping, Bombed; Nord-Ostsee-Kanal by Brunsbüttle, D, Shipping, Bombed; Friedrichskoog, D, Factory, Bombed; Kiel Canal, D, Shipping, Bombed; Kiel, D, Barracks, Bombed; Pellworm Island, D, Village, Bombed; E of Rendsburg, D, Shipping, Bombed; S of Rendsburg, D, Shipping, Bombed; River Eider–Kiel Canal, D, Shipping, Bombed; Tellingstedt, D, Village, Bombed; 04.06: Den Haag [The Hague], NL, Rolling Stock, Bombed; Valkenburg, NL, Aerodrome, Abnd; 07.06: Beat 8 (Ameland/Terschelling Islands), D, Shipping, Bombed; 11.06: NW Germany (Area River Ems-Weser), D, Towns and Villages, Abnd; 14.06: Brest, F, Shipping, Abnd; St Omer (Fort Rouge), F, Aerodrome, Bombed; St Omer (Longueness), F, Aerodrome, Abnd; 15.06: Beat 10 (Mouth of Schelde/Den Haag), NL, Shipping, Bombed; 16.06: Beat B (Between Beats 7 and 8 – East Frisian Islands, and Ameland), NL, Shipping, Bombed; 19.06: Le Havre, F, Docks, Bombed; 21.06: Dutch Coast, NL, Shipping, Abnd; 23.06: Béthune (Chocques), F, Chemical Works, Bombed; Béthune (Chocques), F, Power Station, Bombed; 26.06: Comines, F, Power Station, Abnd; 28.06: Bremen, D, Town and Docks, Abnd; 30.06: Bremen, D, Town and Docks, Abnd; NW of Norderney Island, D, Shipping, Bombed; Terschelling Island, NL, W/T Station, Bombed; S of Terschelling Island, NL, Shipping, Bombed; W Terschelling, NL, Town and Harbour, Bombed.

04.07: Bremen, D, Town and Docks, Bombed; 07.07: Den Haag [The Hague] to Ijmuiden, NL, Shipping, Bombed; 16.07: Rotterdam, NL, Docks, Bombed; 19.07: Off Den Haag [The Hague], NL, Shipping, Bombed.

Malta 1941

The following abbreviations have been used:

G	Greece	M	Malta	I	Italy	Si	Sicily
It	Italian-governed	T	Tunisian-governed	L	Libya		

31.07: Off Pantellaria, It, Shipping, Abnd; 01.08: N of Pantellaria, It, Shipping, NF; Lampedusa Island, It, Shipping in Harbour, Bombed; 02.08: Misratah [Misurata], L, Barracks, Bombed; Tarabulus–Benghazi Road [Tripoli–Benghazi], L, Target Not Known, Bombed.

03.08: Tarabulus [Tripoli], L, Harbour/Shipping, Bombed; 04.08: N of Misratah [Misurata], L, Shipping, Bombed; 05.08: W of Sicily, Si, Shipping, Bombed; Gulf of Sirt [Sirte], L, Shipping, NF; E of Misratah [Misurata], L, Barracks, Bombed; 06.08: Off Lampedusa Island, It, Shipping, Abnd; 07.08: S of Pantellaria, It, Shipping, Bombed; 08.08: Catania, Si, Shipping in Harbour, Abnd; 09.08: Bwayrat Al Hasun–Misratah [Misurata], L, Shipping, NF; Bwayrat Al Hasun, L, Dumps, Bombed; Bwayrat Al Hasun–Misratah [Misurata], L, Packing Cases, Bombed; 09.08: Bwayrat Al Hasun–Misratah [Misurata], L, Petrol Tankers, Bombed; Misratah [Misurata], L, Barracks, Bombed; 10.08: N of Qarqarah Islands [Kerkenna], T, Shipping, Bombed; Catania, Si, Shipping in Harbour, Abnd; 11.08: Cariati, I, Barrack Blocks, Bombed; Crotone, I, Chemical Works, Bombed; 14.08: S of Qarqarah Islands [Kerkenna], T, Shipping, NF; 15.08: Off Bwayrat Al Hasun, L, Shipping, Bombed; 17.08: S of Pantellaria, It, Shipping, Abnd; 18.08: Off Lampedusa Island, It, Shipping, Bombed; 22.08: Misratah [Misurata]–Bwayrat Al Hasun, L, Shipping, NF; W of Bwayrat Al Hasun, L, Motor Transports, Bombed; 23.08: NE of Qarqarah Islands [Kerkenna], T, Shipping, Bombed; 24.08: Ras Angeia (M. el Auègia), L, Shipping, Bombed; 25.08: Off Lampedusa, It, Shipping, Bombed; 26.08: East of Qarqarah Islands [Kerkenna], T, Shipping, Photos/Bombed; 27.08: Ionian Sea, Shipping, NF; Lampedusa Island, It, Shipping in Harbour, Bombed; 28.08: W of Crete, Shipping, Bombed; 30.08: Licata, Si, Chemical Works, Bombed; Licata, Si, Power Station, Bombed; Ionian Sea, Shipping, Recce;

01.09: Crotone, I, Chemical Works, Bombed; Crotone, I, Railway Siding, Bombed; Crotone, I, Shipping in Harbour, Bombed; Ionian Sea, Shipping, Recce; 02.09: Location Not Known, Shipping, Recce; 03.09: Ionian Sea, Shipping, Recce; 04.09: Crotone, I, Shipping in Harbour, Bombed; 06.09: Ionian Sea, Shipping, Recce; 08.09: Off Syracuse, Si, Shipping, NF; 09.09: SE Coast off Sicily, Si, Shipping, NF; 11.09: Ionian Sea, Shipping, Bombed; South Tunisian Coast, T, Shipping, Recce; Off Qarqarah Islands [Kerkenna], T, Shipping, NF; 12.09: NE of Qarqarah Islands [Kerkenna], T, Shipping, Recce; NNW of Tarabulus [Tripoli], L, Shipping, Bombed; 13.09: Cape Matapan, G, Shipping, Recce; Off Qarqarah Islands [Kerkenna], T, Survivors, Search; 17.09: N of Qarqarah Islands [Kerkenna], T, Shipping, Bombed; 19.09: Bwayrat Al Hasun, L, Ammunition Dump, Bombed; Bwayrat Al Hasun, L, Lorry Convoy, Bombed; 20.09: Location Not Known, Shipping, Recce; Filfla Island, M, Target Practice, Bombed; 22.09: Al Khums [Homs], L, Barrack Blocks, Bombed/Machine-gunned; Al Khums [Homs], L, Dumps Bombed; 25.09: Gulf of Sirt [Sirte], L, Shipping, NF; E of Sirt [Sirte], L, Lorries, Bombed; E of Sirt [Sirte], L, Soldiers, Machine-gunned; 27.09: Bo Rizzo, Si, Aerodrome, Abnd; Porto Empedocle, Si, Granary, Machine-gunned; Porto Empedocle, Si, Granary, Bombed.

APPENDIX III

Aircraft

All aircraft are listed by their manufacturers' serial number. The wartime squadron coding for 105 Squadron was GB and for 107 Squadron, OM. These codes were not always advertised when operating abroad, and occasionally only the individual aircraft code letter was shown on the side of the aircraft.

Where known, the aircraft's single coding identification letter is detailed after the colon. In the event of an aircraft having worn more than one code letter, all letters used are listed in chronological order.

Following use by 105 Squadron, the fate of each aircraft is detailed, although in many cases the ultimate fate of those passed to other units is not listed here. Failed to return in abbreviated as FTR.

The use of asterisks * indicates aircraft which did not apparently fly operationally with 105 Squadron, but which are understood to have been on its charge.

(M) indicates an aircraft flown by 105 Squadron when on Malta. This is followed, where applicable, by the number of any other squadron to which the aircraft may have belonged while being operated by 105 Squadron. When it is uncertain to which squadron an aircraft may have belonged, dual squadron ownership is denoted by, for example, 105/107.

L SERIES
L6764, Passed to 17 OTU; L6796, Passed to 17 OTU; L6812, Passed to 17 OTU; L8788:N, Passed to 88 Squadron; L9020, Passed to 88 Squadron; L9339, FTR Ostend 18.09.41; L9209, Passed to 114 Squadron; L9244:H, Passed to 1416 Flight; L9379:Y, Passed to 88 Squadron.

N SERIES
N6183:W, (M) 107, Passed to 113 Squadron.

P SERIES
P4840:Y, (M) 107, Passed to Middle East; P4918:O, Passed to 5 Air Observers' School.

R SERIES
R3599, Passed to 21 Squadron; R3606:*, Passed to 107 Squadron; R3669:*, Passed to 17 OTU; R3682:G, Crashed (landing) Swanton Morley, 23.03.41; R3688:*, Passed to 107 Squadron; R3707:U, B, FTR Off Ameland, 25.05.41; R3838:M, Passed to 13 OTU; R3844:*, Passed to 88, then to 105, then to 21 Squadron; R3907, Passed to 88 Squadron.

T SERIES
T1814:D, Passed to 21 Squadron; T1826:A, Crashed (overshot) Hendon 24.05.41; T1828:*, Passed to 25 Squadron; T1848:V, Passed to 614 Squadron; T1853, Passed to Overseas Aircraft Delivery Unit, Crashed in sea on approach to Gibraltar 04.11.41; T1877:S, Passed to 102 Maintenance Unit; T1884, Crashed (ran out of fuel) Motram 26.11.40; T1885:F, X, F, Passed to 51 OTU; T1886, Crashed Foxley Wood 26.11.40; T1887:S, Passed to 88 Squadron; T1890, FTR Belgium 15.11.40; T1891, FTR Homberg 28.10 40; T1892:Q, Crashed Birmingham 21.03.41; T1893, FTR Düsseldorf 28.11.40; T1894, FTR Dutch Coast 09.09.40; T1895:F, X, FTR Wilhelmshaven 28.02.41; T1896, FTR Calais 02.10.40; T1897, FTR NW France 11.12.40; T1922:*, Passed to 114 Squadron; T1930:J, X, Passed to 13 OTU; T1931:T, K, Passed to 17

OTU; T1932:T, Passed to 17 OTU; T1936:P, Passed to 13 OTU; T1989:R, Crashed (overshot) Swanton Morley 25.02.41; T1996:*, Passed to Turkish Air Force 27.03.42; T2033:*, Passed to 1482 Flight; T2043:*, Passed to 139 Squadron; T2056, Passed to 25 Squadron; T2118:E, FTR Norwegian Fjord 16.05.41; T2141, FTR English Channel 17.04.41; T2229, Crashed Birch Newton 28.10.40; T2276:*, Passed to 114 Squadron; T2329, FTR Hamburg 16.11.40.

V SERIES

V5384:B, Passed to 17 OTU; V5502:U, FTR Off Ijmuiden 07.07.41; V5821:K, (M) 107, Struck off charge Middle East 11.10.41; V5823:G, Crashed (landing in field) England 01.05.41; V5828:R, FTR Hardangerfjord, Norway 08.05.41; V5899:J, Possibly passed to 45 Squadron; V6014:S, (M), Passed to 203 Squadron; V6028:D, Passed to 88 Squadron; V6032:J, Passed to 88 Squadron; V6039:Q, FTR Hague 19.07.41; V6183:W, (M) 107, Struck off charge 01.04.42; V6316:S, FTR Off Terschelling 07.06.41; V6318:B, FTR Mouth of Schelde 23.04.41; V6319:F, FTR Off the Hague 15.06.41; V6333:*, Passed to 113 Squadron; V6336:H, Crashed (take-off) Swanton Morley 20.06.41; V6370:T, FTR Mouth of Schelde 25.04.41; V6373:O, Passed to 88 Squadron; V6374:V, X, Passed to 88 Squadron; V6380:G, Passed to 88 Squadron; V6399:T, Passed to 88 Squadron; V6420:K, Passed to 13 OTU; V6421:A, Passed to 88 Squadron; V6453:E, Passed to 55 Squadron; V6455:A, Passed to 88 Squadron; V6525:*, Passed to 21 Squadron.

Z SERIES

Z5875:*, Passed to 21 Squadron; Z5899:J, Passed to 17 OTU; Z5903:D, FTR Calais 23.03.41; Z6377:N, (M), FTR 107 Squadron Malta 11.41; Z7298:*, Passed to 88 Squadron; Z7357:U, (M), FTR details unknown; Z7359:*, Passed to 11 Squadron; Z7361:R, Passed to 88 Squadron; Z7366:*, Passed to Air Overseas Delivery Unit; Z7367:L, (M), Crashed (in sea) Off Tripoli 12.09.41; Z7371:*, Crashed (take-off) Swanton Morley 19.07.41; Z7408:K, (M), Struck off charge 18.11.41; Z7409:*, FTR 23.07.41; Z7410:*, Passed to 110 Squadron (Malta); Z7420:M, (M), Left on Malta, Lost 23.02.42; Z7423:H, (M), FTR Al Khums 22.09.41; Z7426:B, FTR Bremen 04.07.41; 7427:*, Passed to 88 Squadron; Z7429:*, Passed to Air Overseas Delivery Unit; Z7430:*, Passed to 114 Squadron; Z7439:H, FTR Off the Hague 19.07.41; Z7445:P, Passed to 88 Squadron; Z7484:K, Passed to 88 Squadron; Z7486:M, FTR Bremen 04.07.41; Z7488:F, Passed to 88 Squadron; Z7494:*, Passed to 226 Squadron; Z7495:*, Possibly passed to 60 Squadron; Z7503:J, (M), crashed (landing) Crotone 11.08.41; Z7504:G, (M), FTR Off Tripoli 12.09.41; Z7508:*, Passed to Lorraine Squadron; Z7511:B, (M), Passed to 107 Squadron; Z7522:E, (M), FTR Off Bwayrat Al Hasun 15.08.41; Z7612:Q, (M) 107, Passed to Jessore; Z7618:O, (M) 107, Left on Malta, Struck off charge 19.10.41; Z7619:Q, (M) 107, Passed to 11 Squadron; Z7627:N, (M) 105/107, Passed to 14 Squadron; Z7638:L, (M) 107, FTR Malta 09.10.41; Z7641:C, (M) 107, Crashed (landing) Luqa 30.08.41; Z7643:R, (M) 107, Transferred to Far East; Z7644:E, (M) 105/107, FTR Malta 09.10.41; Z7654:Y, (M) 107, FTR Malta 04.09.41; Z7682:N, (M) 107, FTR Off Kerkenna 26.08.41; Z7704:J, (M) 107, Struck off charge 31.10.41; Z7754:D, (M) 107, Transferred to Far East; Z7755:O, (M) 107, FTR Misurata 24.09.41; Z7760:G, (M) 107, Damaged beyond repair, Malta 15.01.42; Z7775:K, (M), Left on Malta; Z7848:Y, (M), Left on Malta; Z7852:C, (M) 105/107, Passed to 113 Squadron; Z7854:C, (M) 107, Passed to South African Air Force; Z9574:X, (M), Passed to 11 Squadron; Z9579:F, (M), Passed to 110 Squadron; Z9599:F, (M) 107, Struck off charge 01.10.41; Z9600:P, (M) 107, Passed to 69 Squadron; Z9603:F, (M), FTR Off Tripoli 12.09.41; Z9604:D, (M), FTR Off Bwayrat Al Hasun 15.08.41; Z9605:U, (M), FTR Lampedusa 01.08.41; Z9606:V, (M), Crashed (landing) Luqa 12 09.41; Z9607:S, (M), Passed to 45 Squadron; Z9608:T, (M), Possibly left on Malta; Z9609:T, (M), Passed to 45 Squadron; Z9613:A, (M), Transferred to Far East; Z9708:M, (M) 105/107, Crashed (landing) Luqa 23.10.41; Z9718:Z, (M), Transferred to Far East.

APPENDIX IV

Battle Honours

Date	*Award*	*Rank*	*Name*	*Service No.*
18.06.40	* CDG	F/O	Christopher Francis Gibson	39981
28.06.40	DFM	LAC	Robert William McCarthy	532666
17.01.41	DFC	F/O	Francis Alfred George Lacelles	40398
07.03.41	DFC	S/L	Gordon Cooper Ollif Key	37815
23.05.41	DFC	F/L	George Edward Goode	81675
23.05.41	DFC	P/O	James Frederick Hogan	45523
23.05.41	DFM	Sgt	Geoffrey Serpell Rowland	755633
04.07.41	DFC	W/C	Hughie Idwal Edwards	39005
22.07.41	VC	W/C	Hughie Idwal Edwards	39005
29.07.41	DFC	P/O	Alister Stewart Ramsay	88659
29.07.41	** DFM	Sgt	Gerald Douglas Prior Quinn	543799
29.07.41	DFM	Sgt	William Hugh Anthony Jackson	965484
29.07.41	DFM	Sgt	James Alan Purves	751111
29.07.41	DFM	Sgt	William Noel Williams	NZ40952
08.08.41	DFC	F/L	Arthur Benjamin Broadley	87659
09.09.41	DFC	P/O	Jack Buckley	89082
23.09.41	DFM	Sgt	Henry Gibson	905120
23.09.41	DFM	Sgt	Otto Shufflebotham	745955
30.09.41	DFC	S/L	Bryan William Smithers	41750
30.01.42	DFM	Sgt	James George Bruce	989150
30.01.42	DFM	Sgt	Adam Herd Flett	910709

Date: Date of Notification in *London Gazette*

*CDG: Croix de Guerre avec Palme
**DFM: Bar to DFM

APPENDIX V

Citations

23.05.41 – Blenheim V5823:G (Raid 01.05.41: Rotterdam)

F/L George Edward Goode 81675
P/O James Frederick Hogan 45523
Sgt Geoffrey Serpell Rowland 775633

In May 1941, Flight Lieutenant Goode, Pilot Officer Hogan and Sergeant Rowland were the pilot, navigator and wireless operator/air gunner respectively of an aircraft which, despite the absence of cloud cover, attacked the oil storage tanks to the west of Rotterdam. In the face of intense anti-aircraft fire the bombs were released over the objective from low level. During this attack, Pilot Officer Hogan was severely wounded by a shell which burst on the front of the aircraft. Flight Lieutenant Goode had altered course for home when he was attacked in turn by each of five pursuing enemy aircraft. Pilot Officer Hogan, who had retained consciousness, rendered valuable assistance by giving clear instructions to his pilot who was thus able to adopt skilful evading tactics. Sgt Rowland was wounded in the trigger finger and his starboard gun put out of action. Nevertheless he continued firing with the remaining gun, working the turret by hand as the mechanical control was damaged. The attackers eventually broke away and Flight Lieutenant Goode, although wounded in the hand, flew his damaged aircraft back to this country, where he made a successful forced-landing. Throughout the operation Flight Lieutenant Goode, Pilot Officer Hogan and Sergeant Rowland displayed the greatest courage, fortitude and devotion to duty.

04.07.41 – Blenheim V6028:D (Sweep 15.06.41: Beat 10)

W/C Hughie Idwal Edwards 39005

In June 1941, this officer led a formation of aircraft in an operational sweep against enemy shipping off the Dutch coast. A convoy of eight merchant vessels was sighted at anchor about 3 miles outside The Hague. In the face of intense and accurate pom-pom and machine-gun fire, the formation attacked from a height of only 50ft. Wing Commander Edwards attacked a ship of some 4,000 tons and, after raking the decks with his forward machine-guns, released his bombs from mast high. A considerable explosion followed, debris being thrown into the air while columns of black smoke were emitted. The vessel was certainly severely damaged if not sunk. This officer has completed numerous operational missions over enemy and enemy-occupied country and against their shipping and has at all times displayed great leadership, skill and gallantry.

22.07.41 – Blenheim V6028:D (Raid 04.07.41: Bremen)

W/C Hughie Idwal Edwards 39005

Wing Commander Edwards, although handicapped by a physical disability resulting from a flying accident, has repeatedly displayed gallantry of the highest order in pressing home bombing attacks from very low heights against strongly defended objectives. On July 4th he led an important attack on the port of Bremen, one of the most heavily defended towns in Germany. This attack had to be made in daylight, and there were no clouds to offer concealment. During the approach to the German coast several enemy ships were sighted, and Wing Commander Edwards knew that his aircraft would be reported and that the defences would be in a state of readiness. Undaunted by this misfortune, he brought his formation 50 miles overland to the target, flying at height of little more than 50 feet, passing under high tension cables, carrying away telegraph wires, and finally passing through a formidable balloon barrage. On reaching Bremen he was met with a hail of fire, all his aircraft being hit and four of them being destroyed. Nevertheless, he made a most successful attack, and then with the greatest skill and coolness withdrew the surviving aircraft without further loss. Throughout the execution of this operation, which he had planned personally with full knowledge of the risks entailed, Wing Commander Edwards displayed the highest standard of gallantry and determination."

29.07.41 – Blenheim V6028:D (Raid 04.07.41: Bremen)

P/O Alister Stewart Ramsay 88659
Sgt Gerald Douglas Prior Quinn 543799

On 4th July 1941, Pilot Officer Ramsay and Sergeant Quinn were the air observer/navigator and wireless operator/air gunner respectively of the leading aircraft of a formation which carried out a daylight bombing attack on Bremen. The flight was carried out mostly under conditions of poor visibility. Three changes of course were necessary on the outward journey, of which two were effected on dead-reckoning alone, out of sight of land. Flying through a balloon barrage and meeting with the most determined and accurate fire from the ground, the centre of the town was attacked from a height of about 50 feet. During the action Sergeant Quinn was wounded in the leg but remained at his post maintaining wireless watch and assisting Pilot Officer Ramsay materially in navigating the aircraft safely back to base. Pilot Officer Ramsay displayed exceptional skill and contributed in a large way to the success of this hazardous mission. In this he was ably assisted by Sergeant Quinn who showed great coolness and courage. Both have participated in numerous operational flights against the enemy.

29.07.41 – Blenheim Z7484:K (Raid 04.07.41: Bremen)

Sgt William Hugh Anthony Jackson 965484
Sgt James Alan Purves 751111
Sgt William Noel Williams NZ40952

Sergeants Jackson, Purves and Williams were the pilot, wireless operator/air gunner and air observer/navigator respectively of an aircraft which participated in a daylight attack on Bremen on 4th July 1941. The formation, which flew on to the target at a height of 50 feet, delivered its attack on the centre of the town whilst flying through a balloon barrage in the face of extremely heavy fire from the ground. During the action the aircraft received direct hits and Sergeant Purves was wounded in the thigh and foot while Sergeant Williams received wounds in the leg and foot. In spite of his injuries Sergeant Williams successfully navigated the aircraft back to this country. In this he was assisted by Sergeant Purves, who, although seriously wounded and suffering from considerable loss of blood, kept to his post. Sergeant Jackson, with exceptional skill, successfully landed his aircraft on reaching base within a few yards of the ambulance and fire tender which were standing by. The three airmen displayed great courage and determination under extremely harassing circumstances.

08.08.41 – Blenheim V6370:O (Raid 16.07.41: Rotterdam)

F/L Arthur Benjamin Broadley 87659

One evening in July 1941, this officer participated in a raid against shipping at Rotterdam. The attack was carried out from mast height and Flight Lieutenant Broadley succeeded in obtaining direct hits on an 8,000-ton ship, apparently under construction and nearing completion, in one of the harbour docks. Flight Lieutenant Broadley has participated in twenty-one operational missions and throughout has displayed great skill and courage.

09.09.41 – Blenheim (Serial unknown) (Raid 18.08.41: Lampedusa)

P/O Jack Buckley 89082

In August 1941, this officer attacked a 9,000-ton ship off Lampedusa. Destroyers, torpedo boats and a large number of lighters were moving a cargo of motor transport at the time but Pilot Officer Buckley attacked through a curtain of fire and, although wounded during the run-in, scored hits, setting the ship on fire. Subsequent reconnaissance revealed that a 700-ton sloop was also sunk as a result of the attack.

30.09.41 – Blenheim (Serial unknown) (Raid 01.09.41: Crotone)
Blenheim Z7408:K (Sweep 11.09.41: Ionian Sea)
Blenheim Z9613:A (Convoy 12.09.41: off Tripoli)

S/L Bryan William Smithers 41750

In September 1941, in an attack on Crotone Harbour, this officer obtained a hit on a 4,000-ton merchant vessel which subsequently appeared to be a total loss. In the course of a long patrol some days later, Squadron Leader Smithers led a force of bombers which operated against a convoy of six merchant vessels escorted by seven destroyers. Flying through an intensive barrage, he subsequently attacked the largest ship of the convoy. The vessel which was also damaged by other aircraft afterwards caught fire. Although his aircraft sustained damage, Squadron Leader Smithers flew it skilfully back to base. This officer has at all times shown outstanding gallantry and fearless leadership.

APPENDIX VI

Crews to Malta

The following crews departed Swanton Morley on 12 July 1941 en route to Malta via Watton (Bodney), Portreath and Gibraltar.

Pilot	*Observer*	*WOp/AG*
P/O J. Buckley	P/O D. Ivens	Sgt R. Allen
Sgt T. Williams	Sgt O. Shufflebotham	Sgt Green
Sgt L.T. Weston	Sgt J. Storey	Sgt F.D. Kindell
Sgt G.K. Williams	Sgt R.E. Griffin	Sgt N. Kay

The following crews departed from Swanton Morley on 25 July 1941 en route to Malta via Portreath and Gibraltar.

(Decorations detailed are as announced or awarded prior to departure)

Pilot	*Observer*	*WOp/AG*
W/C H. I. Edwards VC DFC	Sgt W. Knight	F/O F.E. Frayn Sgt G.D.P. Quinn DFM & Bar
S/L G.E. Goode DFC	Sgt F.A. Harbord	P/O E.W. Applebee DFM
S/L B.W. Smithers	Sgt F.K. Hindle	Sgt Fisher
F/L A.B. Broadley	P/O A.S. Ramsay DFC	Sgt V.R. Marsh
F/O H.J. Roe	F/Sgt J.D. Timms	F/Sgt S.R. Samways
P/O B. Hanafin	Sgt C.H. Hill	P/O Cheney
P/O P.H. Standfast	P/O H.C. Sorenson	Sgt D.A.D. Hoare
P/O A.L. Duncan	Sgt E. Smith	Sgt R.W. Lyndall
Sgt R.J. Scott	Sgt W.B. Healy	Sgt S.G. Bastin
Sgt W.H.A. Jackson DFM	Sgt D.R. Scholefield	Sgt A.F. Tuppen
Sgt J. Bendall	Sgt H.A. Nicols	Sgt A. Brown
Sgt J. Bruce	Sgt A.H. Flett	Sgt H. Gibson

APPENDIX VII

Roll of Honour

Great Britain

Date	*Aircraft*	*Rank*	*Name*	*Duty*	*Service Number*
01.09.40	T1877	Sgt	H.H. Duncan	Obs	581442
09.09.40	T1894	Sgt	D.D.R. Hodson	Pilot	566166
		Sgt	E.B. Palmer	Obs	743071
		Sgt	R. Green	WOp/AG	965313
18.09.40	L9339	Sgt	C.W. Bowles	Pilot	580170
		Sgt	V. Radford	Obs	580445
		Sgt	A. Lackenby	WOp/AG	620363
02.10.40	T1896	Sgt	K. Lord	Pilot	517486
		Sgt	F.V. Bundock	Obs	580601
		Sgt	H. Dunbar	WOp/AG	627887
28.10.40	T2229	P/O	I. Prosser	Pilot	41950
		Sgt	A.F. Dallas	Obs	NZ39964
		Sgt	J. Hardcastle	WOp/AG	627887
28.10.40	T1891	S/L	C.W. Grannum	Pilot	26011
		P/O	N.A. Knight	Obs	82736
		Sgt	J.E. Greenwood	WOp/AG	532939
15.11.40	T1890	P/O	D. Murray DFC	Pilot	41050
		Sgt	C.D. Gavin	Obs	580393
		Sgt	T. Robson	WOp/AG	939777
16.11.40	T2329	Sgt	C. Whitfield	Pilot	525569
		Sgt	W.J. Gilmour	Obs	734017
		Sgt	T.E. Ashurst	WOp/AG	751950
26.11.40	T1866	P/O	L.T.J. Ryan	Pilot	41744
		Sgt	S.W. Slade	Obs	749586
		Sgt	R. Meikle	WOp/AG	938736
28.11.40	T1893	F/L	C.D. Swain	Pilot	37658
11.12.40	T1897	F/Sgt	P.R. Richardson	Pilot	565331
		Sgt	J.F. Donlon	Obs	521006
		Sgt	V.C. Gifford	WOp/AG	549511

Date	*Aircraft*	*Rank*	*Name*	*Duty*	*Service Number*
28.02.41	T1895:X	Sgt	S. Jones	Obs	968353
		Sgt	J. Bimson	WOp/AG	970880
21.03.41	T1892:Q	P/O	I.M. Shirlaw	Pilot	81054
		P/O	C.R. Dugdale	Obs	84034
		F/O	J.O. Mair	WOp/AG	78277
23.03.41	Z5903:D	Sgt	C.H. King	Pilot	904527
		Sgt	R.F. Murphy	Obs	755142
		Sgt	F. Gibbs	WOp/AG	755569
17.04.41	T2141	Sgt	I.G. Sarjeant	Pilot	742026
		Sgt	L.L. Evered	Obs	967757
		Sgt	K.G. Gresty	WOp/AG	742026
23.04.41	V6318	Sgt	A.A. Lister	Pilot	754209
		Sgt	W.T. Heaney	Obs	979954
		Sgt	K.W. Porter	WOp/AG	943625
25.04.41	V6370:T	P/O	R. Needham	Pilot	60808
		P/O	T. Keightley-Smith	Obs	89067
		Sgt	F.H. Bridgeman	WOp/AG	911575
08.05.41	V5828:R	W/C	A.L. Christian	Pilot	29160
		F/Sgt	H.F. Hancock	Obs	580443
		Sgt	G. Wade	WOp/AG	751442
16.05.41	T2118:E	P/O	R.A. Richards	Pilot	60819
		Sgt	A.C. North	Obs	965820
		Sgt	E.E.J. Snutch	WOp/AG	751069
25.05.41	R3707:B	P/O	G.E.J. Rushbrooke	Pilot	60816
		Sgt	G.E. Green	Obs	969371
		Sgt	S. Parr	WOp/AG	946264
07.06.41	V6316:S	P/O	L.S. Clayton	Pilot	61217
		P/O	V.E.G. Phillips	Obs	62301
		Sgt	A.J. Stiddard	WOp/AG	1152032
15.06.41	V6319:F	F/O	P.H. Watts	Pilot	41070
		Sgt	D.D. Milroy	Obs	743035
		Sgt	P.B. Murray	WOp/AG	977615
20.06.41	V6336:H	Sgt	D.O. Beacham	Pilot	1182064
		Sgt	P.G. Griffiths	Obs	1150627
		Sgt	N.W. Appleby	WOp/AG	751242
		ACI	G.M. McFadzean	G/C	985467
		LAC	R.C. Ballard	G/C	643070

Date	*Aircraft*	*Rank*	*Name*	*Duty*	*Service Number*
04.07.41	Z7426:B	Sgt	W.A. MacKillop	Pilot	1053612
		Sgt	E.G. Nethercutt	Obs	920591
		Sgt	G.F. Entwistle	WOp/AG	956616
04.07.41	Z7486:M	F/O	M.M. Lambert	Pilot	42132
		Sgt	R. Copeland	Obs	956081
		Sgt	F.W.R. Charles	WOp/AG	949785
07.07.41	V5502:U	S/L	A.A.MacD. Scott	Pilot	40643
		Sgt	R.G.J. Dewin	Obs	745497
		Sgt	P. Conlon	WOp/AG	939928
19.07.41	Z7439:H	Sgt	V.G. Farrow	Pilot	929616
		Sgt	E.C. Saunders	Obs	925661
		Sgt	O.H. Robinson	WOp/AG	967533
19.07.41	V6039:Q	Sgt	R.W. Taylor	Pilot	NZ401790
		Sgt	R.F.G. Witherington	Obs	975504
		Sgt	S. Sparkes	WOp/AG	992848

Malta

Date	*Aircraft*	*Rank*	*Name*	*Duty*	*Service Number*
01.08.41	Z7605:U	P/O	A.S. Ramsay	Obs	88659
15.08.41	Z7522:E	F/O	H.J. Roe	Pilot	79153
		F/Sgt	J.D. Timms	Obs	580630
		F/Sgt	S.R. Samways	WOp/AG	552093
15.08.41	Z9604:D	P/O	P.H. Standfast	Pilot	89357
		P/O	H.C. Sorenson	Obs	66535
		Sgt	D.A.D. Hoare	WOp/AG	956948
26.08.41	Z7682:N	Sgt	R.J. Scott	Pilot	904184
		Sgt	W.B. Healy	Obs	978873
		Sgt	S.G. Bastin	WOp/AG	909151:
04.09.41	Z7654:Y	Sgt	W.H. Wallace	Pilot	1253867
		Sgt	L.D. Parry	Obs	954380
		Sgt	J.E. Jones	WOp/AG	1059799
12.09.41	Z9603:F	S/L	F.R.H. Charney DFC	Pilot	101503
		Sgt	S. Porteous	Obs	984451
		Sgt	D.R. Harris	WOp/AG	976863
12.09.41	Z7504:G	Sgt	Q.E. Mortimer	Pilot	1002556
		Sgt	D.J. Reid	Obs	978132
		F/O	C.D. Owen	WOp/AG	82990

Date	*Aircraft*	*Rank*	*Name*	*Duty*	*Service Number*
17.09.41	P4840:Y	F/Sgt	J. Bendall	Pilot	745763
		Sgt	C.H. Hill	Obs	1154518
		Sgt	A. Brown	WOp/AG	552771
17.09.41	Z7755:O	P/O	P.E.C. Robinson	Pilot	65572
		Sgt	B.F. Brookes	Obs	925829
		Sgt	F. Burrell	WOp/AG	638941
22.09.41	Z7423:H	W/C	D.W. Scivier AFC	Pilot	43073
		F/Sgt	L.M. Barnett	Obs	565063
		Sgt	B. Gray DFM	WOp/AG	537006

BUCKINGHAM PALACE

The Queen and I offer you our heartfelt sympathy in your great sorrow.

We pray that your country's gratitude for a life so nobly given in its service may bring you some measure of consolation.

George R.I.

Mrs. R. Bastin.

A Message of Condolence from HM King George VI. This was the standard wartime expression of sympathy sent to the bereaved next of kin on the death of their loved one. (via Mrs N.A. Scott)

APPENDIX VIII

Tributes

The following tributes were made to the Bristol Blenheims and their crews, in addition to those contained in the text.

Air Marshal Sir Hugh Pughe Lloyd KBE CB CBE MC DFC said of the Blenheim crews whom he commanded on Malta:

> I can never hope to describe all I feel about their courage and determination to kill the really important Axis shipping. It would have been a simple matter to have flown off to chase and sink the small ships which abounded around the Italian coasts; but such shipping was not vital to the African campaign, and they knew it. Those aircrew were the flower of our race; all of them had been given a good education in their youth and were far above the average in intelligence, men who knew what they were doing and why it had to be done, and men who had volunteered to be aircrew in preference to many other far less hazardous tasks. Theirs was a calm and conscious courage. To every one of those volunteers the sinking of ships was their crusade and without any doubt they were the knights of St John – the modern Crusaders.

(Source: *Briefed To Attack*, Hodder & Stoughton, 1949)

Air Chief Marshal Sir Arthur T. Harris KCB OBE AFC wrote of Bomber Command's 2 Group Blenheim operations:

> In March 1941 Blenheims of No. 2 Group began a campaign of low-level bombing against enemy coastal shipping, which could not be attacked by the Navy without risking prohibitive losses by shore-based enemy aircraft. These attacks were hazardous in the extreme; the enemy's anti-aircraft fire was deadly and our losses were very heavy. The gallantry of the Blenheim crews was beyond praise and their determination never wavered though I know many of the men felt that they were being sent to certain death. It proved extremely difficult to estimate the exact degree of success in many of these attacks, because of the very low height from which they were carried out; oblique photographs of the target were taken at the moment of attack and as the aircraft left for home but these could seldom be interpreted with any degree of certainty. It is believed that about seventy ships were sunk in a period of about six months.

A note was appended:

> In the month of April, over 100,000 tons of enemy shipping was sunk by the 2 Group Blenheims, a success greater than that achieved by the whole of the Royal Navy during that month.

(Source: *Bomber Command*, Astra House, via W/C Ron Wood)

Group Captain F.E. 'Teddy' Frayn wrote the following to the author about the Blenheim aircrew:

> Young men of the calibre of your uncle, Stuart Bastin, and the other members of his crew and his many other colleagues who, during those hectic days of 1941, were engaged in an almost hopelessly continual struggle with a well equipped enemy, did more than most people will ever know, to win victory for the freedom of mankind. Attacking shipping at low level was like going into a hornet's nest, weaving in against heavy fire, attacking with determination and pulling up over the mast heads at the very last moment.

Group Captain A. Hesketh wrote on behalf of **Air Vice-Marshal Alan Lees, Air Officer Commanding No. 2 Group**, appraising the Bristol Blenheim aircraft itself:

> Blenheims, originally medium aircraft, are by modern standards classified as light, and although even now they still retain their place in the affections of experienced commanders and pilots, are being superceded by aircraft which carry larger loads and give better performances. That two squadrons are re-forming with Blenheims does not imply a permanent contribution of these aircraft even to a limited extent for these squadrons will be re-equipped when the supply of Blenheims comes to an end. No. 2 Group, with Blenheim aircraft, has had a long record of successful and often outstanding operational service which all ranks in the branches at stations and at Group Headquarters can, in virtue of their own particular contribution, contemplate in retrospect with considerable satisfaction.

(Source: No. 2 Group HQ – No. 2 Group Summary of Events, March 1942: Public Record Office, AIR 14 – 523 Ref: 2G/S.522/2/PRO Dated 9/4/42)

Principal Sources and Selected Bibliography

SOURCES

Public Record Office, Kew, London
[Operations Record Books include RAF Forms 540 and 541]

In particular:

AIR 14/149: Commouflage 1939–1941
AIR 14/523: Summary of Events: 2 Group
AIR 14/3361: Raid Sheets: 2 Group
AIR 14/3362: Raid Sheets: 2 Group
AIR 14/3363: Raid Sheets: 2 Group
AIR 24/908: Malta Headquarters
AIR 27/398: 38 Squadron RAF Operations Record Book
AIR 27/606: 69 Squadron RAF Operations Record Book
AIR 27/829: 105 Squadron RAF Operations Record Book
AIR 27/830: 105 Squadron RAF Operations Record Book
AIR 27/842: 107 Squadron RAF Operations Record Book
AIR 27/1553: 264 Squadron RAF Operations Record Book
AIR 27/1555: 264 Squadron RAF Operations Record Book
AIR 28/302: Luqa Station
AIR 28/790: Swanton Morley Station
AIR 29/658: 17 OTU, Upwood
AIR 37/47: Daylight bombing attacks on Germany and Occupied Territory – photographs 1941
ADM 173/17175: Submarine log – HMS *Utmost*
WO 208/3028: German plans for the capture of Gibraltar

Ministry of Defence – Naval Staff Duties (Historical Section) London

In particular:

SO 36404: Naval Staff History – selected convoys (Mediterranean) 1941–2
: Naval Cypher 2120A – 10th September 1941
: Naval Cypher 1730A – 29th September 1941

BIBLIOGRAPHY

Lt-Col Eddy Bauer *The History of World War II* (Orbis, 1983)
Chaz Bowyer *Bomber Barons* (Book Club Associates, 1983)

Chaz Bowyer *Bristol Blenheim* (Ian Allan, 1984)
M.J.F. Bowyer *No. 2 Group RAF: A Complete History 1936-1945* (Faber & Faber, 1974)
M.J.F. Bowyer *Action Stations 1: Military Airfields of East Anglia* (Patrick Stephens, 1990)
Ernle Bradford *Siege Malta 1940/1943* (Hamish Hamilton, 1985)
Alan Burgess *The Longest Tunnel* (Bloomsbury, 1990)
Charles Carrington *Soldier at Bomber Command* (Leo Cooper, 1987)
W.R. Chorley *Royal Air Force Bomber Command Losses of the Second World War Vol I 1939–1940* (Midland County Publications, 1992)
W.R. Chorley *Royal Air Force Bomber Command Losses of the Second World War Vol II 1941* (Midland County Publications, 1993)
Richard Collier *The War in the Desert* (Time Life Books, 1977)
Len Fearnley *Blenheim Odyssey* (Len Fearnley, 1990)
Norman Franks *Valiant Wings* (William Kimber, 1988)
Frederick R. Galea *Air War Over Malta: The Allies* (Modelaid International, 1988)
R.E. Gillman *The Shiphunters* (John Murray, 1976)
James J Halley *The Squadrons of the Royal Air Force* (Air Britain, 1980)
James J. Halley *Royal Air Force Aircraft: K1000 to K9999* (Air Britain, 1976); *L1000 to L9999* (Air Britain, 1979); *N1000 to L9999* (Air Britain, 1977); *P1000 to P9999*, 1978); *R1000 to R9999* (Air Britain, 1980); *T1000 to T9999* (Air Britain, 1981); *V1000 to V9999; W1000 to W9999*; *X1000 to X9999*; *Z1000 to Z9999* (Air Britain, 1984)
Max Hastings *Bomber Command* (Michael Joseph, 1987)
The Air Battle of Malta (HMSO, 1944)
East of Malta, West of Suez (HMSO, 1943)
The Mediterranean Fleet, Greece to Tripoli (HMSO, 1944)
Destruction of an Army (HMSO, 1941)
Leslie Hunt *A Short History of No. 2 Group RAF* (Private, *c.* 1965)
Kalevi Keskinen, Kari Stenman and Klaus Niska *Bristol Blenheim* (Tietoteos, 1984)
H. T. Lanton & J.J. Colledge *Warships of World War II* (Ian Allan, 1980)
Air Marshal Sir Hugh Pughe Lloyd *Briefed to Attack* (Hodder & Stoughton, 1949)
Ron Mackay *Bristol Blenheim in Action* (Squadron/Signal, 1988)
David Mordey *British Aircraft of World War II* (Temple Press, 1984)
Kenneth Poolman *Night Strike from Malta* (Janes, 1980)
Derek Ransom *Battle Axe – A History of 105 Squadron RAF* (Air Britain, 1967)
Richards/Saunders *Royal Air Force 1939–1945*, Vols I/II (HMSO, 1953–54)
Alan Shepperd *Campaign Series-3. France 1940: Blitzkrieg in the West* (Osprey, 1990)
Christopher F. Shores *Mediterranean Air War* Vol I (Ian Allan, 1972)
John W.R. Taylor *Combat Aircraft of the World* (Embury Press and Michael Joseph, 1969)
Philip Vella *Malta: Blitzed but not Beaten* (Progress Press, 1985)
R. Wallace Clarke *British Aircraft Armament Vol I: RAF Gun Turrets from 1914 to the Present Day* (Patrick Stephens, 1993)
Graham Warner *The Forgotten Bomber* (Patrick Stephens, 1991)
A.B.C. Whipple *The Mediterranean* (Time Life Books, 1981)
W. Alister Williams *The VCs of Wales and the Welsh Regiments* (Bridge Books, 1984)
Robert Woolcombe *The Campaigns of Wavell, 1939–1943* (Cassell, 1959)

Index